D1794723

Rogov's Guide to Israeli Wines
2010

Daniel Rogov

ROGOV'S GUIDE TO ISRAELI WINES

2010

The Toby Press

Rogov's Guide to Israeli Wines 2010
Sixth Annual Edition
The Toby Press LLC

POB 8531, New Milford, CT 06776-8531, USA
& POB 2455, London W1A 5WY, England
& POB 4044, Jerusalem 91040, Israel

www.tobypress.com

ISBN 978 1 59264 262 5, *hardcover*

A CIP catalogue record for this title is
available from the British Library.

Typeset in Chaparral by KPS

Printed in Israel

TABLE OF CONTENTS

FOREWORD

If in twenty years we were to open a time capsule, we would find that 2009 demonstrated itself to be a somewhat schizophrenic year for the Israeli wine industry. On the one hand, at wine exhibits in New York, California, Paris and Bordeaux an increasing number of Israeli wines received rave reviews, and many of those wines earned high scores in internationally renowned magazines and newspapers. On the other hand, more than a few of the smaller wineries in the country folded up their tents and vanished into the night, largely because the fad of opening small wineries has partly run its course, partially because some succumbed to the reality of difficult economic times, and even more failing because their wines did not meet the standards required in a world of increasingly knowledgeable consumers.

All of which is just fine, for on an overall basis those wineries that remain in the game have realized that quality and value for money are critical to their success. For example, 2009 marked a distinct increase in quality of releases of wines in even the lower-level series of the large wineries; a maintenance of often extraordinarily high quality and a moderation of prices from many of the smaller and larger wines; and, no less important, the release of a host of wines that stand comfortably against many of the very best wineries of the U.S.A. and Europe. Equally critical, the wines of the 2008 harvest, m knowost of which have yet to come to market but were tasted from barrels, are proving that 2008 will indeed be a fine vintage year, producing many quality wines that are capable of medium- to long-term cellaring.

The days when Israel was producing primarily sweet red wines for sacramental purposes are long gone, and today Israel is acknowledged as a serious wine producer. Wines are being made from highly prized grape varieties at more than one hundred and fifty wineries scattered all over the country, from the Upper Galilee and the Golan Heights to the Judean Hills and the Negev Desert. The construction of state-of-the-art wineries, the ongoing import and cultivation of good vine stock from California, France and Australia, and the enthusiasm and knowledge of young, well-trained winemakers who are not afraid to experiment with new wine varieties and blends has yielded an abundance of quality wines that can compete comfortably with many of the fine wines of the New and Old Worlds.

The purpose of this book is to provide readers with extensive knowledge about the wineries and wines of Israel, and to serve as a convenient guide for selecting and storing local wines. The introduction supplies the reader with the necessary historical and geographical background, while the major part of the guide is devoted to the wines, offering tasting notes and scores for wines that are now on the shelves or scheduled to appear within the next six to nine months, as well as wines that are still stored in the cellars of wine lovers.

How to Use the Guide

Wineries are arranged in the book by alphabetical order, and in the few cases where wineries may be known by more than one name, especially outside of Israel, readers will find the alternative names listed in the index. Following a brief description of the location, history and production of each winery are the reviews, ranging from the top-level series to the lower. Each series is arrayed from red wines to whites, followed by sparkling and dessert wines. These are further divided into grape varieties such as Cabernet Sauvignon, Merlot, etc. Each variety is arranged according to vintage years, from the most current release to the most mature available or still likely to be found in a fine wine cellar. Each review concludes with a score and a suggested drinking window.

Key to Symbols and Scores

THE WINERIES

***** A WORLD-CLASS WINERY, REGULARLY PRODUC-
ING EXCELLENT WINES

**** CONSISTENTLY PRODUCING HIGH-QUALITY WINES

*** SOLID AND RELIABLE PRODUCER WITH AT LEAST SOME GOOD WINES

** ADEQUATE

* HARD TO RECOMMEND

The ratings of wineries that have been releasing wines for less than three years should be considered as tentative, much depending on the consistency of future releases.

SCORES FOR INDIVIDUAL WINES

96–100	Truly great wines
90–95	Exceptional in every way
85–89	Very good to excellent and highly recommended
80–84	Recommended but without enthusiasm
70–79	Average but at least somewhat faulted
Under 70	Not recommended

Special Note about Tentative Scores:

The scores of wines tasted only from the barrel—that is to say, well before release and sometimes even before final blends have been made—are scored within a range and noted as *tentative*. Wines attaining such scores will be re-tasted and updated in future editions.

DRINKING WINDOWS

A drinking window is the suggested period during which the wine is at its very best. The notation "best 2010–2015," for example, indicates that the wine needs further cellaring before it comes to its peak and will then cellar comfortably through 2015. "Drink now–2012" indicates that although the wine is drinking well now it will continue to cellar nicely until 2012. "Drink now" indicates that the wine is drinking well now but can be held for another year or so. "Drink up" suggests that the wine is at or past its peak and should not be cellared any longer. "Drink from release" refers to wines that are not yet on the market. Some will appear within the coming nine months and others may appear only in two to three years. Such wines were tasted either from bottles as advance tastings or from barrels.

KOSHER WINES

There is no contradiction between making fine wine and the laws of kashrut, as is made apparent in the introduction to this guide. Within the guide, the reviews of all wines that have received a kashrut certificate from a recognized rabbinic authority are followed by the symbol к.

Introduction

The History of Wine in Israel

Ancient Times

The history of wine in the Land of Israel is as old as the history of the people who have inhabited that land over the centuries. As early as five thousand years ago people cultivated vines and made, stored and shipped wines. The first mention of wine in the Bible is in a reference to Noah, who is said to have planted the first vineyard and to have become intoxicated when he drank the wine (Genesis 9:20–21). Another well-known reference concerns the spies sent by Moses to explore the Land of Canaan. They returned after their mission with a cluster of grapes said to have been so large and heavy that it had to be borne on a carrying frame (Numbers 13:23). The vine is also mentioned as one of the blessings of the good land promised to the children of Israel (Deuteronomy 8:8).

Much of the process of winemaking has remained consistent throughout this time. Already in the Bible, we find a list of the necessary steps to care for a vineyard:

> My beloved had a vineyard in a very fruitful hill;
> And he dug it; and cleared it of stones,
> And planted it with the choicest vine,
> And built a tower in the midst of it,
> And also hewed out a vat therein;
> And he looked that it should bring forth grapes.
> He broke the ground, cleared it of stone and
>   planted it with choice vines.
> He built a watchtower inside it,
> He even hewed a wine press inside it.
>
> *(Isaiah 5: 1–2)*

Vintners in ancient times knew as we do today that locating vineyards at higher altitudes, where there are greater temperature changes between night and day, would cause the fruit to ripen more slowly, adding to the sweetness of the fruit and its ability to produce fine wines. Two ways of growing vines were known: in one the vines were allowed to grow along the ground; in the other they were trained upward on trellises (Ezekiel 17:6–8). It was widely accepted then as today that vines cultivated by the second method almost always produce superior grapes.

Remains of ancient wine presses may be found today in all parts of Israel, from the Galilee to Jerusalem and the Negev Desert. In nearly every part of Israel, archaeologists have discovered hundreds of jars for the storage and transportation of wine. Many of these amphorae list in detail where and by whom the wine was made, as well as the year of the vintage, indicating that even in antiquity the source of the grapes and the quality of the harvest were considered important.

It is known today that even during the Bronze Age, Egyptian Pharaohs enjoyed wines that were shipped from Canaan. The growing of grapes and the production of wine was a major agricultural endeavor during the periods of the First and Second Temples, and the kings of Judah and Israel were said to have owned large vineyards as well as vast stores of wine. The vineyards and stores of King David in particular were so numerous that he is said to have appointed two officials, one to be in charge of the vineyards, and the other to be in charge of storage (I Chronicles 27:27).

In biblical times the harvest was a celebratory period as well as a period of courtship. The treading of the grapes was done most often on a *gat* or an *arevah*, the *gat* being a small, generally square, pressing floor that had been cut into bedrock, and the *arevah* a smaller treading surface that could be moved from vineyard to vineyard. From either of these the must (that is to say, the fresh and as yet unfermented grape juice) ran into a *yekev*, which was a vat for collecting the must as it flowed from the treading floor through a hole carved in the stone. When natural bedrock was unavailable, an earthen treading surface lined with mosaics was used. In several areas, caves or large cisterns carved from natural bedrock have been found, which would have served two purposes—first for storing the grapes until they were pressed, and then, because they were cool and dark, for storing the wine while it fermented and then aged in clay jugs.

Once fermentation had been completed, the wines were stored in pottery vessels which were sealed with wood, stone or clay stoppers. For purposes of shipping, the stoppers were wrapped in cloth and coated with clay. Since new clay vessels tend to absorb as much as 20 percent of the wines stored in them, it became common practice to store better wines in older jars. A major development, during the third century BCE, was the discovery that stoppers made from cork were an effective way to seal amphorae.

As much as these wines were prized, it must be understood that they were very different from wines as we know them today. They were often so intense and coarse that they needed a fair amount of "adjustment" before they were considered drinkable. To improve the bouquet, the Romans were known to add spices and scents to their wines. To make the wine sweeter, they added a syrup made by heating grape juice in lead containers for a long period over a low flame. To improve flavors and hide faults it was customary to add honey, pepper, chalk, gypsum, lime, resin, herbs and even sea water.

In the time of the First and Second Temples, wine was widely consumed by the local populace, but the very best wines were set aside for libations in the Temple. The Bible specifies the different types of offerings—a quarter of a *hin* (one *hin* was the equivalent of about 5.7 liters or 1.5 gallons) of wine when offering a sheep; a third of a *hin* for a ram; and half a *hin* for an animal from the herd, such as a cow (Numbers 15:5). In addition, people were required to give tithes of new wine to the Temple (Deuteronomy 12:17). Wines were so central to the culture during that period that those who planted vineyards were exempt from military service, and illustrations of grapes, grape leaves, amphorae and drinking vessels were often used as symbols on seals and coins as well as for decorations on the friezes of buildings.

After the destruction of the Second Temple, wine was integrated into all religious ceremonies including *brit milah* (circumcision), weddings, the Sabbath and high holidays. It is especially central in the Passover *Seder*, where it is customary to drink four glasses of wine.

During the late Roman and Byzantine periods, running from the fourth to the sixth century, the wine industry shifted from Judea to the southern part of the land, where the port towns of Ashkelon and Gaza became centers of wine trading. The wines produced in the area were so coveted by the Romans that they shipped them to their legions throughout the Mediterranean and North Africa, and Christian pilgrims brought them back to Europe.

The Moslem conquest of the Holy Land in the seventh century put an end to this prosperous industry. The Moslem rulers banned the drinking of alcohol and as a result the flourishing local wine industry almost ceased to exist. The only wines allowed were the small amounts that Christians and Jews required for sacramental purposes. Throughout the twelfth and thirteenth centuries, the Crusaders made sporadic attempts to revive the wine industry in the Holy Land, but these were short-lived, as it was easier to ship wines from Europe. It was only with the renewal of Jewish settlement in the nineteenth century that the local winemaking industry was reestablished.

Modern Times

The Jewish philanthropist Sir Moses Montefiore, who visited the Holy Land numerous times in the nineteenth century, encouraged the Jews living there to work the land and replant vines. One person who heeded his call was Rabbi Itzhak Schorr, who founded a new winery in Jerusalem in 1848. Rabbi Abraham Teperberg followed suit, founding the Efrat winery in 1870 in the old city of Jerusalem. In addition, he also opened an agricultural school in Mikveh Israel, not far from Jaffa. This school was financed and run by *Alliance*

Israélite Universelle, a Jewish organization based in France that aimed at training Jewish settlers in agricultural work. The school was the first to plant European grape varieties, and had a winery as well as large wine cellars. Many of its graduates became vine growers.

An important boost to the local industry came about when Baron Edmond de Rothschild, the owner of the famed Chateau Lafite in Bordeaux, agreed to come to the help of the Jewish colonies, and financed the planting of the first vineyards near Rishon Letzion, on the coastal plain. Rothschild hoped that the Holy Land would serve as the source of kosher wines for Jews the world over, and that the wine industry would provide a solid economic basis for the new Jewish communities. He brought in experts from Europe and imported grape varieties from the south of France including Alicante Bouchet, Clairette, Carignan, Grenache, Muscat and Semillon. He also funded the first wineries of the new Jewish settlements—first the Rishon Letzion Winery in 1882, then the Zichron Ya'akov winery in the Mount Carmel area in 1890—thus marking the beginning of the modern wine industry in the Land of Israel. Unfortunately, not all ran smoothly. The first harvests were lost to heat and in 1890–1891 the land was overrun by phylloxera, a plague of aphid-like insects that destroyed all of the vines. The vineyards were dug up, and replanted with vines grafted onto phylloxera-resistant root stocks.

In 1906 Rothschild helped to set up a cooperative of grape growers that managed the two wineries, and in 1957 his heirs sold their share to the cooperative. It took the name Carmel Mizrachi, and continued to be the dominant factor in the local wine industry until the early 1980s.

However, Rothschild's dream that viticulture would provide a major source of income for the region was shattered with the advent of three major events which virtually eliminated the fledgling industry's three largest potential markets: the Russian Revolution, the enactment of Prohibition in the United States, and the banning of imported wines to Egypt. Many vineyards had to be uprooted. While several new wineries opened in the following decades, including Segal, Eliaz and Stock, for the most part they and Carmel continued to produce wines largely destined for sacramental purposes. Records from 1948 testifying to the annual consumption of a mere 3.9 liters of wine per person demonstrate that wine had not yet become part of the culture of life in Israel.

The Israeli Wine Revolution

In 1972, Professor Cornelius Ough of the Department of Viticulture and Oenology at the University of California at Davis visited Israel and suggested that the soil and climate of the Golan Heights would prove ideal for the raising of grapes. In 1976 the first vines were planted in the Golan, and in 1983 the then-newly-established Golan Heights Winery released its first wines. Almost overnight it became apparent that Israel was capable of producing wines of world-class quality. During the early 1980s the Israeli wine industry endured an economic crisis, but the revolution had begun and there was no turning back.

Unfettered by outdated winemaking traditions or by a large stagnant corporate structure, the young winery imported excellent vine stock from California, built a state-of-the-art winery, and added to this the enthusiasm and expertise of young American winemakers who had been trained at the University of California at Davis. Equally important, the Golan winery began to encourage vineyard owners to improve the quality of their grapes and, in the American tradition, paid bonuses for grapes with high sugar and acid content, while rejecting substandard grapes. The winery was also the first to realize that wines made from Grenache, Semillon, Petite Sirah and Carignan grapes would not put them on the world wine map, and focused on planting and making wines from Cabernet Sauvignon, Merlot, Sauvignon Blanc, Chardonnay, White Riesling, Gewurztraminer and other noble grape varieties.

The Golan wines were a success from the beginning, not only within Israel but abroad. This success had a great impact on other Israeli wineries, which have made major steps in improving the quality of their wines. There are now five major wineries, twelve medium-sized wineries and a host of small wineries in the country, many of which are producing wines that are of high quality, and several producing wines good enough to interest connoisseurs all over the world.

The Current and Future State of Wine Production in Israel

Accurate data about the local wine industry is difficult to come by due to lack of coordination between the Israeli Wine Institute, the Ministry of Agriculture, the Export Institute and the Grape Grower's Association. When wineries submit their production and export figures, for example, they make no distinction between exports of table wines, sacramental wines, grape juice and even brandy and liqueurs. It is estimated that today Israel produces about thirty-six million bottles of table wine a year, an amount representing continued growth of five to ten percent annually over the past five years. Approximately forty-eight thousand dunams (twelve thousand acres) of land are currently under grape cultivation, an increase of fifty-five percent in cultivated land area since 1995. Moreover, the development of vineyards is once again on the rise, and several of the medium-sized wineries are planting vineyards that are intended to double or triple their production. Approximately sixty percent of the table wines produced today are dry reds, while as recently as 1995 production was seventy percent whites and only thirty percent reds.

Following an extended period in which the imagination of the wine-drinking public within Israel was captured by boutique wineries and *garagistes*, the years 2003–2008 might be regarded as the years of the larger wineries. On the other hand, 2009 saw a balancing phenomenon, for whereas well over 90% of the better wines in the country are produced by the larger wineries, it is once again the wines of the small and often newer small wineries with which Israelis and those abroad have "fallen in love." In 2003, the Golan Heights Winery released the country's first varietal wines made from

Sangiovese, Pinot Noir and Gamay grapes, as well as the country's first single-vineyard organically grown Chardonnay. Under its Yarden label, the winery also produced the country's first Semillon-botrytis wine. During that same year, Carmel released the first wines from its new boutique winery Yatir, and has continued to give us exciting single-vineyard Cabernet Sauvignon, Syrah and Chardonnay wines. Barkan introduced the country's first Pinotage wine. During 2005, Recanati released the country's first wine made from Barbera grapes and several of the medium-sized wineries gave us the country's first Zinfandel wines. Smaller wineries, on the other hand, especially those focused on unusual varietal wines or equally unusual blends, have no less captured the palates of the more wine-sophisticated among consumers both in Israel and abroad.

Although the Golan Heights Winery, with its Katzrin, Yarden, Gamla and Golan series, remains the obvious quality leader among the large wineries in the country, a great deal of excitement continues to be generated by Clos de Gat, Tabor, Yatir, Pelter, Vitkin and the upper-level series of Carmel. Three other large wineries, Binyamina, Teperberg (until recently known as Efrat) and Zion, have now joined the ranks of those wineries on the way up. Each of these wineries, now with well-trained winemakers aboard, are in the process of modernizing their equipment, gaining better control over their vineyards and producing several series of wines that are successfully capturing the attention of sophisticated wine drinkers.

The Phenomenon of the Boutique Wineries

In recent years, the country has seen a dramatic growth in boutique wineries, *garagistes*, micro-wineries and artisanal producers, each striving, but not all succeeding, to create world-class wines. Such wineries, producing anywhere from under one thousand to one hundred thousand bottles annually, can remain highly personalized affairs, the winemakers having full control over their vineyards, knowing precisely what wine is in what barrel at any given moment and what style they want their wines to reflect. The label of a boutique winery does not, however, guarantee quality. At the top end of the range, a handful of small wineries founded by competent men and women, several of them well-trained professionals, are producing some of the very best wines in the country. At the bottom end are numerous wineries founded by hobbyists that produce wines that are barely acceptable. It is largely the wineries at the lower end of this spectrum that are now closing. Despite this, boutique wineries continue to open, as if to demonstrate that optimism knows no bounds.

Grape Growing Regions

The ideal areas for the cultivation of wine grapes lie in the two strips between 30–50 degrees north and south of the equator. Israel, which is located on the southern side of that strip in the Northern Hemisphere, is thus ideally situated. Considering Israel's specific climate, it is important to note that the vine can thrive in many different types of soil, as well as in regions that receive little rainfall.

Although the land area of Israel is a mere 7,992 square miles (which is five percent of the land area of California), like many wine-growing regions that have a long north-south axis (Italy, Chile or California, for example), the country has a large variety of microclimates. In the north, snow falls in winter and conditions are comparable to those of Bordeaux and the Northern Rhone Valley of France, yet within a few hours' drive one arrives at the Negev Desert, where the climate is similar to that of North Africa.

The country is divided into five vine-growing regions, the names of which are generally accepted by the European community and appear on all labels of varietal wines that are designated for sale both locally and abroad. Each region is divided into sub-regions, encompassing specific valleys, mountains or other locales. Although various governmental and quasi-governmental agencies are considering implementing a more stringent *appellation controlee* system, the major regions today remain as follows:

GALILEE: Located in the northern part of the country, this area extends to the Lebanese border and incorporates the Golan Heights. It is the region most suited for viticulture in Israel. The high altitude, cool breezes, marked day and night temperature changes and rich, well-drained soils make the area ideal for the cultivation of a large variety of grapes. The area is divided into four sub-regions: the Upper Galilee, the Lower Galilee, Tabor and the Golan Heights. Some of the wineries located here are the Golan Heights Winery, Galil Mountain, Chateau Golan, Dalton, Saslove and Tabor. Development of new vineyards continues apace in the area, many of these owned by wineries located in other parts of the country.

SHOMRON (SAMARIA): Located near the Mediterranean coast south of Haifa, it includes the Carmel Mountain Range and the vineyards surrounding the towns of Zichron Ya'akov and Binyamina. This region remains the largest grape growing area in the country. The area has medium-heavy soils and a Mediterranean climate, with warm summers and humid winters. Wineries in the area include Margalit, Tishbi, Binyamina and the Zichron Ya'akov branch of Carmel, all relying at least in part on grapes grown in other areas for their better wines.

SHIMSHON (SAMSON): Located between the foothills of the Jerusalem Mountains and the Mediterranean coast, this region encompasses the central plains, including the area around Rishon Letzion and Rehovot. Although the area boasts many vineyards, the limestone, clay and loamy soils and the coastal Mediterranean climate of warm, humid summers and mild winters do not offer ideal conditions for the cultivation of fine varieties, and many of the wineries in the area rely on grapes from other parts of the country. Among the wineries located here are Carmel, Barkan, Karmei Yosef, and Soreq.

JERUSALEM MOUNTAINS: Sometimes referred to as the Judean Hills, this region surrounding the city of Jerusalem offers a variety of soil conditions and a cool Mediterranean climate due to its relatively high altitude. For many years the region served as home primarily to wineries that specialized in sweet sacramental wines, but about a decade ago it became clear that this area could prove excellent for raising noble varieties. The area underwent strenuous revitalization with the major planting of sophisticated vineyards and the opening of several medium-sized and an increasing number of small wineries. More than twenty-five wineries are found in the area, including Castel, Clos de Gat, Sea Horse, Flam, Ella Valley Vineyards, Mony, Tzora and Teperberg. It is clear that a true *route de vins* is developing in this region.

NEGEV: Ten years ago, few would have thought this semi-arid desert region appropriate for growing grapes, but now, sophisticated computerized drip-irrigation systems have made it possible to grow high quality grapes here, including among others Merlot, Cabernet Sauvignon and Chardonnay. The region is divided into two sub-areas: Ramat Arad, which is situated 600–700 meters above sea level and has impressive night-day temperature changes, where results with noble varieties have been excellent; and the Southern Negev, a lower, more arid area where sandy to loamy soils and very hot and dry summers offer a special challenge to grape growers. Carmel was the first to plant extensive vineyards at Ramat Arad. More recently, Barkan has begun wide-ranging development of vineyards at Mitzpe Ramon in the heart of the Negev. Among the wineries found here, some rely entirely on desert-raised grapes. Others that draw as well on grapes from other areas are Yatir and Sde Boker.

Grape Varieties in Israel

The last two decades have seen a major upheaval in the vineyards of Israel. Prior to 1985 the grapes planted were largely Carignan, Petite Sirah and Grenache for red and rosé wines, and Semillon, Emerald Riesling and Colombard for whites. The wineries focused on light, white and often sweet wines, and only a handful of noble varieties were to be found in the country. The scene shifted dramatically with

MEDITERRANEAN
SEA

Galilee

Katzrin

HAIFA

*Sea of
Galilee*

Zichron Ya'acov

Shomron

TEL AVIV

Rishon Le-Zion

JERUSALEM

Samson

Jerusalem
Mountains

*Dead
Sea*

Tel Arad

BEER SHEVA

Negev

EILAT

ROGOV'S
GUIDE
TO
ISRAELI
WINES

■ **Wine Regions**
Vineyard Areas

Galilee
Upper Galilee
Lower Galilee
Golan Heights

Shomron
Mt. Carmel
Sharon

Samson
Dan
Adulam
Latrun

Jerusalem Mountains
Beit-El
Jerusalem
Southern Jerusalem Mountains

Negev
Northern Negev Hills
Central Negev

the development of vineyards planted with noble varieties, first on the Golan Heights, then in the Upper Galilee. Today, from the Negev Desert to the northernmost parts of the country, the focus is on many of those varieties that have proven themselves throughout the world.

Unlike many of the wine-growing regions, especially in Europe, Israel does not have any indigenous grapes that might be considered appropriate for making wine. The closest the country came to having its own grape was the introduction of the Argaman grape, a cross between Souzao and Carignan grapes. Widely planted in the early 1980s, that experiment proved a fiasco: although the grape yielded wines deep in color, they lacked flavor, depth or body.

White Wine Grapes

CHARDONNAY: The grape that produces the great dry white wines of Burgundy and is indispensable to the production of Champagne. The most popular white wine grape in the world today, producing wines that can be oaked or unoaked, and range in flavors from flinty-minerals to citrus, pineapple, tropical fruits and grapefruit, and in texture from minerally-crisp to creamy.

CHENIN BLANC: Originating in France's central Loire Valley, a grape capable of producing long-lived wines with honeyed notes. Until recently used in Israel to produce ordinary, semi-dry wines but now being shown by several small wineries to produce exciting dry and sweet wines.

COLOMBARD: Known in Israel as French Colombard and producing mostly thin and acidic wines.

EMERALD RIESLING: A cross between the Muscadelle and Riesling grapes developed in California primarily for growth in warm climates, the grape produces mostly semi-dry wines of little interest to sophisticated wine consumers.

GEWURZTRAMINER: This grape originated in Germany, came to its glory in Alsace and has now been transplanted to many parts of the world. Capable of producing aromatic dry and sweet wines that are often typified by their softness and spiciness, as well as distinctive aromas and flavors of litchis and rose petals.

MUSCAT: There are many varieties of Muscat, the two most often found in Israel being the Muscat of Alexandria and Muscat Canelli, both of which are capable of producing wines that range from the dry to the sweet and are almost always typified by their perfumed aromas.

RIESLING: Sometimes known as Johannisberg Riesling, sometimes as White Riesling and sometimes simply as Riesling, this noble German variety has the potential to produce wines, that although light in body and low in alcohol, are highly flavored and capable of long aging. Typified by aromas and flavors of flowers, minerals and lime, and when aged, sometimes taking on a tempting petrol-like aroma. Not to be confused with the definitely inferior Emerald Riesling grape.

SAUVIGNON BLANC: At its best in the Loire Valley and Bordeaux for producing dry white wines, this successful transplant to Israel is capable of producing refreshing, sophisticated and distinctively aromatic and grassy wines, often best consumed in their youth.

SEMILLON: Although this native French grape was used for many years in Israel to produce largely uninteresting semi-dry white wines, its susceptibility to noble rot is now being used to advantage to produce sweet dessert wines with the distinctive bouquet and flavors of melon, fig and citrus. Several small wineries have recently begun producing interesting dry whites from this grape.

TRAMINETTE: A not overly exciting hybrid, a derivative of the Gewurztraminer grape, developed primarily for use in cold weather New York State and Canadian climates.

VIOGNIER: The most recent white wine transplant to Israel, this grape produces the fascinating Condrieu wines of France's Rhone Valley. Capable of producing aromatic but crisply dry whites and full-bodied whites, some of which have long aging potential.

Red Wine Grapes

ARGAMAN: An Israeli-inspired cross between Souzao and Carignan grapes. Possibly best categorized as the great local wine failure, producing wines of no interest. Many of the vineyards that were planted with Argaman continue to be uprooted to make room for more serious varieties.

BARBERA: From Italy's Piedmont region, this grape has the potential for producing wines that although light and fruity are capable of great charm.

CABERNET FRANC: Less intense and softer than Cabernet Sauvignon, most often destined to be blended with Merlot and Cabernet Sauvignon, but even on its own capable of producing dramatically good, leafy, fruity and aromatic reds.

CABERNET SAUVIGNON: The most noble variety of Bordeaux, capable of producing superb wines, often blended with smaller amounts of Merlot and Cabernet Franc. The best wines from this grape are rich in color and tannins, and have complex aromas and depth of flavors, those often typified by blackcurrants, spices and cedarwood. At their best, intriguing and complex wines that profit from cellaring.

CARIGNAN: An old-timer on the Israeli scene, for many years this originally Spanish grape produced largely dull and charmless wines. In recent years, however, several wineries have demonstrated that old-vine Carignan grapes, especially those in fields that have been unwatered for many years, can produce interesting and high quality wines.

GAMAY: The well-known grape of France's Beaujolais region, this fairly recent introduction to Israel is capable of producing light- to medium-bodied wines of fragrance and charm, intended primarily for drinking in their youth.

GRENACHE: Although this grape has traditionally done well in France's Rhone Valley and Spain, for many years it did not yield sophisticated kosher wines, most being somewhat pale, overripe and sweet in nature. Today, however, there is a growing movement to cut back on the yield of the grapes, the result being sometimes concentrated and intense wines of long cellaring potential.

MALBEC: Well known in France's Bordeaux, the Loire and Cahors, and the specialty grape of Argentina, this grape is capable of producing dense, rich, tannic and spicy wines that are remarkably dark in color.

MERLOT: Softer, more supple and often less tannic than Cabernet Sauvignon—with which it is often blended—but capable of producing voluptuous, opulent, plummy wines of great interest. A grape that has proven popular on its own as it produces wines that are often easier to drink and are approachable earlier than wines made from Cabernet Sauvignon.

NEBBIOLO: The grape from which the Barolo and Barbaresco wines of Italy's Piedmont region are made. Still experimental in Israel but with the potential for producing perfumed, fruity and intense wines that are full-bodied, high in tannins, acidity and color, and have the potential for long-term cellaring.

PETIT VERDOT: Planted only in small quantities and used in Israel as it is in Bordeaux, primarily for blending with other noble varieties to add acidity and balance. Capable on its own of producing a long-lived and tannic wine when ripe.

PETITE SIRAH: Related only peripherally to the great Syrah grape, this grape is, at its best, capable of producing dark, tannic and well-balanced wines of great appeal and sophistication. This potential is being realized far more frequently within Israel, especially when the grapes come from older vineyards.

PINOT NOIR: A relatively recent transplant to Israel, this grape, which is responsible for the great reds of Burgundy, is making a very good initial showing. At its best the grape is capable of producing smooth, rich and intricate wines of exquisite qualities, with flavors of cherries, wild berries and violets, which as they age take on aromas and flavors of chocolate and game meat. Also used in Israel, as in the Champagne region of France, to blend with Chardonnay to make sparkling wines.

PINOTAGE: A South African cross between Pinot Noir and Cinsault, capable of being flavorful and powerful, yet soft and full, with a pleasing sweet finish and a lightly spicy overlay.

SANGIOVESE: Italy's most frequently planted variety, found in the simplest Chianti and most complex Brunello di Montalcino wines, this is another grape recently introduced to Israel, showing fine early results with wines that are lively, fruity and full of charm.

SYRAH: Some believe that this grape originated in ancient Persia and was brought to France by the Romans, while others speculate that it is indigenous to France. Syrah found its first glory in France's northern Rhone Valley, and then in Australia (where it is known as Shiraz). Capable of producing deep royal purple tannic wines that are full-bodied enough to be thought of as dense and powerful, but with excellent balance and complex aromas and flavors of plums, berries, currants, black pepper and chocolate. First results from this grape have been exciting and plantings are increasing dramatically.

TEMPRANILLO: The staple grape of Spain's Rioja area, with recent plantings in Israel, this is a grape with the potential for producing long-lived complex and sophisticated wines typified by aromas and flavors of black fruits, leather, tobacco and spices.

ZINFANDEL: Zinfandel (the Italian variety of which is known as Primitivo) is not exactly new in Israel, but until recently the vines that had been planted were capable of producing only mediocre semi-dry blush wines. What is new are recently planted high-quality vines from California that offer the potential for producing full-bodied to massive wines, moderately to highly alcoholic, with generous tannins and the kind of warm berry flavors that typify these wines at their best.

Vintage Reports: 1976–2008

The first formal vintage tables appeared in the 1820s and since then wine lovers have relied on them to help make their buying and drinking decisions. As popular as they are, however, it is important to remember that because all vintage tables involve generalizations, there are no firm facts to be found in them. In a sense, these charts are meant to give an overall picture and perhaps to supply clues about which wines to consider buying or drinking. In making one's decisions it is wise to remember that the quality of wines of any vintage year and in any region can vary enormously between wineries. Also worth keeping in mind is that vintage reports and tables such as those that follow are based on what most people consider "quality wines" and not those made for everyday drinking and thus not intended for aging. More than this, estimates of drinkability are based on wines that have been shipped and stored under ideal conditions. Equally important, whether one enjoys drinking wines when they are young, in their adolescence, during their early adulthood or when they become fully mature is much a matter of personal taste.

Following are short reports on the last five vintage years, these followed by a listing of the years of interest going back to 1976. Vintage years are rated on a scale of 20–100, and these numerical values can be interpreted as follows:

100	=	Extraordinary
90	=	Exceptional
80	=	Excellent
70	=	Very Good
60	=	Good but Not Exciting
50	=	Average but with Many Faulted Wines
40	=	Mediocre/Not Recommended
30	=	Poor/Not Recommended
20	=	Truly Bad/Not Recommended

The following symbols are used to indicate drinking windows (Predictions of drinking windows are based on ideal storage since the wine was released.):

C	=	Worthy of Cellaring
D/C	=	Drink or Cellar
D	=	Drink Now or in the Next Year or So
D–	=	Past Its Prime but Probably Still Drinkable
SA	=	Well Beyond Its Prime and Probably Undrinkable

The Last Five Years

2008 VINTAGE RATING 92

An exceptional year for both reds and whites, advance and barrel-tasting revealing rich, ripe qualities and often age-worthy wines. C

2007 VINTAGE RATING 86

The second not-at-all-exciting vintage in a row, reflecting an especially dry winter and spring. Probably best from high altitudes where night-day temperatures were most dramatic and probably better for whites than reds. D/C

2006 VINTAGE RATING 86

An especially dry winter, a cold rainy April and then rains during mid-harvest in October (five times the seasonal norm) led to an extended harvest lasting from August to November, yielding a surprisingly small crop. Probably better for reds than whites, this was not an exciting year and many of the top-of-the line series and single-vineyard releases will not be released from this vintage. D/C

2005 VINTAGE RATING 90

One of the most promising years in the last decade, with a prolonged harvest of overall high quality, exceptionally good in many parts of the country for reds and whites alike. Barrel tastings reveal wines of excellent balance, structure and aging potential. C

2004 VINTAGE RATING 88

Colder than average temperatures and heavy rainfall during the winter months followed by an unusually warm and dry period during March and April caused early budbreak in warmer vineyards. Relatively cool temperatures returned in May leading to a relatively short and hectic harvest but with an overall excellent crop. A promising year. D/C

Somewhat Older Vintages

2003	90	D/C
2002	82	D

2001	85	D
2000	89	D/C
1999	86	D
1998	85	D
1997	90	D/C
1996	82	D-
1995	90	SA
1994	84	SA
1993	92	D
1992	85	SA
1991	82	SA
1990	91	D
1989	90	SA
1988	85	SA
1987	78	SA
1986	76	SA
1985	90	SA
1984	86	SA
1983	55	SA
1982	55	SA
1979	92	SA
1976	92	SA

Questions of Kashrut

For many years, wines that were kosher had a justifiably bad name, those in the United States being made largely from Concord grapes, which are far from capable of making fine wine, and many of those from Israel following the perceived need for kosher wines to be red, sweet, coarse and without any sign of sophistication. The truth is that those wines were not so much consumed by knowledgeable wine lovers as they were used for sacramental purposes. Such wines are still made but are today perceived largely as oddities. With kosher wines now being made from the most noble grape varieties in state-of-the-art wineries by talented winemakers, there need be no contradiction whatsoever between the laws of kashrut and the production of fine wine.

Some Israeli Wines Are Kosher, Others Are Not

A look at the current Israeli wine scene indicates that the wines of every large winery and the majority of medium-sized wineries in Israel are kosher, but those of the smaller wineries are often not.

For many years, all of the wines produced in Israel were kosher, with the exception of those made in Christian monasteries. The reasons for this were and still are twofold. The first reason relates to the fact that a large proportion of the Israeli population, even among the non-observant, consume only foods and beverages that are kosher. The second, also with a clear economic basis, is that only kosher products can enter the large supermarket chains in the country. Because the majority of wines produced in the country continue to be purchased in supermarkets, no large winery can give up that considerable sales potential. In addition, kashrut is maintained because many of the wineries continue to target their export sales largely toward Jewish consumers worldwide.

The wines of several medium-sized producers and many of the boutique wineries have a somewhat different goal in mind—that of producing upper-end wines that are targeted toward higher-end and not necessarily kashrut-observant wine consumers both in Israel and abroad. The production of kosher wines, which more than anything adds the need for additional staff (for example, rabbinical supervisors), as well as fees to the rabbinical authorities, can add prohibitively to the costs and the eventual retail price of wines, especially for small wineries.

What Makes an Israeli Wine Kosher?

In order for an Israeli wine to be certified as kosher, several requirements must be met. As can easily be seen, none of these requirements has a negative impact on the quality of the wine being produced and several are widely acknowledged to be sound agricultural practices even by producers of non-kosher wines.

1. According to the practice known as *orla*, the grapes of new vines cannot be used for winemaking until the fourth year after planting.

2. No other fruits or vegetables may be grown in between the rows of vines (*kalai hakerem*).

3. After the first harvest, the fields must lie fallow every seventh year. Each of these sabbatical years is known as *shnat shmita*.

4. From the onset of the harvest only kosher tools and storage facilities may be used in the winemaking process, and all of the winemaking equipment must be cleaned to be certain that no foreign objects remain in the equipment or vats.

5. From the moment the grapes reach the winery, only Sabbath-observant Jews are allowed to come in contact with the wine. Because many of the winemakers in the country are not Sabbath observant, this means that they cannot personally handle the equipment or the wine as it is being made and are assisted in several of their more technical tasks by Orthodox assistants and kashrut supervisors (*mashgichim*).

6. All of the materials (e.g., yeasts) used in the production and clarification of the wines must be certified as kosher.

7. A symbolic amount of wine, representing the tithe (*truma vema'aser*) once paid to the Temple in Jerusalem, must be poured away from the tanks or barrels in which the wine is being made.

The Question of Wines That Are Mevushal

Some observant Jews demand that their wines be pasteurized (*mevushal*), especially in restaurants and at catered events, where there is the possibility that a non-Jew may handle the wine. This tradition dates to ancient times, when wine was used by pagans for idolatrous worship: the Israelites used to boil their wines, thus changing the chemical composition of the wine so that it was considered unfit for pagan worship. Wines that are *mevushal* have the advantage that they can be opened and poured by non-Jews or Jews who are not Sabbath observant.

Today, *mevushal* wines are no longer boiled. After the

grapes are crushed, the common practice is to rapidly raise the temperature of the liquids to 176–194 degrees Fahrenheit (80–90 Celsius) in special flash pasteurizing units, hold it there for under a minute and then return the temperature, equally rapidly, to 60 degrees Fahrenheit (15 Celsius).

There is no question that modern technology has reduced the impact of these processes on the quality of the wine, but most winemakers and consumers remain in agreement that, with very few exceptions, wines that have been pasteurized lose many of their essential essences, often being incapable of developing in the bottle and quite often imparting a "cooked" sensation to the nose and palate. It is important to note that since 2008 the best wines of Israeli wineries have not been *mevushal* for local consumption but often undergo that process for wines destined for export.

Some wines are produced in both regular and *mevushal* versions, the *mevushal* editions destined for the export market or for the highly observant within Israel. Because it is almost impossible for anyone outside of the wineries to keep track of and taste all of those wines, no attempt is made within this book to report on such "double bottlings."

Simply stated, a wine that is *mevushal* is no more or less kosher than a wine that is not, and none of the better wines of Israel today fall into this category. Those who are concerned with such issues will find the information they require on either the front or rear labels of wines produced in the country.

A Few Lists

Ten Best Wine Producers
1. Golan Heights Winery (Katzrin, Yarden, Gamla)
2. Yatir
3. Margalit
4. Castel
5. Clos de Gat
6. Flam
7. Chateau Golan
8. Pelter

9. Carmel (Limited Edition, Single Vineyard, Appellation)
10. Galil Mountain

Ten Up-and-Coming Producers

1. Binyamina
2. Tabor
3. Assaf
4. Vitkin
5. Odem Mountain
6. Avidan
7. Psagot
8. Tulip
9. Trio
10. Zion

Ten Best Value Producers

1. Galil Mountain
2. Tabor
3. Dalton
4, Golan Heights Winery (Gamla, Golan)
5. Recanati
6. Saslove
7. Barkan
8. Tishbi
9. Teperberg
10. Zion

The Twenty-Five Best Wines Released in the Last Twelve Months

In earlier editions of this book, I have listed what I consider the ten best wines released in the year preceding publication. This year, a departure in procedure is called for, for if only ten wines were to be named, the list would be dominated largely by the Clos de Gat winery, which released six wines scoring 92 points or higher. In order to add a bit of balance, this year's list is thus of the twenty-five best wines of the year, all scoring between 92 and 94 points. In each score category wineries are listed in alphabetical order.

EARNING 94 POINTS
Chateau Golan, Cabernet Sauvignon, Royal Reserve, 2005
Margalit, Cabernet Sauvignon, Special Reserve, 2007
Yatir, Yatir Forest, 2005

EARNING 93 POINTS
Carmel, Limited Edition, 2005
Carmel, Cabernet Sauvignon, Single Vineyard, Kayoumi, Upper Galilee, 2007
Carmel, Gewurztraminer, Late Harvest, Single Vineyard, Sha'al Vineyard, 2008
Chateau Golan, Geshem, Royal Reserve, 2005
Clos de Gat, Merlot, Sycra, 2006
Clos de Gat, Ayalon Valley, 2005
Clos de Gat, Syrah, Har'el, 2007
Galil Mountain, Yiron, 2005
Golan Heights Winery, Katzrin, 2004
Golan Heights Winery, Cabernet Sauvignon, Elrom Vineyard, 2006
Margalit, Merlot, 2007
Margalit, Cabernet Franc, 2007
Pelter, T-Selection, Cabernet Sauvignon, 2006
Pelter, Petit Verdot, T-Selection, 2006
Yatir, Shiraz, 2007

EARNING 92 POINTS
Binyamina, Merlot, Reserve, 2006
Carmel, Shiraz, Single Vineyard, Kayoumi, 2007
Castel, Grand Vin Castel, 2007
Clos de Gat, Cabernet Sauvignon, Har'el, 2007
Clos de Gat, Chardonnay, 2008
Ella Valley Vineyards, Syrah, Vineyard's Choice, 2007
Margalit, Enigma, 2006
Pelter, Pinot Noir, T-Selection, 2006

Drinking Habits

Within Israel

Since the founding of the state in 1948 and until 1997, annual Israeli wine consumption held steady at about 3.9 liters per capita. Although there is some debate about precisely how much wine is being consumed by Israelis, recent years have seen a major increase, and consumption now stands at about 6 liters annually. This figure puts Israelis far behind the French and Italians, who consume 56 and 49 liters respectively, or even the Australians who consume 20 liters per year. It is also interesting that recent studies show that in Israel there is no significant correlation between wine consumption and either alcoholism or automobile accidents.

The increase in local consumption reflects of course the increasing quality of local wines. However, it also reflects the fact that more and more Israelis are traveling abroad and dining in fine restaurants where wine is an integral part of the meal. Today, many Israelis are touring the fine wineries of Bordeaux, Tuscany and the Napa Valley, and even though such wine appreciation is still limited to the upwardly mobile segment of the population, more and more people now order wine to accompany their meal in a fine restaurant.

In addition to showing a growing appreciation of wine in general, Israelis are moving in several directions that can be seen in many other countries as well. Consumption is shifting from semi-dry to dry wines, from whites to reds, from light to heavier wines and most importantly, there is a movement toward buying higher quality wines. Twenty-five years ago, more than eighty percent of the wines produced in the country were sweet. Today, nearly eighty percent of the wines produced are dry.

Israelis also continue to increase their consumption of imported wines, and the better wine shops of the country stock wines from every region of France, Italy, Australia, New Zealand, California, Washington State, Spain, Portugal, Germany, Austria, Chile and Argentina. Some members of the local wine industry perceive this phenomenon as having a negative impact on the local industry. Others, perhaps with a greater sense of foresight, realize that imported wines pose a challenge to the local wine industry to continue to improve the quality of its products.

Sacramental versus "Wine Culture"

Within Israel, as in nearly every country with a Jewish population, some continue to drink wine entirely for sacramental purposes—as, for example, for the Kiddush blessing that opens the two main meals of the Sabbath and holidays. An increasing number have realized that any kosher wine is appropriate for such purposes, but others hold to the perceived tradition that such wines should be red, thick and sweet. Although such wines hold no interest for sophisticated wine drinkers, several of the large wineries continue to produce Kiddush wines and there are wineries that focus entirely on these consumers.

Within the "Jewish World"

Nearly all of the better wine stores of the major cities of North America, the United Kingdom and France have at least a small section devoted to kosher wines, and in recent years the wines of Israel have taken a more prominent space on those shelves alongside kosher wines from California, France, Spain, Australia, Chile and Argentina. The reception of Israeli wines, both kosher and non-kosher, is gradually getting warmer: They are now being reviewed more regularly in magazines devoted to wine as well as in the weekly wine columns of many critics, and are appearing on the menus of an increasing number of prestigious restaurants.

Israel as a Potential Supplier of "Niche Wines"

Wine lovers enjoy few things more than hunting for previously unknown or little-known wines. So it has been in recent years, for example, with the wines of Sicily, and the Penedes region of Spain: When those wines first arrived on the shelves of wine stores in New York, London and Toronto, they filled an empty "niche." The first wines sold out quickly, those that proved to be of high quality were reordered, and those that came to be accepted as truly excellent moved out of the niche category and onto the regular shelves.

Many, including this critic, feel that Israeli wines are on the verge of being accepted as niche wines, especially in North America and the United Kingdom. When this happens, the wines will move off those shelves limited only to kosher holdings and begin to appear in a special Israeli or Mediterranean section. Their appeal to the broader population will come from their unique qualities, reflecting their Mediterranean and specifically Israeli character.

The Wineries and Their Wines

For many years it was possible to group Israeli wine producers into one of two broad categories—large and small wineries. The last seven years have seen dramatic changes, for during that time five new medium-sized producers have appeared on the local scene, several of the wineries that could be categorized as boutiques have expanded their production, and although some boutique wineries have closed, a host of small wineries continues to open. Within each category there are wineries that produce excellent and often exciting wines.

The wines reviewed in this guide include only those I have tasted—wines already on the market, wines due to be released within the next several months, or those still in the cellars or homes of wine lovers. Also listed are barrel tastings, some being those of wines scheduled to be released only in another two to three years. Not included in the guide are wineries that produce wines primarily for sacramental purposes, as those wines hold no interest for wine consumers at large. Nor, with only a few exceptions, does the guide rate the wines of those wineries producing under 2,500 bottles annually. Ratings for wineries (1–5 stars) are based on current status. For wineries that have been releasing wines for less than three years, their ratings should be considered as tentative, as those ratings might move up or down in the next editions of this guide, much depending on the consistency of future releases.

Those seeking reviews of more mature wines not listed herein are referred to earlier editions of this book. If that is not possible, inquiries may be addressed to the author at rogov@tobypress.com.

Achziv **

Founded in 2005 by the Guberman family, with Mark Guberman as the winemaker, and located on Kibbutz Gesher
Haziv, not far from the city of Nahariya
in the Western Galilee, this small winery
produces red wines from Cabernet Sauvignon, Syrah and Merlot grapes. Current production is about 2,000 bottles
annually.

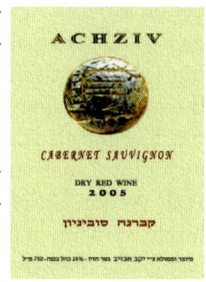

ACHZIV, CABERNET SAUVIGNON, 2007: Dark garnet, full-bodied,
with firm tannins now settling in nicely. Opens with hints of spicy
wood and currants, those yielding to aromas and flavors of wild berries,
dark chocolate and, on the generous finish, a hint of licorice. Drink
now–2011. Score 85.

ACHZIV, CABERNET SAUVIGNON, 2006: Blended with 15% Merlot,
full-bodied, firmly tannic and reflecting its 12 months in French oak
with a light smoky overlay. Opens to reveal traditional blackcurrant
and blackberry fruits, those leading to a moderately long finish with
an appealing hint of dark chocolate. Drink now. Score 86.

ACHZIV, CABERNET SAUVIGNON, 2005: Garnet toward purple,
medium- to full-bodied, with soft tannins, a round and generous wine.
Blended with 12% Merlot, showing spices and vanilla from the wood and
an array of currant, berry and purple plum fruits. Drink now. Score 85.

ACHZIV, MERLOT, 2007: Garnet to royal purple in color, with the addition of a small amount of Cabernet Sauvignon, medium- to full-bodied,
showing wild berry, cassis and blackberry fruits on a gentle background
of earthy minerals. Soft tannins and a gentle wood influence lead to a
long finish. Drink now–2011. Score 87.

ACHZIV, MERLOT, 2006: Dark royal purple in color, an oak-aged
blend of 85% Merlot and 15% Cabernet Sauvignon, showing blackberry,
chocolate and citrus peel, those somewhat marred by rough-edged tannins and a high level of acidity. Drink now. Score 84.

Agur ✳✳✳

Set on Moshav Agur in the Judean plains, this small winery, owned by winemaker Shuki Yashuv, has grown from releasing 1,800 bottles in the 2000 vintage to about 20,000 in the 2008 vintage. The winery has its own vineyards on the moshav and also draws on grapes from the Ella Valley, those including Cabernet Sauvignon, Merlot, Cabernet Franc and Petit Verdot. Grapes from each vineyard are fermented separately, some in stainless steel vats, others in new and used *barriques*. The winery has moved into a new facility, and the wines will be kosher starting with the 2007 vintage.

Special Reserve

SPECIAL RESERVE, 2006: A medium- to full-bodied blend of 60% Cabernet Sauvignon, 35% Merlot and 5% Cabernet Franc, with firm tannins and generously spicy wood integrating nicely to show appealing blackberry, black cherry and sweet herbs on the nose and palate. Long and generous. Drink now–2011. Score 88.

SPECIAL RESERVE, CABERNET SAUVIGNON, 2005: Dark royal purple, medium- to full-bodied, with generous spicy oak integrating with chewy tannins and fruits. A blend of 85% Cabernet Sauvignon with equal parts of Petit Verdot and Merlot, oak-aged for 18 months, the wine is concentrated, showing currant and plum fruits along with hints of cedar, green olives and sage, with the tannins rising on the persistent finish. Drink now. Score 87.

SPECIAL RESERVE, CABERNET SAUVIGNON, 2004: Dark garnet, with firm tannins and spicy oak. Showing currant, blackberry and licorice aromas and flavors, all leading to a gripping and moderately long finish. Drink now. Score 86.

SPECIAL RESERVE, CABERNET SAUVIGNON, 2003: With its once firm tannins now integrating nicely, this dark ruby red is showing generous oak and spicy blackberry and currant fruits. Drink up. Score 86.

Agur

AGUR, CABERNET SAUVIGNON, 2006: Dark garnet, full-bodied, with good balance between dusty wood, blackcurrants and blackberries supported by a potpourri of spices and cedar and a hint of minerals on the firm and complex finish. Drink now. Score 86–88.

AGUR, CABERNET SAUVIGNON, 2004: Dark ruby toward garnet, medium- to full-bodied, with chunky country-style tannins and appealing blackberry, currant, and spicy aromas and flavors. Drink now. Score 86.

AGUR, MERLOT, 2006: Super-dark purple, with gripping tannins that turn supple from mid-palate and reveal cherry cola, black cherry and plum fruits on a background of mocha and spicy oak. The best yet from Agur. Drink from release–2012. Tentative Score 88–90.

AGUR, KESSEM, 2006: A blend of Cabernet Sauvignon, Merlot and Petite Verdot (50%, 30% and 20% respectively). Aged in *barriques* for 12 months, with soft, gently caressing tannins and an appealing overlay of spices, opening to reveal blackberry, blackcurrant and purple plum fruits, those supported nicely by hints of earthy minerals. Drink now–2011. Score 87.

AGUR, KESSEM, 2005: This unfiltered medium-bodied blend of 60% Cabernet Sauvignon, 30% Merlot and about 5% each Cabernet Franc and Petit Verdot was developed in *barriques* for 12 months, and is showing gentle overlays of spices and a hint of vanilla, with soft tannins and generous blackberry, red currant and red plums, all leading to a somewhat acidic but lingering finish. Drink up. Score 87.

AGUR, ROSA, 2008: Dark ruby in color, medium-bodied, with soft tannins. A round, easy-to-drink wine with a basic berry-cherry personality made somewhat more interesting by notes of sweet chewing tobacco that come in from mid-palate. Drink up. Score 85. **K**

AGUR, ROSA, 2007: A rosé wine made from equal parts of Cabernet Sauvignon and Cabernet Franc, fermented in old *barriques* after short skin contact. Medium-bodied, with a light tannic hint, and simple but appealing blackberry, raspberry and strawberry fruits. Drink up. Score 84. **K**

AGUR, BLANCO, 2008: Light straw colored, medium-bodied, a blend of Viognier and Riesling. On the nose and palate tropical and summer fruits come together nicely with a hint of bitter peach pits. Drink now. Score 85. **K**

AGUR, BLANCO, 2007: A light, bright and lively white, showing simple but pleasant summer and tropical fruits. A blend of 70% Viognier and 30% Riesling. Nothing complex here but easy to drink. Drink up. Score 85. **K**

Alexander ✶✶✶✶

Located on Moshav Beit Yitzhak in the Sharon region, the winery, founded in 1996 by Yoram Shalom, receives grapes largely from contract vineyards over which it has full control at Kerem Ben Zimra in the Upper Galilee. Primary output to date has been of Cabernet Sauvignon, Merlot, Chardonnay and Sauvignon Blanc and now coming on line are Syrah and Grenache.

Growth has been steady, increasing from about 12,000 bottles in 2002 to 45,000 in 2005 and 2006. With the 2006 vintage the winery switched over to kosher production and planned output for that and the 2007 harvest is 45,000–50,000 bottles. In addition to producing two top-of-the-line series, Alexander the Great and Alexander, the winery also releases two blended wines, Sandro and Gaston. In addition, the winery produces private label wines for several restaurants.

Alexander the Great

ALEXANDER THE GREAT, CABERNET SAUVIGNON, 2007: Dark, almost impenetrable garnet in color, full-bodied, concentrated and intense. On first attack dried figs and orange peel, those yielding to traditional Cabernet currant and berry notes, all with a sweet chocolate overlay. Drink now–2012, perhaps longer. Score 88. **K**

ALEXANDER THE GREAT, CABERNET SAUVIGNON, 2006: Dark garnet toward royal purple, full-bodied and with still-firm tannins and reflecting its development in *barriques* for 15 months with generous spicy wood, those in fine balance and needing only time to integrate. On the nose and palate blackcurrant, blackberry and dark chocolate notes, all leading to a long, mouth-filling finish. Drink now–2012. Score 89. **K**

ALEXANDER THE GREAT, CABERNET SAUVIGNON, 2005: Made from grapes from 26-year-old vines, this medium- to full-bodied dark garnet-red wine shows soft tannins, spicy wood and a tempting array of mineral, black fruit, herbal and chocolate aromas. On the long finish, cloves and a hint of iodine. Best 2009–2013. Score 90.

ALEXANDER THE GREAT, CABERNET SAUVIGNON, GRAND RE-SERVE, 2004: Reflecting its 48 months in mostly new oak *barriques* with far too generous smoky and vanilla overlays and gripping tannins, those yielding slowly in the glass to reveal moderate levels of plums, blackberries and currants, all with overlays of mocha and herbs. More powerful and intense than elegant, a distinctly overly oaky wine. Drink now–2011. Score 86.

ALEXANDER THE GREAT, CABERNET SAUVIGNON, 2004: Full-bodied and reflecting the *barriques* in which it developed with firm, near-sweet tannins and hints of spicy wood. Generous and long with a complex array of currant, herbal and mineral aromas and flavors. Drink now–2011. Score 90.

Alexander

ALEXANDER, CABERNET SAUVIGNON, 2005: Medium- to full-bodied, dark ruby in color, with soft tannins; showing vanilla and spices from the casks in which it aged. On the nose and palate, rich blackcurrant and blackberry fruits along with hints of earthiness. Drink now. Score 88.

ALEXANDER, CABERNET SAUVIGNON, 2004: Medium- to full-bodied, with gripping tannins and wood nicely balanced by generous black fruits. Drink now. Score 87.

ALEXANDER, MERLOT, 2005: Deep royal purple, with firm but nicely integrating tannins. Hints of spicy wood and tobacco balanced nicely by a generous array of black plum, raspberry, cassis and chocolate aromas and flavors. Drink now. Score 89.

ALEXANDER, MERLOT, 2004: Dark cherry toward garnet, medium-bodied, with soft tannins integrating nicely. Round and generous, with cassis, blackberry and black cherry fruits accompanied by hints of pepper and nutmeg. Drink now. Score 86.

ALEXANDER, SYRAH, 2005: Dark royal purple, full-bodied, with deep but remarkably soft tannins. Hints of smoky wood, freshly turned earth and spices on a background of black fruits and, on the finish, light smoked meat. Drink now. Score 89.

ALEXANDER, MERLOT-SYRAH-GRENACHE, 2004: Deep royal purple, full-bodied, with soft tannins integrating nicely and showing an appealing array of plum, cassis and orange peel fruits, those backed up by Mediterranean herbs. Lingers nicely on the palate. Drink now. Score 90.

ALEXANDER, CHARDONNAY, LIZA, 2007: Wet golden straw in color, medium-bodied, with light spicy notes setting off citrus, pear and melon fruits. Reflecting 18 months of oak-aging, a rather woody wine lacking liveliness or complexity. Drink up. Score 84. **K**

ALEXANDER, SAUVIGNON BLANC, LIZA, 2007: Developed partly in stainless steel and partly in *barriques* for several months, a simple but pleasant wine showing pineapple, guava and green apple notes. A bit more acidity would have added liveliness. Drink up. Score 82. **K**

Sandro

SANDRO, 2006: Dark ruby, medium- to full-bodied, a blend of Merlot, Cabernet Sauvignon and Sauvignon Blanc (70%, 25% and 5%, respectively). Reflecting 14 months in oak, dusty wood and soft, gently gripping tannins, those parting to show appealing currant, berry and orange peel notes. Drink now. Score 87. **K**

SANDRO, 2005: A medium-bodied blend of Cabernet Sauvignon and Merlot, with soft tannins and light spicy wood, opening in the glass to reveal traditional blackberry and currant fruits. Soft and round. Drink up. Score 87.

Gaston

GASTON, GMS, 2005: A blend of 76% Merlot and 12% each of Grenache and Syrah. Dark garnet, medium- to full-bodied, aged in *barriques* for 12 months. On first attack generous wood on both nose and palate, but that recedes nicely to reveal currant, wild berry and plum fruits on a just spicy-enough background. Well balanced and long. Drink now. Score 88.

GASTON, 2004: An oak blend of 76% Merlot and 12% each of Grenache and Syrah. Dark, nearly inky-garnet in color, with intense almost jam-like cherry and berry fruits, those supported by Oriental spices. On the moderately long finish an attractive herbal-earthiness. Drink up. Score 87.

Aligote **

Established by Tsvika Fante and located on Moshav Gan Yoshiya on the central Coastal Plain, the first wines released by this winery were 800 bottles from the 2002 harvest. Production is currently 4,000 bottles annually.

ALIGOTE, CABERNET SAUVIGNON, 2006: Garnet toward royal purple, medium- to full bodied, with gripping tannins that yield slowly in the glass. Currant and blackberry fruits, those overlaid by spicy wood and notes of Mediterranean herbs. Drink now. Score 85.

ALIGOTE, CABERNET SAUVIGNON, 2005: Traditional Cabernet aromas and flavors of blackberries and currants, those matched nicely by hints of green olives, spices and espresso coffee. Drink up. Score 84.

ALIGOTE, MERLOT, 2006: Dark garnet, medium-bodied, with somewhat chunky country-style tannins. Opens to show appealing blackberry, black cherry and spices, with oak and tannins rising on the finish. Drink now. Score 84.

ALIGOTE, MERLOT, 2005: Dark ruby toward garnet, medium-bodied, with soft tannins. Generous cherry, berry and spice flavors with a hint of sandalwood on the finish. Drink up. Score 84.

ALIGOTE, SANGIOVESE, 2005: Ruby toward purple, medium-bodied, with appealing black cherry, blackberry and spicy aromas and flavors. Not complex but a good quaffer. Drink now. Score 84.

Alon **✶✶**

Founded in 2003 and located on Moshav Alonei Aba, north of Haifa, this small winery produced about 5,000 bottles from the 2006 vintage and 3,500 from the 2007. Winemaker Chaim Cachala makes wines primarily from Cabernet Sauvignon, Tempranillo, Cabernet Franc, Carignan, Petit Verdot and Petite Sirah grapes, those predominantly from the Galilee and Jezreel Valley.

ALON, CABERNET SAUVIGNON, 2006: Medium-bodied with gently gripping tannins, this oak-aged red shows appealing red currant and cherry fruits, those with hints of chocolate and licorice. Drink now. Score 84.

ALON, CABERNET SAUVIGNON, 2005: Deep royal purple, medium- to full-bodied, with soft, near-sweet tannins and spicy wood integrating nicely to show appealing black fruits on a background of Mediterranean herbs. Mouth-filling and moderately long. Drink up. Score 85.

ALON, CABERNET SAUVIGNON, 2003: Dark ruby, medium-bodied, with a somewhat woody influence but also showing cassis and berry fruits along with hints of vanilla. Firmly tannic on the finish. Drink up. Score 83.

ALON, CARIGNAN, 2005: Dark garnet and aromatic, this medium-bodied blend of 86% Carignan and 7% each of Tempranillo and Cabernet Sauvignon shows soft tannins that are settling in nicely with berry, black cherry and currant fruits. Hints of chocolate and licorice on the finish. Drink up. Score 82.

ALON, CABERNET FRANC, 2006: Deep ruby toward garnet, medium- to full-bodied, with silky smooth tannins and gentle spicy wood opening to show raspberry, cassis and light herbal aromas and flavors. Drink now. Score 85.

ALON, PETIT VERDOT, 2006: Dark garnet, medium-bodied, with good varietal character showing cassis, tobacco and herbal notes. Not complex but fresh and crisp. Drink now. Score 84.

ALON, PETIT VERDOT, 2005: An oak-aged blend of 88% Petit Verdot and 12% Tempranillo. Royal purple, light- to medium-bodied, with soft tannins and somewhat generous smoke as it first opens, that yields to reveal berry and cherry fruits together with a hint of licorice. Drink up. Score 84.

ALON, TEMPRANILLO, 2005: Blended with 15% Petite Sirah, this ruby-toward-garnet, medium-bodied red shows soft tannins, gentle spiciness and appealing plum and herbal notes. Drink now. Score 85.

ALON, PETITE SIRAH, 2005: A pleasant little country-style wine, coarse and tannic but opening to reveal generous red plum and blueberry fruits. Drink up. Score 84.

Alona ✳✳✳

Founded in 2001 by the Azoulay and Rabau families on Givat Nili, not far from the city of Zichron Ya'akov, the vineyards of this small winery are spread on the slopes above Nachal Taninim, and contain Cabernet Sauvignon and Merlot grapes. Current production is about 8,000 bottles annually.

ALONA, CABERNET SAUVIGNON, 2006: Dark and brooding, full-bodied and concentrated, with firm tannins and spicy wood yielding to show currants, berries and notes of Mediterranean herbs. Drink now. Score 86.

ALONA, CABERNET SAUVIGNON, 2005: Dark garnet, full-bodied, with caressing soft tannins and spicy oak, those in good balance with fresh blackberry and currant aromas and flavors. On the finish a touch of cedar. Drink now. Score 88.

ALONA, MERLOT, 2005: Deep garnet toward royal purple, medium-to full-bodied, with appealing aromas and flavors of spicy plums and currants. Graceful and elegant. Drink now. Score 90.

ALONA, MERLOT, 2004: Dark royal purple in color, medium- to full-bodied, with good concentration and density. Showing blackcurrant, berry, vanilla and creamy notes. Lingers nicely with hints of mocha and cream on the finish. Drink now. Score 90.

ALONA, CABERNET SAUVIGNON-MERLOT, 2005: Medium- to full-bodied, with soft tannins and showing an appealing array of berry and cherry fruits on a lightly spicy background. Lacks complexity but a good quaffer. Drink now. Score 86.

Amphorae ✶✶✶✶

Set in the green and luxuriant mouth of a long-dormant volcano on the western slopes of Mount Carmel, the winery was founded in 2000, and with Gil Shatzberg as winemaker emerged as one of the most promising wineries in the country. In early 2008, Shatzberg moved to Recanati Winery, and several months after that the winery was sold to a group led by David Bar-Ilan of the Keshet winery (a winery that has still to release its first wines). The stars awarded to the winery are thus based on performance up to and including the releases from the 2006 vintage.

Production from the 2000 vintage was 23,000 bottles and production for 2006 was about 80,000 bottles. Because of ownership changes, current production is not known. The winery has released wines in four series, the top of the line Amphorae Reserve, the regular Amphorae releases, the wines in the Rhyton series and those labeled Med.Red or Med. Blend. The first three series are age-worthy, and the Med.Red and Med.Blend wines are meant for youthful consumption. Those residing in the United States should note that all Amphorae wines are being sold there under the "Marvah" label.

Amphorae is the Greek term for tall, double-handled jugs with narrow necks and bases, often made of clay, that were used by the Greeks and later by the Romans for storing and shipping wine. The original rhyton was an ancient Greek cup, most often shaped like a drinking horn.

Amphorae Reserve

Cabernet Sauvignon 2001 **Amphorae**Vineyard

AMPHORAE, CABERNET SAUVIGNON, RESERVE, 2005: Showing dark, full-bodied and soft, gently mouth-coating tannins, those yielding on the nose and palate to reveal generous black fruits. The potential is here for true elegance and great length. Best from release–2012. Tentative Score 92–94.

AMPHORAE, RESERVE, 2003: A blend of Cabernet Sauvignon, Merlot and Cabernet Franc (70%, 15% and 15% respectively). Generously but not offensively oaked, dark garnet to royal purple, deeply aromatic and full-bodied, with caressing tannins. On the nose and palate an elegant array of currant, blackberry, blueberry, cedar and herbs with hints of cola on the long, generous finish. Drink now–2014. Score 93.

AMPHORAE, CABERNET SAUVIGNON, RESERVE, 2000: Deep garnet-red, remarkably rich, complex and aromatic. Excellent balance, with tiers of currant, plum, Mediterranean herbs and sweet oak coming to a long finish. A wine worthy of cellaring. Drink now–2014. Score 93.

Amphorae

AMPHORAE, CABERNET SAUVIGNON, 2006: Medium- to full-bodied, with soft tannins and gentle wood, a supple and velvety wine offering blackcurrant, blackberry and raspberry fruits, those supported nicely by hints of tobacco and anise. Tightly wound, but with time will show complexity and elegance. Drink now–2013. Score 90.

AMPHORAE, CABERNET SAUVIGNON, 2005: Dark garnet, full-bodied with generous smoky and dusty oak on first attack, that happily settling down as the wine sits in the glass. A deep-garnet blend of 90% Cabernet Sauvignon with 5% each of Syrah and Cabernet Franc, showing fine balance between wood, soft tannins and aromas, and flavors of spicy plums, currants and espresso coffee. A long mineral and sage-rich finish. Drink now–2011. Score 90.

AMPHORAE, CABERNET SAUVIGNON, 2004: Deeply aromatic, full-bodied with firm tannins, showing fine balance and structure. On the nose and palate blackberries, currants, and black cherries, those offset by mocha, vanilla and spicy oak. Drink now. Score 91.

AMPHORAE, MERLOT, ORGANIC, 2006: From the organic vineyard at Makura Ranch, this dark ruby red and deeply aromatic wine is made entirely according to organic principles, Medium- to full-bodied, showing still gripping tannins and a fine balance and structure that bode well for the future. On the nose and palate, near-sweet black cherries, blackberries and currant fruits, those showing appealing hints of spices and spring flowers. Plush, open-textured and long. Drink now–2012. Score 91.

AMPHORAE, MERLOT, 2006: Dark ruby toward garnet, medium- to full-bodied, with firm tannins and a gentle hand with the wood. Seductive, showing ripe blackberry, currant and wild berries, those with overlays of dark chocolate and freshly ground coffee. Complex and concentrated but showing elegance and length. Drink now–2013. Tentative Score 90–92.

AMPHORAE, MERLOT, ORGANIC, 2005: Made from organically raised Merlot grapes, aged in French oak for 12 months and bottled unfiltered, this deep, almost inky garnet wine shows full body and generous but soft tannins. Blueberries on the nose, then opening in the glass to reveal aromas and flavors of blackberries, blueberries and ripe plums, those on a spicy and lightly earthy-herbal background. Drink now–2011. Score 90.

AMPHORAE, MERLOT, 2005: Dark garnet, medium- to full-bodied, with its once chewy tannins now settling down nicely and matched comfortably by spicy wood, all in fine balance with currant and black cherry fruits, those supported by hints of chocolate and licorice, and, on the long finish, a hint of sweet cedar. Tight, focused, rich and long. Drink now–2012. Score 91.

AMPHORAE, MERLOT, 2004: Garnet toward royal purple, medium- to full-bodied, with firm tannins integrating nicely with generous wood, all coming together with purple plum, raspberry and briar notes, and all lingering nicely with a tantalizing hint of bitter herbs that rises on the finish. Drink now–2011. Score 90.

AMPHORAE, SYRAH, 2006: Developing in French oak and showing notes of appealing dusty wood. Medium- to full-bodied, opening with traditional Syrah spices, black pepper, leather and earthy minerals, those yielding nicely to blackberry, boysenberry and plums. Long and elegant, with tannins and fruits rising simultaneously on the finish. Drink from release–2014. Tentative score 90–92.

AMPHORAE, SYRAH, 2005: A full-bodied, aromatic and generous wine showing soft, caressing tannins and generous peppery plum, wild berry, exotic spices and hints of roasted meat and earthy minerals. Round, ripe and long with notes of citrus peel and vanilla on the long finish. Drink now–2014. Score 92.

AMPHORAE, SYRAH, 2004: Full-bodied, with firm and well-structured tannins integrating nicely and showing a core of leather, spicy wood and earthiness that highlight rich currant, wild berry, anise and lightly beefy flavors. On the long, elegant finish, generous hints of espresso coffee, violets and toffee. Drink now–2012. Score 91.

AMPHORAE, CABERNET FRANC, 2004: Deep garnet with bright raspberry and plum flavors, this dark, rich and plush wine shows thick, earthy tannins and gamey currant and cedarwood aromas and flavors. Perhaps not elegant but certainly powerful and complex. Drink now–2012. Score 90.

AMPHORAE, ROSÉ, ORGANIC, 2006: Made entirely from organically raised Merlot grapes, with six hours of skin contact and a minimal addition of sulfites. Pink toward light ruby in color, medium-bodied, with an appealing array of raspberry, blueberry and cassis fruits, those on a crisply dry, mineral-rich background. Round, generous and refreshing with just the right hints of complexity. Drink up. Score 88.

AMPHORAE, CHARDONNAY, 2007: Developed partly in *barriques* and partly in stainless steel, light golden in color, showing a light oaky note that yields to citrus, peach and tropical fruits, those on a light mineral background. Drink up. Score 88.

AMPHORAE, VIOGNIER, 2007: The color of damp straw and blended with 5% of French Colombard, this unoaked white shows lively floral, peach and nut flavors, those opening to hints of apricots. Not complex but a good quaffer meant for early drinking. Drink now. Score 86.

Rhyton

Rhyton Red 2001   Amphorae**v**ineyard

AMPHORAE, RHYTON, 2006: Garnet toward royal purple, a blend of Cabernet Sauvignon, Syrah and Merlot with the Cabernet dominating. At this early stage showing a bit flabby, the tannins soft, the fruits holding back, and spicy and chocolate notes dominating. Builds as it sits in the glass, so perhaps better with time. Drink now. Score 86.

AMPHORAE, RHYTON, 2005: Medium- to full-bodied, a blend of Cabernet, Merlot and Syrah (50%, 30% and 20% respectively) opening nicely and offering blackberry, black cherry and currant fruits. Look for hints of chocolate and spices on the generous finish. Drink up. Score 87.

Med.Blend

AMPHORAE, MED.BLEND, 2006: Medium-bodied, garnet with purple reflections, and showing soft, gently mouth-coating tannins. A blend of 78% Cabernet Sauvignon, 18% Syrah and 4% Merlot, showing racy black fruits and spices. Round and ready and easy to drink. Drink now. Score 88.

AMPHORAE, MED.BLEND, 2005: A blend of 56% Cabernet Sauvignon, 22% Syrah and 22% Merlot, oak-aged for 14 months. Medium-bodied, soft and round, with gentle wood and tannins highlighting aromas and flavors of currants, black cherries, raspberries and spices, all with hints of tobacco and chocolate on the finish. Drink now. Score 89.

AMPHORAE, MED.BLEND, 2004: Aged in French oak for 14 months and showing medium- to full-bodied, with soft, gently mouth-coating tannins and a well-measured hand with spicy oak. On first attack red currants and wild strawberries, those leading to bitter cherries, tobacco and appealing herbal overtones. On the finish a tantalizing hint of anise. Drink up. Score 89.

Med.Red

AMPHORAE, MED.RED, 2005: Deep ruby toward garnet, medium-bodied, this blend of Cabernet Sauvignon and Shiraz shows soft tannins and a judicious hand with spicy wood; opens in the glass to reveal appealing berry, currant and black cherry fruits. Drink up. Score 88.

AMPHORAE, MED.RED, 2004: Dark garnet toward royal purple and medium-bodied, this blend of Cabernet Sauvignon, Merlot and Syrah shows silky, well-integrating tannins, in fine balance with gentle spicy wood and black fruits. Soft, round and delicious. Drink up. Score 88.

Amram's *

Founded in 2001 on Moshav Ramot Naftaly in the Upper Galilee by grape grower Amram Azulai and his son Ehud, the team has vineyards of Cabernet, Merlot, Shiraz and Sangiovese grapes in Emek Kadesh. Production from 2004 was 2,800 bottles and current releases are of about 6,000 bottles annually. The winery releases two series— the *barrique*-aged Bresheit (literally "Genesis") and Ramot

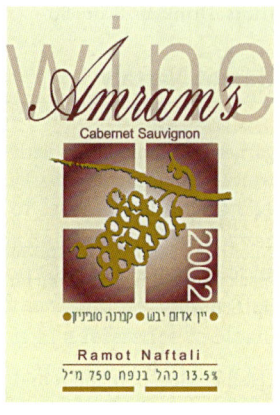

Naftaly, the wines of which are made in large glass containers together with oak chips. Dramatic changes from tasting to tasting lead one to believe that multiple bottlings may have been made.

Bresheit

BRESHEIT, CABERNET SAUVIGNON, 2007: Medium- to full-bodied, showing spicy cedarwood and soft tannins, opens to reveal currant, wild berry and chocolate notes. Round and smooth, a good entry-level wine. Drink now. Score 84.

BRESHEIT, CABERNET SAUVIGNON, 2006: Blended with 7% Merlot and 3% Shiraz and oak-aged for 12 months, this medium- to full-bodied, softly tannic wine shows forward blackberry, currant and cassis notes, those on a background of anise-flavored chocolate, along with a hint of sweetness that may not be appreciated by all. Drink now. Score 83.

BRESHEIT, CABERNET SAUVIGNON, 2005: Dark garnet, with near-sweet tannins, reflecting its 12 months in oak with spices and vanilla. On the nose and palate berries, black cherries and currants. Marred by a hint of sweetness that runs through. Drink now. Score 83.

BRESHEIT, MERLOT, 2005: Dark garnet toward purple in color, medium-bodied, with soft tannins and primarily berry and black cherry fruits. Lacks complexity and showing age. Drink up. Score 78.

BRESHEIT, CABERNET SAUVIGNON-SHIRAZ, 2005: Dark purple, medium-bodied, with chunky tannins and a generous hand with spicy wood, this blend of 75% Cabernet and 25% Shiraz shows plum and berry fruits. Drink up. Score 80.

Ramot Naftaly

RAMOT NAFTALY, CABERNET SAUVIGNON, 2006: Ruby toward garnet, medium-bodied, with soft tannins and showing primarily red fruits. A simple table wine. Drink now. Score 82.

RAMOT NAFTALY, CABERNET SAUVIGNON, 2005: Dark garnet in color but lacking clarity, this medium- to full-bodied wine shows skimpy black fruits hidden under a far-too-generous layer of sweetness. Drink up. Score 75.

RAMOT NAFTALY, MERLOT, 2005: Medium-bodied, a simple but accessible wine. Soft and round with blackberry and blueberry fruits on a lightly spicy background. Drink now. Score 84.

RAMOT NAFTALY, CABERNET SAUVIGNON-MERLOT, 2005: A dark purple blend of 60% Cabernet Sauvignon and 40% Merlot. Medium-bodied, with soft tannins and primarily blueberry aromas and flavors. An acceptable entry-level wine. Drink up. Score 80.

RAMOT NAFTALY, CABERNET SAUVIGNON-SHIRAZ, 2007: Garnet toward royal purple, medium-bodied, with somewhat chunky tannins and too-heavy notes of spicy oak that hide the black fruits that are trying to make themselves felt. Drink now. Score 79.

RAMOT NAFTALY, CABERNET SAUVIGNON-SHIRAZ, 2005: Medium-dark garnet, medium-bodied, with soft tannins. Shows simple berry, cherry fruits on a somewhat overly acidic background. Drink up. Score 78.

RAMOT NAFTALY, CABERNET SAUVIGNON-SANGIOVESE, 2007: Dark but not fully clear ruby in color, medium-bodied, with chunky, country-style tannins. Opens to show wild berry, currant and citrus peel notes. Not complex but easy to drink. Drink now. Score 84.

RAMOT NAFTALY, CABERNET SAUVIGNON-SANGIOVESE, 2006: A blend of 75% Cabernet Sauvignon and 25% Sangiovese, developed with oak chips. Dark garnet, medium-bodied with soft tannins, and showing appealing blackberry and black cherry fruits on a lightly spicy background. Soft and round. A good quaffer. Drink now. Score 85.

Anatot ✴✴

Founded in 1998 by Aharon Helfgot and
Arnon Erez, the winery is located in Anatot,
a community north of Jerusalem, and draws
on grapes primarily from vineyards in the
Lachish and Shiloh regions. Current annual
production is 17,500 oak-aged bottles from
Cabernet Sauvignon, Shiraz and Merlot
grapes. Wines are produced in four series,
Alpha, Shani, Anatot, and Notera.

Alpha

ALPHA, MERLOT-SHIRAZ, 2005: Oak-aged for 18 months, medium- to
full-bodied, with generous wood and gripping tannins that part slowly
to reveal berries and plums on a lightly spicy background. Drink now.
Score 82.

Shani

SHANI, SHIRAZ-CABERNET SAUVIGNON, 2005: Ruby toward garnet,
medium-bodied, with chunky tannins and a few black fruits. A simple
country-style wine that falls somewhat flat on the palate. Oak-aged for
18 months. Drink now. Score 80.

Anatot

ANATOT, CABERNET SAUVIGNON, 2006: Garnet toward royal purple,
medium- to full-bodied, with soft tannins, smoky oak and an appealing
array of wild berry, cassis and citrus peel all on a lightly spicy background. Drink now. Score 85.

ANATOT, CABERNET SAUVIGNON, 2005: Medium- to full-bodied, the
wine has soft tannins, smoky oak and gripping acidity. Opens slowly,
showing black fruits, spices and, on the finish, ripe plums. Drink now.
Score 85.

ANATOT, MERLOT, 2005: Garnet toward purple, medium- to full-
bodied, with chunky tannins that soften as the wine opens and reveals
spicy oak, berries, plums and currant notes. An entry-level wine. Drink
now. Score 83.

ANATOT, SHIRAZ, 2005: Deep royal purple in color, medium-bodied, with soft tannins and spicy wood integrating nicely. Aromas and flavors of plums, berries and hints of tar and licorice. Drink up. Score 84.

Notera

NOTERA, 2005: Medium- to full-bodied, with perhaps too-generous oak that tends to hide the berry, black cherry and currant fruits. Drink up. Score 82.

Asif **

Founded in 2006 and located on Moshav Bnei Atarot on the Central Plain, Asif was set out as the country's first negotiant winery and service winery. In the first role, much as in Burgundy, the winery purchases its own wine by purchasing wines in barrel form from other wineries, and then finishing the wines in the barrel-aging and blending processes. In the second role, as a service winery, the goal is to let other small wineries use the Asif facilities in order to make their own kosher wines. The winery, which is entirely kosher, is also planting several of its own vineyards. Ya'akov Oryah is the winemaker, and the winery is currently releasing about 12,000 bottles annually. Wines are bottled under the Efron's Cave label for export to the U.S.A.

ASIF, CABERNET SAUVIGNON, 2007: Tasted from components. Dark garnet, medium-bodied, with gentle wood influences, soft tannins integrating nicely and good balancing acidity. On the nose and palate red currants, raspberries and blueberries, all lingering nicely. Drink from release. Tentative Score 85–87. **K**

ASIF, CABERNET SAUVIGNON, 2006: A Bordeaux blend of 85% Cabernet Sauvignon, 9% Cabernet Franc and 6% Merlot. Medium- to full-bodied, with gently gripping tannins and notes of sweet-and-spicy cedarwood, opens to reveal ripe plum, blackcurrant and black cherry fruits. Drink now. Score 86. **K**

ASIF, MERLOT, 2005: Dark garnet, blended with 15% of Cabernet Sauvignon, medium- to full-bodied, showing good concentration and balance. Silky tannins and generous wild berry and black cherry notes here along with notes of vanilla and spices, all lingering nicely. Drink now. Score 86. **K**

ASIF, CABERNET SAUVIGNON-CABERNET FRANC-MERLOT, 2005: Garnet, full-bodied with tannins integrating nicely with spicy wood. Oak-aged for 18 months, showing warm and round, with generous blackcurrant and blackberry fruits complemented nicely by notes of Oriental spices, black pepper and green olives. A blend of 85% Cabernet Sauvignon, 9% Cabernet Franc and 6% Merlot. Drink now. Score 88. **K**

ASIF, GRENACHE-SYRAH-MERLOT, 2006: Oak-aged for 18 months, a blend of 45% each of Grenache and Syrah along with 10% Merlot. Ruby toward garnet, medium- to full-bodied, with soft tannins and showing notes of spicy oak. On the nose and palate currant, blackberry and purple plums, those complemented by hints of tobacco, licorice and earthy minerals. Drink now. Score 87. **K**

ASIF, RED BLEND, 2005: A blend of equal parts Zinfandel, Cabernet Sauvignon and Merlot. Medium-bodied, with somewhat chunky tannins that give the wine a sharp edge, but opening in the glass to reveal generous blackberry and currant fruits backed up by a low-key but appealing earthy-herbaceousness. Drink now. Score 85. **K**

ASIF, ROSÉ, 2007: Dark rose-petal pink, a light- to medium-bodied, lively blend of 95% Syrah and 5% Cabernet Sauvignon showing raspberry, strawberry and cassis aromas and flavors. Lively and refreshing. Drink up. Score 85. **K**

ASIF, CHARDONNAY, 2008: The color of damp straw, with an orange tint, a medium-bodied white with a not-complex-but-appealing nose and palate of grapefruit, grapefruit pith and pears, and a light creamy note on the finish. Drink now. Score 86. **K**

ASIF, CHARDONNAY BLEND, 2007: Made entirely from Chardonnay grapes, but called a blend because it was made from grapes from different vineyards. Light golden in color and generously oaky, even though it was aged in *barriques* for only four months. Showing peach, banana and citrus, but not a lively or complex wine. Drink up. Score 83. **K**

ASIF, VIOGNIER, ADAM VEYADAMA, 2008: Bronzed gold in color and despite its youth already taking on a somewhat oxidized note. On the nose and palate citrus peel, Granny Smith apples and hints of earthy minerals. Not for cellaring. Drink up. Score 82. **K**

ASIF, WHITE BLEND, 2008: A somewhat unlikely blend of Sauvignon Blanc, Gewurztraminer and Viognier (64%, 28% and 8% respectively) in which, alas, the varietal traits of each of the grapes is lost. Despite that, a simple but pleasant blend, showing medium-bodied, with lively acidity to highlight grapefruit, spicy and floral notes. Drink now. Score 84. **K**

ASIF, WHITE BLEND, 2007: Light gold in color, a medium-bodied blend of Chardonnay, Sauvignon Blanc and Semillon (42%, 48% and 10% respectively). A rather nondescript blend, reflecting none of the varieties used and lacking in acidity that might have made it more lively. On the nose and palate overripe summer fruits that never come together as a coherent whole. Drink up. Score 78. **K**

Assaf ✶✶✶✶

Founded in 2004 by Assaf Kedem, who was formerly a partner in the Bazelet Hagolan Winery, the winery is located in the village of Kidmat Tzvi on the Golan Heights. Draws on its own vineyards, those containing Cabernet Sauvignon, Cabernet Franc, Shiraz, Zinfandel, Pinotage and Sauvignon Blanc grapes. Production from the 2007 vintage was 25,000 bottles and anticipated production from the 2008 harvest is 35,000 bottles. Wines are bottled in a reserve and a regular series. The same wines sometimes bottled under the Lili label are intended entirely for export.

Reserve

RESERVE, CABERNET SAUVIGNON, 2007: Full-bodied, with soft, almost plush tannins and showing generous currant and cherry fruits, those supported nicely by hints of spicy wood, eucalyptus and bittersweet chocolate. Drink from release–2012. Tentative Score 90–92.

RESERVE, CABERNET SAUVIGNON, 2006: Oak-aged for 14 months, a blend of 93% Cabernet Sauvignon and 7% Cabernet Franc. Dark garnet toward royal purple, full-bodied and with fine balance and structure that bode well for the future. On the nose and palate hints of sweet cedar followed by blackcurrant, purple plum and blackberry fruits, those supported nicely by hints of minted dark chocolate. Drink now–2013. Score 90.

RESERVE, CABERNET SAUVIGNON, 2005: Dark garnet, medium- to full-bodied, with still gripping tannins and generous wood waiting to integrate, but showing fine balance and structure. On the nose and palate black and red berries and blackcurrants supported nicely by spicy tobacco and hints of chocolate. Long and generous. Drink now–2012. Score 90.

RESERVE, CABERNET SAUVIGNON, 2004: Garnet toward deep purple, medium- to full-bodied, this blend of 85% Cabernet Sauvignon and 15% Cabernet Franc was aged in partly French, partly American *barriques* for 12 months. Good balance between mouth-coating tannins, vanilla-tinged spicy oak and acidity. On the palate wild berries, red currants and a light but appealing mineral hint, all lingering nicely. Drink now. Score 90.

RESERVE, SHIRAZ, CAESARIA, 2007: Still young but already showing broad and generous, with generous blackberry, currant and licorice flavors, those with overlays of tar and smoke. Finely tuned balance between wood, tannins and acidity, all leading to a super-long finish. Drink now–2013. Score 90.

RESERVE, SHIRAZ, CAESARIA, 2006: Medium- to full-bodied, ripe, round, soft and generous with blackberry, licorice and mocha notes coming together with hints of smoke and pepper. Oak-aged for 14 months. What cannot help but fascinate is a distinct hint of apricot here. Long, generous and elegant. Drink now–2013. Score 91.

Assaf

ASSAF, CABERNET SAUVIGNON, 2007: Medium- to full-bodied, reflecting its 11 months in oak with gentle notes of sweet cedar and vanilla and soft, well-integrated tannins. On the nose and palate red and black berries and cassis, those complemented nicely by notes of minted chocolate. On the long, mouth-filling finish a hint of red licorice. Drink now–2013. Score 91.

ASSAF, CABERNET SAUVIGNON, 2006: Oak-aged for eight months, dark purple in color, with still-firm tannins, and showing fine balance and structure that bode well for the future. On the nose and palate currants, blackberries, vanilla, dusky herbs and a generously meaty overlay that rises on the long finish. Drink now–2013. Score 90.

ASSAF, CABERNET SAUVIGNON, 2005: Blended with 7% of Cabernet Franc, this medium- to full-bodied, softly tannic, dark garnet-toward-royal purple wine shows fine balance and structure. Seductive, rich and supple, with lush raspberry, blackberry and currant fruits supported nicely by vanilla and, on the long finish, the tannins rising again. Drink now–2011. Score 90.

ASSAF, SHIRAZ, 2006: Blended with 3% Cabernet Sauvignon and oak-aged for 14 months, showing a distinctly Shiraz nose of spicy wood, plums and blackberries, all with a hint of saddle leather. Dark garnet toward royal purple, with just the right notes of spicy wood and fine balance between still firm tannins and fruits. Concentrated and intense but with a distinct touch of elegance and a long finish. Drink now–2012. Score 90.

ASSAF, PINOTAGE, 2007: Made from intentionally early-harvested grapes and developed in used oak barrels. Dark garnet toward royal purple in color, showing blackberry and plum fruits, those supported by generous hints of toast and cedarwood. On the long smooth finish an appealing mineral note. Lively and fresh with just enough complexity to grab our attention. Drink now. Score 89.

ASSAF, 4 SEASONS, 2007: A blend of Pinotage, Syrah, Cabernet Sauvignon and Cabernet Franc and, as unlikely as that sounds, a fine combination, indeed unusual for Israel but not uncommon in South Africa. Reflecting its seven months in oak with light spices and soft, gently caressing tannins, a medium- to full-bodied and round wine, with generous blueberry, fig and licorice notes coming together nicely and lingering comfortably on the palate with a hint of cedarwood rising on the finish. Drink now–2011. Score 89.

ASSAF, SAUVIGNON BLANC, 2008: Light golden straw in color, medium-bodied, with fine balance between acidity and fruits, a lively but complex and elegant wine showing tropical and citrus fruits on a background of freshly cut grass. Drink now–2011. Score 90.

ASSAF, SAUVIGNON BLANC, 2007: Developed for three months in 400-liter casks, this deep golden wine shows earthy, mineral and vanilla aromas and flavors that come together very nicely with citrus, pear and melon fruits. Creamy and intense enough that you might describe this white wine as tannic. Drink now. Score 90.

ASSAF, SAUVIGNON BLANC, 2006: Light straw in color, unoaked and showing fresh and concentrated flavors of grapefruit, lime and a near intense minerality. On the long finish hints of wet gravel, grass and jalapeño peppers. Simultaneously refreshing and complex. Drink up. Score 90.

Avidan ✶✶✶

Founded in 2000 by Shlomo and Tsina Avidan, this boutique winery is located on Kibbutz Eyal in the Sharon region and relies on Chardonnay, Shiraz, Cabernet Sauvignon, Pinot Noir, Grenache, Mourvedre, Carignan, Petite Sirah and Merlot grapes selected from various vineyards in the Upper Galilee, and is currently producing about 30,000 bottles annually. With major expansion and modernization now completed, wines are released in several series—the age-worthy Premium and Reserve wines and the varietal Avidan, and the Blend des Noirs and Petite Soleil, meant for earlier consumption.

Premium

PREMIUM, MERLOT, 2006: Oak-aged for ten months and blended with a small amount of Grenache, with somewhat stinging tannins that seem to not want to integrate quite yet. Opens slowly to show black cherry, plum, nutty and spicy aromas on a light mineral background. Drink now–2011. Score 87.

PREMIUM, GRENACHE, 2008: Ruby toward garnet, medium- to full-bodied, with gentle tannins and a light hand with the oak, but perhaps a bit too much acidity here. Opens in the glass to reveal wild berry and sour cherry fruits, those on a lightly spicy background. Perhaps better with time. Tentative Score 85–87.

PREMIUM, GRENACHE, 2007: Medium-dark garnet in color, made from 30-year-old low yield vines, showing fine concentration and intensity. Medium- to full-bodied (perhaps leaning toward the full), with gently caressing tannins showing black cherry, wild berry, blueberry and peppery aromas and flavors. Drink now–2013, perhaps longer. Score 88.

PREMIUM, GRENACHE, 2006: Rich and concentrated, medium- to full-bodied, with soft tannins integrating nicely and reflecting its ten months in *barriques* with gently spicy oak. On the nose and palate a generous and intriguing array of aromas and flavors, among those currants, blackberries and plums, nutmeg, sage and vanilla, and ending with the tannins and oak rising on the finish together with hints of grilled beef and cloves. Drink now. Score 90.

Reserve

RESERVE, CABERNET SAUVIGNON, 2006: Deep royal purple, medium- to full-bodied, with soft, mouth-coating tannins and generous black fruits supported by earthy minerals. In time it will develop intriguing tobacco and chocolate aromas and flavors. Generous fruits rise on the long finish. Drink now–2011. Score 89.

RESERVE, CABERNET SAUVIGNON, 2005: Oak-aged for 24 months and blended with 15% Merlot, dark garnet, full-bodied and showing generous oak and firm tannins, those in fine balance with blackberry, blackcurrant and citrus peel fruits, all with peppery and anise overtones leading to a long, generous finish. A fine wine, but for those who like their reds on the muscular side. Drink now–2012. Score 91.

RESERVE SHIRAZ, 2006: Made entirely from Shiraz grapes, aged for 16 months in American and French *barriques*, dark garnet to royal purple in color, full-bodied, with soft, gently caressing tannins, opens with a burst of chocolate and leather. Opens slowly in the glass to reveal aromas and flavors of blackberries, red cherries and peppermint, those leading to a long and supple finish. Bright and effusive at this stage and will show greater complexity as it continues to develop. Drink now–2014. Score 91.

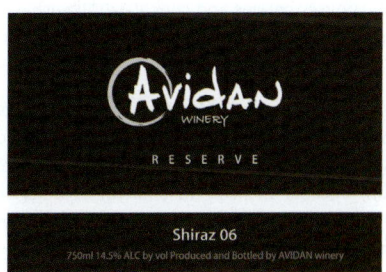

RESERVE, SHIRAZ, 2005: Made from an Australian clone but with a distinctly Rhone nose and palate. Developed for 16 months in French oak, it shows a generous mouthful of blackberry, blueberry, plum and cherry fruits, those overlaid nicely by hints of leather, earth and Oriental spices that go on to a long finish. Drink now–2011. Score 90.

Avidan

AVIDAN, CABERNET SAUVIGNON, 2005: Still in embryonic form but already showing firm tannins well balanced by spicy wood, herbaceousness and currant and plum fruits. Firm but near-elegant. Drink now. Score 87.

AVIDAN, MERLOT, 2005: Soft and round, with silky tannins that allow berry, black cherry and currant notes to make themselves felt on a background of spicy cedar. Drink now. Score 86.

AVIDAN, SHIRAZ, 2006: Dark garnet, medium- to full-bodied, oak-aged for 16 months, showing chunky tannins and skimpy plum and berry fruits. Lacks complexity or depth. Drink now. Score 85.

AVIDAN, SHIRAZ, 2005: Full-bodied but not dense, a rich, polished and thoroughly modern wine, with generous plum and blackberry fruits backed up nicely by dark chocolate, pepper and hints of licorice. Drink now–2010. Score 89.

AVIDAN, SHIRAZ, LIMITED EDITION, 2004: Dark garnet and medium-bodied, this oaked, unfiltered wine shows good balance between soft tannins, spicy oak, and berry, currant and cassis aromas and flavors. Moderately long. Drink now. Score 86.

AVIDAN, PETITE SIRAH, 2006: Deep garnet, full-bodied, with ripe and supple tannins. Opens with a mint-like nose, going on to plums, blueberries and huckleberry fruits, all backed up by light hints of spices and grilled meat. Drink from release–2011. Tentative Score 88–90.

AVIDAN, CARIGNAN, 2008: A juicy, easy-drinking style showing black fruits, currants, boysenberries and chocolate, all with a modest touch of spicy oak and with tannins that are silky smooth. Drink from release. Tentative Score 88–90.

AVIDAN, MOURVEDRE, 2008: My guess is that this one will be destined for a GSM (Grenache-Syrah-Mourvedre) type blend but I'd love to see it as a varietal release. Medium- to medium-full (more perhaps toward the full) bodied, showing fascinating aromas and flavors of blackcurrants and plums supported by generous notes of mint, roasted herbs and white chocolate. Just firm enough tannins promising to integrate nicely. Tentative Score 89–91.

AVIDAN, FRINGE, 2007: Reflecting by its name the winery's proclivity to "play" with labels and with blends. A full-bodied and gently muscular blend of 60% Cabernet Sauvignon and 40% Petite Sirah, showing still-caressing tannins and a comfortable modicum of soft and spicy oak in fine balance with black fruits. On first attack blackberry, currants and vanilla, those yielding to citrus peel, chocolate and mint. Drink now–2013, perhaps longer when it will show both softer and more round. Score 90.

AVIDAN, FLEUR DE LIS, 2005: An oak-aged potpourri of Grenache, Cabernet Sauvignon, Merlot, Tempranillo, and Petite Sirah. Medium- to full-bodied, with generous spicy oak and appealing berry, black cherry and cassis fruits. A pleasant but not complex wine. Drink up. Score 86.

AVIDAN, CHARDONNAY, FRINGE, PETITE SOLEIL, 2008: Not at all aromatic at this stage, but showing fat and creamy with pear and fig notes matched nicely by notes of Oriental spices and earthy minerals. You may like it or you may hate it, but it will make you think. Drink now. Score 87.

AVIDAN, RUBY, N.V.: A brandy-reinforced red wine, one of the few worthwhile red dessert wines made in Israel today. Dark ruby in color, rich and complex, loaded with spices, walnut, nutmeg and espresso coffee on raspberry and cassis fruits. Smooth, well balanced, with no syrupy sensation . Drink from release. Tentative Score 88–90.

AVIDAN, GOLD, N.V.: A white dessert wine based on Chardonnay grapes, and reinforced with brandy to a 17% alcohol level. Generous maple syrup sweetness set off nicely by spices, orange peel and an appealing floral hint that lingers nicely. Not complex but enjoyable. Drink from release. Tentative Score 86–88.

Blend des Noirs

BLEND DES NOIRS, TAGADOM (RED LABEL), 2007: Oak-aged for 12 months, this medium-bodied blend of Petite Sirah, Cabernet Sauvignon and Shiraz (45%, 35% and 20% respectively), shows super-dark garnet in color. Opens with a fresh, black fruit nose, and goes on in the glass to reveal currants and raspberries, those supported by hints of mint, licorice and espresso coffee. Soft and gently mouth-coating tannins rise comfortably on the finish. Drink now–2012. Score 88.

BLEND DES NOIRS, TAGKATOM (ORANGE LABEL), 2007: Medium-dark garnet in color, medium- to full-bodied, showing spicy oak and somewhat sharp and stinging tannins at this stage of its development. Beneath the tannins lightly peppery currant and black cherry fruits. Give this one a bit of time for the tannins to settle down. A blend of 45% Cabernet Sauvignon, 30% Merlot and 25% Grenache, oak-aged for 12 months. Best from 2010. Score 87.

BLEND DES NOIRS, TAGSAGOL (PURPLE LABEL), 2007: Dark garnet toward royal purple, medium- to full-bodied, showing silky tannins and a gentle hand with the oak. On the nose and palate wild currants and wild berries, those supported by notes of mint and bitter-sweet chocolate. On the moderately long finish an appealing hint of saddle leather. Drink now–2012. Score 89.

BLEND DES NOIRS, RED, 2006: Aged in French and American oak for ten months, a blend of Shiraz, Cabernet Sauvignon and Petite Sirah (45%, 35% and 20% respectively). Medium- to full-bodied, with chunky, somewhat coarse tannins, showing straightforward berry and currant notes. A pleasant country-style wine. Drink now. Score 85.

BLEND DES NOIRS, ORANGE, 2006: Garnet toward royal purple, an oak-aged blend of Cabernet Sauvignon, Cabernet Franc and Merlot. Medium- to full-bodied, with ripe blackberry and cassis fruits, those opening to show notes of orange peel and chocolate. Drink now. Score 86.

BLEND DES NOIRS, PURPLE, 2006: A blend of 40% Cabernet Sauvignon, 35% Merlot and 25% Shiraz. Developed in oak for ten months, garnet toward youthful royal purple, medium- to full-bodied with near-sweet tannins in fine balance with spicy wood. On the nose and palate a generous array of berry, currant and plum fruits, those with hints of espresso and leather. Drink now. Score 87.

BLEND DES NOIRS, MERLOT-CABERNET-SHIRAZ, 2005: Oak-aged for ten months, dark garnet toward royal purple in color, this blend (50%, 35% and 15% respectively as listed on the label) shows medium- to full-bodied, with firm, almost gripping tannins, those opening to reveal aromas and flavors of blackberries, currants and espresso coffee, all leading to a medium-long, near-sweet finish. Drink up. Score 86.

BLEND DES NOIRS, CABERNET SAUVIGNON-CABERNET FRANC-MERLOT, 2006: Soft and round but with plenty of muscle, reflecting its time in oak with spices and vanilla, and opening to reveal aromas and flavors of blue- and blackberries, red currants, red licorice and, on the long finish, gentle hints of green olives. Drink now–2011. Score 90.

BLEND DES NOIRS, GRENACHE-PETITE SIRAH-MERLOT, 2005: A blend of equal amounts of Grenache, Petite Sirah and Merlot, each oak-aged separately for ten months. Medium- to full-bodied, dark garnet, with tannins now integrating nicely and showing spicy wood, an appealing array of currant, plum and berry fruits, those supported by hints of tobacco and saddle leather. Drink up. Score 87.

Petite Soleil

PETITE SOLEIL, ROSÉ, 2008: A true potpourri, this deep cherry red rosé is a blend of Cabernet Sauvignon, Merlot, Shiraz, Grenache, Carignan and Pinot Noir. Although it seems that just about everything "left over" was used here, the result is a success, the medium-bodied wine showing a fruity nose and appealing raspberry, cassis and cranberry fruits. Think of this not so much as a true rosé but as a light and refreshing red. A fun and easy-to-drink wine. Drink now. Score 87.

PETITE SOLEIL, CHARDONNAY, 2006: Made from late-harvested Chardonnay grapes, with a nice hint of wood from six months of aging in Burgundy-style barrels; showing citrus, tropical and crème brûlée aromas and flavors. Intentionally off-dry but lively, and with just enough complexity. Drink now. Score 87.

Bar **

Established in 2002 by Ilan Bar in the town of Binyamina in the Sharon area and drawing largely on grapes from the surrounding vineyards, this family-owned winery produces Cabernet Sauvignon, Merlot, Carignan, Sauvignon Blanc and Chardonnay wines as well as Jonathan Red, a blend of Merlot and Cabernet. The winery is currently producing about 4,500 bottles annually.

BAR, CABERNET SAUVIGNON, 2006: Garnet in color, medium-bodied, with spicy and vanilla-rich wood and chunky, country-style tannins. On the nose and palate berries, currants and spices. Lacks complexity. Drink now. Score 84.

BAR, CABERNET SAUVIGNON, 2005: Ruby toward garnet, medium-bodied, with gripping tannins and spicy wood opening to reveal not-overly-generous red and black berry fruits, this wine is somewhat one-dimensional. Drink now. Score 82.

BAR, CABERNET SAUVIGNON, 2004: Dark ruby, medium-bodied, with generous smoky wood and firm tannins hiding the black fruits that struggle to make themselves felt. Drink now. Score 83.

BAR, JONATHAN RED, 2005: Medium-bodied, garnet in color, with chunky, country-style tannins. On the nose and palate berries, black cherries and hints of spices. Drink up. Score 84.

BAR, JONATHAN RED, 2004: A country-style, medium-bodied blend of Merlot and Cabernet Sauvignon with chunky tannins and spicy cedar. Aromas and flavors of wild berries, cassis liqueur and herbaceousness. Showing age. Drink up. Score 83.

Baram ✶✶

Located on Kibbutz Baram in the Upper Galilee, this small winery released its first wines from the 2004 vintage. Winery-owned vineyards contain Cabernet Sauvignon and Merlot grapes. First release was of 1,800 bottles, increasing to 5,500 bottles from the 2008 vintage.

BARAM, CABERNET SAUVIGNON, 2006: Medium- to full-bodied, with chunky, country-style tannins and generous smoky wood somewhat hiding the black fruits that are underneath. Drink now. Score 84.

BARAM, CABERNET SAUVIGNON, 2005: Dark garnet toward royal purple, medium-bodied, with gripping tannins and spicy wood integrating nicely and revealing berry, black cherry and fresh herbal aromas and flavors. Drink now. Score 86.

BARAM, MERLOT, 2005: Dark ruby toward garnet, medium-bodied, with soft, near-sweet tannins and showing appealing raspberry and cherry fruits on a lightly spicy background. Drink now. Score 86.

BARAM, CABERNET SAUVIGNON-MERLOT, 2006: An oak-aged blend of ⅔ Cabernet Sauvignon and ⅓ Merlot. Medium-bodied, with softly caressing tannins, appealing hints of spices and vanilla from the oak and showing generous black fruits. Round and moderately long. Drink now. Score 85.

Barkai **

Headed by winemaker Ettai Barkai, the winery is located on Moshav Roglit in the Ella Valley at the foothills of the Jerusalem Mountains, and relies on Cabernet Sauvignon, Merlot and Shiraz grapes from its own vineyards. Production for 2002 and 2003 was under 1,000 bottles annually. The winery is currently producing about 4,000 bottles annually. A new winery is currently being constructed with a capacity for 10,000 bottles annually.

BARKAI, CABERNET SAUVIGNON-MERLOT, 2006: Medium-bodied, with gently mouth-coating tannins and showing appealing wild berry, black cherry and spicy wood. Drink now. Score 84.

BARKAI, CABERNET SAUVIGNON-MERLOT, 2005: Garnet toward royal purple, medium-bodied, with soft tannins. On the nose and palate berries, cherries and sweet cedarwood. Drink now. Score 84.

BARKAI, CABERNET SAUVIGNON-MERLOT, 2004: Deep ruby toward garnet, medium-bodied with generous near-sweet tannins and flavors and aromas of sur-ripe berries, cherries and cassis. Drink up. Score 84.

Barkan ✦✦✦

Founded in 1990 by Shmuel Boxer and Yair Lerner with the buyout of the former wine and liqueur producer, Stock, the winery was first located in the industrial area of Barkan, not far from Kfar Saba on the Trans-Samaria Highway. In 1999 Barkan began planting extensive vineyards in Kibbutz Hulda, on the central plain near the town of Rehovot, where it now has a state-of-the-art winery. From mid-2008, the full operations of the winery have been at Hulda. Under the supervision of winemakers Ed Salzberg, Yotam Sharon and Irit Boxer, the first of whom studied in California, the second in France, and the third in Australia, this is now the second-largest winery in Israel, with current production at 7.5–9 million bottles annually and projected growth to 10 million by 2010.

Barkan, whose main ownership is now in the hands of the soft-drink company Tempo, has a current investment exceeding $20 million, and includes the winery, the adjoining vineyards (1500 dunams owned jointly by the winery and the kibbutz, making this the largest single vineyard in the country), a visitors' center and a new barrel room currently under construction. Barkan is also the parent company of Segal Wines.

The winery releases varietal wines in four series: Superieur, Reserve (of which the Altitude wines may be considered a sub-label), Classic and Domaine. In addition, the winery is currently developing a vineyard of 150 dunams (75 acres) at Mitzpe Ramon in the Negev Desert, and will release wines from there under the label Negev Project.

Superieur

SUPERIEUR, CABERNET SAUVIGNON, 2003: Dark, almost impenetrable royal purple in color, firm and concentrated, this is one of the best ever from Barkan. Full-bodied, with gently mouth-coating tannins and a judicious hand with spicy oak, shows intense aromas and flavors of blackcurrants, blackberries and black cherries, those complemented by hints of dates, sage and near-sweet cedarwood. A long finish bursting with minerals and black fruits. Drink now. Score 91. **K**

SUPERIEUR, CABERNET SAUVIGNON, 2002: Full-bodied, with generous spicy oak and lively acidity. Features a core of ripe blueberry, cassis and blackcurrant fruits, those matched nicely by overlays of spices and cocoa and, on the long finish, appealing hints of minerals and licorice. Drink up. Score 87. **K**

SUPERIEUR, MERLOT, 2004: Medium- to full-bodied, with soft tannins integrating nicely; showing smoky blackberry, berry, black cherry and cassis fruits, those on a light background of red peppers and vanilla, all leading to a long, smooth, mouth-filling finish. Drink now. Score 89. **K**

Reserve

RESERVE, CABERNET SAUVIGNON, 2007: Dark and ripe, with crisp tannins and an array of near-sweet black cherry, smoky and creamy notes. A bit too soft on the opening but intensity rises on the finish. Perhaps better with time. Drink now. Score 86. **K**

RESERVE, CABERNET SAUVIGNON, 2006: Garnet-red, medium- to full-bodied, developing in French and American oak and showing near-sweet tannins opening to reveal raspberry, currant and earthy minerals leading to a medium-long finish. Drink now. Score 87. **K**

RESERVE, CABERNET SAUVIGNON, 2005: Reflecting 20 months in American, French and

Hungarian *barriques* with a generous overlay of spicy wood, showing mouth-coating tannins and with a relatively high alcohol content (15.5%), one might expect this full-bodied red to be somewhat overpowering. Happily, however, the elements come together nicely, opening to show a solid base of blackcurrants and black and red berries, those with appealing bittersweet notes that linger nicely on the finish. Drink now–2011. Score 88. **K**

RESERVE, CABERNET SAUVIGNON, 2004: A distinctly Old World style of wine. Dark garnet in color, medium- to full-bodied, but showing fine concentration with generous layers of currants, berries and red plums supported by now well-integrating tannins and a gentle hand with the wood. On the finish, look for a tempting note of Mediterranean herbs. Drink now. Score 90. **K**

RESERVE, MERLOT, 2006: Dark garnet, medium- to full-bodied, with soft, near-sweet tannins and hints of spicy wood from the 14 months it spent in new French *barriques*. Opens to show blackberries and purple plums, those parting in the glass to make way for red fruits, cassis and notes of citrus peel. On the finish hints of what at one moment seem like mint, at the next of licorice. Generous and appealing. Drink now–2011. Score 88. **K**

RESERVE, MERLOT, 2005: Aged in oak for 14 months, dark garnet, medium- to full-bodied, with gripping tannins on first attack which yield in the glass to reveal good balance between gentle wood and cassis, red plum and wild berry fruits complemented by hints of pepper, vanilla and chocolate. Lingers nicely on the palate. Drink now. Score 87. **K**

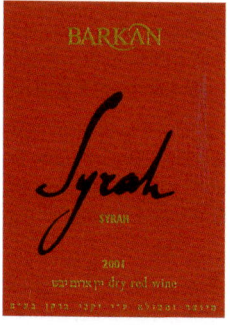

RESERVE, SHIRAZ, 2006: Deep and youthful garnet toward royal purple in color, reflecting its year in French and American *barriques* with appealing spicy notes. A full-bodied wine, with still gripping tannins and a tempting note of bitter herbs that runs through. Blended with 4% each of Cabernet Sauvignon and Petit Verdot, opens to show appealing red berry and cherry fruits, those complemented by hints of white pepper and licorice. Drink now–2011. Score 88. **K**

RESERVE, SHIRAZ, 2005: Oak-aged for 14 months, medium- to full-bodied, dark garnet, firm, and faithful to the Shiraz variety, this red shows oak-accented berry, cherry and licorice flavors backed up by light hints of leather and mint. Lingers nicely. Drink now. Score 88. **K**

RESERVE, PINOTAGE, 2007: A good effort for the vintage, concentrated, with plum grape and blackberry notes along with sweet and spicy notes that run through this medium- to full-bodied wine. Drink now. Score 86. **K**

RESERVE, PINOTAGE, 2006: Dark, but somehow not glistening, garnet toward purple in color, showing near-sweet tannins and berry, plum and currant fruits and, always in the background, notes of earthy minerals and tobacco. On the finish fruits rise along with notes of cloves. Drink now. Score 87. **K**

RESERVE, PINOTAGE, 2005: Garnet toward purple, medium-bodied with soft, near-sweet tannins and reflecting its 12 months in oak with generous spicy wood. Opens to show straightforward berry, cherry and plum fruits on a lightly spicy background. Neither complex nor deep. Drink up. Score 84. **K**

RESERVE, TEMPRANILLO, 2005: Dark ruby in color, with firm tannins now softening and integrating nicely and showing an appealing array of plum, cherry, licorice and tobacco aromas and flavors, all reflecting 16 months in oak with sweet cedarwood. Drink up. Score 88. **K**

RESERVE, CHARDONNAY, 2007: Showing light spicy and vanilla notes from the oak in which it was aged for a short while, lively golden in color and showing an appealing array of tropical fruits and red grapefruit. Bright and zesty. Drink now. Score 86. **K**

RESERVE, CHARDONNAY, 2006: Light gold in color, one-third of this medium-bodied white was aged in oak. Shows appealing peach, melon and citrus fruits, those complemented by gentle hints of wood. Crisp, fruity and mouth-filling. Drink up. Score 87. **K**

RESERVE, SAUVIGNON BLANC, 2008: Unoaked, crisp and lively, a medium-bodied white showing citrus, tropical fruits and an appealing light grassy note. Drink now. Score 87. **K**

RESERVE, EMERALD RIESLING, 2008: Blended with 5% Muscat of Alexandria grapes, semi-dry, fruity and floral, with pineapple, citrus and apple notes. A simple entry-level wine. Drink up. Score 84. **K**

Altitude

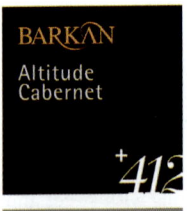

ALTITUDE, CABERNET SAUVIGNON, 412, 2005: Dark garnet in color, medium- to full-bodied, with soft, near-sweet tannins and reflecting its 14 months in oak with spicy wood. On the nose and palate red plums, berries and currants, those with hints of chocolate and tobacco on the finish. Drink now. Score 88. **K**

ALTITUDE, CABERNET SAUVIGNON, 624, 2005: Deep, almost impenetrable garnet in color, this medium- to full-bodied wine shows on first attack firm, drying tannins and spicy oak, but those receding in the glass to add a near-sweetness to the black and red fruits, Oriental spices and hints of freshly picked mushrooms and green olives. Long and generous. Drink now. Score 90. **K**

ALTITUDE, CABERNET SAUVIGNON, 720, 2005: Opens with a smoky, spicy nose, and goes on to deliver appealing plum, blackberry and currant fruits, those overlaid with Oriental spices. Soft, caressing tannins and gentle wood add to the complexity of the wine. Look as well for a tantalizing hint of earthy bitterness that comes in on the long finish. Drink now–2012. Score 91. **K**

ALTITUDE, CABERNET SAUVIGNON, +720, 2003: Made from grapes from the Har Godrim vineyard near the Lebanese border and aged for 12 months in primarily French oak casks, this full-bodied, concentrated wine is dark garnet toward royal purple in color, with firm tannins that are integrating nicely. Showing generous red currants and plums on a tantalizing earthy-herbal and lightly minty background. Drink now. Score 90. **K**

RESERVE, CABERNET SAUVIGNON, ALTITUDE +624, 2003: Deep, almost impenetrable garnet in color, this medium- to full-bodied wine shows on first attack firm, drying tannins and spicy oak but those receding in the glass to add a near-sweetness to the black and red fruits, Oriental spices and hints of freshly picked mushrooms and green olives. Long and generous. Drink now. Score 90. **K**

RESERVE, CABERNET SAUVIGNON, ALTITUDE +412, 2003: Made from grapes from two vineyards—85% harvested at Avnei Eitan on the Southern Golan Heights and 15% at Kerem Dishon in the Upper Galilee—this deep garnet, full-bodied wine was aged in primarily French *barriques* for 14 months. Near-sweet tannins and a gentle influence of the wood reveal generous cassis, blackberry and raspberry fruits, those backed up by spices and a light mineral overlay. Drink now. Score 89. **K**

Classic

CLASSIC, CABERNET SAUVIGNON, 2007: Medium-bodied, with soft tannins and traditional blackcurrant and blackberry fruits. Drink now. Score 85. **K**

CLASSIC, CABERNET SAUVIGNON, 2006: Medium, perhaps medium- to full-bodied, with notes of spicy oak and soft tannins integrating nicely and showing appealing blackberry, black cherry and currant fruits. Drink now. Score 85. **K**

CLASSIC, MERLOT, 2007: Medium-bodied, soft, round and showing a basic cherry-berry personality. A good entry-level wine. Drink now. Score 84. **K**

CLASSIC, MERLOT, 2006: Soft and round, with a bare hint of spicy wood and straightforward berry, cherry and cassis fruits. Drink up. Score 85. **K**

CLASSIC, SHIRAZ, 2007: Made entirely from Shiraz grapes, unoaked, showing medium-bodied with soft tannins and opening to show raspberries, red currants and cherry notes, those with a light overlay of white chocolate. A good quaffer. Drink now. Score 85. **K**

CLASSIC, SHIRAZ, 2006: Royal purple in color, medium-bodied, with soft, gently mouth-coating tannins and good acidity to keep it lively. Few varietal traits here, but appealing black and red fruits on a lightly spicy background make this a good quaffer. Drink now. Score 85. **K**

CLASSIC, PINOT NOIR, 2006: Lightly oaked, medium-bodied, with soft tannins integrating nicely. On the nose and palate red currants, wild berries and red plums, those supported by notes of licorice and cigar tobacco. Drink now. Score 87. **K**

CLASSIC, PINOTAGE, 2007: Dark garnet toward royal purple, with near-sweet tannins and opening to show plum, currant jelly, eucalyptus and smoky notes. Drink now. Score 87. **K**

CLASSIC, PINOTAGE, 2005: Garnet-red in color, medium-bodied, with plum, strawberry jam and toasty notes along with hints of smoke and cocoa on the finish. Easy to drink. Drink up. Score 85. **K**

CLASSIC, SHIRAZ ROSÉ, 2007: Blush pink, light- to medium-bodied, soft, round and lively with berry, cherry and tutti-frutti notes that make for ideal breakfast or warm-weather quaffing. Drink up. Score 86. **K**

CLASSIC, CHARDONNAY, 2008: Golden straw in color, light- to medium-bodied, an unoaked wine showing lively tropical and citrus fruits along with a hint of spiciness. Drink up. Score 84. **K**

CLASSIC, CHARDONNAY, 2007: Light gold in color and medium-bodied, this unoaked Chardonnay shows aromatic and generous on the palate with citrus, pineapple and light spicy notes. A good quaffer, but turns acidic and fades quickly in the glass. Drink up. Score 80. **K**

CLASSIC, SAUVIGNON BLANC, 2008: Pale straw in color, a simple little white with citrus, citrus peel and floral notes. Drink up. Score 84. **K**

CLASSIC, SAUVIGNON BLANC, 2007: Light straw colored, unoaked, light- to medium-bodied, with tropical fruits, citrus peel and a nice hint of spiciness. Simple but appealing. Drink up. Score 84. **K**

CLASSIC, EMERALD RIESLING, 2008: As light in color as in body, semi-dry, with citrus, pineapple and floral notes. A simple entry-level wine. Drink up. Score 80. **K**

Domaine

DOMAINE, CABERNET SAUVIGNON, 2008: Light, with soft tannins and simple but pleasant berry, black cherry and currant fruits. Drink now. Score 80. **K**

DOMAINE, MERLOT, 2008: Dark ruby toward garnet, with light herbal overtones highlighting berry and black cherry fruits. An entry-level wine. Drink now. Score 82. **K**

DOMAINE, SHIRAZ, 2008: Dark garnet, medium-bodied, with soft tannins and showing plum, wild berry and leathery notes. Drink now. Score 84. **K**

DOMAINE, PETITE SIRAH, 2008: Garnet toward purple, medium-bodied, a simple country-style wine with blackberry, blueberry and spicy notes. Drink now. Score 84. **K**

Bashan ★★★

Founded by Uri Rapp and Emmanuel Dassa, the winery is located on the southern Golan Heights and produces the country's only kosher bio-organic wines, those from grapes raised in its own vineyards. The first releases were from the 2004 vintage, and to date are based entirely on Cabernet Sauvignon and Merlot grapes. Current releases are 10,000–15,000 bottles annually, and tentative plans are to grow to production of 50,000–100,000 bottles.

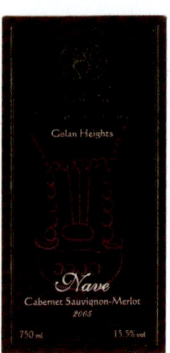

BASHAN, CABERNET SAUVIGNON, EITAN, 2006: Dark royal purple and firmly tannic but showing fine balance and structure that bode well for the future. Well focused, with currant and plum fruits highlighted by mineral and herbal notes and, on the moderately long finish, a hint of toasty oak. Drink now. Score 86. **K**

BASHAN, CABERNET SAUVIGNON, EITAN, 2005: Medium- to full-bodied, this organic wine shows good balance between sweet oak, generous yeasts and, on the nose and palate, appealing ripe and spicy black fruits. Drink now. Score 88. **K**

BASHAN, MERLOT, EITAN, 2006: Garnet toward royal purple, medium-bodied, with soft tannins. Showing generous berry, black cherry and milk chocolate aromas and flavors. A caressing, if not long, finish. Drink now. Score 86. **K**

BASHAN, MERLOT, EITAN, 2005: Dark ruby toward garnet, reflecting its 16 months in oak with firm tannins and spicy wood, those yielding in the glass to show black fruits, eucalyptus and black olives all coming to a medium-long finish. Drink up. Score 86. **K**

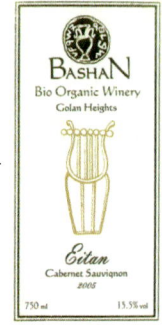

BASHAN, CABERNET SAUVIGNON-MERLOT, NAVE, 2005: A dark garnet, medium- to full-bodied blend of 70% Cabernet Sauvignon and 30% Merlot that spent 14 months in oak. Opens with a light bottle stink, but that passes quickly to reveal a clean, well-balanced wine with soft tannins and appealing currant, berry and eucalyptus aromas and flavors. Not complex but quite appealing. Drink now. Score 86. **K**

Bazelet Hagolan ✳✳✳

Founded in 1998 by Yo'av Levy and Assaf Kedem on Moshav Kidmat Tzvi in the Golan Heights, the first facility of this winery was located in a cow shed and initial production from that vintage year was 1,800 bottles. Today, entirely under the auspices of Levy, the winery is currently producing about 30,000 bottles annually, half of those from grapes grown in its own vineyards on the Golan Heights. Until 2005 the winery released only Cabernet Sauvignon wines. The winery's first Merlot was released from the 2006 vintage.

The wines are in two series: Reserve and Bazelet Hagolan, the first aged in oak for about 20 months, the second for 8–10 months. Production has been kosher since the 2004 vintage.

Reserve

RESERVE, CABERNET SAUVIGNON, 2006: Dark garnet toward royal purple, full-bodied and deeply aromatic, with firm tannins in fine balance with wood and fruits. On the nose and palate spicy blackberry, currant and citrus peel, and, on the long finish, a generous hint of espresso coffee. Drink now. Score 86. **K**

RESERVE, CABERNET SAUVIGNON, 2005: Rich, ripe, smooth, generous and well balanced with currant, berry and plum flavors coming together with near-sweet tannins and tempting smoky oak lingering nicely. Drink now–2012. Score 88. **K**

RESERVE, CABERNET SAUVIGNON, 2004: Dark garnet toward royal purple, full-bodied, with firm tannins in fine balance with acidity, spicy wood and fruits. On first attack, blackcurrants and black licorice, those followed by wild berries, earthy minerals and Mediterranean herbs. Long and generous. Drink now–2011. Score 90. **K**

RESERVE, MERLOT, 2006: Oak-aged, with a generous 15.5% alcohol content. Full-bodied and intense, almost thick on the palate with soft tannins integrating to show appealing black, near-jammy fruits. Finishes sweet and hot. Drink now. Score 85. **K**

Bazelet Hagolan (Bronze)

BAZELET HAGOLAN, CABERNET SAUVIGNON, 2006: Medium- to full-bodied, with chunky country-style tannins and a hint of sweet cedarwood that runs throughout. Opens to show traditional Cabernet currant and blackberry fruits, those matched by hints of light earthiness and sweet herbs. Drink now. Score 87. **K**

BAZELET HAGOLAN, CABERNET SAUVIGNON, 2005: Youthful garnet toward royal purple, medium- to full-bodied, with soft tannins integrating nicely and showing a pleasing array of currant, blackberry, vanilla and, on the long finish, minerals and a layer of toasty oak. Spoiled somewhat by a rising musky aroma that comes in from mid-palate. Drink now. Score 85. **K**

BAZELET HAGOLAN, MERLOT, 2006: Garnet toward royal purple, medium- to full-bodied, with near-sweet tannins and spicy oak highlighting plum and currant fruits. In the background, light toasty bread and smoked meat. A 15% alcohol content gives a fairly hot finish. Drink now. Score 85. **K**

Beit-El ✶

Established by California-trained winemaker Hillel Manne in 2001 and located in Beit-El, north of Jerusalem, this small winery has been producing Cabernet Sauvignon and Merlot wines from its own vineyards. The winery is currently producing about 8,000 bottles annually, nearly all of those destined for export to the United States.

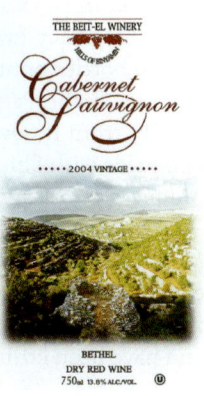

BEIT-EL, CABERNET SAUVIGNON, 2006: Full-bodied enough to be thought thick, with searing tannins and spices hiding stewed plum fruits. Tentative Score 65–67. **K**

BEIT-EL, CABERNET SAUVIGNON, 2005: Medium-bodied, with chunky country-style tannins and aromas and flavors of cooked fruits on a sweet, alcoholic and coarse background. Score 65. **K**

BEIT-EL, MERLOT, 2007: Dark ruby toward garnet in color, medium-bodied with chunky, country-style tannins. Opens to show perhaps too-generous overlays of spicy oak and vanilla that tend to hide plum and black cherry fruits, those leading to a sweet-and-sour finish. Drink up. Score 76. **K**

BEIT-EL, MERLOT, 2005: Medium-bodied, showing signs of oxidation despite its youth, and with stewed, sweet fruits on the palate. Drink up. Score 70. **K**

Benhaim ✳✳✳

Founded in 1997 on Moshav Kfar Azar in the Sharon region, this family-owned winery is currently producing about 35,000 bottles annually from Cabernet Sauvignon, Merlot, Cabernet Franc, Petite Sirah, Chardonnay and Muscat grapes largely from its own vineyards. Under development are vineyards with Shiraz and Traminette, and the winery also produces a Port-style wine.

With vineyards now planted on the eastern slopes of Mount Meron in the Upper Galilee, the winery is planning to expand its production to 50,000 bottles. Wines are released in three series—Grande Reserve, Reserve and Tradition—and have been kosher since the 2001 vintage.

Grande Reserve

GRANDE RESERVE, CABERNET SAUVIGNON, 2005: Dark garnet toward royal purple, showing generous toasty wood and firm tannins that yield in the glass to reveal appealing blackberry, currant and citrus peel notes, those on a background of dark chocolate and cigar tobacco. Drink now–2011. Tentative Score 88. **K**

GRANDE RESERVE, CABERNET SAUVIGNON, 2003: Reflecting more than two years in new oak with full-body, generous spicy and dusty wood, and firm tannins that tend to overpower the fruits. Given time in the glass, the wine opens to reveal currant, purple plum and chocolate, the wood rising again on the finish. Drink now. Score 86. **K**

Reserve

RESERVE, CABERNET SAUVIGNON, 2006: Showing dark royal purple toward garnet, medium- to full-bodied, with generous soft tannins and abundant spicy and dusty oak. On the nose and palate blackcurrants, berries and plums, with light herbal and green olive overtones. Round and well balanced. Drink now–2011. Score 88. **K**

RESERVE, CABERNET SAUVIGNON, 2005: Dark garnet, medium- to full-bodied, a blend of Cabernet Sauvignon, Merlot and Petite Sirah (90%, 7% and 3% respectively). Tannins now showing more firmly than at an earlier tasting, in fact almost lip searing, and with generous dusty and spicy oak from its 20–24 months in oak. As the wine opens it shows spicy blackcurrant and berry fruits on a background of saddle leather. Drink now. Score 85. **K**

RESERVE, MERLOT, 2005: Reflecting its oak aging in new American and French *barriques* for 20 months with generous cedarwood, spicy and vanilla overtones. Dark garnet in color, full-bodied, with firm tannins that part slowly to reveal black fruits and notes of freshly picked herbs. Drink now–2011. Score 85. **K**

Tradition

TRADITION, CABERNET SAUVIGNON, 2006: Garnet toward dark purple, medium-bodied, with firm tannins and spicy wood. Opens to show wild berries, currants and notes of tobacco. Drink now. Score 85. **K**

TRADITION, CABERNET SAUVIGNON, 2005: Dark garnet, medium- to full-bodied with soft, mouth-coating tannins and spicy wood. On the nose and palate currant, berry and exotic spices. Drink now. Score 85. **K**

TRADITION, MERLOT, 2006: Medium-bodied, with soft, mouth-coating tannins and spicy wood. Youthful royal purple in color, opens on the palate to show generous wild berries, spices and a hint of chocolate. Drink now. Score 85. **K**

TRADITION, MERLOT, 2005: Garnet toward ruby, medium-bodied, and reflecting its 18 months in oak with firm tannins and generous sweet and spicy cedarwood. Blended with about 10% of Cabernet Franc, opens to reveal blackberry and black cherry fruits, those complemented by a hint of chocolate that lingers nicely on the medium-long finish. Drink now. Score 85. **K**

TRADITION, CHARDONNAY, 2007: Showing dramatically different than at earlier tastings. Golden straw in color, an unoaked medium-bodied wine with clean and crisp aromas and flavors of lemon and grapefruit. Drink up. Score 84. **K**

TRADITION, MUSCAT, DEMI-SEC, 2007: Unoaked and generously floral on the nose, but with its citrus and tropical fruits carrying an unwanted overlay of what appears to be Brett, that giving the wine a muddled persona. Drink up. Score 78. **K**

TRADITION, MOSCATELLE, 2007: Light golden straw in color, a wine that boasts sweet rosewater, violets and vanilla on the nose and not much in the way of fruits. Drink up. Score 78. **K**

Benhaim

BENHAIM, LA PETITE SIRA, 2004:
Not a typographical error, the *sira* in question being a small boat, reflecting the family's love of sailing. A blend of 60% Petite Sirah and 40% Merlot, aged in oak for 12 months. Super-dark garnet, medium-bodied, showing silky tannins and generous black fruit. Drink up. Score 83. K

BENHAIM, ROSÉ, VIN JEUNE, 2007:
A blend of 90% Merlot and 10% Cabernet Franc, those with short skin contact, opens with what seems to be dusty wood on the nose, that going on to a too generously acidic background. Muddled berry and red cherry notes here. Drink up. Score 70. K

BENHAIM, CHARDONNAY, VIN JEUNE, 2007: A super-young unoaked release, with no label and meant for light, easy drinking. Alas, too much like a blend of lemon and pineapple juice, to which has been added an artificial sweetener. Drink up. Score 72. K

Ben Hanna ✳✳✳

Located on Moshav Gefen, on the plains between Beit Shemesh and Kiryat Malachi, and receiving Cabernet Sauvignon, Merlot, Grenache, Petit Verdot, Cabernet Franc,
Viognier and Argaman grapes from the Judean Mountains,
this winery is the venture of Shlomi Zadok. The winery's first
release was of 2,500 bottles. Current production is about
6,000 bottles, and plans are to grow slowly to releases of
about 60,000 bottles annually.

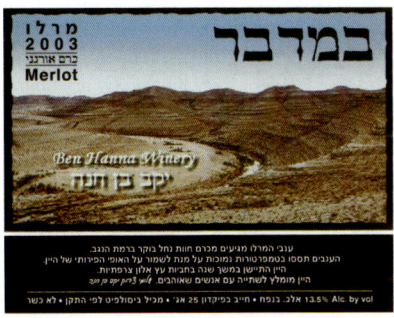

BEN HANNA, CABERNET SAUVIGNON, 2006: Developed in French
oak *barriques*, this medium- to full-bodied wine opens with surprisingly
soft tannins but those build nicely together with spicy oak as the wine
sits on the palate. Traditional Cabernet blackberry and currant fruits
unfolding to reveal hints of mocha and cigar tobacco that linger on the
long, fruity finish. Drink now–2012. Score 89.

BEN HANNA, CABERNET SAUVIGNON, SHALEM, 2005: A blend of
Cabernet Sauvignon, Cabernet Franc and Merlot (80%, 15% and 5%
respectively), aged in French oak *barriques* for 21 months and showing
soft, round and aromatic. On the nose and palate raspberry and red
currant fruits on a background of herbs and mint. Long and generous.
Drink now–2011. Score 89.

BEN HANNA, CABERNET SAUVIGNON, 2005: Dark royal purple,
full-bodied, with soft tannins integrating nicely and showing fine balance between spicy wood, acidity and fruits. On the nose and palate
blackcurrants, blackberries, a hint of green olives and, on the long finish,
fine spices. Drink now–2011. Score 89.

BEN HANNA, MERLOT, 2007: Deep garnet, medium- to full-bodied with soft, gently mouth-coating tannins and appealing notes of spicy oak. Shows a generous array of blackberry, black cherry and blueberry fruits, those complemented by hints of Oriental spices. Drink from release–2013. Score 90.

BEN HANNA, MERLOT, 2006: Garnet-red with purple reflections and, in accordance with the winemaker's philosophy, soft and round. On the nose and palate black cherries and wild berries. Easy to drink but with just the right touch of complexity. Drink now–2011. Score 86.

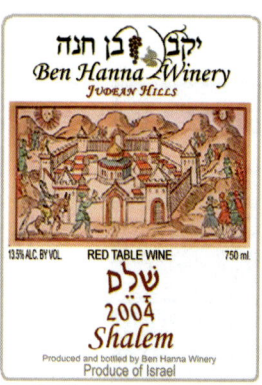

BEN HANNA, MERLOT, SHALEM, 2004: Dark garnet, medium-bodied, reflecting its 19 months in oak with generous spices and medium-firm tannins, but opening nicely in the glass to reveal cherry, blackberry, vanilla and toasty oak. Drink now. Score 86.

BEN HANNA, MERLOT, SINGLE HUMPED, 2004: The "Humped" refers to the picture of a camel on the label. Based largely on grapes from the Negev, this is a soft, round and generous wine showing blueberry, blackberry and currant notes along with hints of mint and sweet herbs, all coming together harmoniously. Drink now. Score 90.

BEN HANNA, CABERNET FRANC, 2006: Medium- to full-bodied, with velvety smooth tannins and appealing floral-scented plum, blueberry and currant fruits on a gentle background of spicy wood and just the barest hint of Brett to add charm. Drink from release–2011. Tentative Score 89–91.

BEN HANNA, CABERNET FRANC, LA MARIÉE, 2005: Broad, dense and concentrated, yet caressing and not at all heavy. Opens with generous raspberries and dried currants highlighted by gentle black and red chili peppers. Moves on to plum and floral aromas and flavors with soft tannins rising on the long, spicy and fruit-rich finish. Best yet from the winery. Drink now–2011. Score 91.

BEN HANNA, CABERNET FRANC, 2005: Developed in French oak, this medium- to full-bodied wine shows soft, near-sweet tannins integrating nicely and blackcurrant, berry and hints of citrus. On the long finish, hints of what seems one moment to be mint and another black licorice. Drink now. Score 88.

BEN HANNA, PETIT VERDOT, 2006: Deep garnet toward royal purple, this full-bodied, oak-aged red shows plush and supple, with currant, blackberry, cola, vanilla and black pepper aromas and flavors, those in fine balance with spicy wood and nicely integrating tannins, all leading to a near-sweet finish. Drink now–2013. Score 91.

BEN HANNA, PETIT VERDOT, LA MARIÉE, 2005: Reflecting 12 months in French oak with gently mouth-coating tannins and hints of spices and vanilla, this medium- to full-bodied wine shows ripe, rich and supple. Dark purple, with generous cherry and currant fruits and, on the long finish, a tantalizing hint of green olives. Drink now–2011. Score 90.

Petit Verdot 2005
La Mariée

Ben Hanna Winery
JUDEAN HILLS
Produce of Israel
Red Israeli Wine

BEN HANNA, PETIT VERDOT, SINGLE HUMPED, 2005: Medium- to full-bodied with silky smooth tannins, this round and well-balanced wine is showing plum and raspberry fruits, those highlighted nicely by generous acidity and a light gamey touch on the long generous finish. Drink now. Score 90.

BEN HANNA, SHALEM, 2006: Dark ruby toward garnet, this oak-aged blend of 70% Cabernet Sauvignon, 20% Merlot and 10% Cabernet Sauvignon shows medium- to full-bodied, with soft tannins and gently spicy wood. On the nose and palate blackberry, currant and blueberries, those on a background of espresso coffee and chocolate. Drink now. Score 88.

BEN HANNA, MEDITERRANEAN BLEND, 2005: An oak-aged blend of 50% Grenache, 33% Petit Verdot, 12% Syrah and 5% Cabernet Franc. Soft, round, with tantalizing hints of spicy oak and sweet cedar and showing an appealing array of blackberry, currant and wild berry aromas and flavors. Long and elegant. Drink now. Score 88.

BEN HANNA, MEDITERRANEO, 2005: Deep, brooding garnet in color, full-bodied, with still-firm tannins and generous spicy wood waiting to settle down, but showing fine balance and simply needing a bit of time. A blend of Grenache, Petit Verdot, Syrah and Cabernet Franc (50%, 33%, 12% and 5% respectively), aged in French oak for 22 months, opening to show a generous mouthful of black cherry, dried raspberries, eucalyptus and cinnamon. Drink now–2011. Score 91.

Ben-Shoshan ✳

Established by agronomist Yuval Ben-Shoshan on Kibbutz Bror Hail in the northern Negev Desert, this winery released its first wine from the vintage of 1998. Desert-raised grapes include Cabernet Sauvignon and Merlot, and other grapes are drawn from the area of Kerem Ben Zimra in the Galilee. The winery produces wines in three series, Kfar Shamai, Har'el and Avdat. Production is currently about 10,000 bottles annually.

Kfar Shamai

KFAR SHAMAI, CABERNET SAUVIGNON, 2005: Aged in French and American oak *barriques* for 16 months, showing generous dusty wood and chunky tannins. Opens to show skimpy black fruits on an acidic and medicinal background. Showing signs of premature aging. Drink up. Score 75.

KFAR SHAMAI, MERLOT, 2005: Dark garnet, medium- to full-bodied, with chunky, country-style tannins. Fading quickly, the once youthful red and blackcurrants and wild berry fruits now all but hidden under distinct medicinal aromas and flavors. Score 70.

KFAR SHAMAI, CABERNET SAUVIGNON-MERLOT, 2005: A blend of equal parts of Cabernet Sauvignon and Merlot, oak-aged for 14 months. Dark garnet, medium- to full-bodied, with soft, near-sweet tannins and showing sur-ripe raspberry and red plum fruits on a background of freshly turned earth and tobacco. Drink now. Score 87.

Har'el

HAR'EL, CABERNET SAUVIGNON, 2005: Dark royal purple, medium- to full-bodied, with chunky country-style tannins and appealing currant, berry and black cherry fruits. Drink now. Score 82.

HAR'EL, CABERNET SAUVIGNON, 2004: Dark royal purple, medium- to full-bodied, with chunky country-style tannins and aromas and flavors of plum compote. Drink up. Score 76.

Avdat

AVDAT, CABERNET SAUVIGNON, 2004: Oak-aged for 14 months, medium- to full-bodied, with soft tannins integrating nicely and showing appealing black fruits on a lightly spicy and earthy-mineral background. Drink now. Score 85.

AVDAT, MERLOT, 2005: Oak-aged for 14 months, garnet red, medium-bodied, with soft tannins and a strong, unwanted hint of medicinal sweetness that overlays the black fruits. Drink up. Score 78.

AVDAT, MERLOT, 2004: Garnet toward royal purple, medium- to full-bodied, with chunky, country-style tannins and generous spicy oak. Opens in the glass to reveal black and red berries and a pleasing earthy overtone. Drink up. Score 83.

Ben-Zimra **

Founded by vintner Yossi Ashkenazi on Moshav Ben Zimra in the Upper Galilee, with Assaf Kedem now serving as the winemaker, this boutique winery has been producing two wines, a reserve and a regular edition of Cabernet Sauvignon since 2003. The winery's vineyards, near the moshav at 870 meters above sea level, are among the best in Israel. Current production is about 10,000 bottles annually, and the winery is planning on growing to 20,000 bottles starting with the 2008 vintage.

Reserve

RESERVE, CABERNET SAUVIGNON, 2007: Dark and deep, medium- to full-bodied with good concentration. Somewhat rustic with a touch of heat on the finish, but showing appealing currant, cherry and berry fruits with hints of anise and spring flowers. Drink now. Score 85.

RESERVE, CABERNET SAUVIGNON, 2006: Not complex but smooth and round. Medium- to full-bodied, well balanced with currant, plum and black cherry fruits and a generous spicy overlay from the oak in which it aged for 14 months. Turns dry and picks up a strong cedarwood note on the finish. Drink now. Score 85.

RESERVE, CABERNET SAUVIGNON, 2005: Dark garnet toward royal purple, full-bodied, with firm tannins just starting to settle down, and reflecting its 14 months in *barriques* with spicy wood. Shows an appealing array of currants, blackberries and eucalyptus, those marred somewhat by a high (15.2%) alcohol level that adds an unwanted sweet note and leads to a hot finish. Drink now. Score 84.

Ben-Zimra

BEN-ZIMRA, CABERNET SAUVIGNON, 2007: Dark and deep, medium- to full-bodied with good concentration. Oak-aged for nine months, somewhat rustic with a touch of heat on the finish, but showing appealing currant, cherry and berry fruits with hints of anise and spring flowers. Drink now. Score 83.

BEN-ZIMRA, CABERNET SAUVIGNON, 2006: Made entirely from Cabernet Sauvignon grapes, oak-aged in new *barriques* for nine months, a straightforward and fruity wine marred somewhat by a too-generous bitter aftertaste. Drink now–2010. Score 84.

BEN-ZIMRA, CABERNET SAUVIGNON, 2005: Dark garnet, medium- to full-bodied, with soft, mouth-coating tannins, reflecting its ten months in oak with gentle spices and a hint of smoke. Slow to open but when it does shows appealing berry, currant and black cherry fruits. Moderately long. Drink now. Score 85.

Binyamina ✳✳✳✳

First established in 1952 as Eliaz Wineries, the winery is located in the town of Binyamina at the foothills of the Carmel Mountains. In 1994 a group of investors bought out and renamed the outdated winery, replacing the existing management. They continued to introduce modern technology and equipment, and in recent years, thanks to increasing quality control in the vineyards and fine winemaking practices, the wines have improved dramatically and are making major steps forward in the realm of quality. In 2008 the winery changed hands again, and the new owners are making major investments in the physical plant, equipment and vineyards.

Under the supervision of senior winemaker Sasson Ben-Aharon and winemaker Assaf Paz, the winery is now the fourth largest in the country and produces about 2.6 million bottles annually from a large variety of grapes, those from vineyards in nearly every part of the country.

The winery releases several series: Avnei Hachoshen, Reserve (until 2006 known as Special Reserve), Yogev, Tiltan and Teva, their basic series originally known as Binyamina. In Hebrew, *Avnei Hachoshen* refers to the precious stones that adorned the vest of the high priest in the days of the Temple; *Tiltan* is the Hebrew name for clover, a plant that has three distinct leaves on every branch (the logic being that these wines are blends of three different vintage years); *Yogev* is the Biblical term for a farmer, in this case a clear bow to the grape-growers; and *Teva* means nature.

Avnei Hachoshen

AVNEI HACHOSHEN, CABERNET SAUVIGNON, 2008: Intensely dark, deeply aromatic and tannic, but well balanced enough to promise roundness and elegance. Opens to show traditional cassis and blackberry fruits on a peppery and earthy-mineral background, and, on the long finish, a hint of After Eight mints. Best 2011–2016, perhaps longer. Tentative Score 91–93. K

AVNEI HACHOSHEN, CABERNET SAUVIGNON, TARSHISH, 2007: Dark garnet toward royal purple, full-bodied with still-firm tannins waiting to integrate, but already showing appealing cassis and black-berry fruits, those complemented by hints of minted chocolate. Drink from release–2013. Tentative Score 87–89. **K**

AVNEI HACHOSHEN, CABERNET SAUVIGNON, TARSHISH, 2006: Almost impenetrably dark gar-net in color, full-bodied, with spicy wood and firm tannins in fine balance, showing rich and well struc-tured. If ever there has been a wine that was "black fruits all the way," this is that wine—opening to show blackcurrant, blackberry, black cherry and deep earthy overtones, those matched nicely by notes of black pepper and star anise, all lingering long and comfortably. Drink now–2014. Score 91. **K**

AVNEI HACHOSHEN, CABERNET SAUVIGNON, TARSHISH, 2005: Dark garnet with purple and or-ange reflections, and aged in new French oak for 16 months. Opens with super-soft tannins, those firming as the wine develops in the glass, medium-bodied, with appealing currant and red plums on the nose and palate, those backed up by a hint of sweet herbs on the moderately long finish. Drink now–2011. Score 89. **K**

AVNEI HACHOSHEN, CABERNET SAUVIGNON, TARSHISH, 2004: Full-bodied, with spicy, vanilla-rich wood and near-sweet tannins in good balance with blackcurrant, wild berries and minerals, all leading to a long and appealing spicy finish. Drink now. Score 88. **K**

AVNEI HACHOSHEN, CABERNET SAUVIGNON, TARSHISH, 2003: Deep garnet toward purple, full-bodied, with mouth-coating tannins that are opening to show harmony, and in addition to traditional blackcurrants, sweet berries and spices, generous mineral, toasty and vanilla notes. Drink now–2011. Score 91. **K**

AVNEI HACHOSHEN, SYRAH, ODEM, 2008: Impenetrably dark garnet toward inky black in color, a deeply aromatic, concentrated and ripe wine showing complexity and remarkable depth. Opens with ripe blackberry and wild berry fruits, goes on to show cherry jam and boysenberries and then to reveal peppery, meaty aromas and flavors. Finishes with a hint of cherry-jam. Full-bodied, with firm tannins set-tling down nicely now, destined for a muscular elegance. Best 2011–2016. Tentative Score 92–94. **K**

AVNEI HACHOSHEN, SYRAH, ODEM, 2007: Showing beautifully. Full-bodied, soft, round and both spicy and juicy, with a generous array of blueberries, blackberries, purple plums and a mélange of fresh herbal notes that lead to a long finish. Drink now–2013. Score 90. **K**

AVNEI HACHOSHEN, SYRAH, ODEM, 2006: Blended with 2–3% of Viognier, dark, dense and concentrated, with fine balance and structure. Firm tannins integrating with spicy wood to show black and red berries, cherries and licorice flavors, all lingering on a long fruity finish. Drink now–2013. Score 90. **K**

AVNEI HACHOSHEN, SYRAH, ODEM, 2005: Blended with 2–3% of Viognier, intensely dark garnet in color, medium- to full-bodied, with generous near-sweet tannins and smoky oak integrating nicely. Shows red berries, cherries and red plums along with hints of leather and meatiness. Long and generous. Drink now–2011. Score 90. **K**

AVNEI HACHOSHEN, SYRAH, ODEM, 2004: With 15 months in oak, showing medium- to full-bodied, soft well-integrated tannins and light herbal-earthy aromas and flavors complemented nicely by plum, berry and cassis fruits. Hints of tobacco and chocolate on the finish. Drink now. Score 87. **K**

AVNEI HACHOSHEN, SYRAH, ODEM, 2003: Blended with 2% of Viognier, full-bodied, firm and concentrated, dark garnet in color, with firm and mouth-coating tannins opening in the glass to reveal near-sweet berry, plum, meaty and earthy aromas and flavors, all leading to a long finish. Drink now–2011. Score 91. **K**

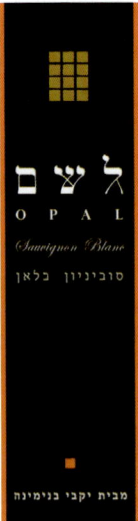

AVNEI HACHOSHEN, CABERNET SAUVIGNON-SHIRAZ-MERLOT, 2006: Dark garnet, aromatic and with tannins that coat the mouth gently. Opens to reveal black cherries, blackberries and notes of sweet and spicy cedarwood. Complex and long. Drink now–2012. Score 90. **K**

AVNEI HACHOSHEN, CABERNET SAUVIGNON-SHIRAZ-MERLOT, SAPIR, 2005: As it was last year, a blend of 40% Cabernet Sauvignon, 35% Shiraz and 25% Merlot. Oak-aged for 15 months, showing dark ruby toward garnet, opening with licorice and mint on the nose and palate, those going to bittersweet chocolate and Mediterranean herbs and then to red plums, cassis and spicy notes. Drink now–2010. Score 89. **K**

AVNEI HACHOSHEN, CABERNET SAUVIGNON-SHIRAZ-MERLOT, SAPIR, 2004: This blend of 40% Cabernet Sauvignon, 35% Shiraz and 25% Merlot spent 15 months in French oak. Dark garnet, medium-bodied, with soft tannins and ripe currant and plum fruits backed up by Oriental spices and pepper. Easy drinking but lacking complexity. Drink now. Score 87. **K**

AVNEI HACHOSHEN, CABERNET SAUVIGNON–SHIRAZ–MERLOT, SA-PIR, 2003: A full-bodied, firmly tannic blend of 40% each of Cabernet and Shiraz and 20% Merlot. Oak-aged for 15 months, showing good balance between wood, tannins and a tempting array of aromas and flavors, those including chocolate, tobacco, dusty-oak and minerals, all on a warm background of blackcurrants, blackberries and spices. Drink now. Score 90. **K**

AVNEI HACHOSHEN, CHARDONNAY, SHOHAM, 2008: Developed partly in 225 liter *barriques* and partly in 300 liter barrels. Light golden in color, combining earthy and flinty minerals that complement citrus, white peach and melon aromas and flavors. Promising elegance. Drink from release–2012. Tentative Score 89–91. **K**

AVNEI HACHOSHEN, CHARDONNAY, SHOHAM, 2007: Gold with orange tints, developed *sur lie* for 12–14 months in oak, showing a generous but gentle wood influence and fine balancing acidity. Opens in the glass to show generous peach, pear and citrus fruits all on a light mineral background. Drink now–2011. Score 89. **K**

AVNEI HACHOSHEN, CHARDONNAY, SHOHAM, 2006: Light gold with green and orange tints, reflecting its 12 months *sur lie* with spicy wood and light toasty overtones, those not hiding but complementing citrus, pear and tropical fruits, all on a light earthy-mineral background. Drink up. Score 88. **K**

AVNEI HACHOSHEN, SAUVIGNON BLANC, LESHEM, 2007: Damp straw in color, developed on its lees for 4–5 months in 2–3-year-old barrels, giving it a light and tantalizing fume note. Opens on the palate to show sweet pea, herbal and grassy notes highlighting summer and citrus fruits and closes with a lightly creamy finish. Drink up. Score 87. **K**

AVNEI HACHOSHEN, CHARDONNAY-SAUVIGNON BLANC-VIOG-NIER, YASHFEH, 2007: A blend of Chardonnay, Sauvignon Blanc and Viognier (40%, 35% and 25% respectively), gently oak-aged, showing crisply dry with fine balancing acidity. On the nose and palate peach, melon, citrus and light spicy notes leading to a long, refreshing finish. Drink now–2011. Score 89. **K**

Reserve

RESERVE, CABERNET SAUVIGNON, 2006: Dark garnet in color, deeply aromatic and showing full body and generous but comfortably yielding tannins, those in fine balance with fruits, wood and acidity.

Reflecting oak-aging for 18 months with spicy overtones, and opening in the glass to reveal blackberry, currant and purple plum fruits, those supported nicely by hints of black pepper. Medium- toward full-bodied, mouth-filling and long. Drink now–2012. Score 91. K

RESERVE, CABERNET SAUVIGNON, 2005: Medium- to full-bodied, with soft tannins integrating nicely with spicy and lightly smoky wood, those yielding to generous red berries, cassis and spices. Lacks complexity but easy to drink. Drink now. Score 87. K

RESERVE, MERLOT, 2006: A Merlot with a unique and charming personality. Full-bodied, reflecting its 14 months in oak with notes of vanilla and spices as well as a cigar-box note that runs through. On the nose and palate opens with strawberries and raspberries, those yielding comfortably to blackberries and currants, all with a generous peppery note that lingers nicely on the long finish. Give this one some time to develop in the bottle and it will show some licorice and smoked meat aromas and flavors as well. One of the best ever from Binyamina. Drink now–2013. Score 92. K

RESERVE, MERLOT, 2005: Dark garnet, medium- to full-bodied, reflecting its development in French oak barrels with hints of spicy wood and generous near-sweet tannins. On the nose and palate raspberry, strawberry and vanilla, those supported nicely by herbal and spicy notes. Drink now. Score 88. K

RESERVE, SHIRAZ, 2006: Developed for 12 months in French and American oak, a full-bodied, dark garnet, aromatic Shiraz blended, as seems to be the wont these days, with 2% of white Viognier grapes, the small amount of which adds both liveliness and flavor. On the nose and palate light notes of smoky wood to match black and red berries, cherries and spices, the tannins coating the mouth gently and then lingering on the generously fruity finish. Drink now–2013. Score 91. K

RESERVE, ZINFANDEL, 2007: Opens with California muscles but those settle down quickly in the glass to reveal a Zinfandel faithful to its variety. Developed in American and French oak for 12 months, with a moderate 14% alcohol content and gently caressing tannins, opens in the glass to reveal wild berry, blackcurrant, raspberry and pepper notes, those matched by notes of chocolate and an appealing hint of dusty wood that rises on the finish. Well done. Drink now–2012. Score 89. K

RESERVE, CHARDONNAY, 2007: Light gold in color, medium-bodied, with a gently spicy oak overlay, opens to reveal appealing citrus and tropical fruits, those on a near creamy background. On the moderately long finish an appealingly bitter herbal note. Drink now. Score 86. **K**

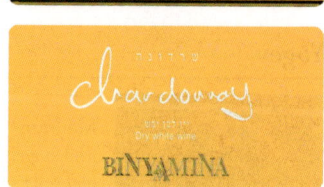

RESERVE, CHARDONNAY, UN-OAKED, 2007: Light golden straw in color, a perhaps too simple wine that, although showing some citrus and tropical fruits, lacks the crisp minerality or liveliness one hopes for in an unoaked Chardonnay. Drink up. Score 84. **K**

RESERVE, SAUVIGNON BLANC, 2008: Light- to medium-bodied, and unoaked, once the wine does open, aromas and flavors of citrus and pineapple, those matched nicely by hints of asparagus (yes, asparagus, not unusual with the variety) and earthy minerals. Drink now or in the next year or so. Score 87. **K**

RESERVE, SAUVIGNON BLANC, 2007: Light gold, medium- to full-bodied, with gentle oak influences and showing citrus, pear and tropical fruits with an appealing hint of bitterness that comes in on the medium-long finish. Drink up. Score 86. **K**

RESERVE, GEWURZTRAMINER, LATE HARVEST CLUSTER SELECT, 2008: Light gold in color, showing deep Gewurztraminer aromas and flavors of litchis and rose petals. To those add the charm of tangerines and passion fruit. A concentrated and intense dessert wine with just the vaguest hint of botrytis (a small number of the grapes were impacted upon by this noblest of rots), those hints possibly to rise nicely as the wine develops in the bottle. Competes with the very best dessert wines in the country. Drink now–2013, perhaps longer. Score 93. **K**

RESERVE, GEWURZTRAMINER, 2008: An appealing light to medium-bodied Gewurztraminer, half-dry but with fine balancing acidity to keep it lively. In addition to traditional litchi and rosewater notes look for hints of pink grapefruit here. Not overly complex but easy to drink, especially as an aperitif or to match noodle-based dishes or wraps. Drink now. Score 87. **K**

RESERVE, GEWURZTRAMINER, 2007: Medium-bodied, light golden in color, with spicy and floral Gewurztraminer traits and appealing citrus and tropical fruits. Off-dry and best as an aperitif or with Oriental cuisine. Drink up. Score 86. **K**

Yogev

YOGEV, CABERNET SAUVIGNON, 2005: Medium- to full-bodied, with soft tannins and sur-ripe plums, berry fruits and generous alcohol that give the wine a near-sweet finish. Drink up. Score 85. **K**

YOGEV, CABERNET SAUVIGNON-MERLOT, 2007: Dark garnet, medium-bodied, with generous spicy wood and appealing notes of blackberries, red and blackcurrants on a background of tobacco and Mediterranean herbs. Drink now. Score 87. **K**

YOGEV, CABERNET SAUVIGNON-MERLOT, 2006: Medium-bodied, with light oak influences and firm tannins. Opens to reveal currant, berry, and black cherry fruits. Not complex but a good quaffer. Drink now. Score 85. **K**

YOGEV, CABERNET SAUVIGNON-MERLOT, 2005: A medium-bodied blend of 50% each of Cabernet and Merlot, aged in oak for eight months. Generous currant, raspberry, red plum and cedar aromas and flavors yield a smooth-textured appealing wine with a moderately long, lightly herbal finish. Drink up. Score 86. **K**

YOGEV, CABERNET SAUVIGNON-SHIRAZ, 2007: Reflecting its six months in oak with light spicy and vanilla overtones, a medium- to full-bodied wine with soft tannins and appealing berry, black cherry and cassis fruits highlighted nicely by a light peppery overtone. Drink now. Score 87. **K**

YOGEV, CABERNET SAUVIGNON-SHIRAZ, 2006: Medium- to full-bodied, with soft tannins and hints of vanilla from the oak in which it aged. On the nose and palate berry, black cherry and a light meaty overtone. Drink now. Score 87. **K**

YOGEV, CABERNET SAUVIGNON-SHIRAZ, 2005: Medium-bodied, with light, spicy oak and bright cherry, and red and black berry aromas and flavors that linger nicely. Ripe and open and, on the moderately long finish, appealing hints of licorice. Drink up. Score 88. **K**

YOGEV, CABERNET SAUVIGNON-ZINFANDEL, 2008: Ruby toward garnet, medium-bodied, with soft tannins and appealing black fruits on the nose and palate. A blend of equal parts of Cabernet Sauvignon and Zinfandel. A good quaffer. Drink now. Score 85. **K**

YOGEV, CABERNET SAUVIGNON-PETIT VERDOT, 2007: A blend of 80% Cabernet and 20% Petit Verdot. Medium- to full-bodied with chunky tannins, a pleasant but not complex country-style wine with black fruits, spices and spicy oak notes. Drink now. Score 86. **K**

YOGEV, CABERNET SAUVIGNON-PETIT VERDOT, 2006: A medium-bodied, softly tannic blend of 80% Cabernet Sauvignon and 20% Petit Verdot, opening on the palate to reveal gentle spicy wood and black-berry and currant fruits, those complemented by a light herbal note. Round and moderately long. Drink now. Score 89. **K**

YOGEV, ROSÉ, 2008: Light rose-petal pink in color, opens quietly but develops nicely after a few minutes in the glass. Good acidity here to keep the raspberry, strawberry and citrus peel notes lively and refreshing. Rosé as rosé should be. Drink now. Score 87. **K**

YOGEV, SAUVIGNON BLANC-CHARDONNAY, 2008: A light- to medium-bodied unoaked blend, this year with 70% Sauvignon Blanc. Crisply dry, with an array of grapefruit, pineapple and citrus peel notes. A good quaffer. Drink up. Score 85. **K**

YOGEV, SAUVIGNON BLANC-CHARDONNAY, 2007: Unoaked, light- to medium-bodied, with crisply clean aromas and flavors of citrus, pineapple, tropical fruits and a near-sweet finish. Not complex but appealing. Drink up. Score 85. **K**

Tiltan

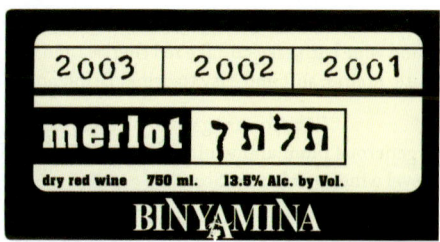

TILTAN, N.V.: A blend not of different grape varieties but of Cabernet Sauvignon grapes from three different vintage years, in this case from 2004, 2005 and 2006. Developed in *barriques* for 18 months, showing generous but not offensive sweet cedarwood and moderately gripping tannins that yield nicely to show blackberry, blackcurrant and orange peel notes, all on a light background of green olives and eucalyptus. Drink now–2011. Score 88. K

TILTAN, N.V.: Made from Cabernet Sauvignon grapes harvested in the 2003, 2004 and 2005 harvests, each developed in wood for a different period of time. Full-bodied, with soft, caressing tannins and a moderate hand with peppery wood, the wine opens on the palate to reveal currants, black cherries and herbal aromas and flavors, all of which are concentrated but not heavy. Finishes with generous tannins and an appealing hint of sage. Drink now–2012. Score 90. K

TILTAN, N.V.: Made from Cabernet Sauvignon grapes from the 2002, 2003 and 2004 vintages, this medium- to full-bodied blend shows generous wood and tannins, those in good balance with spicy and lightly earthy black fruits. On the finish, nice hints of herbs and vanilla. Showing first signs of aging. Drink up. Score 86. K

Teva

TEVA, CABERNET SAUVIGNON, 2008: With just a bit of Merlot blended in, dark ruby toward garnet, medium-bodied, with gently caressing tannins and opening to show red currants, plums and raspberry notes. Not complex but appealing. Drink now. Score 86. K

TEVA, CABERNET SAUVIGNON, 2006: Dark cherry red toward garnet in color, medium-bodied, with light hints of spicy oak and an appealing cherry, blackberry personality. On the short, fruity finish an appealing hint of tobacco. Drink now. Score 85. K

TEVA, MERLOT, 2006: Ruby toward garnet, medium-bodied with soft tannins. Not at all complex but with pleasant blackberry and black cherry fruits on a light spicy background. Drink now. Score 84. K

TEVA, SHIRAZ, 2008: Dark cherry red, medium-bodied, with silky tannins, a round wine with easy-to-take red cherries and berries on the nose and palate. Round, soft and easy to drink. Drink now. Score 86. K

TEVA, SHIRAZ, 2007: Ruby toward garnet, medium-bodied, with soft tannins and generous plum and wild berry fruits. Soft and round, a good entry-level wine. Drink now. Score 85. K

TEVA, PINOTAGE, 2007: Medium-bodied, dark and youthful, royal purple in color at this stage, and showing a generous core of blackberry, wild berry and cherry fruits, those on a background of firm but ripe tannins. Drink now. Score 86. K

TEVA, PINOTAGE, 2006: Bright royal purple in color, medium-bodied, with soft tannins balanced by lively acidity and just a hint of spicy wood. On the nose and palate cherries and an intimation of cassis, those matched by a light touch of white pepper. Nothing complex but a round, easy-to-drink quaffer. Drink up. Score 84. K

TEVA, TEMPRANILLO, 2007: Dark royal purple, with near-sweet tannins, a soft, round red with aromas and flavors of blackberries, vanilla, toast and minerals. A thoroughly modern Tempranillo. Drink now. Score 86. K

TEVA, TEMPRANILLO, 2006: Blended with 15% of Cabernet Sauvignon, treated lightly to American oak *barriques*, this medium-bodied and softly tannic wine shows appealing black cherries, purple plums and hints of cigar tobacco leading to a round and moderately long finish. Drink up. Score 85. K

TEVA, CABERNET BLUSH, 2007: Semi-sweet, bright pink in color with generous red fruits. A bit more balancing acidity would have helped. Drink up. Score 82. K

TEVA, CHARDONNAY, 2008: Golden straw in color, an unoaked, crisply dry with fine acidity and showing appealing tropical and citrus fruits. Not at all complex but a very pleasant quaffer, and fine value for money. Drink now. Score 86. K

TEVA, MOSCATO, 2008: Lightly *frizzante*, gives the sensation of floating on the palate. Moderate sweetness balanced by lively acidity and showing citrus and summer fruits. Aromatic and very easy to drink, especially when served as well chilled as you would a Champagne. Drink now. Score 86. K

Birya ✶✶

Founded by Moshe Porat in the community of Birya near the town of Safed in the Galilee, the winery draws on grapes from Ramot Naftaly in the Upper Galilee, and released its first wines from the 2003 vintage. Production for the 2005 vintage was 4,000 bottles Because of damage during the Israel-Hezbollah war during the summer of 2006, no wines were produced from that vintage.

BIRYA, CABERNET SAUVIGNON, 2005: Dark ruby toward garnet, this medium- to full-bodied wine shows soft tannins and generous currant, blackberry and mint on the nose and palate. On the moderately long finish a hint of fresh herbs. Drink up. Score 85. **K**

BIRYA, CABERNET SAUVIGNON, 2004: Deep garnet toward royal purple in color, medium- to full-bodied, with soft tannins integrating nicely with wood and fruits. Aromas and flavors of blackcurrants and berries on a light herbal background. Drink up. Score 84. **K**

BIRYA, CABERNET SAUVIGNON, PORAT WINE, 2003: Medium- to full-bodied with firm but well-integrating tannins and traditional Cabernet fruits of blackcurrants and berries with hints of herbs and spices on the finish. Drink up. Score 85. **K**

BIRYA, MERLOT, 2005: Generous blackberry, purple plum and black cherry fruits on a medium-bodied, softly tannic frame. A good quaffer. Drink up. Score 85. **K**

BIRYA, MERLOT, 2004: Medium-bodied, soft and round, with forward berry, black cherry and currant fruits. Drink up. Score 85. **K**

Bustan ✶✶✶✶

Founded in 1994 by Ya'akov Fogler, this microwinery situated on Moshav Sharei Tikva in the Shomron region draws Cabernet Sauvignon, Merlot and Syrah grapes from the Jerusalem and Judean Mountains, and produces about 3,000 bottles annually. The winery has earned a good name for its distinctly French-style wines, which have had a formal kashrut certificate since 1999.

BUSTAN, CABERNET SAUVIGNON, 2005: Deep, almost inky garnet in color, full-bodied, with intensity and concentration. Generous but remarkably soft tannins and spicy wood meld comfortably into the background to highlight traditional Cabernet aromas and flavors of blackcurrants, blackberries and spices, those with appealing overlays of minted chocolate and earthy minerals. On the long finish an appealing hint of near-sweet cedar. Approachable now, but best 2011–2015. Score 92. **K**

BUSTAN, CABERNET SAUVIGNON, 2004: Dark, almost impenetrable royal purple in color, full-bodied and powerful, with soft, mouth-coating tannins along with aromas and flavors of blackcurrants, blackberries, plums and spices, all with notes of chocolate, minerals and spicy cedarwood. Long and generous. Drink now–2014. Score 91. **K**

BUSTAN, CABERNET SAUVIGNON, 2003: Dark ruby to garnet, medium-bodied, with soft tannins integrating well and with generous but not overwhelming spicy oak. Spicy currant and berry fruits along with chocolate and tobacco on the powerful but elegant finish. Drink now–2011. Score 90. **K**

BUSTAN, MERLOT, 2005: Full-bodied, with deep, near-sweet and gently mouth-coating tannins, a muscular but simultaneously elegant Merlot. On the nose and palate, wild berries, currants, spices, Mediterranean herbs and *garrigue*, all coming together as a coherent whole. Long and generous. Approachable now, but will show its elegance only starting in 2011, and then cellar well until 2014. Score 92. **K**

BUSTAN, MERLOT, 2004: Aged in *barriques* for 22 months, dark, almost impenetrable garnet in color, but despite that casting purple and orange reflections. Full-bodied, with big but velvety smooth tannins and showing a tempting array of blackberries, spices, dark chocolate, green olives and a light note of grilled meat. Luscious and long. Drink now–2012. Score 92. **K**

BUSTAN, MERLOT, 2003: Deep, dark, rich and aromatic. Full-bodied, with soft tannins, this smooth and round wine opens to reveal generous blueberry, cherry and currant fruits on a spicy floral background, all lingering nicely on the generous finish. Drink now–2012. Score 91. **K**

BUSTAN, SYRAH, 2006: Not Australia and not the Rhone, but Syrah with a distinctly Mediterranean note. Full-bodied, with generous but gently mouth-coating tannins in fine balance with spicy wood and fruits. On first attack wild berries and plums, those yielding comfortably to notes of blackberries and cassis and, in the background, tantalizing hints of leather and game meat. Long, generous and mouth-filling. Best 2011–2015. Score 92. **K**

BUSTAN, SYRAH, 2005: Full-bodied, with super-soft tannins and opening with a burst of sweet and savory tannins, those parting in the glass to reveal layer after layer of blackberry, plum and citrus peel notes, complemented by notes of black tea, white pepper and, on the long finish, a hint of peppermint. Concentrated, intense, well focused, supple and harmonious with a super-long finish. Drink now–2013. Score 92. **K**

BUSTAN, SYRAH, 2004: Dark garnet, full-bodied, with firm tannins and gentle smoky wood influences. On the nose and palate black fruits, exotic spices and hints of saddle leather and earthy minerals. Long and generous. Drink now–2012. Score 90. **K**

BUSTAN, SYRAH, 2003: Aromatic enough to be thought of as perfumed, this full-bodied, chewy and richly tannic wine offers up flavors of blackberries, currants, and boysenberry jam, those with tempting overlays of pepper, wet earth, and just a hint of grilled meat. Deep and intense, with a long, complex finish. Drink now–2011. Score 90. **K**

Bustan Hameshusheem *

Located on Moshav Had Ness on the Golan Heights, winemaker-owner Benny Josef released his first wines to the market from the 2001 vintage. Production of 8,000 bottles annually is primarily of Cabernet Sauvignon, Merlot, Barbera and Sangiovese, and the grapes are drawn from the Upper Galilee and nearby vineyards.

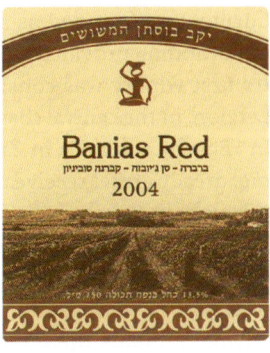

BUSTAN HAMESHUSHEEM, CABERNET SAUVIGNON, 2006: Medium- to full-bodied, a country-style wine with generous black fruits and Mediterranean herbs, but sharp tannins and a distinct note of volatile acidity. Drink up. Score 78.

BUSTAN HAMESHUSHEEM, CABERNET SAUVIGNON, 2005: Full-bodied, with chunky, country-style tannins and smoky oak holding back the black fruits and spices. Drink up. Score 80.

BUSTAN HAMESHUSHEEM, CABERNET SAUVIGNON, 2004: Dark in color, with generous firm tannins, those balanced nicely by spicy oak, currant and wild berry aromas and flavors. Drink up. Score 80.

BUSTAN HAMESHUSHEEM, SANGIOVESE-CABERNET SAUVIGNON, 2005: Light in body, color and tannins, with a stewed fruit nose and overly sweet on the palate. Drink up. Score 75.

BUSTAN HAMESHUSHEEM, BARBERA-SANGIOVESE-CABERNET SAUVIGNON, BANIAS RED, 2004: As light in color as in body, reflecting its eight months in oak with only the barest hint of spiciness and stingy and overripe black fruits. Drink up. Score 75.

Carmel ★★★★

Carmel was founded as a cooperative of vintners in 1882 with funding provided by the Baron Edmond de Rothschild. Its first winery was constructed that same year in Rishon Letzion, in the central coastal region of the country, followed in 1890 by a winery in Zichron Ya'akov, in the Mount Carmel area. Carmel receives grapes from about 300 vineyards throughout the country, some owned by the winery, others by individual vintners and by kibbutzim and moshavim. Even though their share of the local wine market has dropped from over 90% in the early 1980s to somewhat under 50% today, Carmel remains the largest wine producer in the country, currently producing over 13 million bottles annually.

For many years, Carmel was in a moribund state, producing wines that, while acceptable, rarely attained excellence and failed to capture the attention of more sophisticated consumers. In the last six years, Carmel has taken dramatic steps to improve the level of its wines. Under the guidance of senior winemaker Lior Laxer and CEO Israel Ivzan, the winery is developing new vineyards in choice areas of the country and gaining fuller control over contract vineyards. In the 1990s Carmel was the first winery to plant major vineyards in the Negev Desert, and a new state-of-the-art winery has been partly completed at Ramat Dalton in the Upper Galilee. Carmel is also the owner of the Yatir boutique winery. Despite all of this, it is no secret that Carmel continues to undergo serious logistic difficulties and, with many relatively new faces at the helm of the company, one now waits patiently to see precisely what the future holds in store.

Current releases include the top-of-the-line varietal Limited Edition, the Single Vineyard series, and the Regional series (sometimes referred to as the Appellation Series), the wines in these series earning the winery's stars. Following these are the wines in the Private Collection series, Reches series (labeled as Ridge outside of Israel), Zichron Ya'akov series, Selected series (sometimes known as Vineyards or Vineyards Selected Series outside of Israel) and the popularly priced Young Selected series. The vineyards mentioned in the tasting notes of the Single Vineyard Wines—Zarit, Ben Zimra and Kayoumi—are located in the Upper Galilee, and Sha'al is on the Golan Heights.

Limited Edition

LIMITED EDITION, 2007: Full-bodied and concentrated but not at all bombastic, developed in Burgundy-sized barrels (45% of which are new), showing fine balance and structure that bode well for the future. A blend of 57% Cabernet Sauvignon, 31% Petit Verdot, 5% each of Merlot and Malbec, and 2% Cabernet Franc, with a generous array of blackcurrant, blackberry and dark plum fruits, those supported by gentle notes of spicy oak and fresh acidity. Needs time for all of the elements to come together. Approachable on release but best 2011–2018. Score 93. **K**

LIMITED EDITION, 2005: A Bordeaux blend of Cabernet Sauvignon, Petit Verdot, Merlot and Cabernet Franc (65%, 17%, 15% and 3% respectively). Dark ruby toward garnet, medium- to full-bodied, with generous soft tannins and reflecting its 15 months in *barriques* with light toasty and spicy oak. Blackberry and black cherry fruits on first attack, yielding to blackcurrants and appealing hints of lead pencil and vanilla and, on the moderately long finish, a near-sweet and elegant tobacco note. Drink now– 2013. Score 92. **K**

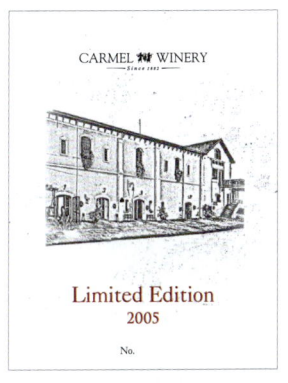

LIMITED EDITION, 2004: This blend of 65% Cabernet Sauvignon, 20% Petit Verdot and 15% Merlot shows soft tannins and generous but gentle wood, those in fine balance with currant, blackberry and black cherry fruits, all melding together with light hints of pepper, anise and cigar-box aromas and flavors. Round and caressing, elegant and long. Drink now–2013. Score 93. **K**

LIMITED EDITION, 2003: A full-bodied blend of 50% Cabernet Sauvignon, 32% Petit Verdot, 17% Merlot and 1% Cabernet Franc. Deeply aromatic, with soft tannins and generous wood in fine balance with fruits and well-tuned acidity. On the nose and palate blackcurrants, blackberries, spices and sweet cedar, all leading to a remarkably long and elegant finish. Drink now–2015. Score 93. **K**

LIMITED EDITION, 2002: Deep royal purple in color, with orange reflections, a Bordeaux blend of 60% Cabernet Sauvignon, 30% Merlot and 10% Cabernet Franc, each variety vinified separately and developed for 14 months in French oak. Medium- to full-bodied, with soft tannins and good balance between sweet and smoky wood, aromas and flavors of blackcurrants, berries and dark chocolate, all leading to a long cigar-box finish. Throwing sediment now. Decant or pour carefully. Drink now. Score 90. **K**

Single Vineyard

SINGLE VINEYARD, CABERNET SAUVIGNON, KAYOUMI, UPPER GALILEE, 2007: Oak-aged for 15 months, a distinctive full-bodied Cabernet, showing cherry, raspberry and red currant fruits on a background of freshly turned earth and tobacco, all leading to a finish that goes on seemingly without end. Well focused and with excellent integration between fruits, tannins and wood. Drink now–2015. Score 93. **K**

SINGLE VINEYARD, CABERNET SAUVIGNON, KAYOUMI, UPPER GALILEE, 2006: Super-dark garnet in color, with a traditional Cabernet nose, a long, round and concentrated wine, medium- to full-bodied with generous but gently mouth-coating tannins, opening to show currant, wild berry, chocolate and espresso coffee notes. Deep, round, nearly chewy and with a deep fruit finish. Drink now–2014. Score 91. **K**

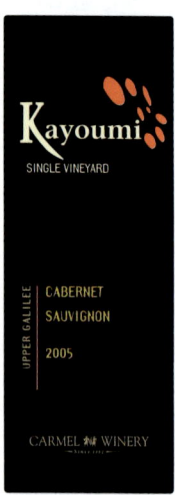

SINGLE VINEYARD, CABERNET SAUVIGNON, KAYOUMI, 2005: Dark garnet with green and orange reflections, full-bodied, open textured and generous showing a spicy, peppery mouthful of blackberry, currant, coffee and black olive notes all leading to a long, round and mouth-filling finish. As this one develops look for an appealing hint of smoked meat rising. Drink now–2013. Score 91. **K**

SINGLE VINEYARD, CABERNET SAUVIGNON, KAYOUMI, 2004: Aged in oak for 15 months, the wine is dark, almost impenetrable purple in color. Firm tannins and smoky wood come together with currant, blackberry, plum and mineral aromas and flavors, those showing hints of Mediterranean herbs and light Oriental spices. Long and generous. Drink now–2012. Score 91. **K**

SINGLE VINEYARD, CABERNET SAUVIGNON, KAYOUMI, 2003: Luscious and elegant, deep garnet, full-bodied and softly tannic. The nose and palate are still showing the blackcurrant, berry and spicy wood that were here but now these are complemented by hints of smoked meat, together with Oriental spices and tobacco. Long and complex. Drink now–2014. Score 92. **K**

SINGLE VINEYARD, CABERNET SAUVIGNON, ZARIT, 2004: Deep garnet toward royal purple, reflecting its 15 months in *barriques* with judicious oak integrating nicely with solid tannins. Opens with currants and dusty wood, moving on to spices and blackberries, and from first sip to last, hints of vanilla, freshly hung tobacco leaves and an intimation of mint. Long and generous. Drink now–2011. Score 91. **K**

SINGLE VINEYARD, CABERNET SAUVIGNON, ZARIT, 2003: Dark garnet, with firm, near-sweet tannins that yield nicely in the glass to reveal an appealing touch of rustic earthiness that adds dimension to rich, ripe black fruits. Complex, concentrated and elegant. Drink now–2011. Score 90. **K**

SINGLE VINEYARD, CABERNET SAUVIGNON, ZARIT, 2002: Dark cherry red, this medium- to full-bodied wine shows soft tannins and generous vanilla and smoky overtones. First impressions are of berries and eucalyptus, those yielding to currants, vanilla, black tea, green peppers and a light spiciness that lingers nicely on the moderately long finish. Warm, round and well balanced. Drink now. Score 90. **K**

SINGLE VINEYARD, CABERNET SAUVIGNON, ZARIT, 2001: Made entirely from Cabernet Sauvignon grapes and aged in French oak *barriques* for 12 months, the wine has a lively cherry-ruby color. The opening impression on the nose is of eucalyptus and black fruits, and on the palate, of sweet berries. Medium-bodied and with soft tannins, the wine opens nicely in the glass and has a medium-long finish. Drink now. Score 87. **K**

SINGLE VINEYARD, CABERNET SAUVIGNON, BEN ZIMRA, 2002: Deep garnet-purple toward black, full-bodied, reflecting its 14 months in oak with generous tannins and spicy oak well balanced by berry, plum and currant fruits, set off nicely by notes of vanilla and eucalyptus. On the long, round finish look for hints of tobacco and green olives. Drink now. Score 90. **K**

SINGLE VINEYARD, CABERNET SAUVIGNON, SCHECH, 2004: From a not-yet-well-known vineyard on the Golan Heights, this red lives up nicely to the stereotypes of what makes a wine "feminine." Soft, round and caressing, elegant without being intense, full-bodied without being muscular, with tempting aromas and flavors of black cherries, currants and anise. Drink now–2012. Score 90. **K**

SINGLE VINEYARD, MERLOT, BEN ZIMRA, 2004: Dark toward inky garnet in color, full-bodied enough to be thought of as dense, with firm tannins integrating now to show fine structure and balance. Opens with a strong gamey aroma, but that fades quickly in the glass to reveal blackcurrants, purple plums and black olives, those highlighted by reined acidity and notes of tar and smoky oak. Long, with meaty flavors and fruits rising on the juicy finish. Drink now–2012. Score 91. **K**

SINGLE VINEYARD, SHIRAZ, KAYOUMI, UPPER GALILEE, 2007: Almost impenetrably dark garnet in color, a big, bold and expressive wine, showing generous black cherry, red plum and raspberry fruits, those on a background of Oriental spices. Concentrated and generous, opening in layers on the palate and then lingering long and comfortably on the palate. Well crafted. Drink now–2015. Score 92. **K**

SINGLE VINEYARD, SHIRAZ, KAYOUMI, UPPER GALILEE, 2006: Deep garnet with hints of royal purple and casting orange and green reflections, a concentrated wine, full-bodied and deeply extracted yet showing remarkably soft tannins and spicy wood that almost melts on the palate. On first attack plums and currants, those making way for black cherries, hints of saddle leather and notes of asphalt. On the long and generous finish with tannins rising a comfortable overlay of freshly roasted herbs and cedar wood. Approachable now but what a waste as this one will start showing its best only in 2011. Cellar comfortably until 2017. Score 93. **K**

SINGLE VINEYARD, SHIRAZ, KAYOUMI, 2005: Dark, almost impenetrable garnet, full-bodied, with silky tannins and showing fine balance and structure. Opens with a burst of dark plum and currant fruits, those yielding to notes of asphalt, bitter herbs and sweet-and-spicy cedarwood. Comes together as elegant, complex and long. Drink now–2012. Score 91. **K**

SINGLE VINEYARD, SHIRAZ, KAYOUMI, 2004: Full-bodied, intense and concentrated, with soft tannins integrating nicely and showing layer after layer of spicy oak, smoked meat and tar, those highlighting red berries, black cherries and licorice. Drink now–2012. Score 91. **K**

SINGLE VINEYARD, SHIRAZ, KAYOUMI, 2003: Firm and well structured, a soft, caressing and elegant wine. Generous soft tannins highlight a tempting array of currant, plum, blackberry and anise flavors and aromas, all of which culminate in a long, mouth-filling finish. Drink now–2011. Score 91. **K**

SINGLE VINEYARD, SYRAH, RAMAT ARAD, 2003: Oak-aged for about nine months, this dark cherry red-toward-purple, medium- to full-bodied wine shows excellent balance between soft tannins, smoke, spices, and aromas and flavors of currants, plums and chocolate. Long, smooth and generous. Drink now. Score 90. **K**

SINGLE VINEYARD, CHARDONNAY, KAYOUMI, 2006: With 75% developing in stainless steel and 25% in 300 liter Burgundy oak, this white is showing an aromatic Chablis-like personality, with minerals and light spices backing up hazelnuts, pears, figs and citrus. On the long finish a hint of toasted brioche. Drink now. Score 90. **K**

SINGLE VINEYARD, CHARDONNAY, KAYOUMI, UPPER GALILEE, 2005: Gentle pressing and cold fermentation, aged partly in new and partly in one-year-old 300 liter French barrels. Showing elegance and focus. Crisp and fresh, and on the nose and palate rich apple, pear, fig and light toasty notes coming together very nicely indeed. Drink up. Score 89. **K**

SINGLE VINEYARD, SAUVIGNON BLANC, RAMAT ARAD, 2006: Shining light straw in color, light- to medium-bodied, this aromatic wine opens to reveal apple and citrus fruits. Not complex but lively and refreshing. Drink now. Score 86. **K**

SINGLE VINEYARD, JOHANNISBERG RIESLING, KAYOUMI, 2006: Bright and juicy, more off-dry than sweet, with tangy acidity highlighting green apple, grapefruit and mineral aromas and flavors. Good concentration in a medium-bodied wine that seems to float gently on the palate. Drink now. Score 89. **K**

SINGLE VINEYARD, JOHANNISBERG RIESLING, KAYOUMI, UPPER GALILEE, 2005: Off-dry but bright and lively, with fine focus and balancing acidity. Unoaked, with tempting peach and apple flavors set off nicely by floral and mineral edges. Elegant and satisfying. Drink now. Score 90. **K**

SINGLE VINEYARD, GEWURZTRA-MINER, LATE HARVEST, SHA'AL VINEYARD, GOLAN, 2008: Generously sweet but with fine balancing acidity, a rich dessert wine, with honey and floral notes to highlight notes of litchi, lemon curd and spices. Complex, long and rich, delicious and complex enough not to accompany dessert but as dessert.

Drink now–2016, perhaps longer. Score 93. **K**

SINGLE VINEYARD, GEWURZTRAMINER, LATE HARVEST, SHA'AL, 2007: Gold, with orange and green tints, medium- to full-bodied, with generous sweetness balanced by lively acidity. Shows litchi, ripe peaches, rose petals, honey, and pineapple aromas and flavors, all coming together in a harmonious whole and, on the long finish, notes of freshly baked pecan pie. Drink now–2011. Score 90. **K**

SINGLE VINEYARD, GEWURZTRAMINER, LATE HARVEST, SHA'AL, 2006: Made from grapes harvested in the upper Golan Heights, some affected by botrytis. Moderately sweet, with rose petal and orange peel overtones and honeyed pear, apricot and litchi fruits. Succulent, with a long-lingering finish. Drink now. Score 90. **K**

SINGLE VINEYARD, GEWURZTRAMINER, LATE HARVEST, SHA'AL, 2005: This medium- to full-bodied white shows generous sweetness and fine balancing acidity along with traditional Gewurztraminer litchis and spiciness, those matched by peach and nectarine fruits and, on the long finish, hints of rosewater and honey. Drink now. Score 91. **K**

Regional (Appellation)

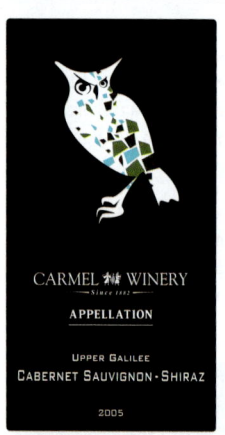

REGIONAL, CABERNET SAUVIGNON, UPPER GALILEE, 2007: Full-bodied, with silky tannins and generous but well-balanced spicy and vanilla-rich wood, those parting to reveal traditional blackcurrant and blackberry fruits, and those complemented nicely by notes of grilled Mediterranean herbs. On the long finish, generous fruits with a hint of near-sweet kirsch liqueur. Drink now–2012. Score 90. **K**

REGIONAL, CABERNET SAUVIGNON, UPPER GALILEE, 2006: Dark garnet with orange reflections, medium- to full-bodied, with firm tannins now settling in nicely. On the nose and palate, spicy wood, currant and blackcurrant fruits along with hints of Mediterranean herbs and dark chocolate. Drink now. Score 88. **K**

REGIONAL, CABERNET SAUVIGNON, UPPER GALILEE, 2005: Blended with 7% Cabernet Franc, this firm, concentrated red shows bright, juicy currant and raspberry fruits, those with overlays of near-sweet cedarwood and sage and, on the long finish, a hint of licorice. Drink now. Score 89. **K**

REGIONAL, CABERNET SAUVIGNON, UPPER GALILEE, 2004: Deep garnet, medium- to full-bodied, with soft tannins and gentle wood highlighting aromas and flavors of currants, wild berries and, on the medium-long finish, a hint of sweet cedar. Drink now. Score 87. K

REGIONAL, MERLOT, UPPER GALILEE, 2007: A dark garnet blend of 85% Merlot and 15% Petit Verdot, reflecting its 12 months in oak with gentle spicy wood, and still firm tannins, those starting to settle in comfortably. Filtered roughly, opens in the glass to show an appealing array of blackberry, blueberry and citrus peel, those matched by notes of Oriental spices. Full-bodied, long and generous. Drink now–2011. Score 89. K

REGIONAL, MERLOT, UPPER GALILEE, 2006: Dark garnet toward royal purple, with soft tannins integrating nicely with spicy wood. Medium- to full-bodied, opens with a plum-rich nose shifting on the palate to berry, black cherry and cassis fruits all supported nicely by hints of white pepper and eucalyptus. Drink now–2011. Score 89. K

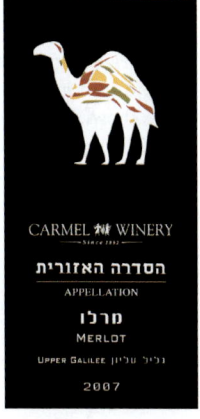

REGIONAL, MERLOT, UPPER GALILEE, 2005: Made from old vine Merlot blended with 7–10% of Cabernet Franc, this medium- to full-bodied wine shows soft, near-sweet tannins integrating nicely and tempting aromas and flavors of ripe berries, plums, chocolate and licorice. Rich, round and delicious. Drink now. Score 89. K

REGIONAL, CABERNET FRANC, UPPER GALILEE, 2007: With grapes from the Netua and Alma vineyards in the Upper Galilee, developed for ten months in oak, some new and some used. Blended with 8% of Petit Verdot and 7% Malbec, a medium- to full-bodied, deep garnet wine showing soft tannins and gentle spicy oak influences integrating nicely and opening to show red fruits and vanilla as well as a clear cigar-box note. Drink now–2012. Score 90. K

REGIONAL, CARIGNAN, OLD VINES, ZICHRON YA'AKOV, 2007: Made from thirty-year-old and older vines, blended with 10% Petit Verdot, oak-aged (minimal new oak) for 14 months. Dark garnet, a fruit-forward blend showing blackcurrant, vanilla and violet notes on a background of fine tannins. Full-bodied, with abundant fruits and fine balance, needs a bit of time for the elements to come together. But best starting in 2011. Score 91. K

REGIONAL, CARIGNAN, OLD VINES, ZICHRON YA'AKOV, 2006: A super-dark garnet blend of 85% Carignan and 15% Petit Verdot, the Carignan from 35–40-year-old, very low-yield wines with no irrigation.

A blockbuster on first attack, but the firm tannins and generous wood settling down nicely to reveal a rich array of plum, red cherry, raspberry and currant fruits all supported nicely by hints of cocoa and spices. Look as well for a generous mocha-rich finish. Drink now–2011. Score 90. **K**

REGIONAL, CARIGNAN, OLD VINES, ZICHRON YA'AKOV, 2005: Blended with 10% Petit Verdot and oak-aged for 12 months. Medium- to full-bodied, with soft, caressing tannins and spicy wood in fine balance with blackberry, cherry and peppery chocolate aromas and flavors, those leading to a medium-long espresso-rich finish. Drink now–2011. Score 91. **K**

REGIONAL, CARIGNAN, ZICHRON YA'AKOV, 2004: Made from old vine Carignan grapes (30–40 years old), blended with 10% of Petit Verdot and aged in French oak for 12 months. Still-firm tannins here but those showing signs of integrating nicely and already revealing raspberry, cherry and cassis fruits, highlighted by hints of dark chocolate and espresso coffee. Drink now. Score 89. **K**

REGIONAL, PETITE SIRAH, OLD VINES, JUDEAN HILLS, 2007: Aged for 14 months in oak, partly new, partly used, made from 35+-year-old vines, a concentrated and full-bodied red, showing royal purple in color and with generous tannins in fine balance with spicy and vanilla-rich wood. On the nose and palate a fine array of red and black fruits, those complemented by notes of black pepper, olives and Mediterranean herbs. Drink now–2012. Score 90. **K**

REGIONAL, PETITE SIRAH, OLD VINES, JUDEAN HILLS, 2006: A big wine, full-bodied, deep garnet toward royal purple, with gripping tannins just starting to settle down but showing fine balance between tannins, wood and fruits. Ripe plum, blackberry and boysenberry notes on a background of minerals, minted chocolate and spicy cedarwood. Drink now–2012. Score 90. **K**

REGIONAL, PETITE SIRAH, JUDEAN HILLS, 2005: Developed in French oak for 12 months, made from grapes from 35-year-old vines, this almost impenetrably dark purple, still-firmly tannic wine opens in the glass to reveal a rich array of dark plum, blueberry, peppery, herbal and spicy cedar notes. Dense enough to be thought of as chewable but opens to show harmony and grace. Drink now–2012. Score 91. **K**

REGIONAL, CABERNET SAUVIGNON-SHIRAZ, UPPER GALILEE, 2007: A blend of equal parts of Cabernet Sauvignon and Shiraz, those developed for 12 months in 30% new oak, the balance being older, showing gentle sweet and spicy oak. With the Shiraz clearly dominant, showing full-bodied, with soft tannins and opening to reveal red and black berries, plums and a hint of saddle leather. Finishes long and spicy. Drink now–2012. Score 90. **K**

REGIONAL, CABERNET SAUVIGNON-SHIRAZ, UPPER GALILEE, 2006: A medium- to full-bodied blend of 50% of each of the varieties, those oak-aged for 12 months in French oak barrels of which about 30% were new. Dark garnet in color, with soft, gently mouth-coating tannins parting to reveal a tempting array of blackberry and plum fruits, those on a background of spices and, coming in near the finish and lingering nicely, hints of leather and vanilla. Drink now. Score 88. **K**

REGIONAL, CABERNET SAUVIGNON-SHIRAZ, UPPER GALILEE, 2005: A blend of 60% Cabernet and 40% Shiraz, this medium- to full-bodied, softly tannic wine fills the palate beautifully. On first attack, light earthy-meaty aromas and flavors, those yielding to blackberries, currants and black cherries and finally, on the long finish, returning to appealing earthy overtones. Drink now. Score 89. **K**

REGIONAL, CHARDONNAY, UPPER GALILEE, 2007: Light golden with green tints, medium-bodied, showing an appealing array of citrus, green apple and tropical fruits on a mineral-rich background. Drink now. Score 88. **K**

REGIONAL, CHARDONNAY, UPPER GALILEE, 2006: Developed *sur lie* in *barriques* for six months, light golden in color, medium-bodied, with appealing tropical fruits, roasted nuts and flinty minerals. Drink up. Score 88. **K**

REGIONAL, SAUVIGNON BLANC, UPPER GALILEE, 2008: Unoaked, showing light golden straw in color, freshly aromatic and on the nose and palate citrus, tropical fruits and citrus peel notes. Not a complex wine but one that is lively and remarkably full of flavor and charm. Drink now. Score 89. **K**

REGIONAL, SAUVIGNON BLANC, UPPER GALILEE, 2007: With only 7% of the wine aged in new 300 liter French barrels and the rest cold fermented and developed in stainless steel, the wine guards the varietal nature of the grape. Bright and lively, with passion fruit, pink grapefruit, green apple, and just-tart-enough citrus fruits. Drink now. Score 89. **K**

REGIONAL, VIOGNIER, UPPER GALILEE, 2008: With 25% of the wine developed in oak, the rest in stainless steel, some of the grapes early harvested and other late harvested, a ripe, creamy near full-bodied white showing concentrated citrus, pear and green apple notes, those on a background of dried apricots and, even though crisply dry, a tantalizing honeyed note. Fine balance between fruits and acidity lead to a long and delicate finish. Drink now–2011. Score 90. **K**

REGIONAL, VIOGNIER, UPPER GALILEE, 2007: With 75% cold fermented in stainless steel and the remainder in *barriques*, that aged *sur lie* for four months. Shows a bare, tantalizing hint of spicy oak on the nose as it opens, yielding to an array of spicy pear, grapefruit and tangerine fruits all on a supple and just-spicy-enough frame. Refreshing and rich. Drink now. Score 88. **K**

REGIONAL, JOHANNISBERG RIESLING, UPPER GALILEE, 2008: Unoaked, medium-bodied, with fine aromatics. Categorized (the law is strange) as off-dry but with a hint of sweetness so gentle that in Germany the wine would be labeled as *trocken* (i.e., dry), and on the palate generous green apple, grapefruit, lemon curd, minerals and a nice hint of white pepper to add to its charm. Drink now–2012. Score 91. **K**

REGIONAL, JOHANNISBERG RIESLING, UPPER GALILEE, 2007: Late harvested, having undergone cold fermentation and developed entirely in stainless steel. Opens with a petrol-rich nose, that going on to reveal green apple, lemon custard and mineral flavors and aromas, all leading to a rich pink-grapefruit finish. Off-dry but with good balancing acidity. Drink now. Score 89. **K**

REGIONAL, GEWURZTRAMINER, UPPER GALILEE, 2008: An off-dry, unoaked white, made from grapes selected from the Kayoumi and Sha'al vineyards. Light gold with green tints, showing typical Gewurztraminer litchi and spicy notes, those matched nicely by notes of ripe peaches and apricots. Fine balancing acidity and a comfortably long finish. Drink now–2011. Score 90. **K**

REGIONAL, GEWURZTRAMINER, UPPER GALILEE, 2007: Off-dry, lively and well balanced with peach, apricot and citrus peel notes highlighted by a light hint of spiciness. Appealing floral and citrus peel on the finish. Drink now. Score 88. **K**

REGIONAL, CARMEL VINTAGE, FORTIFIED PETITE SIRAH, JUDEAN HILLS, 2004: With Tawny-Port-style chocolate, raisins and spice box aromas, this rich dessert wine opens to reveal coffee and a hint of bitter almonds to balance the sweetness. Drink now. Score 89. **K**

Private Collection

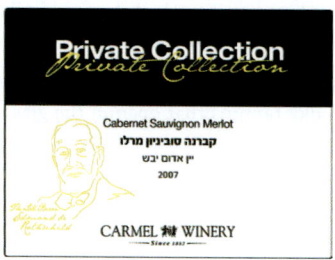

Note: The Private Collection wines made for the U.S.A. and U.K. prior to 2007 were *mevushal* (flash pasteurized), while those distributed in Israel were kosher but not *mevushal*. Because *mevushal* wines cellared a year or longer tend to show "cooked" flavors and aromas, they should be consumed in their youth. Starting with the 2007 harvest, the Private Collection wines will no longer be *mevushal*. The tasting notes that follow are for non-*mevushal* wines.

PRIVATE COLLECTION, CABERNET SAUVIGNON, 2007: Made entirely from Cabernet Sauvignon grapes, developed partly in stainless steel and partly in French and American oak *barriques* for eight months. Full-bodied, with somewhat gripping tannins, opens with a blueberry nose and then goes on to reveal currant and plum fruits on a lightly spicy background with a hint of espresso coffee that makes itself felt. Drink now. Score 86. K

PRIVATE COLLECTION, CABERNET SAUVIGNON, 2006: Medium- to full-bodied, with soft tannins and bare hints of spicy and vanilla-rich oak. Shows berry, black cherry and currant fruits. Not complex but good with food. Drink now. Score 86. K

PRIVATE COLLECTION, CABERNET SAUVIGNON, 2005: Garnet toward royal purple, medium- to full-bodied, with soft tannins integrated nicely. Opens with blackberries and currants, those yielding to blueberries and spices and, on the moderately long finish, hints of black licorice. Drink up. Score 85. K

PRIVATE COLLECTION, MERLOT, 2007: Aged partly in stainless steel and partly in *barriques*, medium- to full-bodied, with gently mouthcoating tannins and notes of spicy cedarwood. On the nose and palate wild berry, cherry and currant fruits, those supported nicely by hints of licorice and chocolate. Drink now. Score 87. K

PRIVATE COLLECTION, MERLOT, 2006: Dark ruby toward garnet, medium- to full-bodied, with soft mouth-coating tannins and spicy wood. Shows blackberry, cassis and herbal aromas and flavors, but lacks depth or complexity. Drink now. Score 84. **K**

PRIVATE COLLECTION, MERLOT, 2005: Dark royal purple, medium-bodied, with chunky tannins that open in the glass to reveal berry, cherry and currant fruits. A country-style wine but easy to drink. Drink up. Score 84. **K**

PRIVATE COLLECTION, SHIRAZ, 2007: Developed partly in stainless steel and partly in *barriques* for eight months. Dark garnet, medium- to full-bodied with chunky, somewhat country-style tannins, appealing cedarwood overtones and opening in the glass to reveal blackberry, plum and leathery notes. Not complex but sits comfortably with food. Drink now. Score 86. **K**

PRIVATE COLLECTION, SHIRAZ, 2005: Medium- to full-bodied, dark garnet-red, with soft tannins well balanced by vanilla and spicy wood. Look for plum and raspberry fruits, those with light vegetal and leathery aromas and flavors. Drink now. Score 87. **K**

PRIVATE COLLECTION, CABERNET SAUVIGNON-MERLOT, 2007: A blend of 50% each Cabernet Sauvignon and Merlot, aged partly in stainless steel and partly in French and American oak. Medium- to full-bodied, with soft tannins and a gentle spicy wood influence, opening in the glass to show black and red berries and notes of purple plums on a background that hints of vanilla and cinnamon. Drink now. Score 87. **K**

PRIVATE COLLECTION, CABERNET SAUVIGNON-MERLOT, 2006: Medium-bodied, with hints of spicy oak and basic currant and berry fruits. Pleasant but lacks complexity or depth. Drink now. Score 84. **K**

PRIVATE COLLECTION, CHARDONNAY, 2007: Golden straw in color, lightly oaked, with peaches, summer fruits and green apples on a lightly spicy and mineral-rich background. Drink now. Score 88. **K**

PRIVATE COLLECTION, CHARDONNAY, 2006: Lightly oaked, this pale golden straw, medium-bodied white shows nectarine and citrus fruits backed up nicely by a hint of spiciness that runs throughout. Drink up. Score 87. **K**

PRIVATE COLLECTION, SAUVIGNON BLANC, 2007: Light golden with green tints, medium-bodied, with good balancing acidity. Aromatic, with appealing summer fruits and citrus on a lightly grassy background. Refreshing and with just the right notes of complexity. Drink now. Score 87. **K**

PRIVATE COLLECTION, EMERALD RIESLING, 2007: Light- to medium-bodied, with moderate sweetness set off by lively acidity. Flowery on the nose and showing tropical and citrus fruits. Drink up. Score 84. **K**

PRIVATE COLLECTION, CHARDONNAY-SAUVIGNON BLANC, 2006: A blend of about 55% Chardonnay and 45% Sauvignon Blanc. Light golden straw in color, medium-bodied, reticent when first poured but opening to show aromas and flavors of white peaches, melon, apricots and, toward the finish, hints of citrus peel and spices. Drink up. Score 85. **K**

PRIVATE COLLECTION, BRUT, N.V.: Made by the Charmat method (with the second fermentation accomplished in pressurized stainless steel tanks), a blend of French Colombard, Chardonnay and Viognier (50%, 40% and 10% respectively), with a portion of the Chardonnay oak-aged, shows simple but appealing aromas and flavors of apples, pears and citrus. A short mousse and sharp but not well-focused bubbles here make one think more of Spanish Cava than of French Champagne. Drink now. Score 86. **K**

Reches (Ridge)

RECHES, RED, ZICHRON YA'AKOV, 2007: Dark royal purple, medium-bodied, with soft tannins, a blend of Carignan, Shiraz, Petite Sirah and Cabernet Sauvignon (60%, 20%, 13% and 7% respectively). Berry, black cherry and currant notes on a lightly spicy background. An entry-level wine. Drink now. Score 83. **K**

RECHES, RED, ZICHRON YA'AKOV, 2006: An unoaked potpourri of Petite Sirah, Cabernet Sauvignon, Merlot, Shiraz and Carignan. Soft, round and simple with primarily black fruits on the nose and palate. Drink up. Score 82. **K**

RECHES, ROSÉ, GALILEE, 2007: A blend of Carignan and Shiraz grapes, light- to medium-bodied and barely off-dry with strawberry, raspberry and gooseberry fruits. Pleasant "as is" but a delight with a few ice cubes added to the wine when it is already well chilled. Drink up. Score 84. **K**

RECHES, WHITE, ZICHRON YA'AKOV, 2007: An unoaked blend of Sauvignon Blanc, Chardonnay, French Colombard and Semillon (40%, 30%, 20% and 10% respectively) come together in a medium-bodied and dry wine, but so super-fruity that many will think it near-sweet. A good entry-level wine. Drink up. Score 85. **K**

Selected (Vineyard)

SELECTED, CABERNET SAUVIGNON, 2007: Medium-dark garnet, medium-bodied, with soft tannins. Shows black fruits along with hints of spicy wood. An entry-level wine. Drink now. Score 83. **K**

SELECTED, CABERNET SAUVIGNON, 2006: Garnet to purple, showing a light hint of spicy oak and currant, berry and black cherry fruits. A good quaffer. Drink now. Score 84. **K**

SELECTED, MERLOT, 2007: Garnet toward purple, medium-bodied, with soft tannins and a generous cherry-berry personality. An entry-level quaffer. Drink now. Score 84. **K**

SELECTED, MERLOT, 2006: Medium-bodied, soft and round. Look for aromas and flavors of cherries and red and black berries. Drink now. Score 84. **K**

SELECTED, ZINFANDEL BLUSH, 2006: A nice little white Zin. Rose-petal pink, light- to medium-bodied, off-dry but with fine balancing acidity to keep it lively, and showing appealing berry and cherry aromas and flavors. Drink up. Score 85. **K**

SELECTED, CHARDONNAY, 2007: Not showing varietal traits but a pleasant enough little wine with aromas and flavors of citrus and tropical fruit. Drink now. Score 84. **K**

SELECTED, CHARDONNAY, 2006: A simple little white wine with pineapple, citrus and tropical fruits. An entry-level quaffer. Drink up. Score 83. **K**

SELECTED, SAUVIGNON BLANC, 2007: Light straw-colored, with generous acidity to keep it lively and an appealing array of citrus and summer fruits. Drink now. Score 84. **K**

SELECTED, SAUVIGNON BLANC, 2006: Light gold in color, light- to medium-bodied, with crisp acidity and an appealing array of pineapple, green apple and tropical fruits. An easy-to-drink wine. Drink up. Score 86. **K**

SELECTED, EMERALD RIESLING, 2007: Light, flowery and aromatic with green apple and citrus notes, and its moderate sweetness balanced nicely by fresh acidity. Drink now. Score 83. **K**

Carmey Avdat ✶✶

Founded by Eyal Izrael, this small winery is based on a private farm on the heights of the Negev Desert not far from Kibbutz Sde Boker. The winery's vineyards of Cabernet Sauvignon and Merlot grapes are planted in a wadi and rely on water from 1,500-year-old water terraces built by the Nab-

bateans. The winery's first releases were 4,500 bottles from the 2005 vintage, which rose to 6,000 bottles from the 2006 and 2007 vintages.

CARMEY AVDAT, CABERNET SAUVIGNON, 2007: Dark garnet, medium-bodied, with softly caressing tannins and notes of spicy wood in good balance with currant, berry and cherry fruits, those on a light earthy background. Drink now. Score 85.

CARMEY AVDAT, CABERNET SAUVIGNON, 2006: Deep garnet toward purple, medium-bodied, with soft tannins and a gentle wood influence. On the nose and palate berries, black cherries and currants, those with light vanilla and earthy-herbal overlays. Drink now. Score 85.

CARMEY AVDAT, MERLOT, 2007: Deep ruby toward garnet, medium-bodied, with somewhat sharp tannins and a perhaps too-generous impact of the oak. Opens to show purple plum, black cherry and chocolate notes. Drink now. Score 84.

CARMEY AVDAT, MERLOT, 2006: Dark, youthful purple, medium- to full-bodied, with still gripping tannins and generous wood influences but those in good balance with fruits and acidity. On the nose and palate berries, cherries, cassis and appealing chocolate and peppery overlays that linger nicely. Drink now. Score 86.

Castel ✶✶✶✶✶

Starting as a micro-winery, the Domaine du Castel grew gradually and now produces approximately 100,000 bottles annually. Since the release of a mere 600 bottles of his first wine in 1992, owner-winemaker Eli Ben Zaken—who now works with his son Ariel—has consistently made some of the very best wines in the country. The winery, with its exquisitely designed barrel room holding more than 500 *barriques*, is located on Moshav Ramat Raziel in the Jerusalem Mountains. The winery relies entirely on grapes grown in the area, mostly in its own vineyards, some in vineyards under its full supervision. Grape varieties include Cabernet Sauvignon, Merlot, Petit Verdot, Cabernet Franc, Malbec and Chardonnay.

The winery produces three wines annually. The first, Grand Vin Castel, is a superb Bordeaux-style blend; the fine second label, Petit Castel, is meant for earlier drinking; and "C" has often been one of the most exciting Chardonnay wines produced in Israel. The winery produced a first kosher version of its Grand Vin in 2002, and from the 2003 vintage all of Castel's wines have been kosher.

Grand Vin Castel

GRAND VIN CASTEL, 2007: Full-bodied, with generous, gently caressing tannins and notes of spicy oak that part to make way for blackcurrant, blackberry and blueberry fruits, those supported by notes of mocha, orange peel and a delicate note of black olives that comes in on the long finish. Long, generous and coherent. Drink now–2014. Score 92. **K**

GRAND VIN CASTEL, 2006: A blend focused on Cabernet Sauvignon and Merlot, those flushed out with Petit Verdot and Malbec. Firm, solid and intense, dark garnet in color, full-bodied and opening to show a generous array of blackberries, black cherries, currants and dark chocolate. Dense, rich and complex, with hints of near-sweetness that toy comfortably on the palate, with tannins that grip comfortably and in fine balance with wood and fruits. Long and generous, muscular and intense but with a distinct note of elegance. Drink now–2013. Score 92. **K**

GRAND VIN CASTEL, 2005: Dark toward inky garnet with firm tannins now integrating nicely with spicy and smoky oak. Opens slowly in the glass to show a nose and palate of blackcurrant, blackberry and purple plum fruits on a background of generous Mediterranean herbs and near-sweet tobacco. On the long finish hints of citrus peel, anise and dark chocolate. Drink now–2011. Score 92. **K**

GRAND VIN CASTEL, 2004: Super-dark garnet toward inky black, full-bodied, with deep and still-firm tannins integrating nicely with smoky and spicy wood and fruits. Opens with blackberries and chocolate, those yielding to currants and raspberries and finally to an array of licorice and tobacco that play on the palate. Long, generous and elegant. Drink now–2011. Score 93. **K**

GRAND VIN CASTEL, 2003: Opens with a somewhat medicinal-iodine aroma, that yielding to licorice, meaty notes and spices. Dark garnet, full-bodied, with its tannins now integrated nicely and opening to reveal blackcurrants and black and red berries, those with overlays of sweet herbs and green olives. On the long finish, an appealing earthy-herbal note. Losing its fresh fruit nature and showing notes of maturity. Drink up. Score 90. **K**

GRAND VIN CASTEL, 2002: Remaining rich and round, continuing to show black fruits, anise and hints of olives and cedarwood, but sliding past its peak and not for further cellaring. Drink up. Score 90.

GRAND VIN CASTEL, 2002 (KOSHER EDITION): Maturing nicely, its once-exuberant currant, cherry and plum fruits now more subdued though still pronounced, and yielding to the minerals and cedar that were once in the background. Full-bodied, with wood, tannins and fruits nicely balanced and taking on a more earthy-herbal note. Drink up. Score 90. **K**

GRAND VIN CASTEL, 2001: Maturing and now showing earthy currant, black cherry, sage and cedarwood aromas and flavors. Full-bodied and concentrated, the wine possesses great elegance and features long lingering flavors rich in hints of coffee and chocolate. A bit of earthy funk creeping in. Showing signs of age. Drink up. Score 91.

GRAND VIN CASTEL, 2000: With once firm tannins now well integrated, this medium- to full-bodied wine is showing excellent balance between spicy blackcurrant, plum and blackberry fruits, those matched nicely by hints of Mediterranean herbs and clean earthy aromas and flavors. Muscular, with firm tannins as well as a long, spicy finish. Somewhat past its peak. Drink up. Score 90.

GRAND VIN CASTEL, 1999: This full-bodied, deep ruby-toward-dark purple wine continues to show good balance between generous, well-integrated tannins and currant, plum and blackberry fruits. Not aging as gracefully as once predicted and now showing a bit flabby on the palate. Past its peak and maturing rapidly. Drink up. Score 87.

GRAND VIN CASTEL, 1998: A near-elegant wine, slow to open during its youth and now aging somewhat more quickly than anticipated. With now softened tannins, some spicy-smoky wood and plum and currant fruits, all leading to a moderately long vanilla-flavored finish. Showing signs of caramelization and age . Drink up. Score 87.

GRAND VIN CASTEL, 1997: Perhaps Castel's most luxurious wine in its youth, with remarkably intense blackcurrant and black cherry fruits, Mediterranean herbs, an abundant but very well-balanced oak and a long finish with pepper and anise. Supple and harmonious but now well past its peak and fading rapidly. Drink up. Score 87.

Petit Castel

PETIT CASTEL, 2006: A blend of Merlot, Petit Verdot and Cabernet Sauvignon. On first attack green and herbal notes, with cedary oak and tobacco flavors dominating, but then opening in the glass to show currants, purple plum and sage notes, the tannins rising on the finish. Drink now–2013. Score 89. K

PETIT CASTEL, 2005: A blend primarily of Merlot, supplemented by Cabernet Sauvignon. Aged in oak for 16 months, this appealing dark red-ruby aromatic wine opens with red berries and spices going on to black cherries, licorice and chocolate. Generous and with a tantalizing hint of sweetness on the long finish. Drink now–2011. Score 91. K

PETIT CASTEL, 2004: Medium- to full-bodied and with soft tannins, this caressing red opens with a chocolate and berry-rich nose, joined by cassis, black cherries, dark plums, bittersweet chocolate and pepper, all lingering on a long, polished and round finish. Elegant and supple. Drink now. Score 92. K

PETIT CASTEL, 2003: Garnet, with a bit of clearing at the rim, opens with a slightly medicinal-iodine note, but that blows in the glass, and then shows medium- to full-bodied, with generous blackcurrant, blackberry and purple plum fruits, those on a softly tannic background. As the wine develops in the glass, look as well for wild berry and a light earthy-herbal note. Drink now. Score 90. K

PETIT CASTEL, 2002: Dark ruby toward garnet, this medium-bodied red shows soft, well-integrated tannins and generous currant and wild berry fruits together with generous touches of sweet cedar, spices and herbs on the moderately long finish. Fully mature and showing signs of age. Drink up. Score 88.

"C" Chardonnay

"C", CHARDONNAY, BLANC DU CASTEL, 2007: Gold, with green and orange tints, deeply floral, full-bodied and with generous but not overpowering oak that parts comfortably to reveal a complex array of citrus peel, summer fruits, hazelnuts, vanilla and crisp minerals. Lively and complex, opening nicely at this stage and showing a near creamy personality, that with a most welcome note of bitterness to enchant. Drink now–2011. Score 90. K

"C", CHARDONNAY, BLANC DU CASTEL, 2006: Showing marginally better than at earlier tastings. Deep golden in color, slow to open, with aromas and flavors hidden for at least ten minutes and then showing now as in its extreme youth a somewhat generous dose of wood. On that background, notes of green apples, citrus, buttery hazelnuts, nutmeg and raisins. Full-bodied, concentrated and intense, but lacking vibrancy. Drink now. Score 88. K

"C", CHARDONNAY, BLANC DU CASTEL, 2005: Bright gold, full-bodied and concentrated, with light but not imposing buttery and spicy sensations. Rich, complex and opulent, with layers of citrus, figs, pears, summer fruits and toasty oak. Shows finesse and elegance. Drink up. Score 92. K

The Cave ✷✷✷

Releasing its first red wine from the 2000 vintage as the boutique arm of Binyamina Wineries, this small winery has its barrel storage facilities in a cave at the foothills of Mount Carmel, not far from the town of Zichron Ya'akov. It should be understood that The Cave is not so much an independent winery as it is an extension of Binyamina, the wines made by the same winemakers, vinified at the main winery and only then transferred to *barriques* for barrel-aging in an artificial cave, that built in the sixteenth century. The cave itself is breathtaking—ninety meters long and nine to ten meters high, with stone-lined walls and roof, and maintaining a constant natural temperature and humidity. The winery is currently releasing 20,000 bottles annually of a Cabernet Sauvignon-Merlot blend. The grapes come from a single vineyard in Kerem Ben Zimra in the Upper Galilee.

THE CAVE, CABERNET SAUVIGNON-MERLOT-PETIT VERDOT, 2007: Dark garnet toward youthful royal purple in color, with generous blackberry, purple plum and peppery notes here, those supported by hints of smoke and saddle leather on the finish. Drink now–2014. Score 88. **K**

THE CAVE, CABERNET SAUVIGNON-MERLOT, 2006: Full-bodied, with firm tannins and an array of currant, berry and black cherry fruits. Good balance and structure here leading to a moderately long finish. Drink now–2012. Score 88. **K**

THE CAVE, CABERNET SAUVIGNON-MERLOT, 2005: Full-bodied, with soft tannins integrating nicely and showing a moderate dose of spicy cedarwood, all in fine balance with fruits and acidity. A blend of 65% Cabernet Sauvignon and 35% Merlot, those vinified separately before the final blend was made near bottling time. Dark garnet toward royal purple in color, with currant, blackberry, spices and hints of bitter orange peel all coming together as a long and coherent whole. Drink now–2011. Score 90. **K**

THE CAVE, CABERNET SAUVIGNON-MERLOT, 2004: Medium-bodied, with soft tannins integrating well with acidity and a generous dose of wood from its 26 months in French oak. Dark royal purple in color, with aromas and flavors of red berries and cassis, with the wood and tannins rising on the finish at this stage. Drink now. Score 87. **K**

Chateau Golan ★★★★★

A fully modern winery located on Moshav Eliad on the Golan Heights, Chateau Golan released their first wines from the 2000 vintage under the hand of Oregon and California-trained winemaker Uri Hetz. Vineyards owned by the winery currently yield Cabernet Sauvignon, Merlot, Cabernet Franc, Petite Sirah, Petit Verdot, Grenache, Sauvignon Blanc, Mourvedre, Rousanne, Grenache Blanc and Viognier grapes. Production is currently between 70,000–75,000 bottles and future production is estimated at somewhat over 100,000 bottles annually. The winery releases wines in one series, Royal Reserve, that including the proprietary blend known as Eliad.

Royal Reserve

ROYAL RESERVE, CABERNET SAUVIGNON, 2008: Young and concentrated, super-dark garnet in color, full-bodied, already showing generous alcohol, tannins and wood. Put that all together and you might have a California wine, but the balance and structure are all here and do not at all hide a tempting array of black and red currants, purple plums and notes of sweet cedarwood. Needs time for the elements to come together, but as those do, a lovely wine in the waiting. Best starting in 2011. Tentative Score 90–92.

ROYAL RESERVE, CABERNET SAUVIGNON, 2007: A medium- to full-bodied blend of 85% Cabernet Sauvignon, 7% each Cabernet Franc and Syrah, and a 1% smidgeon (I always wanted to use that word in a tasting note) of Petite Sirah. Deep garnet and reflecting its 12 months in oak with gently mouth-coating tannins. Opens to show appealing aromas and flavors of blackberries, blackcurrants and violets, and, on the generous finish, a gentle hint of bittersweet chocolate. Drink now–2014. Score 90.

ROYAL RESERVE, CABERNET SAUVIGNON, 2006: Cabernet Sauvignon blended with 9% Cabernet Franc, 3.5% Syrah and 1.5% Petit Verdot. Oak-aged for 12 months, medium-dark garnet, with a hint of sweetness on the nose, turning firm on the palate with mouth-coating tannins and hints of wood. Opens to light oak and mocha, which support currants, blackberries and a hint of vanilla bean that adds a nice touch; tannins, alcohol and a note of sweet chewing tobacco rising on the finish. Drink now–2013. Score 90.

ROYAL RESERVE, CABERNET SAUVIGNON, 2005: Almost impenetrably dark garnet in color, this wine is both concentrated and elegant. A blend of 89% Cabernet Sauvignon and 11% Cabernet Franc, opening with spicy, mocha-tinged blackcurrants, those yielding to blackberries, herbs and light oak. Hints of light sea salt and leather on the super-long finish make the wine intriguing. Perhaps the best yet from the winery. Drink now–2015. Score 94.

ROYAL RESERVE, CABERNET SAUVIGNON, 2004: Blended with 15% Cabernet Franc, and aged in French and American oak for 12 months, this medium- to full-bodied wine's tannins and lightly smoky wood are integrating nicely to highlight blackberry, currant and purple plum fruits, those opening to hints of strawberries and spices. Drink now–2012. Score 91.

ROYAL RESERVE, CABERNET SAUVIGNON, 2003: Deep, young and tight, but showing excellent focus and concentration. Full-bodied and packed with nicely integrating tannins, the wine shows aromas and flavors of currants, black cherries and anise, along with attractive earthy-herbal overtones and hints of green olives. Drink now–2011. Score 90.

ROYAL RESERVE, MERLOT, 2008: I rather like the winemaker's comment: "If my 2007 Merlot was a dragon, this one is a teddy bear." Medium- to full-bodied, with generous but round gently caressing tannins, a distinctly Old World wine, opening slowly in the glass to reveal a blackberry, raspberry and floral personality. Big but gentle, with hints of chocolate and citrus peel on the long finish. Drink from release–2014. Tentative Score 90–92.

ROYAL RESERVE, MERLOT, 2007: A full-bodied blend of 86% Merlot, 9% Petite Sirah and 5% Syrah. Oak-aged for 13 months, calling to mind the 2001 release from the winery, both being deeply extracted, muscular and intense. Generous soft tannins along with notes of near-sweet cedarwood in fine balance with blackberry, raspberry and cassis fruits, those on a background of licorice and bittersweet chocolate. Tannins and a note of toasty oak rise on the long finish. A powerhouse, but one with grace. Drink now–2014. Score 90.

ROYAL RESERVE, MERLOT, 2006: Showing more full-bodied than at earlier tastings, with soft, near-sweet tannins. Opens with a somewhat veggie nature, but shifts quickly to show tempting black fruits, damson plums and crushed berries, those complemented nicely by an exotic near-sweet spicy note that lingers through the finish. Drink now–2011. Score 90.

ROYAL RESERVE, MERLOT, 2005: A thoroughly modern but still Old-World wine, with good acidity, gentle wood and fruits in fine balance.

Showing a bit green now, but opening to currant and blueberry fruits, those complemented nicely by mocha, chocolate and vanilla. Look for a long, lightly spicy finish. Balance, harmony and finesse here. Drink now. Score 90.

ROYAL RESERVE, MERLOT, 2004: A blend of Merlot, Syrah and Cabernet Franc (89%, 6% and 5% respectively) aged in oak for 13 months, this medium-dark garnet wine shows near-sweet tannins and a light earthy minerality, those supporting generous red currant, berry and cherry aromas and flavors. On the long finish tantalizing hints of sage and anise. Drink now–2012. Score 92.

ROYAL RESERVE, MERLOT, 2003: Aged in oak for 12 months, this deep garnet-toward-royal purple, medium- to full-bodied blend of Merlot, Syrah and Cabernet Sauvignon (86%, 13% and 1% respectively) shows fine balance between generous tannins, spicy wood and currants, berry fruits and herbaceousness. On the long finish hints of licorice and green olives. Concentrated and well focused. Drink now. Score 90.

ROYAL RESERVE, SYRAH, 2008: Full, round and rich, supple, generous and concentrated, even at this very early stage showing a generous range of mineral flavors to complement red berries, dark plums, tobacco and earthy-mineral notes. An intense wine, true to its variety and with the tannins already submerging to reveal the complexity of the wine. Approachable on release, but best 2012–2018. Tentative Score 92–94.

ROYAL RESERVE, SYRAH, 2007: A full-bodied blend of 95% Syrah and 5% Mourvedre, those aged for 12 months in oak and showing a generous but well-balanced 14.6% alcohol content that yields to an appealing hint of sweetness. Opens on the palate to reveal purple plums, wild berries and notes of both licorice and lead pencil. On the long finish, with tannins rising, a pleasing note of violets. Drink now–2014. Score 91.

ROYAL RESERVE, SYRAH, 2006: Medium-dark garnet toward royal purple in color, full-bodied, this blend of 89% Syrah, 8% Grenache and

3% Petite Sirah was aged in oak for 12 months. Generous but soft tannins and spicy wood along with a fairly high alcohol content (14.7%), those in fine balance with fruits and acidity. On the nose and palate ripe blackberries, raspberries and red plums, those matched nicely by spices and hints of citrus peel and saddle leather. Drink now–2012. Score 90.

ROYAL RESERVE, SYRAH, 2005: Blended with 3% Cabernet Sauvignon and aged in large French barrels for 11 months. Dark, rich and plush from first attack, opening to show a tempting array of spicy blackberry, raspberry, red currants and pomegranate fruits, those matched nicely by hints of citrus peel. Bold, with distinctly Old-World charm, showing a light greenness, minerality and tantalizing meaty notes. Long and generous. Drink now–2012. Score 92.

ROYAL RESERVE, SYRAH, 2004: Aged in large oak barrels for 14 months, this medium- to full-bodied and firmly tannic wine opens beautifully in the glass to reveal ripe blackberry, currant and raspberry fruits, all with a delicate hint of near-sweetness and spring flowers. On the long and generous finish hints of spices, licorice and smoked meat. Drink now–2011. Score 90.

ROYAL RESERVE, SYRAH, 2003: Blended with 15% Grenache, this is a classic and elegant Syrah with distinct Mediterranean overtones. Fine balance between wood and soft tannins, a generously gamey wine that offers up smoke and black pepper along with deep raspberry and floral aromas and flavors. Drink now. Score 90.

ROYAL RESERVE, SYRAH, 2002: Tasted from the winery's library, my most recent tasting note holds firmly. Big, dense and tannic, continuing to show round and rich. Deep garnet-to-purple color with a bit of clearing now appearing at the rim, showing generous plum, herbal and earthy aromas and flavors. Drinking well but fully mature and not for further cellaring. Drink up. Score 90.

ROYAL RESERVE, CABERNET FRANC, 2007: This could be a textbook Loire Valley Cabernet Franc, especially when one considers the area of Chinon. Smooth and velvety, with plenty of tannins, but those soft and gently mouth-coating and opening to show black cherry, currant, blueberry and tobacco notes, those complemented by hints of tobacco. As this one develops look for hints of green olives and briar. Drink from release–2013. Tentative Score 90–92.

ROYAL RESERVE, CABERNET FRANC, 2005: Subtle and seductive, with generous tannins integrating nicely. On the nose and palate fresh currant, dark berry and black cherry fruits matched nicely by bell peppers, cigar box and lead pencil notes. Good length, depth and a distinct note of elegance. Drink now–2011. Score 90.

ROYAL RESERVE, CABERNET FRANC, LIMITED EDITION, 2003:
Full-bodied, earthy and aromatic with an appealing array of currant, plum and wild berry fruits, those backed up nicely by vanilla and spices from the oak as well as an appealing hint of earthiness on the moderately long finish. Rich and concentrated. Drink now. Score 90.

ROYAL RESERVE, GRENACHE, 2005: Ripe, rich and with generous oak-accented blackberry, black cherry, spicy and black pepper flavors. True to its variety, with an attractive hint of greenness. Drink now. Score 90.

ROYAL RESERVE, GRENACHE, 2003: Loyal to its varietal traits, this attractive, pale ruby wine is medium-bodied, with soft tannins and tempting blackberry, black cherry and red currant fruits as well as spicy oak. Drink now. Score 89.

ROYAL RESERVE, GESHEM RED, 2008: Grenache and Mourvedre, the Grenache dominating nicely and giving the still very young wine a Grand Marnier nose. Full-bodied, with ample but gently gripping tannins, opens with a distinct note of sweetened chewing tobacco, then going on to show generous red fruits and huckleberries, all with light hints of anise and tar that come in and linger on a long and broad finish. Best 2011–2018. Tentative Score 92–94.

ROYAL RESERVE, GESHEM RED, 2007: Plenty of alcohol here, but that showing neither heat nor sweetness as it is in fine balance with spicy wood, near-sweet tannins and fruits. Full-bodied, rich and deep, showing almost incense-like anise notes and then opening to reveal berry, black cherry and currant fruits. A blend of 70% Grenache with 15% each of Mourvedre and Syrah, oak-aged for 13 months, with a tempting *liquoreux* finish. Drink now–2015. Score 91.

ROYAL RESERVE, GESHEM, 2006: A blend of 80% Grenache, 14% Syrah and 6% Mourvedre, each developed separately and having spent a total of 13 months in *barriques*. Medium garnet in color, medium- to full-bodied, opening quietly on the nose but showing very nicely indeed on the palate, opening to reveal raspberry, cherry and red currant fruits, those supported well by vanilla and hints of spices and bittersweet chocolate. Long and generous. Drink now–2012. Score 91.

ROYAL RESERVE, GESHEM, 2005: Medium-dark garnet, a blend of 70% Grenache and 30% Syrah, reflecting its aging in French oak for 12 months with a light, pleasingly musky overtone. Opens with a near-raspberry liqueur nose, that settling down to reveal oak-accented aromas and flavors of blackberries, cherries and black pepper. Deep and long. Drink now–2013. Score 93.

ROYAL RESERVE, GESHEM, 2004: The first blend of Syrah and Grenache from the winery (62% and 38% respectively). Dark ruby toward garnet, medium- to full-bodied, with soft, ripe tannins integrating well and showing currant and berry fruits, those matched nicely by spices, freshly crushed herbs and, as the wine sits on the palate, hints of orange peel and black tea. Long, super-fruity finish. Drink now. Score 91.

ROYAL RESERVE, ROSÉ, 2008: Almost a twin to the 2007 wine. Pale toward blushing pink in color, made entirely from Cabernet Franc grapes, partly developed in stainless steel and for a short while in used *barriques*. Medium-bodied, with appealing red and black berries, strawberries and red currants, those on a spicy background. Plenty of good acidity here. A more than usually complex rosé. Drink now. Score 89.

ROYAL RESERVE, ROSÉ, 2007: As is the tradition of the winery, a rosé made entirely from Cabernet Franc grapes, that developed partly in stainless steel and part for a short while in old *barriques*. Blushing peach in color, medium-bodied, with appealing wild berries, cassis and notes of strawberries, those on a lightly spicy background. Mouth-filling and generous for a rosé. Drink up. Score 88.

ROYAL RESERVE, SAUVIGNON BLANC, 2008: Lively gold in color, with green and orange tints, developed partly in oak and partly in stainless steel, a wine that is simultaneously lively and refreshing as well as complex and thought provoking. With traditional Sauvignon Blanc aromas and flavors (think of Jancis Robinson's "cat's pee on a gooseberry bush") complemented by grassy, citrus and tropical fruits, those on a background of well-tuned acidity. Long and generous. Drink now–2011, perhaps longer. Score 91.

ROYAL RESERVE, SAUVIGNON BLANC, 2007: 60% of this wine was fermented and developed *sur lie* in old 350 liter barrels, and 40% in stainless steel for about six months. Medium-bodied and aromatic with generous notes of citrus, pineapple and orange peel. Drink now. Score 87.

ROYAL RESERVE, GESHEM BLANC, 2008: Light golden straw in color, a medium-bodied and nicely aromatic blend of Viognier, Grenache Blanc and Roussanne (58%, 37% and 5% respectively). A distinctly Mediterranean blend (you can almost feel the sunshine here), opening with an appealing floral nose and then going on to show apple, nectarine and quince fruits, all supported by fine balancing acidity. A tantalizing hint (perhaps merely an illusion) of sweetness on the long finish. Drink now–2012. Score 91.

ROYAL RESERVE, GESHEM WHITE, 2007: A gently oak-aged blend of Viognier, Grenache Blanc, French Colombard and Roussanne (63%, 29%, 7% and 1%, respectively), calling to mind the white wines of the Rhone Valley. Opens with a floral, almost honeysuckle nose, and then goes on to show melon, white peach, almond and buttery notes on the nose and palate. Full-bodied, smooth and creamy in texture, a quiet and elegant wine, but lacking the mineral and acidity in the backbone that might have elevated the wine to a far higher level of enjoyment. Drink now. Score 88.

Eliad

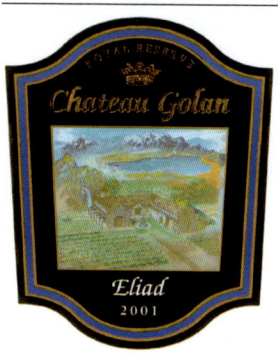

ELIAD, 2007: 89% Cabernet Sauvignon, 7% Petit Verdot and 4% Merlot. Almost inky dark in color, a distinctly Old World wine in its elegance. On first attack blackberries and black cherries, those yielding comfortably to notes of toasty oak and bittersweet chocolate, and, on the long finish, as we have come to know with this wine, hints of olives and Mediterranean herbs. Not at all a "blockbuster" but that's just as well, for given time this one will indeed show elegance. Best 2011–2016, perhaps longer. Score 90.

ELIAD, 2006: Dark garnet, full-bodied and with fine balance and structure, a blend of 93% Cabernet Sauvignon and 3.5% each of Merlot and Petit Verdot, oak-aged for 12 months. Opens with red and black berries, those joined by blackcurrant and black cherries supported by a light note of spicy oak, sweet cedarwood and milk chocolate. Ripe, round and generous, will most assuredly call to mind Bordeaux with a Mediterranean hint added by notes of fresh herbs and black olives. Drink now–2013. Score 91.

ELIAD, 2005: Aged in French oak for 13 months, this blend of 94% Cabernet Sauvignon and 6% Syrah opens with rich, almost syrup-like fruits on the nose, and goes on to show depth and grace. Soft tannins, light smoky wood, fine-grained tannins in good balance with berry, black cherry, currants and licorice. Drink now–2012. Score 93.

ELIAD, 2004: A blend of Cabernet Sauvignon, Merlot, Cabernet Franc and Petit Verdot (70%, 21%, 3% and 6% respectively), this may be the most intense wine released to date by the winery. Dark garnet in color, ripe and complex, showing deep plum, berry, floral, coffee, peppery and earthy aromas and flavors all coming together beautifully in a long and graceful finish. Drink now–2012. *Score* 92.

ELIAD, 2003: Oak-aged, this deep garnet blend of 66% Cabernet Sauvignon, 20% Merlot and 14% Cabernet Franc is already showing rich, intense and complex. Concentrated plum, berry, currant and spicy oak aromas and flavors matched nicely by spices and a hint of tobacco. Drink now–2012. Score 92.

Chillag ★★★★

After studying oenology in Piacenza, Italy, and working at the Antinori wineries in Tuscany, Orna Chillag released her first wines in Israel in 1998. Now located in a new facility in the industrial area of the town of Yahud, on the central plain, the winery relies on Merlot and Cabernet Sauvignon grapes from the Upper Galilee and the Judean Mountains and recently planted its own Syrah, Petit Verdot and Petite Sirah. Production has grown from 4,000 bottles in 2002 to about 15,000 annually in 2007 and 2008.

Until 2005 the winery released wines in two series, Primo Riserva and Giovane. More recently the wines have been appearing in Primo, Solo and Vivo series, the first two meant for cellaring and the second released early and meant for drinking in their youth.

Primo and Primo Riserva

PRIMO, CABERNET SAUVIGNON, UPPER GALILEE, 2005: Blended with 10% Merlot, reflecting its 22 months in French oak with generous but judicious spicy wood in fine balance with soft tannins and opening to show a tempting array of blackberries, currants and Oriental spices, all leading to a rich, long and blueberry-laden finish. Drink now–2012. Score 91.

PRIMO, CABERNET SAUVIGNON, UPPER GALILEE, 2004: Dark royal purple, oak-aged for 18 months, a full-bodied blend of 90% Cabernet Sauvignon and 10% Merlot. Generous smoky cedarwood notes here, but those in fine balance with soft tannins and fruits. Opens with blackcurrants and blackberries, goes on to reveal raspberries, strawberries and notes of dark chocolate and licorice. Long and elegant. Drink now–2012. Score 91.

PRIMO RISERVA, CABERNET SAUVIGNON, 2003: Aged in French oak for 18 months, this full-bodied red with its youthful tannins now nicely tamed, shows appealing and forward aromas and flavors of blackcurrants, purple plums and ripe berry fruits, those matched nicely by spicy oak and, on the long finish, tantalizing hints of freshly turned earth and mushrooms. Needs a bit of time to let the tannins settle in. Drink now–2011. Score 90.

PRIMO RISERVA, MERLOT, 2005: Supple and round with fine structure, Chillag's best to date. Blended with 10% of Cabernet Sauvignon, aged for 22 months in French *barriques*, showing dark garnet in color. Full-bodied with tannins integrating nicely with spicy wood, fresh acidity and generous fruits. On the nose and palate black cherries, plums, toasty oak and roasted coffee, finishing with plum and lead-pencil notes. Drink now–2012. Score 92.

PRIMO RISERVA, MERLOT, 2004: Medium- to full-bodied, with now soft, round tannins, minerals and generous toasty oak reflecting the 21 months the wine spent in *barriques*. Comes together to show appealing blueberries, blackberries and mineral aromas and flavors that linger comfortably. Drink now. Score 89.

Solo

SOLO, CABERNET SAUVIGNON, UPPER GALILEE, 2005: Medium- to full-bodied (leaning toward the full), a blend of 90% Cabernet Sauvignon and 10% Merlot. Aged in new and one-year-old French *barriques* for 18 months and shows a distinct Tuscan flair. Dark garnet, with soft tannins and an appealing array of wild berries and currants on a spicy background. Lingers nicely on the palate. Drink now–2011. Score 90.

SOLO, MERLOT, JUDEAN MOUNTAINS, 2005: Deep garnet toward royal purple, a full-bodied blend of 90% Merlot and 10% Cabernet Sauvignon. Developed in French oak for 18 months, showing generously spicy wood, that in fine balance with mouth-coating tannins and fruits. On the nose and palate ripe plums, wild berries, a hint of cherry liqueur, and, on the long finish, a generous touch of bittersweet chocolate. Drink now–2011. Score 90.

Vivo

VIVO, MERLOT, JUDEAN MOUNTAINS, 2006: Medium-bodied, reflecting its 12 months in new and one-year-old French *barriques* with gently spicy cedar notes and opening to reveal purple plums, wild berries and notes of spices on the moderately long finish. Not complex but fills the mouth nicely and a good match to food. Drink now. Score 87.

VIVO, BLEND, JUDEAN MOUNTAINS, 2006: Garnet toward royal purple, medium- to full-bodied with soft tannins and notes of spicy wood. Opens to reveal appealing plum and raspberry fruits, those supported nicely by notes of milk chocolate and café au lait. Drink now. Score 88.

Giovane

GIOVANE, CABERNET SAUVIGNON, 2007: Tasted as components. Showing dark garnet toward royal purple, medium- to full-bodied, with soft tannins and at this embryonic stage showing a gentle hint of spicy French oak. Opens to reveal traditional Cabernet aromas and flavors of blackcurrants and blackberries, those matched nicely by hints of tobacco and chocolate. Drink from release. Tentative Score 88–90.

GIOVANE, MERLOT, 2006: A blend of 86% Merlot, 12% Cabernet Sauvignon and 2% Petite Sirah. Developed for ten months in French *barriques*, showing medium- to full-bodied with soft, gently mouth-coating tannins and opening to reveal plum and blackberry fruits, those highlighted by notes of sweet toast, vanilla and minerals. Drink now. Score 89.

GIOVANE, CABERNET SAUVIGNON-PETITE SIRAH, 2005: A blend of equal parts Cabernet Sauvignon and Petite Sirah. Oak-aged for 20 months, showing medium- to full-bodied and with still-firm near-sweet tannins, those just starting to settle down and opening to reveal generous black fruits, those on a light background that hints nicely of licorice and bitter almonds. Easy to drink but with just enough complexity to grab and hold our interest. Drink now. Score 90.

Clos de Gat ★★★★★

Located on Kibbutz Har'el in the Jerusalem Mountains, this joint project of the kibbutz and Australian-trained wine-maker Eyal Rotem released its first wines from the 2001 vintage. The name "Clos de Gat" is a play on words—the French *clos* is an enclosed vineyard surrounded by stone walls or windbreaks, while the Hebrew *gat* is an antique wine press. Grapes come from the winery's own vineyards, which now include Cabernet, Merlot, Petit Verdot, Syrah and Chardonnay. Production is currently about 50,000 bottles annually.

The winery releases wines in three series, Sycra (Aramaic for "bright red"), the Bordeaux-blend Clos de Gat, and Har'el. From the 2003 vintage, the wines have been made with wild yeasts.

Sycra

SYCRA, MERLOT, 2006: Full-bodied, reflecting its 20 months in new oak with generous spicy wood and equally generous but softly mouth-coating tannins, those in fine balance with fruits and acidity. Opens with currant, purple plum and mocha notes, those yielding to blackberry, citrus peel and light herbal and tobacco overtones. Drink now–2014. Score 93.

SYCRA, MERLOT, 2003: With 24 months in wood and a generous 15% alcohol content, this super-dark garnet-colored wine is full-bodied enough to be chewy and shows tannins that, although gripping, seem soft and comforting. On the nose and palate touches of spice and freshly-turned earth supporting currant, blackberry and floral notes, all leading to a finish that goes on and on. Drink now–2013. Score 93.

SYCRA, SYRAH, 2006: An opulent wine, almost impenetrably deep garnet in color, full-bodied, with silky-smooth tannins that caress gently and opening in the glass to reveal aromas and flavors of wild berries, grilled meat and spices, those leading to a fruit-rich finish on which you will find tempting chocolate and vanilla undertones. Long, round and generous. If this one does not make you fall in love you're a hard-hearted wine lover indeed. One of the best wines ever from Israel. Approachable now, but best 2011–2016. Score 95.

SYCRA, SYRAH, 2004: Oak-aged for 20 months. Full-bodied, with oak that at one moment seems spicy and at the next smoky but never dominating; with firm tannins integrating nicely now. A dense, almost muscular wine, but one that sits gently and opens to show a tempting array of cherry, berry and currant fruits, those on a just-spicy-enough background to highlight hints of freshly roasted coffee. Well focused, intense and long. Drink now–2014. Score 93.

Clos de Gat

CLOS DE GAT, AYALON VALLEY, 2005: A Bordeaux blend of Cabernet Sauvignon, Merlot and Petit Verdot (63%, 30% and 7%), given a distinct Mediterranean note by touches of black olives and mint. Dark garnet, opens with a sweet red nose, that overlaid with notes of spicy cedarwood. Showing soft, mouth-coating tannins, opens to reveal currant, blackberries and notes of slate. On the long and generous finish, look for notes of raspberries and mocha. Drink now–2014. Score 93.

CLOS DE GAT, AYALON VALLEY, 2004: Dark, full-bodied, firmly tannic, with generous spicy wood, this blend of 65% Cabernet Sauvignon, 30% Merlot and 5% Petit Verdot shows fine harmony but still needs time to integrate. The wine opens to reveal currant, blackberry, spicy oak and hints of licorice and light earthiness. Drink now–2012. Score 93.

CLOS DE GAT, 2003: Predominantly Cabernet Sauvignon, fleshed out with Merlot and Petit Verdot. Dark garnet, medium- to full-bodied, with firm tannins integrating nicely, this elegant wine shows blackcurrant, black cherry and berry fruits, those supported well by hints of vanilla and licorice, all leading to a long spicy finish. Drink now–2012. Score 92.

CLOS DE GAT, 2002: With generous but soft tannins, this dark red-toward-black, medium- to full-bodied blend of 70% Cabernet Sauvignon and 30% Merlot reflects its 18 months in oak with spicy but not exaggerated wood. On the nose and palate ripe currants and plums matched nicely by hints of coffee, sweet cedar, vanilla and Mediterranean herbs. Drink now. Score 90.

CLOS DE GAT, CABERNET SAUVIGNON-MERLOT, AYALON VALLEY, 2001: A deep ruby-garnet, full-bodied unfiltered blend of 70% Cabernet Sauvignon and 30% Merlot, with generous, soft tannins that integrate beautifully, a wine that can honestly be said to reflect its *terroir*. Overlaying traditional Cabernet blackcurrants are generous hints of green olives, basil, tarragon and other Mediterranean herbs. The wine shows good balance and structure, with chocolate and leather coming in on the long finish. Maturing nicely. Drink now–2011. Score 90.

CLOS DE GAT, CHARDONNAY, 2008: Already showing rich, complex and opulent, with generous fig, citrus and melon fruits on a full-bodied background of minerals and butterscotch. On the long and mouth-filling finish, a tempting and delicate note of kumquats. Drink now–2014. Score 92.

CLOS DE GAT, CHARDONNAY, 2007: Deep bright gold in color, full-bodied, reflecting its 12 months *sur lie* in oak with no *battonage*, with a near creamy texture, opening with delicate honeyed green apple and pear notes, those concentrated and well focused and showing fine balance with just enough acidity to keep the wine fresh. Closes with an earthy-mineral overlay that lingers nicely. Generous, mouth-filling and almost extravagant. Drink now–2015. Score 93.

CLOS DE GAT, CHARDONNAY, 2006: Developed *sur lie* for 12 months in French oak, wisely using only 25% of new oak before the final blend was made, and thus showing a light, almost tantalizing hint of the wood. Medium- to full-bodied, with fine balance between wood, acidity and fruits. Opens with citrus, citrus flowers and citrus rind, those yielding to hints of melon and spiced apples all lingering long and comfortably on the finish. Hedonistic, elegant and complex. Drink now–2011. Score 92.

CLOS DE GAT, CHARDONNAY, 2005: Dark gold, full-bodied, but so well balanced that it floats on the palate. Reflects its year in oak with generous spicy wood that turns creamy on the palate and with citrus and green apple notes that develop into peaches, apricots, ginger and lightly chalky-mineral notes that linger comfortably through the long finish. Drink now–2011. Score 92.

CLOS DE GAT, CHARDONNAY, 2004: Deep but lively gold, full-bodied, simultaneously floral and creamy, with fine balancing acidity to show off citrus, pear, green apples and, on the long finish, hints of figs and ginger. Long, generous and mouth-filling. Drink up. Score 92.

CLOS DE GAT, CHANSON BLANC, 2008: Showing light gold in color, medium-bodied, with crisp acidity to highlight citrus, pear and melon fruits. A blend of Chardonnay, Semillon, Viognier and Chenin Blanc, with generous mineral overtones. Refreshing and with just enough complexities. Drink now–2011. Score 90.

CLOS DE GAT, CHANSON, 2007: A well-crafted unoaked blend of Chardonnay, Semillon, Viognier and Chenin Blanc (about 75%, 15%, 7% and 3% respectively). Pale gold in color with orange reflections, medium-bodied, opening with minerals and citrus fruits, those opening in the glass to reveal passion fruits and ripe melon. Long, lively and thought-provoking. Drink now. Score 91.

CLOS DE GAT, CHANSON, 2006: A blend of 70% Chardonnay, 15% Semillon, and 7–8% each of Viognier and Chenin Blanc that comes together in ways that delight. Light gold, medium-bodied, with fine balancing acidity and showing an array of lemon, quince, green apple, stony minerals, and floral aromas and flavors that go on to a long and lively finish. Easy to drink but surprisingly complex. Drink now. Score 92.

Har'el

HAR'EL, CABERNET SAUVIGNON, 2008: Deep, dark and intensely tannic, a rich, full-bodied red showing fine balance and structure, with spicy and vanilla-tinged oak and still firm tannins yielding to highlight well-focused blackberry, blackcurrant and black cherry fruits. On the long finish, with chewy tannins rising, tempting notes of licorice and mint. Best 2012–2017. Tentative Score 93–95.

HAR'EL, CABERNET SAUVIGNON, 2007: A blend of 87% Cabernet Sauvignon, 9% Merlot and 4% Petit Verdot. Deep garnet in color, medium- to full-bodied (leaning toward the full) and firmly tannic, opens with an unusual but very appealing light musky note and then goes on to well-focused red currants and cherries, those supported nicely by notes of freshly turned earth and Mediterranean herbs. Supple, rich and deep, with a finish that goes on seemingly without end. Drink now–2016. Score 92.

HAR'EL, CABERNET SAUVIGNON, 2006: Dark, almost inky-garnet in color, full-bodied, with tannins that are firm on first attack but yield nicely in the glass to reveal fine balance with a genteel hand, with spicy oak, good balancing acidity and fruits. Blended, Bordeaux style, with 9% Merlot and 4% Petit Verdot. On the nose and palate opens with raspberries, those then going to purple plums, blackberries and currants, all intertwined with a pleasing overlay of Mediterranean herbaceousness. Well crafted. Drink now–2012. Score 91.

HAR'EL, CABERNET SAUVIGNON, 2005: Blended with 8% of Merlot and 3% of Petit Verdot and aged in oak for 12 months, this deep garnet-toward-royal purple, full-bodied red shows generous, fine-grained tannins that highlight lightly spicy wood and generous red currant and black cherry fruits. On the moderately long finish, an appealing mineral streak. Drink now–2012. Score 90.

HAR'EL, CABERNET SAUVIGNON, 2004: Full-bodied and firmly tannic, reflecting its 12 months in oak with spicy wood which yields in the glass to reveal currants, black cherries and purple plums, those supported nicely by hints of chocolate and cigar tobacco. Fine balance and structure. Drink now–2012. Score 90.

HAR'EL, CABERNET SAUVIGNON, 2003: Dark garnet, full-bodied, with its tannins now showing soft and nicely integrated. Opens with a rich fruity nose that hints of tar and goes on to reveal generous red berry, cherry and blackcurrant fruits all on a background of gentle oak, anise and a note of iodine. Drinking nicely now, but not for longer cellaring. Drink now. Score 90.

HAR'EL, MERLOT, 2008: Round, ripe, concentrated and generous, showing full-bodied, with still gripping tannins needing time to settle down. On the nose and palate ripe blackberry, black cherry and currant fruits, those matched nicely by hints of toasted rye bread and spices that linger on the long and fruity finish. Approachable on release, but best 2011–2016. Tentative score 92–94.

HAR'EL, MERLOT, 2007: Royal purple toward black, muscular, with bold tannins and spicy oak integrating nicely. Made entirely from Merlot grapes, aged in *barriques* for 14 months. On first attack near-sweet plum and cocoa aromas and flavors, those yielding to notes of currant jam and licorice. A solid finish on which arise notes of citrus peel. Drink now–2015. Score 92.

HAR'EL, MERLOT, 2005: Deep and dark, full-bodied, with still gripping tannins integrating well and with generous spicy wood all coming together to show round and generous. Deeply aromatic, opens to reveal aromas and flavors of red currants, raspberries and chocolate, those yielding later to generous hints of chocolate and toasted rye bread. On the long, intense finish look for hints of minerals and licorice. Drink now–2012. Score 92.

HAR'EL, MERLOT, 2004: Deep and dark, opening with a chocolate-rich nose and firm tannins, those opening to show near-sweet oak and generous currants, plums and berries. A long, mouth-filling and deeply aromatic finish that picks up notes of smoke. Drink now–2012. Score 90.

HAR'EL, MERLOT, 2003: A dense, muscular wine that needs time to settle down but promising to be deep, dark and absolutely beautiful. Complex oak-accented blackberry, currant and black cherry aromas and flavors on a background of chewy tannins, sweet cedar and hints of pepper and vanilla, all of which linger beautifully. Drink now–2012. Score 92.

HAR'EL, SYRAH, 2008: Full-bodied and supple, with fine balance between wood, tannins and a loamy earthy note. Opens to reveal currant and wild berry fruits, those followed by blackberries and black cherries, all supported by a gentle spicy note. Tempting on release, but best 2011–2017. Tentative Score 93–95.

HAR'EL, SYRAH, 2007: Dark, almost impenetrable royal purple, full-bodied, with generous soft tannins integrating nicely. Blended with 15% of Cabernet Sauvignon and oak-aged for 15 months, a generously spicy wine opening to show wild berry, plum and black cherry fruits, those going on to reveal notes of sage, minerals and dark chocolate. Deep and complex, with a long finish on which tannins, red cherries and floral notes make themselves comfortably felt. Drink now–2015. Score 93.

HAR'EL, SYRAH, 2006: Dark garnet toward royal purple, blended with 15% of Cabernet Sauvignon and oak-aged for 15 months (about ⅓ new oak). Full-bodied, with soft, gently mouth-coating tannins and fine balance and structure. Opens slowly in the glass at this stage but when it does, it does so with gusto, showing plum, red berry and cassis fruits, those on a generous but well-proportioned spicy background. Long, round and elegant. Drink now–2013. Score 93.

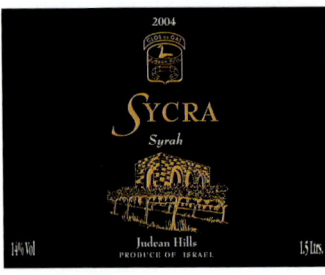

HAR'EL, SYRAH, 2005: Blended with 7% Cabernet Sauvignon, this dark royal purple, deeply aromatic, mouth-filling and lush red shows medium to full-bodied, and boasts tannins that are soft but comfortably gripping. A generous array of plum, cherry and berry fruits, those backed up by juniper and white pepper. On the long finish hints of leather and citrus peel. Drink now–2012. Score 93.

HAR'EL, SYRAH, 2004: Dark garnet, this medium- to full-bodied blend of 85% Syrah and 15% Cabernet Sauvignon shows soft, round tannins and a fruit-forward style on which you will find a fine array of plum, blueberry and blackberry, those complemented by spices and appealing hints of fresh herbs and toffee. Drink now. Score 92.

HAR'EL, SYRAH, 2003: Deep ruby colored, this blend of 85% Syrah and 15% Cabernet Sauvignon shows generous peppery overtones. Medium- to full-bodied, with firm but nicely integrating tannins and complex plum, red berry and earthy aromas and flavors, all with a hint of leather on the finish. Drink now. Score 91.

Dalton★★★★

Founded by the Haruni family in 1993, this fully modern winery located in the industrial park of Dalton in the Upper Galilee has vineyards in Kerem Ben Zimra and several high altitude sites along the Lebanese border. Australian and Californian-trained winemaker Na'ama Mualem is currently producing wines in seven series, the age-worthy Single Vineyard, Reserve, Safsufa Vineyards and Dalton Estate wines, and the Alma, Dalton and Canaan series, those of similar varieties but which are intended for early drinking. With the 2006 vintage, a wine under the Matatia label was released, that perhaps destined to become the winery's flagship wine. Grapes include Cabernet Sauvignon, Merlot, Shiraz, Barbera, Zinfandel, Chardonnay, Sauvignon Blanc and Muscat. First production was 50,000 bottles, current production is about 880,000 and the target for 2010 is one million bottles. Dalton has earned a consistently good name for high quality wines, providing excellent value for money.

Matatia

MATATIA, 2006: A Bordeaux blend of 80% Cabernet Sauvignon, 15% Merlot and 5% Cabernet Franc. Developed in new French oak, showing deep and dark but not at all mysterious. On first attack aromas of mint, tar and a hint of iodine, those remarkably and perhaps surprisingly pleasing. Yields in the glass to reveal generous blackberry, blackcurrant and bitter orange peel notes, and finally, on the long finish, hints of espresso coffee. With fine balance between wood, acidity, tannins and fruits, a thought-provoking and delicious wine. Produced in a limited edition of 6,000 bottles. If I had to find a single word to describe the wine, that word would be "scrumptious." Drink now–2014. Score 93. **K**

Single Vineyard

SINGLE VINEYARD, CABERNET SAUVIGNON, MERON, 2004: Deep youthful cherry toward garnet, medium- to full-bodied, this well-balanced wine was aged in French oak for eight months and then bottled without filtration. Generous soft tannins and ample wood, those already integrating nicely to reveal a very appealing array of red currant, raspberry and citrus peel on a peppery, lightly herbal, minty background. Round, long and mouth-filling. Drink now. Score 92. **K**

SINGLE VINEYARD, MERLOT, MERON, 2005: Supple, rich and generous. Aged in oak for 16 months, with soft, near-sweet, mouth-coating tannins and fine balancing acidity to add liveliness to the blueberry and currant fruits. Hints of spices and mint run through to the long finish. Ripe, round and polished. Drink now–2011. Score 91. **K**

Reserve

RESERVE, CABERNET SAUVIGNON, 2007: Dark garnet toward youthful royal purple, showing still firm tannins and generous spicy wood, but with fine balance and structure that bode well for the future. Opens to reveal traditional Cabernet blackcurrants and blackberries, those supported nicely by notes of tobacco and chocolate. Long and mouth-filling. Best from 2011. Tentative Score 90–92. **K**

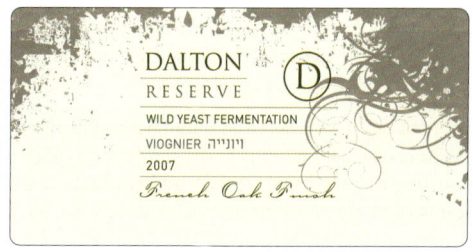

RESERVE, CABERNET SAUVIGNON, 2006: Super-dark in color, firmly tannic, showing good structure and fine balance between wood, tannins and fruit that bodes well for the future. A full-bodied, rich and concentrated wine, with dense blackberry and blackcurrant fruits, notes of freshly roasted coffee and gentle layers of currants, spices, green olives and cedarwood. Drink now–2013. Score 92. **K**

RESERVE, CABERNET SAUVIGNON, 2005: Dark garnet with orange and green reflections, medium- to full-bodied, with still-firm tannins integrating nicely and showing light spicy oak. Opens with currants and plums, goes on to wild berries and hints of black licorice and chocolate. Long, round and generous. Drink now–2011. Score 91. **K**

RESERVE, CABERNET SAUVIGNON, 2004: Medium- to full-bodied, with a layer of spicy and toasty wood to show for its 18 months in oak, this dark garnet-toward-royal purple wine shows moderately soft tannins and acidity coming together nicely. On the nose and palate blackberries, currants and an intimation of purple plums, those complemented by hints of spices and minty chocolate on the long finish. Drink now–2012. Score 91. **K**

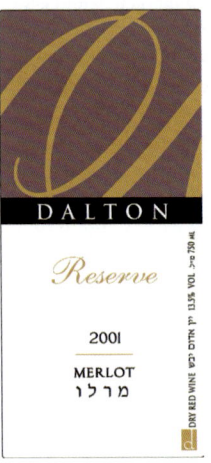

RESERVE, MERLOT, 2007: Developing in French *barriques*, half of which are new, showing soft tannins, a gentle influence of spicy cedar and generous wild berry, purple plum and cassis notes. Finishes with hints of tobacco and Mediterranean herbs. Drink from release–2013. Tentative Score 88–90. **K**

RESERVE, MERLOT, 2006: Oak-aged for 18 months, dark, youthful royal purple in color, full-bodied, with soft, gently mouth-coating tannins integrating nicely with light spices and vanilla from the oak in which it is aging. Opens to reveal ripe and generous red plum, raspberry and coffee aromas and flavors, those supported nicely by a tantalizing hint of cigar tobacco. Long, ripe and generous. Drink now–2013. Score 90. **K**

RESERVE, MERLOT, 2005: Soft and round but well focused, opening in the glass to reveal silky tannins and a gentle touch with the wood, those supporting currant, berry, cocoa and light hints of mint, all of which linger very nicely on the palate. Drink now. Score 89. **K**

RESERVE, MERLOT, 2004: Medium- to full-bodied, with tannins that have firmed up somewhat but still remain in fine balance with wood, acidity and fruits. On the nose and palate, generous red and black berries and ripe red plums on a light tobacco and herbal background. Look as well for an appealing hint of vanilla that creeps in on the finish. Drink now–2011. Score 90. **K**

RESERVE, SHIRAZ, 2008: Blended and fermented together with 6.5% Viognier, the blend developed in 60% of New French oak, showing forward blackberry, currant and purple plums, those matched by a generous note of black licorice. Long, concentrated and, given time, will show elegance. Best starting in 2011. Tentative Score 90–92. **K**

RESERVE, SHIRAZ, 2007: Dark garnet in color, opening with an appealing bitter-nutty nose, that going on to show spicy wood and gently mouth-coating tannins. On the palate a generous array of black and purple fruits, those complemented nicely by notes of freshly tanned leather and cigar tobacco. Drink now–2014. Score 91. **K**

RESERVE, SYRAH, 2005: Blended with 10% of Viognier, nearly black in color, but a wine of remarkable elegance. Aromatic, with spicy and floral scents on first attack, those yielding to aromas and flavors of berries and plums, all backed up by hints of white pepper, and on the long finish, surprising notes of peaches and apricots. Drink now–2011. Score 91. **K**

RESERVE, CABERNET SAUVIGNON-MERLOT, 10TH ANNIVERSARY EDITION, 2003: Dark cherry toward garnet, medium-bodied, this gently oaked wine shows an appealing array of aromas and flavors. On first attack blackberries and a hint of mint, those yielding to strawberries, cherries, licorice and earthy minerals. Nicely balanced and moderately long. Drink now. Score 89. **K**

RESERVE, CHARDONNAY, 2007: Developed in French *barriques* for four months, showing light gold in color, with a tantalizing note of toasty oak to highlight crisp citrus, apple and quince fruits, and blossoming on the finish to show hints of cantaloupe melon. A fine food wine, lingering nicely on the palate. Drink now. Score 88. **K**

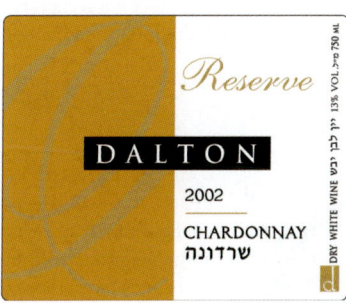

RESERVE, SAUVIGNON BLANC, 2008: An unoaked white, developed on its lees in stainless steel tanks. The color of damp straw, light- to medium-bodied, showing crisp and refreshing with its grapefruit, pineapple and gooseberry fruits complemented nicely by notes of stony minerals and freshly cut grass. Drink now. Score 88. **K**

RESERVE, SAUVIGNON BLANC, 2007: Unoaked, developed on its lees in stainless steel tanks, a crisp, lively and just-complex-enough wine. Lovely fruit here, with grapefruit running through but also showing citrus peel and a hint of grassiness on a light mineral background. Drink up. Score 89. **K**

RESERVE, VIOGNIER, 2008: Light gold in color, fermented with wild yeasts and highly aromatic. Rich ripe and generous, showing appealing honeyed nectarine and pineapple fruits all with a hint of pepper. Rich and harmonious. Drink now–2013. Score 91. **K**

RESERVE, VIOGNIER, 2007: Perhaps the Israeli Viognier most loyal to the grape to date. Fermented partly with wild yeasts, developing in *barriques* on its lees, showing intense, vibrant and complex with spice, floral, fig and melon aromas and flavors. Deep and rich with a long, broad finish. Drink now–2011. Score 91. **K**

RESERVE, VIOGNIER, 2006: Light gold in color, having spent only four months in oak to maintain fresh aromas and flavors, this medium-bodied white is showing aromatic on the nose, with an appealing array of white peaches, apricots and a distinct floral character, those backed up by hints of caramel and, on the long finish, a note of cinnamon. Drink up. Score 88. **K**

Dalton Estate

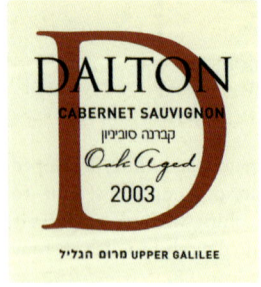

DALTON ESTATE, CABERNET SAUVIGNON, 2008: Deep garnet in color, opens with a fruit-rich nose, goes on to show generous wild berries, blackcurrants and spices, those on a medium- to full-bodied frame with gently gripping tannins and light cedar notes. Drink from release–2013. Tentative Score 88–90. **K**

DALTON ESTATE, CABERNET SAUVIGNON, 2007: Just complex enough to grab attention, showing ripe and distinctive for cherry, blackberry, blueberry and herbal aromas and flavors framed by gentle notes of sweet-and-spicy oak. Medium-bodied with soft tannins, and lingering nicely on the palate. Drink now–2011. Score 90. **K**

DALTON ESTATE, CABERNET SAUVIGNON, 2006: Dark ruby toward garnet, medium-bodied, with soft tannins integrated nicely with lightly spicy wood. Opens to reveal traditional Cabernet blackcurrants and blackberries along with generous hints of berries, mint and vanilla. Not overly complex but soft, round and generous. Drink now. Score 87. **K**

DALTON ESTATE, CABERNET SAUVIGNON, 2005: Developed for 12 months in French and American *barriques*. Dark garnet, medium-bodied, with somewhat chunky country-style tannins that yield in the glass to reveal plum, blackberry and currant fruits, those with a somewhat heavy mineral-earthy overlay. Drink up. Score 85. **K**

DALTON ESTATE, MERLOT, 2008: Still in its infancy but already showing dark garnet and deeply aromatic. Medium- to full-bodied, with gentle wood influences to highlight blackberries, black cherries and chocolate-coated citrus peel. Long and mouth-filling. Drink from release–2013. Tentative Score 89–91. **K**

DALTON ESTATE, MERLOT, 2007: Lightly gripping tannins on a medium- to full-bodied frame, showing fine balance and reflecting its ten months in oak with generous but gentle sweet cedar. Opens to show generous wild berry, cassis and spices, all lingering nicely. Drink now–2011. Score 88. **K**

DALTON ESTATE, MERLOT, 2006: Garnet toward royal purple, medium-bodied and generously aromatic, showing soft, well-integrated tannins and lightly spicy oak. On the nose and palate wild berries, currants and a hint of white chocolate on the long, round finish. Drink now. Score 88. **K**

DALTON ESTATE, MERLOT, 2005: Dark royal purple, medium-bodied, with firm tannins matched nicely by vanilla and cloves from the French oak *barriques* in which it developed. A vibrant and lively young red with currant, raspberry and plum aromas and flavors matched nicely by a hint of exotic spices that runs throughout. Drink now. Score 88. **K**

DALTON ESTATE, SHIRAZ, 2008: Dark garnet with purple reflections, full-bodied, with softly caressing tannins and gentle notes of spicy wood. Opens to show spicy black fruits complemented by hints of saddle leather and black tea. Drink from release–2012, perhaps longer. Tentative Score 89–91. **K**

DALTON ESTATE, SHIRAZ, 2007: Made entirely from Shiraz grapes, a distinctly New World wine, fruit forward, medium- to full-bodied, with generous but not-at-all overpowering oak and soft, near-sweet tannins in fine balance with fruits. At first sip a virtual attack of berry and plum fruits, those yielding on the palate to blackberries and peaches (yes, peaches!) and an array of spices. Long and generous. Drink now–2012. Score 90. **K**

DALTON ESTATE, SHIRAZ, 2006: Dark, almost impenetrable garnet, medium- to full-bodied, and with soft and gently mouth-coating tannins in good balance with fresh acidity and fruits. On the nose and palate blackberries, purple plums, licorice, black pepper and hints of saddle leather and vanilla that come in on the generous finish Drink now. Score 87. **K**

DALTON ESTATE, SHIRAZ, 2005: Dark, almost inky garnet, medium-bodied, with soft mouth-coating tannins balanced nicely by hints of vanilla and spices from the American oak in which it aged for ten months. On the nose and palate, appealing cherry, plum and berry fruits, those matched nicely by undertones of earthiness, cardamom and white pepper. Ripe, round and generous. Drink now. Score 88. **K**

DALTON ESTATE, BARBERA, 2008: Deep royal purple, shows somewhat generous acidity on first attack, but that resides (and will do so further with time) and opens to reveal a gentle hint of spicy oak to highlight red currant and cherry fruits. Finishes on an appealing red licorice note. Drink from release. Tentative Score 86–88. **K**

DALTON ESTATE, BARBERA, 2007: Dark ruby toward garnet, medium-bodied, with soft tannins and a bright and lively set of cherry, berry and citrus peel aromas and a background of light spicy oak. Aged in used French oak for ten months, showing generous fresh fruit on a medium finish. Drink now. Score 87. **K**

DALTON ESTATE, BARBERA, 2006: Oak-aged for ten months, dark ruby toward garnet in color, medium-bodied, soft and round, showing a light hand with the oak and generous raspberry, plum and currant fruits on a gently spicy finish. Drink now. Score 88. **K**

DALTON ESTATE, BARBERA, 2005: Lightly oak-aged, royal purple in color, with generous acidity, soft tannins and moderate wood influences, those well in balance with fruits. Opens with wild berries and spring flowers, those going to cassis, blackberries and a nice hint of licorice. Round, soft and satisfying. Drink up. Score 88. **K**

DALTON ESTATE, FUMÉ BLANC, 2008: With the addition of 9% Viognier to add body, medium-bodied and reflecting its four months in oak with light hints of spices and a tantalizing smoky note. On the nose and palate citrus fruits, nectarines and what at one moment seems like papaya and another like mango. Round and generous. Drink now. Score 88. **K**

DALTON ESTATE, FUMÉ BLANC, 2007: With a light note of oak, refreshing acidity and an appealing floral note on both nose and palate. On first attack grapefruit, peach and nectarine fruits, those turning toward papaya and mango. Crisp and refreshing with a rich, smooth texture. Drink up. Score 88. **K**

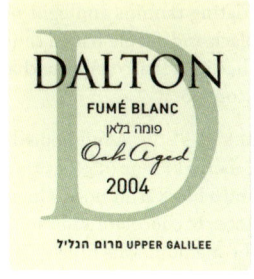

Safsufa Vineyards

SAFSUFA VINEYARDS, CABERNET SAUVIGNON, 2006: Dark garnet with purple reflections, medium- to full-bodied, reflecting its 12 months in used French oak *barriques* with gentle notes of spices. On the nose and palate, traditional Cabernet blackcurrant and blackberry fruits, those on a light background of near-sweet cedar and minted chocolate. Drink now–2011. Score 88. **K**

SAFSUFA VINEYARDS, CABERNET SAUVIGNON, 2005: Oak-aged for 12 months, medium- to full-bodied, and with soft, yielding tannins. Showing currant and berry fruits, those on a background of vanilla and stewed plums. Lacking balance and with a lightly cooked hint creeping in. Drink up. Score 85. **K**

SAFSUFA VINEYARDS, MERLOT, 2006: Deep royal purple, medium- to full-bodied, showing appealing hints of vanilla and spices from its 12 months in used French oak. Soft tannins highlight aromas and flavors of red berries, cherries and cassis, all coming to a near jammy fruit finish. Drink now–2011. Score 87. **K**

SAFSUFA VINEYARDS, SHIRAZ, 2005: Inky-garnet in color, full-bodied and with firm tannins integrating nicely. Aged in oak for 12 months and showing dark berry fruits, leather and citrus peel on the palate, but faulted by a far-too-distinct hint of stewed fruit compote that comes in on the finish. Drink now. Score 85. **K**

SAFSUFA VINEYARDS, SAUVIGNON BLANC-CHARDONNAY, 2007: A lively, unoaked blend, not complex but showing appealing grapefruit, citrus peel and pineapple notes. An enjoyable summertime quaffer. Drink up. Score 85. **K**

Alma

ALMA, 2007: Almost impenetrably dark garnet in color, a full-bodied blend of 65% Cabernet Sauvignon, 22% Merlot and 13% Cabernet Franc. Developed in French *barriques* for 14 months, showing gently mouth-coating tannins and light notes of sweet cedarwood, opens with ripe black and purple fruits, those on a background of chocolate and sweet chewing tobacco. Approachable and enjoyable now, but best 2011–2014. Score 90. **K**

ALMA, 2006: A full-bodied blend of Cabernet Sauvignon, Merlot and Cabernet Franc (56%, 25% and 19% respectively), showing soft tannins and a black fruit nose. Opens to reveal wild berries, purple plums and notes of chocolate and vanilla along with a hint of jammy sweetness on the medium-long finish. Drink now–2012. Score 89. **K**

ALMA, 2005: Garnet toward purple, medium- to full-bodied, this blend of 65% Cabernet Sauvignon and 35% Merlot spent 16 months in French oak. Firm tannins integrating nicely with spicy oak. On the nose and palate blackberries, purple plums and a teasing hint of bitter oranges, the fruits backed up nicely by Oriental spices. Still-firm tannins, spicy oak and acidity in fine balance. Drink now. Score 89. **K**

Dalton

DALTON, ZINFANDEL, 2008: Dark garnet toward royal purple, blended with 12% of Petite Sirah, oak-aged in 70% new French oak for 16 months, showing fine balance between wood, soft tannins and fruits. On the nose and palate ripe wild berry, blackberry and boysenberry fruits. Elegant and polished, generously mouth-filling without ever feeling heavy. Drink from release–2013. Tentative Score 90–92. **K**

DALTON, ZINFANDEL, 2007: Deep, almost impenetrable garnet in color, developed in new American oak and blended with about 7% Merlot. Generously aromatic, with gently gripping tannins and not at all imposing oak notes, those in fine balance with black and red fruit, including red currants, blackberries, blueberries and huckleberries, all on a generously spicy background. Although the wine boasts a 15.5% alcohol content it manages to keep nicely in balance and shows elegance. Drink now–2012. Score 90. **K**

DALTON, ZINFANDEL, 2006: As has become traditional at the winery, a single vineyard wine. Blended with about 7% of Merlot but fully faithful to the variety, with full body, wild berries, plums, vanilla and notes of white chocolate and cinnamon, all with a bare and tantalizing hint of sweetness. Aged in new American *barriques* for 12 months, showing fine balance between sweet and spicy oak, notes of black pepper, soft tannins and fruits. 15% alcohol here but not a hot spot to be found. Drink now–2011. Score 90. **K**

DALTON, ZINFANDEL, 2005: This dark royal purple wine spent 12 months in new American oak. Full-bodied, with generous near-sweet tannins and smoky and vanilla oak, it opens on the palate to reveal black cherry, raspberry and plum fruits, those backed up by hints of chocolate, vanilla and espresso coffee. A generous and mouth-filling finish. Drink now. Score 89. **K**

DALTON, ROSÉ, 2008: As has become traditional at Dalton, made entirely from Cabernet Sauvignon grapes with a very short skin contact. Peach-blossom pink, with wild berry and cassis fruits matched by an appealing hint of grapefruit peel. Off-dry and lively, fine on its own or a good match to fish, seafood and chicken salads. Drink now. Score 87. **K**

DALTON, ROSÉ, 2007: Made entirely from Cabernet Sauvignon grapes, rose-petal pink toward orange, with red berry, dried cherry and a hint of what might be citrus that comes in. Barely off-dry with plenty of acidity to keep it lively and with a pleasing light *frizzante* note, a refreshing wine. Drink up. Score 86. **K**

DALTON, LIQUEUR MUSCAT, N.V.: Deep gold toward bronze in color, a late harvest wine fermented for a short time, the fermentation stopped by the addition of neutral spirits and then developed in old barrels. At this stage showing generous sweetness, that balanced by natural acidity, and on the nose and palate, honeyed summer fruits, citrus and even notes of guava. A contemplation wine to sip quite slowly, not with dessert but in the late hours of the evening. Eventually to become part of a solera system. Drink from release. Score 91. **K**

DALTON, MOSCATO, 2008: A very pleasant little lightly *frizzante* wine, showing moderate sweetness, fine acidity and an appealing array of floral, citrus and citrus peel notes. Drink well chilled. Drink up. Score 86. **K**

Canaan

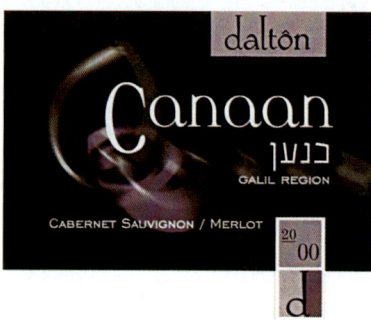

CANAAN, CABERNET SAUVIGNON, 2008: Dark royal purple in color, medium-bodied, with gently caressing tannins and a bare hint of spicy wood, showing cassis, raspberries and red plums, those opening to show notes of green olives and mint. An appealing Mediterranean wine. Drink now–2011. Score 85. **K**

CANAAN, MERLOT, 2008: Deep ruby toward garnet, medium-bodied, reflecting its four months in used oak with light notes of spicy wood, soft tannins and generous plums and blackberries, all on an appealingly spicy background. Drink now–2011. Score 86. **K**

CANAAN, RED, 2008: Dark royal purple, medium-bodied, softly tannic, a blend of 64% Cabernet Sauvignon and 24% Merlot, the rest of Petite Sirah and Shiraz. Light tannins and good acidity in fine balance with spicy purple plum and blackberry fruits. Drink now. Score 85. **K**

CANAAN, RED, 2007: Dark ruby toward garnet, medium-bodied, with soft tannins and generous berry, black cherry and red currant fruits on a lightly spicy background. A good quaffer. Drink now. Score 85. **K**

CANAAN, RED, 2006: This blend of Cabernet Sauvignon, Shiraz and Merlot (70%, 10% and 20% respectively) is soft and round, medium-bodied, with gentle tannins and forward berry, plum and raspberry fruits matched by a spicy note that runs throughout. Not complex but quite pleasant. Drink up. Score 85. K

CANAAN, WHITE, 2008: A floral blend of Sauvignon Blanc and Chardonnay with a bit of Muscat tossed in. Off-dry, with its sweetness set off by natural acidity and showing pleasant citrus and mango flavors and aromas. Drink now. Score 84. K

CANAAN, WHITE, 2007: A blend of Sauvignon Blanc, Chardonnay and White Riesling. Lively and fresh with citrus and green apple fruits. A good entry-level wine. Drink up. Score 84. K

Ein Nashut *

Situated on Kibbutz Kidmat Tzvi on the Golan Heights, this small winery released its first wines from the 2007 vintage. The winery relies on Cabernet Sauvignon, Merlot and Shiraz grapes from its own vineyards.

EIN NASHUT, CABERNET SAUVIGNON, 2007: A blend of Cabernet Sauvignon, Merlot and Shiraz (85%, 10% and 5% respectively), cold fermented and then exposed to oak chips for 14 months. Medium-bodied, showing raspberry, cherry and wild strawberry fruits. Somewhat chunky tannins and a hint of raisined fruits make this a simple but pleasant enough little country-style wine. Drink now. Score 84.

EIN NASHUT, FRENCH SHIRAZ, 2007: Precisely how the winery chose to name this particular wine is not known. A medium- to full-bodied blend of 85% Shiraz with 15% of Cabernet Sauvignon, oak-aged for 14 months, showing red plums and white pepper but those struggling to make themselves felt through a simultaneously too astringent and too bitter background. Drink up. Score 79.

Ein Teina ✴✴

Founded by Yotam Ben-Tzvi on Moshav Givat Yoav on the southern Golan Heights, this small winery released its first wines in 2004. First year's releases were of 900 bottles, and in 2006 production was about 2,500 bottles. The winery relies on Cabernet Sauvignon, Merlot and Syrah grapes from the southern Golan.

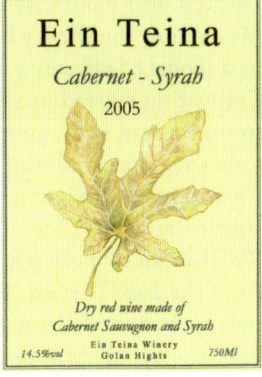

EIN TEINA, CABERNET SAUVIGNON, 2007: Developed in French oak for 12 months, dark garnet in color, showing black fruits and wild berries on a background of tobacco and fresh herbs. Medium- to full-bodied, with good balance and structure, with a sweet nose and a surprising but quite pleasant note of cloves coming in on the long finish. Drink now. Score 88.

EIN TEINA, CABERNET SAUVIGNON-SYRAH, 2006: Medium-bodied, with soft tannins and a generous hint of smoky wood, opens to show generous aromas and flavors of currants, blackberries and blueberries, those on a background of Oriental spices. Drink now. Score 86.

EIN TEINA, TALIA'S BLEND 2006: A blend of Cabernet Sauvignon, Merlot and Syrah. A simple country-style wine with chunky, almost coarse tannins and a bit of bottle stink that never quite blows off, that hiding the fruits that try to make themselves felt. Drink up. Score 79.

EIN TEINA, TALIA'S BLEND, 2005: A ruby-toward-garnet blend of Cabernet Sauvignon, Merlot and Syrah. Medium- to full-bodied, with soft tannins integrating with spicy wood. Bold aromas and flavors of blackberries and currants, those on a background of mocha and orange peel, with gentle peppery notes that run through to a long ripe finish. Drink now–2009. Score 89.

EIN TEINA, CABERNET SAUVIGNON-SYRAH, 2005: Medium-bodied, with soft, near-sweet tannins and hints of spicy wood. On first attack raspberry and currant fruits on a lightly earthy background, those yielding to hints of figs and cigar tobacco. Drink now–2009. Score 88.

Ella Valley Vineyards ✦✦✦✦

Located on Kibbutz Netiv Halamed Hey in the Jerusalem Mountains, the winery has vineyards that might well serve as a model of efficiency and beauty anywhere in the world. Cultivation started in 1997 in the Ella and Adulam Valleys in the Judean Hills, and now includes Cabernet Sauvignon, Cabernet Franc, Merlot, Shiraz, Pinot Noir, Petite Sirah, Chardonnay, Sauvignon Blanc, Semillon and Muscat grapes. Under the supervision of French-trained winemaker Doron Rav Hon, the winery released its first wines, 90,000 bottles, from the 2002 harvest. Production in 2007 was of 200,000 bottles, but 2008, because it was a *shmita* year (a sabbatical year in which the vineyards lie fallow for many kosher wineries), yielded only 150,000 bottles.

Wines are released in three series: Vineyard's Choice, Ella Valley Vineyards and Ever Red, the first two destined for moderately long cellaring and the third for early drinking.

Vineyard's Choice

VINEYARD'S CHOICE, CABERNET SAUVIGNON, 2005: Full-bodied, with moderately firm tannins, a gentle wood influence, and fine balance. Blended with 10% of Merlot, this soft, round wine opens with near-sweet berries and spices, those yielding to reveal lush currant and blackberry aromas and flavors. Drink now–2013. Score 91. K

VINEYARD'S CHOICE, CABERNET SAUVIGNON, RR, 2004: Deep garnet toward royal purple in color, aged in French oak for 17 months, showing fine balance between spicy wood, soft tannins that are integrating nicely, and fruits. On the nose and palate blackcurrants, purple plums and blackberries, those supported by gentle notes of white pepper and Mediterranean herbs. Drink now–2014. Score 91. K

VINEYARD'S CHOICE, CABERNET SAUVIGNON, 2003: Blended with 3% of Cabernet Franc and aged in oak for 17 months, this is a deep and brooding wine. Dark royal purple, full-bodied, with ripe, rich fruits showing harmony and finesse. Layers of currants, juicy cherries and tempting oak shadings. Drink now–2011. Score 91. **K**

VINEYARD'S CHOICE, MERLOT, 2005: Deep and dark, with blockbuster tannins that promise to soften with time to show the wine's complexity and balance. A tempting array of black cherry, blackberry and currant flavors all coming together in a long finish. Drink now–2012. Score 91. **K**

VINEYARD'S CHOICE, MERLOT, 2004: Dark garnet, with firm tannins integrating nicely now and showing sweet-and-spicy cedar notes, and opening to reveal red and black berries, currants and light tobacco and herbal notes that come in on the long finish. Drink now–2011. Score 90. **K**

VINEYARD'S CHOICE, MERLOT, 2003: Its youthful royal purple color and generous black cherry, berry and spices show this to be an exuberant wine, but as those come together in the glass showing full body and firm structure, one begins to feel the elegance. Softening nicely now and showing long and round with an appealing spicy oak note that rises on the finish. Drink now. Score 90. **K**

VINEYARD'S CHOICE, SYRAH, 2007: Notably dark garnet in color, full-bodied, with fine balance between still gripping tannins and wood, and just waiting patiently for all of its elements to come together. On first attack currants, wild berries and an appealing loamy note, those opening to reveal hints of bay leaves, juniper berries and mint, all leading to a long and intense finish. Drink now–2016, perhaps longer. Score 92. **K**

VINEYARD'S CHOICE, CABERNET SAUVIGNON-MERLOT, 2005: Dark garnet toward purple, deeply aromatic, a full-bodied blend of 60% Cabernet Sauvignon and 40% Merlot. Muscular and tannic at this time but with balance and structure that bode well for the future. Currant, cherry and berry fruits with generous hints of toasty oak on an appealing base of exotic spices. Overtones of cedar come in on the long finish. Drink now–2012. Score 90. **K**

VINEYARD'S CHOICE, MERLOT-CABERNET SAUVIGNON, 2004: A blend of 60% Merlot and 40% Cabernet Sauvignon, oak-aged for 16 months. Showing generous oak, firm but well-integrating tannins, plums and black cherries on a spicy and harmonious background and with hints of vanilla that rise on the moderately long finish. Drink now. Score 88. **K**

VINEYARD'S CHOICE, MERLOT-CABERNET FRANC, 2006: A full-bodied blend of 80% Merlot and 20% Cabernet Franc, dark ruby toward garnet in color, and reflecting its time in oak with Oriental spices and firm tannins. Opens nicely in the glass to reveal blackberry, raspberry and dried currant fruits. Generously spicy, with a tantalizing hint of red chili rising on the super-long finish. Drink now–2013. Score 92. **K**

VINEYARD'S CHOICE, CHARDONNAY, 2005: Reflecting its 11 months in oak with gentle vanilla, buttery and spice notes, this sparkling clear golden straw-colored wine shows a complex and concentrated array of green pineapple, citrus and ripe pear fruits all leading to a long and generous finish. Showing first signs of age. Drink up. Score 88. **K**

Ella Valley Vineyards

ELLA VALLEY VINEYARDS, CABERNET SAUVIGNON, 2008: Medium- to full-bodied, with soft tannins integrating nicely. Opens with a bare and tantalizing hint of freshly cut Mediterranean herbs, and then goes on to generous cherry and currant fruits. Supple and generous. Drink from release–2013. Tentative Score 90–92. **K**

ELLA VALLEY VINEYARDS, CABERNET SAUVIGNON, 2007: Rich and ripe, full-bodied with near-sweet tannins and a judicious hand with spicy oak. Blended with 10% Merlot and 5% Petite Sirah, opens with a nose of freshly turned damp earth and plums, those yielding in the glass to aromas and flavors of ripe currants, blueberries, dark cherries and roasted Mediterranean herbs. Long and generous. Drink now–2015. Score 91. **K**

ELLA VALLEY VINEYARDS, CABERNET SAUVIGNON, 2006: Medium- to full-bodied, with soft, gently mouth-coating tannins and gently spicy wood reflecting its 14 months in oak. A blend of 86% Cabernet Sauvignon and 14% Merlot showing currants, berries and hints of pepper, all leading to an aromatic and fruity finish. Drink now–2012. Score 90. **K**

ELLA VALLEY VINEYARDS, CABERNET SAUVIGNON, 2005: Dark royal purple, medium- to full-bodied, with tannins and wood in fine balance with fruits. On first attack blackcurrants, blackberries and a light earthy overlay, those opening to reveal spicy oak and hints of dark cocoa. Long, generous and elegant. Drink now–2011. Score 89. **K**

ELLA VALLEY VINEYARDS, CABERNET SAUVIGNON, 2004: Full-bodied, ripe and complex, with soft tannins integrating nicely and showing currant and red plums along with intimations of anise, black pepper and spicy oak. On the finish hints of earthiness and freshly tanned leather. Round and long. Well crafted. Drink now–2011. Score 91. K

ELLA VALLEY VINEYARDS, CABERNET SAUVIGNON, 60TH ANNIVERSARY EDITION, 2004: Vinified separately from the regular release, but a near-twin to that wine (see above). Full-bodied, dark garnet, with soft tannins integrating nicely with spicy wood and fruits. On the nose and palate blackcurrants, plums and blackberries, those supported nicely by notes of Oriental spices and black pepper along with a hint of earthy minerality that comes in on the long finish. Drink now–2011. Score 91. K

ELLA VALLEY VINEYARDS, MERLOT, 2008: Deep garnet in color, full-bodied with still gripping tannins but already showing fine balance and structure that bode well for the future. Rich and round, a fruity red with an abundance of blackberry, raspberry and currant notes, those showing an appealing floral note. From mid-palate on to the long finish, hints of citrus peel and milk chocolate. Drink from release–2014. Tentative Score 90–92. K

ELLA VALLEY VINEYARDS, MERLOT, 2007: Blended with 15% Cabernet Sauvignon, opens with a hint of dusty wood and near-sweet tannins. A full-bodied and firm Merlot showing round and well balanced, the tannins complemented nicely by light spicy oak. On the nose and palate generous blackberry, currant, wild berry and exotic spices highlighted nicely by notes of minerals and light toasty oak. Drink from release–2013. Score 90. K

ELLA VALLEY VINEYARDS, MERLOT, 2006: Full-bodied, a solid, almost muscular wine, but with gently gripping tannins in fine balance with spicy wood. Dark ruby toward garnet, showing a tempting array of raspberries, cherries and spices on a tempting earthy-mineral overlay. Long and generous. Drink now–2011. Score 90. K

ELLA VALLEY VINEYARDS, MERLOT, 2005: Dark and brooding, with still gripping tannins, this dense wine offers up generous currant and black cherry aromas and flavors. Showing muscular elegance. Drink now–2012. Score 92. K

ELLA VALLEY VINEYARDS, MERLOT, 2004: Blended with 5% of Cabernet Sauvignon, deep royal purple toward garnet in color, a firm but round and well-balanced wine showing black cherry, blackcurrant and spicy cedarwood, all coming to a long finish on which the fruits rise nicely. Drink now–2011. Score 90. **K**

ELLA VALLEY VINEYARDS, SYRAH, 2008: Tasted from several components, those from the Nes Harim and Netiv Halamed Hey vineyards. Dense and muscular, with firm tannins enclosing a rich core of wild berries, blackberries and sweet cedarwood notes. Opens in the glass to reveal an appealing black cherry note that lingers nicely. Drink from release–2015. Tentative Score 91–93. **K**

ELLA VALLEY VINEYARDS, SYRAH, 2006: Blended with 3% each of Merlot and Cabernet Sauvignon, dark, almost inky-garnet in color, medium- to full-bodied, deeply aromatic and showing a generous array of blackberry, black cherry and currant notes. Long and mouth-filling. Drink now–2012. Score 92. **K**

ELLA VALLEY VINEYARDS, SHIRAZ, 2004: Full-bodied, dark, rich and complex with an array of spicy, smoky and meaty plum, berry, currant and anise notes set off nicely by near-sweet tannins. Well balanced and flavorful. Drink now. Score 89. **K**

ELLA VALLEY VINEYARDS, PINOT NOIR, 2008: Dark cherry red, medium- to full-bodied with fine tannins and spices. A well-focused wine, elegant and stylish showing wild berry, black cherry and cassis fruits, with a tantalizing bitter-herbal finish that rises on the long, generously fruity finish. Drink from release–2014. Tentative Score 90–92. **K**

ELLA VALLEY VINEYARDS, PINOT NOIR, 2005: Ruby toward garnet in color, medium-bodied, with soft, caressing tannins and generous cherry, cassis, strawberry and cranberry aromas and flavors, those backed up nicely by minerals, hints of white pepper and vibrant acidity. Drink now–2012. Score 92. **K**

ELLA VALLEY VINEYARDS, CABERNET FRANC, 2008: Tasted from components, showing medium- to full-bodied, with soft tannins and gentle wood offset comfortably by fresh acidity. Opens to reveal red cherry, blackberry, tobacco and mineral notes, the fruits and a light nutty flavor rising on the long finish. Drink from release–2013, perhaps longer. Tentative Score 90–92. **K**

ELLA VALLEY VINEYARDS, CABERNET FRANC, 2007: Blended with 5% each of Cabernet Sauvignon and Merlot, dark royal purple, medium- to full-bodied with softly caressing tannins. Opens with a distinct veggie Cabernet Franc note, that yielding comfortably to cherry, blackberry, licorice and citrus peel on the long and generous finish. Drink now–2013. Score 90. K

ELLA VALLEY VINEYARDS, CABERNET FRANC, 2006: Blended with 3% each of Merlot and Cabernet Sauvignon, dark garnet in color, medium- to full-bodied, deeply aromatic and showing a generous array of blackberry, black cherry and currant notes. Long, round, rich and mouth-filling. Drink now–2012. Score 92. K

ELLA VALLEY VINEYARDS, CABERNET FRANC, 2005: Blended with 12% of Merlot, oak-aged for 15 months, this dark garnet, medium- to full-bodied wine shows appealing vegetal aromas on first attack, those parting to reveal gently spicy cedarwood, raspberries, blackberries, red currants and generous hints of herbaceousness and white chocolate that come in on the long, well-balanced finish. Drink now–2011. Score 91. K

ELLA VALLEY VINEYARDS, CABERNET FRANC, 2004: Intensely dark royal purple, opens with a somewhat funky and loamy nose, but that passes quickly and reveals a medium- to full-bodied wine, showing appealing red fruits, those supported nicely by notes of vanilla and cinnamon. From mid-palate on, notes of cigar box and traditional Cabernet Franc veggie notes. Long and generous. Drink now–2011. Score 91. K

ELLA VALLEY VINEYARDS, CABERNET FRANC, 2003: Blended with 15% of Cabernet Sauvignon, this almost impenetrably dark garnet, oak-aged, full-bodied red shows firm tannins and generous wood influence, those balanced nicely by a generous array of black fruits, coffee, white chocolate and tobacco, all leading to a long leathery finish. Drink now. Score 91. K

ELLA VALLEY VINEYARDS, PETITE SIRAH, 2007: The winery's first release of a Petite Sirah varietal wine. Made from grapes from ten–year-old vines, intensely dark royal purple in color, showing generous tannins and fine fruit concentration. On the nose and palate blackberries, raspberries and loganberry fruits, those matched nicely by notes of mint and tobacco. Firm and chewy with a long, near muscular finish. Drink now–2012. Score 90. K

ELLA VALLEY VINEYARDS, CABERNET SAUVIGNON-SYRAH, 2005: Dark purple toward brick red, full-bodied, with soft tannins, this blend of 65% Cabernet Sauvignon and 35% Syrah is young, generous and remarkably lively, with cherry, raspberry and plum aromas and flavors, those with overlays of cedarwood, freshly turned earth and spices. Drink now. Score 89. K

ELLA VALLEY VINEYARDS, CABERNET SAUVIGNON-SYRAH, 2004: Deep garnet toward purple, this full-bodied blend of 70% Cabernet

Sauvignon and 30% Shiraz reflects its 13 months in oak with spices and vanilla. With tannins settling in nicely now, showing generous blackberry and black cherry fruits, those supported by hints of spicy cedar and herbs and, creeping in comfortably on the long finish, a hint of grilled meat. Drink now. Score 89. **K**

ELLA VALLEY VINEYARDS, MERLOT-PETITE SYRAH, 2006: Deep purple, medium- to full-bodied, with somewhat chunky tannins that give the wine a few sharp edges but showing generous plum and black-currant fruits. An appealing country-style quaffer. Drink now–2011. Score 87. **K**

ELLA VALLEY VINEYARDS, CHARDONNAY, 2008: The color of golden straw after a light rain, showing medium-bodied, vibrant and full of life, with light smoky oak notes of ripe pears and lime that linger nicely on an expressive finish. Drink now–2011. Score 89. **K**

ELLA VALLEY VINEYARDS, UNOAKED CHARDONNAY, 2008: Light and glistening golden straw in color, developed on its fine lees in stainless steel tanks and with no racking, a medium-bodied white. Generous lemon curd, lime and green apple notes. Crisp and tangy enough to make you smile with pleasure. Drink now. Score 87. **K**

ELLA VALLEY VINEYARDS, CHARDONNAY, 2007: Developed partly in *barriques*, partly in stainless steel for 11 months, a medium-bodied, crisply freshly and aromatic wine. Freshly dampened golden straw in color, showing a gentle hand with the wood, with the nose and palate opening with hints of honey, flaky pastry and minerals, and goes on to show yellow plum and citrus blossoms. Well structured, long and elegant. As the wine develops in bottles look for a gentle honeyed and creamy hint that will creep in. Drink now–2011. Score 90. **K**

ELLA VALLEY VINEYARDS, UNOAKED CHARDONNAY, 2007: Light gold in color, medium-bodied, with crisp acidity to support appealing tropical and citrus fruits, those on a background of light, near-flinty minerals and finishing with a hint of white pepper. Calls to mind Petit Chablis. Drink up. Score 88. **K**

ELLA VALLEY VINEYARDS, SAUVIGNON BLANC, 2008: Blended with a small quantity of Semillon, the wine oak-aged in small part, showing light gold in color with lively and crisp acidity. Opens with notes of kiwis, guava and grapefruit, those supported nicely by light hints of freshly cut grass, all with just enough complexity to grab our attention. Drink now. Score 88. **K**

ELLA VALLEY VINEYARDS, SAUVIGNON BLANC, 2007: Light straw in color, a bright and lively wine with pear, passion fruit and grapefruit showing nicely on the nose and palate and with some appealing floral, anise and sage notes in the background. Fresh and appealing. Drink up. Score 89. **K**

ELLA VALLEY VINEYARDS, MUSCAT DESSERT WINE, 2006: Full-bodied with lots of glycerin, avoiding the sometimes too-too flowery nature of the Muscat grape, and with fine balancing acidity to set off the generous sweetness. Dark gold in color, sitting almost thickly but comfortably on the palate and showing both fresh and dried honeyed apricots, those yielding to pear and raisin compote. Generous and long. Perhaps best not with dessert but as dessert. Drink now. Score 90. **K**

ELLA VALLEY VINEYARDS, MUSCAT DESSERT, 2003: Medium-bodied, unabashedly sweet but with fine balance between sugar, acidity and alcohol. On the nose and palate aromas and flavors of honeyed summer fruits, stewed pears, sesame seeds and spring flowers. Generous, mouth-filling and long. Drink now. Score 90. **K**

Ever Red

EVER RED, 2007: A medium-bodied blend, gently tannic red, this year of 60% Merlot and 40% Cabernet Sauvignon. Developed for 14 months in *barriques*, shows appealing berry, currant and black cherry fruits, those on a background of light and just-spicy-enough oak. Not complex but comfortable drinking. Drink now. Score 87. **K**

EVER RED, 2006: A medium-bodied blend of Cabernet Sauvignon, Merlot and Petite Sirah (45%, 45% and 10% respectively) that was developed for 14 months in *barriques*. Soft near-sweet tannins integrating nicely with red berries, red currants and light oak, all showing a gentle spicy note. Drink now. Score 88. **K**

Erez **

Founded in 2003 by Erez Sadon, this boutique winery is located in Rehelim in the Shomron and has vineyards on Mount Bracha at an elevation of 840 meters. The winery is currently producing about 8,000 bottles annually, those primarily from Cabernet Sauvignon, Merlot and Chardonnay grapes.

EREZ, CABERNET SAUVIGNON, 2005: Dark royal purple, medium- to full-bodied, with somewhat chunky, country-style tannins and generous wood parting to show currant, blackberry and chocolate notes. Drink now. Score 85.

EREZ, CABERNET SAUVIGNON, 2004: Reflecting generous spicy wood from its 20 months in oak, medium- to full-bodied, with firm tannins integrating nicely now. Opens to reveal traditional currant, berry and spices. Drink up. Score 85.

EREZ, MERLOT, 2005: Dark garnet, medium- to full-bodied, with somewhat coarse tannins and generous wood that seem not to want to integrate, and thus tend to hide the black fruits that struggle to make themselves felt. Drink now. Score 80.

EREZ, MERLOT-CABERNET SAUVIGNON, 2003: A blend of 65% Merlot and 35% Cabernet Sauvignon, oak-aged for 18 months and showing generous spicy wood that tends to dominate the black fruits that fail to make themselves fully felt. Drink up. Score 82.

Essence **

Located in the community of Ma'aleh Tsvia in the Western Galilee, the winery was founded by Yaniv Kimchi, Eitan Rosenberg and Itzhak Avramov, and released its first wines in 2001. Grapes, including Cabernet Sauvignon and Merlot, are raised in the winery's organic vineyards at the foothills of Mount Kamon, and the wines are made in accordance with international organic standards. The winery's

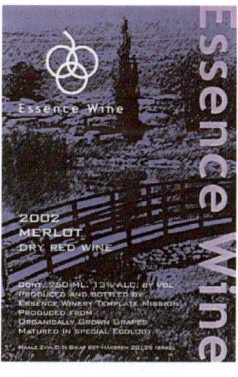

output is currently about 10,000 bottles annually.

ESSENCE, CABERNET SAUVIGNON, 2006: Garnet toward royal purple, medium-bodied, with firm but nicely integrating tannins and revealing currant, wild berry and blackberry fruits. Drink now. Score 84.

ESSENCE, CABERNET SAUVIGNON, RESERVE, 2005: Dark ruby toward garnet, medium- to full-bodied, with chunky country-style tannins and generous spicy wood. Opens to reveal berry, black cherry and cassis fruits. Drink now. Score 85.

ESSENCE, CABERNET SAUVIGNON, 2004: Garnet-red, medium-bodied, with firm tannins integrating nicely. On the nose and palate berry and currant fruits with hints of toasted oak. Drink up. Score 85.

ESSENCE, MERLOT, 2006: Showing generous spicy and smoky wood, with chunky, country-style tannins, those settling down slowly to reveal blackberry, raspberry and citrus peel. Drink now. Score 83.

ESSENCE, MERLOT, 2005: Oak-aged for 14 months, with now-soft tannins and once-generous wood now integrating, this medium-bodied red opens in the glass to show berry and cherry fruits. A pleasant quaffer. Drink now. Score 84.

ESSENCE, ELECTRUM, 2005: Aged in *barriques* for 24 months, this medium-bodied blend of equal parts of Cabernet Sauvignon and Merlot shows drying tannins and a distinctly bitter note that overlays black cherry and currant notes. Drink now. Score 84.

Flam ✶✶✶✶✶

Located in a state-of-the-art facility not far from the town of Beit Shemesh at the foothills of the Jerusalem Mountains, the Flam winery has produced consistently excellent and exciting wines since its first releases from the 1998 vintage. Established by brothers Golan and Gilad Flam; Golan, having trained and worked in Australia and Tuscany, is the winemaker; Gilad is in charge of the business aspects. The winery is currently producing age-worthy varietal Cabernet Sauvignon and Merlot wines in their Reserve and Superiore series; a second wine, Classico, which is a blend of Cabernet Sauvignon and Merlot that is meant for relatively early drinking; and a label for white wine, Flam. Production from the 2004 and 2005 vintages was of 55,000 bottles, and for 2006–2008 about 100,000 bottles annually.

Grapes come primarily from vineyards over which the winery has full control, in the Judean Mountains and the Galilee. In addition to current reliance on Cabernet Sauvignon, Merlot, Syrah, Chardonnay and Sauvignon Blanc, other varieties including Cabernet Franc, Petit Verdot and Mourvedre are soon to come on line.

Reserve

RESERVE, CABERNET SAUVIGNON, 2008: Potentially the best ever from a fine winery. Intensely dark garnet, full-bodied, with silky soft tannins, showing a rich nose of spring and citrus flowers, opening in the glass to revel in traditional Cabernet currant and blackberry fruits. Give the wine a few more moments and it unfolds to reveal notes of spiced plums and a tantalizing hint of *garrigue*. Best from 2012. Tentative Score 93–95.

RESERVE, CABERNET SAUVIGNON, 2007: Dark, almost inky-garnet in color, full-bodied, with softly caressing tannins. Still in its extreme youth but already showing round and complex with currant, blackberry and citrus peel notes on first attack, those yielding to a light undercurrent of Mediterranean herbs. Long and generous. Drink now–2014. Score 91.

RESERVE, CABERNET SAUVIGNON, 2006: Oak-aged for about 16 months, a full-bodied, gently tannic and concentrated blend of 87%

Cabernet Sauvignon, 10% Merlot and 3% Petit Verdot. Dark, almost impenetrable garnet, with soft, near-sweet tannins and notes of spicy wood, opens with a mélange of black cherry, blackberry and currant notes, and reveals hints of red berries and brown spices. Long, broad and elegant. Approachable now, but will show its elegance best from 2011–2015. Score 92.

RESERVE, CABERNET SAUVIGNON, 2005: Blended with 6% each of Merlot and Petit Verdot and oak-aged for 18 months, this deep garnet, full-bodied red's chewy tannins are now integrating nicely but still showing generous wood. On the nose and palate a complex and elegant array of blackcurrant, black cherry, anise and Mediterranean herbs and, on the long finish, hints of vanilla and sage. Firm but yielding and lingering long on the palate. Drink now–2013. Score 93.

RESERVE, CABERNET SAUVIGNON, 2004: Deep garnet toward black, full-bodied, with once searing tannins now integrating nicely. This blend of 88% Cabernet Sauvignon and 12% of Merlot reflects its 18 months in *barriques* with spicy wood and tannins in fine balance with natural acidity and currant, plum and blackberry fruits. On the long finish hints of mint and spices. Drink now–2012. Score 91.

RESERVE, CABERNET SAUVIGNON, 2003: This full-bodied, dark garnet-toward-inky purple wine, blended with 7% of Merlot, was oak-aged for about 14 months. Generous blackcurrant and cherry fruits come together elegantly with mineral, herbal and light earthy aromas and flavors, all with a hint of smoky-toasty oak. Super-smooth tannins and a long finish. Drink now–2014. Score 93.

RESERVE, MERLOT, 2008: Intensely dark garnet, opening with generous floral and minty notes on the nose and then opening to reveal currant, wild berry and black cherry fruits all on a lightly spicy veggie note. Best from 2011–2016. Tentative Score 91–93.

RESERVE, MERLOT, 2007: A tentative blend of 92% Merlot and 4% each of Cabernet Sauvignon and Petit Verdot. Dark, full-bodied and with still gripping tannins starting to settle in nicely. On the nose and palate appealing blackberry, blueberry and bittersweet chocolate. Look as well for a hint of cherry liqueur on the finish. Best from 2011–2015. Score 90.

RESERVE, MERLOT, 2006: Dark garnet, a full-bodied blend of 86% Merlot and 14% Petit Verdot, reflecting generous but not-at-all exaggerated oak-aging with still firm tannins and notes of vanilla and spices. On first attack black fruits, those opening to reveal raspberries and blueberries, and those on a background of mocha and sweet cedar. Give this one time and it will show fine balance between tannins, wood and fruits. Has the structure for aging. Drink now–2015. Score 92.

RESERVE, MERLOT, 2005: Dark garnet toward royal purple, medium- to full-bodied, reflecting its 18 months in oak with soft, mouth-coating tannins and spicy wood. Look for a tempting light earthiness that supports blackberries, currants, and a touch of spiciness that weaves its way through the wine and then lingers nicely on a long, elegant finish. Drink now–2012. Score 92.

RESERVE, MERLOT, 2004: Dark garnet with orange and green reflections. Made entirely from Merlot grapes, full-bodied and tannic. On first attack peppery wood reflecting 16 months in oak, that opening slowly to reveal firm mouth-coating tannins, then showing a tempting array of currant, berry and black cherry fruits, those backed up nicely by spices and, on the long finish, a hint of crème Anglaise. Continuing to develop nicely. Drink now–2012. Score 92.

RESERVE, MERLOT, 2003: Blended with 7% Cabernet Sauvignon, dark, deep and intense, with soft, almost sweet tannins and layer after layer of berry, black cherry, anise and spice aromas and flavors that linger nicely on the palate. The once-marked wood influence is now receding and the wine is showing soft, round and long. Drink now–2012. Score 92.

RESERVE, SYRAH, 2008: Developing primarily in older oak, showing deep garnet in color, full-bodied, with generously mouth-coating tannins waiting to settle down. Already showing a fruit-forward nose and opening to reveal plum and wild berry fruits along with notes of saddle leather and mocha. Promises elegance. Best 2011–2016. Tentative Score 91–93.

RESERVE, SYRAH, 2007: Dark garnet with purple reflections, medium- to full-bodied with round, gently caressing tannins and a generously fruity personality. Look for raspberries and red currants on a lightly meaty and spicy background, all lingering nicely on the palate. Drink now–2013. Score 90.

RESERVE, SYRAH, 2005: Dark garnet in color, with hints of dusty wood on first attack, those yielding to appealing plum, wild berry and mint. Full-bodied and chewy but soft and elegant. Drink now. Score 90.

RESERVE, SYRAH, 2004: Youthful royal purple, aged in French and American *barriques*, this aromatic, medium- to full-bodied wine shows firm but yielding tannins, gentle wood and a tempting array of berry and plum fruits, those backed up by hints of Oriental spices, chocolate and light earthiness. Drink now. Score 90.

Superiore

SUPERIORE, 2007: Dark ruby toward garnet, medium- to full-bodied, with gently mouth-coating tannins, a blend of 72% Syrah and 28% Cabernet Sauvignon. Aromatic, with black fruits and a note of leather on the nose, opens to reveal blackberry, currant and vanilla notes. Soft, round and comfortably elegant. Drink now–2012. Score 91.

SUPERIORE, 2006: A blend of 86% Syrah and 14% Cabernet, oak-aged for 12 months in French and American oak. Medium- to full-bodied, with soft tannins integrating nicely and a nice "bite" of spicy wood. Concentrated on the palate, showing purple plum, blackberry and raspberry fruits, those supported by tantalizing hints of leather and smoked meat. Drink now–2012. Score 91.

SUPERIORE, 2005: A blend of 81% Syrah and 19% Cabernet Sauvignon. After 12 months in oak, this dark ruby red is medium- to full-bodied, with fine-grained tannins and lively cherry, raspberry and cassis fruits, those supported nicely by hints of herbs, cedar and spring flowers. Drink now. Score 90.

SUPERIORE, 2004: A blend of 80% Syrah and 20% Cabernet Sauvignon showing toasty oak, smoke and generous but soft tannins, those matched nicely by spicy plum, berry and black cherry fruits. A long, round and elegantly near-sweet finish. Drink now. Score 90.

Classico

CLASSICO, 2008: A blend of equal parts of Cabernet Sauvignon and Merlot, oak-aged in American oak for six months. Dark royal purple in color, opens to show light notes of toasty wood that complement appealing cherry, berry and currant fruits. Soft, round and generous with just enough complexity to catch our attention. Drink now–2011. Score 89.

CLASSICO, 2007: A gently oak-aged blend of Cabernet Sauvignon and Merlot, showing light hints of tobacco, chocolate and spicy cedarwood to highlight currant, blackberry and black cherry fruits. Medium- to full-bodied, with soft tannins throughout and, on the long finish, a hint of Mediterranean herbs. Drink now. Score 89.

Flam

FLAM, SAUVIGNON BLANC-CHARDONNAY, 2008: A blend this year of 80% Sauvignon Blanc and 20% Chardonnay, those wisely unoaked to maintain the wine as crisply fresh and aromatic. Shows tropical and citrus fruits along with citrus flowers and flinty minerals. Fine balance here between fruits and acidity to make the wine both lively and fascinating. Drink now. Score 90.

FLAM, SAUVIGNON BLANC-CHARDONNAY, 2007: An unoaked blend of 70% Sauvignon Blanc from the Upper Galilee and 30% Chardonnay from the Jerusalem Hills. Light golden straw in color, medium-bodied, with a deeply aromatic citrus and tropical fruit nose. Opens on the palate to show melon, pineapple and green apples. Crisp, lively, just complex enough and with a long fruity finish. Drink now. Score 89.

Gad ✶

Located on Moshav Sdot Micha in the Ella Valley, this boutique winery was founded by Amir Baruch in 2000. Production, primarily from Cabernet Sauvignon, Merlot, Syrah and Petite Sirah grapes from vineyards in Karmei Yosef, is currently about 10,000 bottles annually.

GAD, CABERNET SAUVIGNON, RESERVE, 2006: Dark but not clear garnet in color, with gripping tannins and searing alcohol, already oxidizing and showing Port-like aromas and flavors. Lacks balance or charm. Score 65. K

GAD, CABERNET SAUVIGNON, 2006: Dark ruby, with too-generous dusty and smoky oak reflecting the simultaneous use of oak barrels and oak chips for five months. Muddy flavors hold back whatever fruits may be lurking here. Score 70. K

GAD, CABERNET SAUVIGNON, RESERVE, 2005: An oak-aged blend of 90% Cabernet Sauvignon and 10% Merlot. Medium-bodied, with coarse tannins and a far-too-generous dose of wood on the palate and nose. Lacks balance. Score 72. K

GAD, CABERNET SAUVIGNON, 2005: Garnet-red, with chunky, country-style tannins and spicy berry-black cherry fruits. Lacks depth, breadth or length. Drink up. Score 78. K

GAD, MERLOT, 2005: Dark ruby red, light- to medium-bodied, with chunky tannins, a few berry, cherry fruits and a too-herbal finish. One-dimensional. Drink up. Score 76. K

GAD, BLEND, 2005: A potpourri of Cabernet Sauvignon, Merlot, Syrah, Petite Sirah and Argaman grapes. Medium-bodied, with flabby tannins, far too acidic and not fruity enough. Score 70. K

Galai **

GALAI

ESTATE WINE

2002

Cabernet Sauvignon

12.5% vol.   Unfiltered   ℮750ml.

Sigalit and Asaf Galai established this small winery at Moshav Nir Akiva in the northern part of the Negev Desert in 2002. The winery has vineyards containing Cabernet Sauvignon and Merlot as well as experimental sections of Cabernet Franc, Shiraz and Zinfandel. Current production is about 7,000 bottles annually.

GALAI, CABERNET SAUVIGNON, 2007: Medium- to full-bodied, with somewhat chunky country-style tannins and generous wood. On the nose and palate blackberries, cherries and currants supported by notes of freshly roasted herbs. A not complex but appealing country-style wine. Drink now. Score 85.

GALAI, CABERNET SAUVIGNON, 2006: Garnet toward royal purple, medium-bodied, with firm tannins and generous wood needing time to settle in. Opens in the glass to reveal black cherry, blackberry and peppery notes that linger nicely. Drink now. Score 85.

GALAI, CABERNET SAUVIGNON, 2005: Dark garnet and medium-bodied, with firm but yielding tannins and light smoky oak. On the nose and palate generous blackcurrant, red and black berries and a hint of white pepper that comes in on the finish. Drink now. Score 85.

GALAI, MERLOT, 2007: Dark royal purple in color, with soft, gently caressing tannins, and opening to show wild berry, cassis and smoky herbal notes. Drink now–2011. Score 86.

GALAI, MERLOT, 2006: Medium- to full-bodied, dark garnet, with silky tannins and showing appealing black fruits on a lightly smoky and spicy background. Drink now. Score 85.

GALAI, MERLOT, 2005: Deep garnet in color, with soft, mouth-coating tannins and light spicy cedarwood in good balance with berry, black cherry and plum notes and, on the moderately long finish, nice hints of Mediterranean herbs. Drink up. Score 87.

Galil Mountain ✶✶✶✶

With its physically beautiful state-of-the-art winery located on Kibbutz Yiron in the Upper Galilee, this joint venture between the Golan Heights Winery and the kibbutz has vineyards located in some of the best wine-growing areas of the Upper Galilee, including Yiron, Meron, Misgav Am, Yiftach and Malkiya. Winemaker Micha Vaadia produces distinctly *terroir*-based wines in two series. The first label, Yiron, is a blend of Cabernet Sauvignon and Merlot, and the second, Galil Mountain, contains varietal releases of Cabernet Sauvignon, Merlot, Pinot Noir, Syrah, Sangiovese, Chardonnay and Sauvignon Blanc. Production from the 2000 vintage was about 300,000 bottles. Since then the winery has grown to an output of 900,000 bottles annually.

Yiron

YIRON, 2005: A Bordeaux-plus wine—that is to say, 50% Cabernet Sauvignon, 44% Merlot and 2% Petit Verdot, plus 4% Syrah. Full-bodied and concentrated but simultaneously soft and elegant, with generous cassis and black fruits, velvety tannins, and reflecting its 16 months in French oak with gently spicy and dusty wood, all of which lead to a super-long finish. Perhaps the best to date from the winery. Drink now–2015. Score 93. **K**

YIRON, 2004: A blend of 72% Cabernet Sauvignon, 25% Merlot and 3% Syrah. Intense garnet toward royal purple, full-bodied, with firm, near-sweet tannins integrating nicely with smoky and vanilla-tinged wood. Opens with wild berries on the nose and palate, those yielding to black cherry, cassis and spices, and finally, on the long finish, a tantalizing hint of bitterness. Drink now–2013. Score 91. **K**

173

YIRON, 2003: A blend of Cabernet Sauvignon and Merlot. Full-bodied, with mouth-coating tannins and spicy wood in fine proportion. Deep ruby toward royal purple in color, showing appealing blackberry, black cherry and currant fruits, those with light earthy-herbal overtones. Long, mouth-filling and elegant. Drink now. Score 90. **K**

YIRON, SYRAH, 2005: Dark, almost inky-garnet in color, medium- to full-bodied, with fine balance between soft tannins, spicy wood and fruits. On first attack raspberries and chocolate, those yielding to blackberries, currants and a rich floral note. On the long finish the tannins rise along with fruits and an appealing hint of red licorice. Drink now–2013. Score 91. **K**

YIRON, SYRAH, 2004: Dark royal purple with orange and green reflections, opening with a rich fruity and floral nose. Full-bodied, with bold but soft tannins integrating nicely with spicy wood and showing black fruits, dusty wood and light meaty and earthy overlays. Long and deep. Drink now–2012. Score 91. **K**

YIRON, SYRAH, 2003: Full-bodied, showing soft tannins with just enough grip to catch the attention, those yielding nicely to light spicy wood. Dark garnet in color, aromatic, with blackberries, purple plums and hints of white pepper and chocolate as well as a light meaty-earthy sensation that comes in on the round and comfortably medium-long finish. Drink now–2012. Score 91. **K**

Galil Mountain

GALIL MOUNTAIN, CABERNET SAUVIGNON, 2007: Dark ruby toward garnet, medium-bodied, with soft, gently caressing tannins, and showing an appealing array of blackberries, blackcurrants and fruits on a background that hints nicely of minted chocolate. Drink now–2011. Score 87. **K**

GALIL MOUNTAIN, CABERNET SAUVIGNON, 2006: Super-dark garnet, showing moderate spicy and vanilla notes and soft, near-sweet tannins. On the nose and palate blackberries and blueberries, currants and, coming in from mid-palate, hints of earthiness and freshly turned mushrooms. Drink now–2011. Score 90. **K**

GALIL MOUNTAIN, CABERNET SAUVIGNON, 2005: Deep garnet with orange reflections, medium- to full-bodied, with appealing near-sweet tannins integrating nicely to reveal aromas and flavors of blackcurrants, wild berries and minerals, all lingering nicely on the palate. Drink now. Score 89. **K**

GALIL MOUNTAIN, MERLOT, 2007: Unoaked, with soft, near-sweet tannins and showing inky-garnet in color. On the nose and palate red and black berries, cassis and hints of Oriental spices and dark chocolate. Drink now. Score 88. **K**

GALIL MOUNTAIN, MERLOT, 2006: Dark ruby toward garnet, medium- to full-bodied, with firm tannins settling in nicely now. On the nose and palate an array of red and black berries, purple plums and orange peel notes, those on a light background of Mediterranean herbs. Drink now. Score 90. **K**

GALIL MOUNTAIN, MERLOT, 2005: Deep, almost inky black-garnet, full-bodied, with firm but comfortably yielding tannins. Ripe berry, currant, green pepper and light herbal aromas and flavors, those coming together in a deep and complex *terroir*-driven wine. Drink now. Score 89. **K**

GALIL MOUNTAIN, SYRAH, 2008: Even at this early stage of its development showing super-dark, well-extracted and with generous soft tannins yielding to red and black berries, plums and Oriental spices. Destined to develop a generous grilled meaty overtone and has the potential for gently muscular elegance. Best 2011–2014. Tentative Score 90–92. **K**

GALIL MOUNTAIN, SHIRAZ, 2007: Medium- to full-bodied, oak-aged for 13 months, with gently mouth-coating tannins and showing an appealing array of cherry, wild berry and peppery notes, with a hint of bitter almonds on the long finish. Drink now–2011. Score 89. **K**

GALIL MOUNTAIN, SHIRAZ, 2006: Dark garnet, medium- to full-bodied, and aromatic with soft tannins integrating nicely and showing a generous array of red and black berries, cherries and plums, those on a lightly spicy background. Easy to drink but with enough complexity to command our attention. Drink now. Score 86. **K**

GALIL MOUNTAIN, PINOT NOIR, 2008: Developing in year-old French barriques, dark garnet, medium- to full-bodied, with fine density and still gripping tannins, but already showing fine balance and structure. Opens with black cherries on the nose and then goes on to reveal aromas and flavors of red and black berries, cassis and spices, those complemented nicely by a gentle hint of sweet-and-spicy wood. As the wine develops, look as well for stony minerals and a subdued hint of mint. Complex, generous and long. Approachable and enjoyable on release, but best 2011–2014. Tentative Score 90–92. **K**

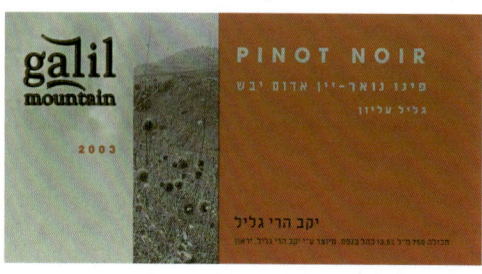

GALIL MOUNTAIN, PINOT NOIR, 2007: Developed in one-to-three-year-old French barrels, those imparting gentle spicy and vanilla notes. Dark cherry red, medium-bodied, with soft tannins integrating nicely and opening to reveal red and black berries, cherries and earthy minerals. Soft and round, with just enough complexity to keep our attention. Drink now–2012. Score 88. **K**

GALIL MOUNTAIN, PINOT NOIR, 2006: Dark cherry red toward garnet, medium-bodied, with its once firm tannins now settling in nicely, opens to show a complex array of red berry, cherry, blueberry and spices, those supported nicely by light toasty vanilla and, on the finish, a hint of minerality. Drink now. Score 89. **K**

GALIL MOUNTAIN, SANGIOVESE, 2005: Dark, almost impenetrable garnet in color, rich, complex and with remarkable finesse for a pure Sangiovese. On the nose and palate plum, cherry, blackberry, anise, currants and wild berries. Drink up. Score 88. **K**

GALIL MOUNTAIN, BARBERA, 2008: Neither Barbera d'Asti nor Barbera d'Alba, but a distinct Barbera de Galilee wine. Tasted from components still in tanks before being transferred to its nine months' anticipated stay in *barriques*, but already showing great charm. Dark garnet toward royal purple, with almost muscular concentration, with firm near-sweet tannins and opening to show a dark chocolate nose, and, on the palate, black and blue berries, purple plums and floral notes.

Destined to be a concentrated wine, but as it continues to develop it will soften comfortably. Drink from release. Tentative Score 90–92. **K**

GALIL MOUNTAIN, BARBERA, 2007: Reflecting its nine months in French oak with notes of smoky oak, medium-dark garnet in color, opening with a quiet nose but going on to reveal a generous array of berries, black cherries, purple plums and spring flowers. Tannins and oak rise along with a hint of bitter almonds on the finish, so give this one a bit of time for its elements to come together. Drink now–2012. Score 89. **K**

GALIL MOUNTAIN, BARBERA, 2006: Developed for nine months in French oak, dark, almost inky ruby toward garnet in color, with its impressive 15% alcohol content in fine balance with wood, tannins and fruit. On the nose and palate blackberries, blueberries, plums and violets supported nicely by notes of vanilla, milk chocolate and, rising on the long finish, notes of black pepper. Gently mouth-coating tannins and fine concentration. Drink now–2011. Score 91. **K**

GALIL MOUNTAIN, SHIRAZ-CABERNET SAUVIGNON, 2007: A blend of 58% Shiraz and 42% Cabernet Sauvignon, aged in American oak for ten months and close to bottling at this tasting. Deep garnet toward royal purple, with generous but soft and gently mouth-coating tannins and fine concentration. Opens to reveal a medium- to full-bodied wine with plum, berry and cassis notes on a lightly spicy smoked-meat background. Drink now–2012. Score 88. **K**

GALIL MOUNTAIN, SHIRAZ-CABERNET SAUVIGNON, 2006: Smooth, round and aromatic, reflecting its ten months in American oak with gently spicy wood and hints of vanilla. Opens in the glass to show a generous mouthful of currant, blackberry, cherry and licorice notes. On the finish look for a hint of pomegranates. Drink now–2011. Score 89. **K**

GALIL MOUNTAIN, SHIRAZ-CABERNET SAUVIGNON, 2005: Dark and concentrated, full-bodied, showing a light herbal and spicy oak nose and opening to reveal currant, blackberry and black cherry fruits, all coming together in a long, chocolate-rich and elegant finish. Drink now–2011. Score 90. **K**

GALIL MOUNTAIN, ROSÉ, 2008: Light- to medium-bodied, with refreshing acidity, a crisply dry, rose-petal pink-colored wine showing an appealing tutti-frutti array of red fruits. Drink now. Score 87. **K**

GALIL MOUNTAIN, ROSÉ, 2007: A blend of 82% Sangiovese, 10% Cabernet Sauvignon and 8% Barbera. Baby-blanket pink in color with generous raspberry and cherry fruits along with hints of blueberries. Crisp and refreshing. Drink up. Score 87. **K**

GALIL MOUNTAIN, CHARDONNAY, 2008: Lightly oaked, with a lively golden color, opens with a distinct peachy nose and goes on to show appealing citrus, apple and white peach fruits, all with a fine overlay of minerality. Look as well for a note of peach and cherry pits that comes in on the finish. Drink now. Score 89. **K**

GALIL MOUNTAIN, CHARDONNAY, 2007: Developed partly in oak, partly in stainless steel vats. Golden straw in color, medium-bodied, with a gentle hint of spicy oak and showing citrus, apple and pear fruits, those with a tempting hint of bitterness that creeps in on the finish. Drink now. Score 88. **K**

GALIL MOUNTAIN, SAUVIGNON BLANC, 2008: An unoaked white, light straw in color, with a generously aromatic nose and crisply refreshing acidity, showing a tempting array of melon, citrus and kiwi fruits, those on a background that hints nicely of freshly mown grass. Drink from release–2010. Score 88. **K**

GALIL MOUNTAIN, SAUVIGNON BLANC, 2007: Fresh and aromatic. Light straw-colored, with melon, apricot and lime fruits, a crisply refreshing wine that lingers nicely on the palate. Drink now. Score 88. **K**

GALIL MOUNTAIN, VIOGNIER, 2008: Developed in new French oak barrels, with a light toasted white bread overlay. Light golden straw in color, with fine balancing acidity to highlight citrus and summer fruits, those hinting of a buttery overlay and peach pits. Medium-bodied but seems to float comfortably on the palate and finishing generous and long. Drink now–2011. Score 90. **K**

GALIL MOUNTAIN, VIOGNIER, 2007: Medium-bodied, dark golden straw with orange and green reflections, showing good balance between wood, acidity and fruit. On the nose and palate floral, light mineral, summer fruits and melon come together nicely. Drink now. Score 89. **K**

GALIL MOUNTAIN, VIOGNIER, 2006: Lightly golden with greenish tinges, this medium-bodied, lightly oaked white opens with a lively and spicy nose, then reveals enticing aromas and flavors of peaches, nectarines, pears and apples backed up by spring flowers and minerals, all complemented by hints of white pepper that play nicely on the palate. Drink now. Score 90. **K**

GALIL MOUNTAIN, AVIVIM, 2007: Medium-bodied, light golden straw in color, a blend of 69% Viognier and 31% Chardonnay, those aged on their lees in new French oak *barriques* for nine months. Youthful and zesty, with lightly spicy cedarwood notes highlighting an array of tropical fruits, pears and honeydew melon. Lurking comfortably in the background a hint of red grapefruit. Drink now. Score 90. **K**

GALIL MOUNTAIN, AVIVIM, 2006: A blend of 74% Viognier and 26% Chardonnay, aged in French oak for nine months. Full-bodied, with a buttery hint on first attack and then opening to show ripe pears, summer and tropical fruits on a generous but not imposing vanilla and oaky background. On the moderately long finish, vanilla, and, creeping in quietly but distinctly, a hint of bitterness that will be appreciated by some and not by others. Drink up. Score 88. **K**

Gat Shomron ✴

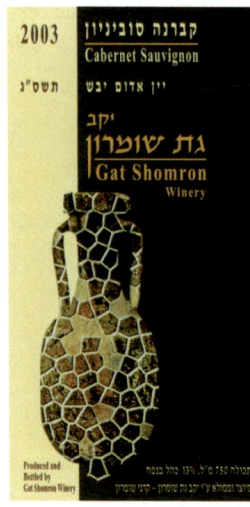

Founded by Avigdor Sharon and Lior Nachum on Karnei Shomron, not far from Kfar Saba, in 2003, this small winery released its first wines from that harvest in 2005, and is currently producing about 7,000 bottles annually of oak-aged Cabernet Sauvignon, Merlot and Chardonnay. Grapes are sourced from the areas of Shomron and the Upper Galilee.

GAT SHOMRON, CABERNET SAUVIGNON, GALILEE, 2006: Aged for one year in 300 liter oak casks, medium-bodied, with somewhat chunky, country-style tannins and opening to reveal berry, currant and black cherry fruits on a lightly spicy background. Drink now. Score 84. K

GAT SHOMRON, CABERNET SAUVIGNON, SHOMRON, 2006: Deep garnet in color, full-bodied, with still-firm tannins needing time to integrate. Opens in the glass to show plum, blackberry and blueberry notes, those complemented by hints of cedarwood and tobacco, all leading to a medium-long finish. Drink now. Score 85. K

GAT SHOMRON, CABERNET SAUVIGNON, 2005: Medium-bodied, with chunky, country-style tannins and skimpy aromas and flavors of spicy berries and black cherries. One-dimensional. Drink up. Score 82. K

GAT SHOMRON, MERLOT, GALILEE, 2006: Super-dark garnet in color, full-bodied, with firm tannins, generous spicy wood and a whopping 15.8% alcohol content. Opens with a marked alcoholic nose but that yields to berry, black cherry and plum fruits, those on a light spicy background. With tannins and alcohol rising, finishes hot. Drink now. Score 83. K

GAT SHOMRON, MERLOT, 2005: Garnet toward purple, with soft tannins and spicy oak opening in the glass to reveal berry and plum fruits. A simple entry-level wine. Drink now. Score 80. K

GAT SHOMRON, SYRAH, 2005: Aged in French and American *barriques* for 14 months, ruby toward garnet, medium to full-bodied with soft, well-integrated tannins and a gentle hand with the oak. Showing appealing berry, black cherry, raspberry and blackberry fruits, those with notes of tar and charcoal. Round and satisfying. Drink now. Score 87. **K**

GAT SHOMRON, RED BLEND, 2007: A potpourri of Cabernet Sauvignon, Cabernet Franc, Syrah, Merlot and Petit Verdot, oak-aged for six months. Medium-bodied, with chunky tannins that give the wine a somewhat country style, but that pleasant enough with berry, cherry and currant notes making themselves felt nicely along with hints of Mediterranean herbs. Drink up. Score 85. **K**

Gesher Damia ✶

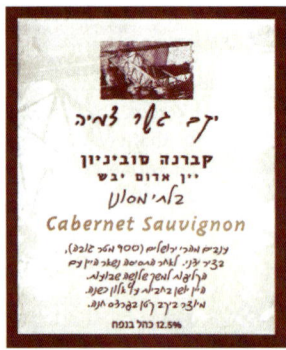

Founded in 1999 by Moshe Kaplan in the town of Pardes Hannah on the northern Coastal Plain, this small winery receives Cabernet Sauvignon, Merlot, Argaman, Petite Shiraz, Gewurztraminer and Chardonnay grapes from Gush Etzion, the Jerusalem Hills and the center of the country. Production is currently about 6,000 bottles annually.

GESHER DAMIA, CABERNET SAUVIGNON, 2006: Garnet-red, medium-bodied, with soft tannins, hints of peppery wood and a basic berry-black cherry personality. Drink up. Score 79.

GESHER DAMIA, CABERNET SAUVIGNON, 2005: Ruby toward garnet, light- to medium-bodied, with almost unfelt tannins, spicy oak and a few blackberry fruits. Drink up. Score 78.

GESHER DAMIA, CABERNET SAUVIGNON, 2004: Dark ruby, medium-bodied, with chunky tannins, smoky oak and skimpy black fruits. Drink up. Score 79.

GESHER DAMIA, MERLOT, 2006: A simple country-style wine with chunky tannins, and near-sweet sur-ripe berry, cherry and cassis notes. Drink up. Score 79.

GESHER DAMIA, MERLOT, 2005: Medium-bodied, with almost unfelt tannins and stewed plum and berry fruits. Drink up. Score 78.

GESHER DAMIA, MERLOT, 2004: Medium-bodied, with soft, near-sweet tannins and blackberry, cherry and cassis fruits, those on a lightly spicy background. Drink up. Score 80.

Ginaton **

Founded in 1999 by Doron Cohen and Benju Duke on Moshav Ginaton on the Central Plain not far from the city of Lod, the winery draws Cabernet Sauvignon, Muscat and Chardonnay grapes from Karmei Yosef and Kerem Ben Zimra. The first commercial releases were 3,000 bottles from the 2000 vintage. Current annual production is about 5,500 bottles.

GINATON, CABERNET SAUVIGNON, 2006: Dark ruby toward garnet, medium- to full-bodied, with soft tannins and a hint of sawdust on the nose. Opens to show currant and berry fruits. An entry-level wine. Drink now. Score 84.

GINATON, CABERNET SAUVIGNON, 2005: Youthful royal purple, medium-bodied, with once firm tannins integrating nicely and showing lightly spicy black fruits. Drink now. Score 84.

GINATON, CABERNET SAUVIGNON, 2004: Garnet toward royal purple, medium-bodied, with soft tannins integrating nicely to show blackberry and currant fruits on a light spicy background. Drink up. Score 84.

GINATON, CABERNET SAUVIGNON, HAR BRACHA, NUMBERED SERIES, 2003: Reflecting its 18 months in oak with generous spicy and smoky cedar and moderately firm tannins. Medium- to full-bodied, with some black fruits. Lacking complexity. Drink up. Score 84.

GINATON, CABERNET SAUVIGNON, KEREM BEN ZIMRA, 2003: Clear ruby toward purple, medium-bodied, with soft, almost unfelt tannins. Aromas and flavors of berries, cassis and black cherries on a lightly herbaceous background. Drink up. Score 84.

GINATON, MERLOT, 2005: This medium-bodied wine shows generous, spicy and vanilla-rich oak with soft tannins rising on the finish. Opens slowly to reveal plum, blackberries and black cherry fruits that linger nicely. Not complex but easy to drink. Drink now. Score 85.

Givon ∗

Established by Nir Ernesti and Shuki Segal in the village of Givon Hachadasha, north of Jerusalem in the Judean Mountains, and relying on Cabernet Sauvignon and Merlot grapes from nearby vineyards, this winery released its first wines from the 2002 vintage. Current production is about 5,000 bottles annually.

GIVON, CABERNET SAUVIGNON, 2005: Somewhat cloudy dark garnet, medium- to full-bodied, with chunky tannins, generous smoky oak and currant, berry and black cherry fruits. A simple country-style wine. Drink now. Score 84.

GIVON, CABERNET SAUVIGNON, 2004: Dark cherry red, medium-bodied, with soft tannins and appealing black cherry and plum fruits. Not typical for the variety but an acceptable quaffing wine. Drink up. Score 83.

GIVON, MERLOT, 2005: Garnet toward purple, with soft tannins and spicy wood reflecting its 16 months in *barriques*, this medium-bodied wine is showing appealing plum, berry and cherry fruits. Drink up. Score 83.

GIVON, MERLOT, 2004: Medium-bodied, low in tannins and on the simple side, with only skimpy berry and plum fruits. Drink up. Score 80.

Golan Heights Winery *****

From the moment they released their first wines in 1984, there has been no doubt that the Golan Heights Winery was and is still today largely responsible for placing Israel on the world wine map. The winery, with its state-of-the-art facilities located in Katzrin on the Golan Heights, and fine vineyards on the Golan and in the Upper Galilee, is owned by eight of the kibbutzim and moshavim that supply them with grapes. Maintaining rigorous control over the vineyards and relying on a combination of New and Old World knowledge and technology, senior winemaker Victor Schoenfeld and his staff of winemakers, all of whom trained in California or France, produce wines that often attain excellence.

The winery has three regular series, Yarden, Gamla and Golan, the wines in the first two series often being age-worthy while those in the Golan series are meant for early drinking. Within the Yarden series the winery occasionally releases single vineyard wines, and those often prove to be among the best wines in the country. There is also the top-of-the-line Katzrin series that includes an often superb red Bordeaux-style blend that is released only in years considered exceptional, and a Chardonnay that has been released annually since 1995.

The winery is currently producing more than six million bottles annually and of this production nearly thirty percent is destined for export. Among the regularly released varietal wines are Cabernet Sauvignon, Merlot, Pinot Noir, Gamay, Sangiovese, Sauvignon Blanc, Chardonnay, Johannisberg Riesling, Muscat Canelli and Gewurztraminer, and the winery is currently cultivating experimental plantings of Nebbiolo and Malbec. The winery also produces sparkling Blanc de Blanc and Brut, both made in the traditional *Champenoise* method; Heightswine (a play on the words Ice Wine); and several dessert wines.

Katzrin

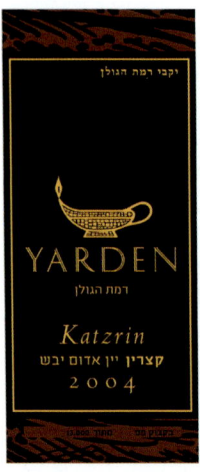

KATZRIN, 2004: Aged in new French *barriques* for 18 months, 94% Cabernet Sauvignon with the addition of 6% Merlot. Dark garnet toward royal purple, with orange and violet reflections. Shows still generous oak and firm tannins, those in fine proportion and well balanced by blackberry, blackcurrant and cherry fruits, on a background of white pepper, Mediterranean herbs and tobacco, and, on the long and generous finish, hints of vanilla and peppermint. Approachable now, but best 2011–2018, perhaps longer. Score 93. **K**

KATZRIN, 2003: Dark garnet, a full-bodied blend of 83% Cabernet Sauvignon, 14% Merlot and 3% Cabernet Franc, with gently mouth-coating tannins and smoky oak integrating nicely. Shows layers of blackcurrant, black cherry and berry fruits, those yielding and coming together with peppery and herbal aromas and flavors culminating in a long blueberry and white chocolate finish. Drink now–2018. Score 93. **K**

KATZRIN, 2000: A blend of 89% Cabernet Sauvignon, 9% Merlot and 2% Cabernet Franc. Showing beautifully now, its blackberry, cherry and currant fruits supported by spicy oak, notes of cigar tobacco and hints of freshly turned earth. Dense, deep and intense, with finely tuned balance and structure, a simultaneously bold and elegant wine. Drink now–2015. Score 92. **K**

KATZRIN, 1996: Vibrant and complex, with an array of aromas and flavors that include currants, cherries and plums overlaid by smoky oak, chocolate, spices and tobacco, this full-bodied, young tannic red is only now beginning to reveal its charms. Excellent integration between fruit, tannins and oak indicates that the wine will continue to develop beautifully. Drink now–2015. Score 93. **K**

KATZRIN, 1993: Deep, broad, long and complex, this full-bodied Cabernet-Merlot blend continues to live up to its promise. Abundant tannins are well balanced by wood and fruits that include cassis, black cherries and orange peel, along with generous overlays of milk chocolate and toasty oak. Elegant and graceful. Drink now–2012. Score 94. **K**

KATZRIN, 1990: A blend of 90% Cabernet Sauvignon and 10% Merlot, this deep, elegant, full-bodied wine has a dark garnet color and excellent balance between fruits, wood, acidity and tannins. Look for a complex array of aromas and flavors, including blackcurrants, cherries, vanilla, cloves and chocolate. Lingers long on the palate. Drink now. Score 93. K

KATZRIN, CHARDONNAY, 2007: Dark, almost bronzed in color, full-bodied, with a generous dose of creamy wood that runs through. Sounds like a wine dominated by wood, but the balance is there, the wood matched at first by notes of butterscotch and then by pear, pineapple, spices, and hazelnuts, all of which come together as a concentrated and well-focused whole. Best from 2011–2016, perhaps longer. Score 92. K

KATZRIN, CHARDONNAY, 2005: A creamy and buttery Chardonnay, deep, almost bronzed gold in color and marked from first attack to its long finish with super-generous toasty oak and hazelnuts. Opens slowly on the palate to reveal fig, melon and pear fruits, but those always under the oaky notes. A good wine, but not up to the Katzrin standards and mostly for those who can take the intense oak. Drink now–2012. Score 88. K

KATZRIN, CHARDONNAY, 2004: Dark golden-yellow, full-bodied and concentrated. Developed in new oak for ten months, notably yeasty on first attack but that yielding beautifully to a buttery, oak-rich texture and opening to reveal nutty, fig, pear, tropical fruits and butterscotch, all on a spicy background. Rich, long and complex. Drink now–2012. Score 92. K

KATZRIN, CHARDONNAY, 2003: Rich, ripe, concentrated and complex with generous layers of figs, tangerines, summer fruits and hazelnuts. Generous but not imposing oak on the finish makes it especially elegant, as does a hint of butterscotch that comes in on the long finish. Drink now. Score 92. K

KATZRIN, CHARDONNAY, 2002: As full-bodied and complex as in its youth but now maturing nicely and reflecting only the barest hint of smoky oak, that serving as a backdrop for summer fruits, pears and citrus. Look as well for roasted nuts, minerals and a hint of cream that play nicely on the palate. Drink up. Score 91. K

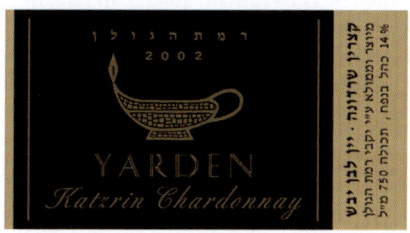

Yarden

YARDEN, CABERNET SAUVIGNON, 2008: A component tasting from the Elrom vineyard. Super-dark garnet toward royal purple, full-bodied with still gripping tannins, those in fine balance with wood and fruits. On first attack a generous array of currants and blueberries, those yielding to spicy plum and near-sweet cedarwood, and, on the long finish, a broad array of spices. Best 2012–2022. Tentative Score 91–93. **K**

YARDEN, CABERNET SAUVIGNON, 2007: Tasted from a component from Yonathan vineyard. Already showing a clean, fresh mineral note that runs through. Full- to medium-bodied, with soft, nicely integrating tannins and gentle hints of sweet-and-spicy wood, opens to reveal generous ripe currant and berry fruits. Approachable on release and capable of cellaring until 2019. Tentative Score 89–91. **K**

YARDEN, CABERNET SAUVIGNON, 2006: Even better than at an earlier tasting. Full-bodied, with soft, gently mouth-coating tannins and sweet cedarwood integrating nicely. On the nose and palate ripe black and red berries and currants on a background of spicy oak, all touched with hints of spices, vanilla and light mineral-earthy overtones. Drink now–2018. Score 92. **K**

YARDEN, CABERNET SAUVIGNON, 2005: Brooding dark ruby red, full-bodied, with near-sweet tannins and spicy oak wrapped around blackcurrants, berries, spices and a hint of dark chocolate. Look as well for enchanting hints of citrus peel and vanilla on the long finish. Fine balance and structure bode well for the future. Drink now–2018. Score 92. **K**

YARDEN, CABERNET SAUVIGNON, ELROM VINEYARD, 2004: Full-bodied, with still-firm tannins and spicy wood well on the way to integrating and already showing elegance and finesse. Look for layer after layer of currant, blackberry and wild berry fruits, those supported beautifully by notes of cedar, sage and tar, all leading to a near-sweet fruity finish that lingers on and on. Drink now–2018. Score 94. **K**

YARDEN, CABERNET SAUVIGNON, 2004: Dark, almost impenetrable garnet, with generous wood in fine balance with acidity and fruits. Opens to show currants and crushed berries, those yielding to cranberries, ripe purple plums and dark chocolate, all on a background of spices, asphalt and earthiness. Drink now–2016. Score 92. **K**

YARDEN, CABERNET SAUVIGNON, ELROM VINEYARD, 2003: Intensely dark ruby toward royal purple, full-bodied, with caressing tannins and a moderate oak influence. Opens with blackcurrants, blackberries and minerals, goes to meaty, earthy and herbal aromas and flavors, and then to spices and a long and elegant fruity finish. Firmly structured with excellent grip and complexity. Drink now–2020. Score 95. **K**

YARDEN, CABERNET SAUVIGNON, 2003: Aged in French oak for 18 months and showing generous but gentle wood influence. Soft mouth-coating tannins support generous blackberry, black cherry and plum fruits, and on the long finish, hints of Oriental spices and a light herbal-tobacco sensation. Drink now–2014. Score 93. **K**

YARDEN, CABERNET SAUVIGNON, 2002: Dark garnet, full-bodied, with once firm tannins and spicy oak now settled in nicely and opening to show aromas of red currants, black cherries and berries on first attack, those giving way to layers of sweet cedar, vanilla, leather, and on the long finish, hints of Mediterranean herbs. Rich, generous and elegant. Drink now–2012. Score 92. **K**

YARDEN, CABERNET SAUVIGNON, ELROM VINEYARD, 2001: Dark, almost impenetrable garnet-purple, full-bodied, with finely tuned balance between generous well-integrated tannins and judicious oak, this exquisite wine shows complex tiers of aromas and flavors of red currants, berries and spices on the first attack, those opening to include light earthy and herbal overlays. Plush and opulent, with a long, complex finish. Among the best ever made in Israel. Drink now–2013. Score 95. **K**

YARDEN, CABERNET SAUVIGNON, 2001: Full-bodied with finely tuned balance between wood, tannins and fruits. Showing plum, wild berry and spicy currant fruits, and reflecting its 18 months in oak with appealing overlays of vanilla, cedar, tobacco and cocoa. Drink now–2013. Score 91. **K**

YARDEN, CABERNET SAUVIGNON, 2000: Full-bodied, still youthful, with firm tannins and generous oak well balanced by currants, blackberries and spicy cedarwood, those opening to plums and black cherries, all matched nicely with vanilla and an appealing herbal overlay followed by a long finish. Drink now–2011. Score 92. **K**

YARDEN, CABERNET SAUVIGNON, 1999: With once firm tannins now softened, showing fine balance between wood and fruits, opens beautifully on the palate. Deep royal purple toward garnet in color, with delicious aromas and flavors of black berries and cherries on a background of vanilla and sweet cedarwood, as well as a hint of freshly roasted coffee on its long finish. Drink now–2011. Score 92. **K**

YARDEN, CABERNET SAUVIGNON, 1998: Full-bodied, deep in color and intense, with aromas and flavors of currant, plum, black cherry, vanilla and lightly toasted oak. Finely tuned balance between fruits, wood and tannins. On the long finish, mineral-earthy overtones and an appealing hint of anise. Developing beautifully. Drink now. Score 91. **K**

YARDEN, CABERNET SAUVIGNON, 1997: This traditional Yarden blend of 94% Cabernet Sauvignon, 5% Merlot and 1% Cabernet Franc is now fully mature but continues to show an overall firm structure and good balance between soft tannins, fruits, wood and acidity. Plenty of Cabernet currants along with blackberries and plums on the first attack, those yielding to gentle overlays of spices and Mediterranean herbs. Not for further cellaring. Drink now. Score 89. **K**

YARDEN, CABERNET SAUVIGNON, 1996: A dark-garnet blend of 98% Cabernet Sauvignon and 2% Cabernet Franc, this concentrated and intense medium- to full-bodied wine with sweet tannins is now showing plum, currant and cherry fruits, those complemented nicely by vanilla and anise on the mid-palate, and appealing herbal sensations on the finish. Drinking very nicely. Drink now. Score 91. **K**

YARDEN, CABERNET SAUVIGNON, 1995: The wine needs time to open in the glass, but doing so it reveals luscious layers of aromas and flavors of blackcurrants, plums, tobacco and vanilla. Full-bodied, with concentrated but well-integrated tannins, and a hint of raspberries on the long finish. Still delicious but now fully mature and not for further cellaring. Drink up. Score 92. **K**

YARDEN, CABERNET SAUVIGNON, 1994: As 1994 was not a great vintage year in Israel, this wine never attained the heights of the best of this series. Medium-bodied, it shows flavors of stewed prunes, black fruits and floral-earthy overtones. Fully mature, drinking well but not for further cellaring. Drink up. Score 87. **K**

YARDEN, CABERNET SAUVIGNON, 1993: No surprises here, this now 16-year-old wine still drinking beautifully. Dark royal purple, full-bodied, concentrated and powerful wine, showing graceful maturity having attained enviable levels of roundness, depth and complexity along with impeccable balance and an elegant bouquet. Silky tannins that give the wine just the right bite, flavors that unfold comfortably on the palate. Drink now–2011. Score 94. **K**

YARDEN, MERLOT, KELA (SHA'AL) VINEYARD, 2008: Full-bodied, concentrated and well-focused, showing layer after layer of blackberries, plums, espresso coffee and fresh sage and roasted herbs. Give this one time and it will show hints of leather. An intense wine but with the potential for elegance. Best 2012–2018, perhaps longer. Tentative Score 92–94. **K**

YARDEN, MERLOT, 2007: The most full-bodied Yarden Merlot in recent years, with gripping but velvety smooth tannins and toasty oak. On first attack ripe raspberries and currants, those making way for light herbal and earthy notes and finally plums and Oriental spices, all culminating in a long, mineral-rich finish. Drink from release–2016. Score 91. **K**

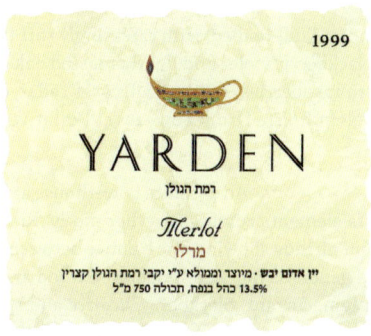

YARDEN, MERLOT, ODEM ORGANIC VINEYARD, 2007: Dark garnet, full-bodied, with silky tannins and gentle spicy wood influences. Opens to reveal a generous array of ripe red currants, black cherries, mocha and spices, with the tannins rising on the finish. Opulent and bold. Drink from release–2016, perhaps longer. Tentative Score 91–93. **K**

YARDEN, MERLOT, 2006: Showing much as at barrel tastings. Almost impenetrably dark garnet, medium- to full-bodied, with soft, gently mouth-coating tannins and opening to show blackberry and raspberry fruits, those supported nicely by notes of minerals and licorice. As this continues to develop look as well for notes of cigar tobacco. Drink from release–2013. Score 90. **K**

YARDEN, MERLOT, ODEM ORGANIC VINEYARD, 2006: Made from organically raised grapes. Deep, dark and mysterious, as the wine is still in its prenatal state, but already showing sweet, smoky and spicy oak well matched by mouth-coating tannins. Opens to reveal sweet black cherries, those followed by blackberries and currants and hints of Mediterranean herbs. Drink now–2015. Score 91. **K**

YARDEN, MERLOT, KELA (SHA'AL) VINEYARD, 2006: Dark garnet toward royal purple, full-bodied, with gently gripping tannins and an appealing underlying note of spicy and vanilla rich oak that plays throughout and yields nicely to an array of wild berry, cassis, bitter citrus peel, and, on the long finish, a note of milk chocolate. Best 2011–2016. Score 91. **K**

YARDEN, MERLOT, 2005: Medium- to full-bodied, with spicy wood and firm mouth-coating tannins in fine balance with fruits. On the nose and palate ripe purple plums and blackcurrants with overlays of smoke and roasted Mediterranean herbs. Long and elegant. Drink from release–2014. Score 91. **K**

YARDEN, MERLOT, TEL PHARES VINEYARD, 2005: Fully faithful to earlier tasting notes. Full-bodied, with caressingly soft tannins and an abundance of blackberry, violet and lightly toasted oak on first attack, those opening to raspberries, mocha and sweet cedar, all building to a long and succulent finish. Drink now–2014. Tentative Score 91. **K**

YARDEN, MERLOT, KELA VINEYARD (FORMERLY KNOWN AS SHA'AL VINEYARD), 2005: An absolute powerhouse at barrel tastings but now with its elements coming together nicely. Rich, intense and concentrated, but already showing fine balance between firm but yielding tannins and generous but well-moderated wood and bold aromas and flavors of plum, currant, blackberry, licorice and spices, all rising to a long tannic and mineral-rich finish. Best 2011–2017. Score 92. **K**

YARDEN, MERLOT, 2004: Dark garnet toward purple, medium- to full-bodied, with tannins and spicy wood now integrated nicely and showing a generous array of berry, cassis and plum fruits, those supported by minerals, sweet cedarwood and, rising on the medium-long finish, an overlay of spices and tobacco. Drink now–2012. Score 90. **K**

YARDEN, MERLOT, ORTAL VINEYARD, 2004: Showing as splendidly as ever! Dark garnet toward inky black, full-bodied, with once firm tannins and generous spicy wood integrating nicely now. Opens to reveal a tempting array of blackberry, raspberry, plum and cassis fruits, those supported nicely by hints of smoky cedarwood and chocolate, all leading to a gently spicy and notably long finish. Simultaneously complex, concentrated and elegant. Drink now–2018. Score 93. **K**

YARDEN, MERLOT, 2003: Dark garnet, full-bodied and with generous tannins, a well-polished wine showing a generous array of cherry, currant and berry fruits, those supported nicely by layers of Mediterranean herbs, vanilla and a gentle hand with smoky oak. On the long finish a tantalizing hint of green olives tiptoes in nicely. Drink now–2014. Score 91. **K**

YARDEN, MERLOT, 2002: Dark garnet, with once firm tannins well integrated with now gently spicy wood. Showing plum and berry fruits on herbal, citrus peel and white chocolate notes. Still drinking nicely, showing deep and concentrated but with first clear signs of aging. Not for further cellaring. Drink up. Score 88. K

YARDEN, MERLOT, 2001: Dark, almost inky purple in color, continuing to show the generous spicy wood that it did in its youth but with the tannins now soft and well integrated. On the nose and palate ripe plums and blackberries complemented by chocolate, spices and vanilla. On the long finish, a hint of earthiness that is on the rise. Not for further cellaring. Drink now. Score 89. K

YARDEN, MERLOT, ORTAL VINEYARD, 2001: My most recent tasting note holds firmly. Deeply aromatic, reflecting its 14 months in mostly new French barrels with generous spicy oak, that in harmony with ample but seamless tannins, all coming together in a dense but plush and luxurious wine. Full-bodied, showing appealing aromas and flavors that open in layer after layer, those including blackberries, near-jammy plums, chocolate, fresh herbs, and on the long finish, a rising hint of Oriental spices all with a light herbal bitterness, that offset comfortably by a hint of orange peel. Drink now–2014. Score 94. K

YARDEN, SYRAH, ORTAL VINEYARD, 2008: Not so much an infant as it remains in embryonic form, but one need have no fear of this wine, which is already showing its potential for future development. With firm tannins just starting to settle in, opens slowly in the glass at this stage to reveal richness, intensity and depth of flavor, opening with blackberry and currant fruits, moving on to plums and wild berries and then opening to reveal minerals, spices, *garrigue* and sage, all coming to a long and firmly tannic finish. Best 2012–2020. Tentative Score 92–94. K

YARDEN, SYRAH, TEL PHARES VINEYARD, 2007: Still in its infancy but already showing fine balance and structure. Still tight, gripping and intense tannins but those settling in nicely with creamy and spicy oak. With fine balance, opens even now to reveal blackberry, blueberry and red currant fruits, those on a background of generously peppered smoked meat and roasted herbs. Give this one time and it will show notes of saddle leather and mocha. Drink from release–2018. Tentative Score 91–93. **K**

YARDEN, SYRAH, TEL PHARES VINEYARD, 2006: Showing even better than at barrel tastings. Full-bodied with now silky tannins and spicy wood integrating nicely. Opens to reveal a complex array of plum, currant and berry fruits, those supported nicely by notes of earthy minerals, and generously peppered game meat with tannins and fruits rising comfortably on the long, round finish. Drink from release–2016. Score 91. **K**

YARDEN, SYRAH, 2005: Showing much as at barrel tastings. Garnet toward inky-black, full-bodied, with spicy oak and generous soft tannins, showing fine structure and balance and happily avoiding being a blockbuster in favor of elegance. Opens with raspberry and red currant notes, those going on to show generous hints of black pepper, anise and wild berries all coming to a long and generous chocolate and smoky finish. Drink from release–2014. Score 91. **K**

YARDEN, SYRAH, ORTAL VINEYARD, 2004: Perhaps the best Syrah ever in Israel. Extraordinarily deep ruby, full-bodied, with near-sweet tannins integrating nicely with spicy wood. Opens with a burst of almost jammy raspberries and kirsch liqueur, those yielding to blackberry, cherry and plum fruits. In the background generous hints of anise and Oriental spices and a hint of freshly tanned leather. Drink now–2018. Score 94. **K**

YARDEN, SYRAH, 2004: Medium-dark ruby toward garnet, with firm tannins and spicy oak integrating nicely. Shows a generous array of near-jammy raspberries, blackberries, black cherries and plums, those supported nicely by hints of spices, herbs and a hint of polished leather. Drink now–2013. Score 90. **K**

YARDEN, SYRAH, 2003: Dark garnet in color, with soft, mouth-coating tannins and an appealing overlay of spicy wood reflecting its 18 months in oak. Opens with blackberry, purple plums and chocolate notes, those yielding to near-jammy raspberries, hints of earthy minerals and a note of peach pit. Long and generous with hints of spring flowers on the long finish. Drink now–2013. Score 92. **K**

YARDEN, PINOT NOIR, MAROM GALIL VINEYARD, 2008: Deeply aromatic, a lighter than usual style Pinot from Yarden, showing red berries, cherries, sage and minerals. Medium-bodied, with light tannins that linger nicely through and lead to a long persistent finish. Drink from release–2016. Tentative Score 89–91. **K**

YARDEN, PINOT NOIR, EIN ZIVAN VINEYARD, 2008: Full-bodied, ripe black cherries, plums and spices, and picking up a mineral edge on a long finish. Ripe, pure and fleshy. Drink from release–2016. Tentative Score 90–92. **K**

YARDEN, PINOT NOIR, 2007: Medium- to full-bodied, with gently mouth-coating tannins, a supple, fragrant and graceful wine. On the nose and palate near-jammy blackberry and blackcurrant fruits on a background of white pepper, and, on the moderately long finish, hints of sandalwood and black cherries. Drink from release–2013. Score 90. **K**

YARDEN, PINOT NOIR, 2006: Intense ruby toward garnet, medium- to full-bodied, with well-focused cherry fruits at the core, those opening to reveal plums, dark chocolate and espresso coffee, all leading to a long blackberry-rich finish. Generous, balanced and long, with wood and tannins nicely integrated. Drink now–2013. Score 90. **K**

YARDEN, PINOT NOIR, 2005: Dark ruby, full-bodied enough to be thought of as fleshy, and with spicy wood and gentle tannins in fine balance with acidity and fruits. Opens with near-sweet, liqueur-like berry aromas and flavors, those yielding in the glass to reveal a crisply dry wine on which you will feel hints of kirsch, dark chocolate and lightly smoked meat, all climaxing in a long and generous blackberry finish. Drink now–2013. Score 93. **K**

YARDEN, PINOT NOIR, 2004: Super-dark garnet, medium- to full-bodied, with firm but well-integrated tannins and showing a generous array of blackberry, plum and black cherry fruits, those supported very nicely by hints of pine nuts. On the fruity finish tantalizing hints of earthiness and anise. Drink now–2012. Score 90. **K**

YARDEN, PINOT NOIR, 2003: Garnet-red, medium- to full-bodied, with soft, mouth-coating tannins and a moderate hand with spicy oak. On the nose and palate, forward but elegant black cherry, blackberry and cassis fruits supported nicely by hints of lightly spicy floral and earthy notes. Drink now–2011. Score 90. **K**

YARDEN, NEBBIOLO, 2008: Still in its infancy but already showing full-bodied, with still gripping, almost chunky lip-sealing tannins, but showing fine balance and structure that bode well for the future. On first attack purple plums, those yielding to blackberries and earthy minerals, and, on the long finish, notes of prunes and what seems at one moment licorice and at the next dark chocolate. Possibly a varietal release, possibly for use as a blending agent. Tentative Score 89–91. **K**

YARDEN, NEBBIOLO, 2006: Developing nicely. Smooth and supple, with licorice, tar and plums on the nose, those yielding to blackberries, strawberries and freshly picked porcini mushrooms. Complex for a young-vine wine and surprises now with a generous note on the long chewy finish. Possibly a varietal release; possibly destined as a blending agent. Tentative Score 88–90. **K**

YARDEN, MOUNT HERMON RED, 2008: Dark ruby toward garnet, medium-bodied with soft tannins, this blend of Merlot, Cabernet Sauvignon, Cabernet Franc, Malbec and Petit Verdot shows forward cherry, berry and cassis fruits. A very pleasant, easy-to-drink wine, well suited to Italian and Mediterranean dishes. Drink now–2011. Score 87. **K**

YARDEN, MOUNT HERMON RED, 2007: Dark cherry toward garnet, medium-bodied, with already well-integrated soft tannins. A blend of Merlot, Cabernet Sauvignon, Cabernet Franc, Malbec and Petite Sirah, opening nicely on the palate to show raspberry, currant and cassis fruits. Not complex but soft, round and generous, the best of this series in quite a few years. A good bet for everyday drinking. Drink now. Score 87. **K**

YARDEN, CHARDONNAY, 2007: Medium-dark gold in color, full-bodied, with vanilla-rich wood on first attack but that integrating nicely in the glass to show a lively and complex wine. On the nose and palate melon, figs and ripe peaches, all coming together as a complex but most refreshing whole. Long and mouth-filling. Drink from release–2012. Score 90. **K**

YARDEN, CHARDONNAY, ODEM ORGANIC VINEYARD, 2007: Full-bodied, deep golden with a distinct tint of orange that plays in the glass, a wine reflecting generous wood but that in fine proportion to acidity and fruits. Opens with pears, grilled nuts and pie crust notes, those going on to show ripe fig, pineapple and baked apple aromas and flavors. Long and creamy with the oak rising on the finish. Elegance on a grand scale. Meant for cellaring, approachable on release, but best 2011–2016. Score 92. **K**

YARDEN, CHARDONNAY, ODEM ORGANIC VINEYARD, 2006: Full-bodied, opening with subtle aromas of figs, pears and apples, going on to show a generous dash of smoky, toasty oak and then blossoming forth with pineapple, citrus peel and minerals leading to a long finish that is simultaneously creamy and bright. Drink now–2013. Score 92. **K**

YARDEN, CHARDONNAY, 2006: Lightly golden in color, with ripe apple, citrus and spices, opening to a touch of charred oak. Medium-bodied, but light, crisp and rich on the palate and showing fine balance along with a long and lively finish. Drink now. Score 89. **K**

YARDEN, CHARDONNAY, ODEM ORGANIC VINEYARD, 2005: Full-bodied, opening with floral and citrus, those going on to tropical fruits and figs, all set off by hints of smoky oak, ginger and, on the long finish, ripe pears. Drink now–2012. Score 91. **K**

YARDEN, CHARDONNAY, 2005: Oak-aged for seven months, full-bodied, bright gold in color, with nutty, floral and woody notes highlighting ripe tropical fruits, pears and citrus. On the background a nice hint of white pepper, all leading to a long finish. Drink now. Score 89. **K**

YARDEN, CHARDONNAY, ODEM ORGANIC VINEYARD, 2004: With its once generous oak now subdued, rich and complex, full-bodied and creamy, with pears, ripe apricots, citrus and mango fruits backed up by light spicy and mineral overtones. Drink now. Score 91. **K**

YARDEN, CHARDONNAY, ODEM ORGANIC VINEYARD, 2003: Lightly burnished gold in color, rich and elegant, with ripe pear, honeysuckle and melon flavors coming together beautifully with generous oak, minerals and nutmeg. On the long finish a hint of hazelnuts. Drink up. Score 90. **K**

YARDEN, CHARDONNAY, 2003: Showing medium- to full-bodied, with a complex array of apricot, pear and fig fruits on first attack, those yielding comfortably to citrus, pineapple, minerals and spicy oak. Showing signs of age. Drink up. Score 89. **K**

YARDEN, CHARDONNAY, ODEM ORGANIC VINEYARD, 2002: Continues to show its buttery-oak pattern. Maturing gracefully and showing a bright golden straw color. Ripe and complex flavors of pears, tropical fruits, hazelnuts and spices opening on the palate to reveal flinty and floral overtones along with generous but well-integrated oak and a long, vanilla-cream finish. Drink up. Score 92. **K**

YARDEN, SAUVIGNON BLANC, 2008: Light golden straw in color, light- to medium-bodied, a crisply refreshing wine with just enough complexity to catch our attention. On the nose and palate generous green apple, lime and grapefruit, those complemented nicely by hints of pine needles and freshly cut grass, all lingering nicely on the finish. Drink now–2011. Score 89. **K**

YARDEN, SAUVIGNON BLANC, 2006: Medium-bodied, light golden straw in color, with grapefruit, yellow plum, apricot and floral aromas and flavors. Lively, dry and pleasant, with a hint of pineapple arising on the finish. Drink now. Score 88. **K**

YARDEN, SAUVIGNON BLANC, 2005: Well balanced and aromatic, with a personality bursting with spices, herbs and peppery wood, those matched nicely by pear, apple, melon and mineral aromas and flavors. Drink now. Score 89. **K**

YARDEN, SAUVIGNON BLANC, 2004: Light straw in color, medium-bodied, with straightforward aromas and flavors of lemon, lime, and ripe peaches. Marred somewhat by unwanted hints of bitterness and earthiness that develop on the palate. Drink up. Score 85. **K**

YARDEN, VIOGNIER, 2008: True to the varietal traits and showing a light floral nose, and then notes of spicy wood, tropical and summer fruits, those including pineapple, guava and peaches. Rich, ripe and lush, with a long, simultaneously refreshing and complex finish. Drink from release–2013. Score 92. **K**

YARDEN, VIOGNIER, 2007: Medium-bodied, showing a bare and tantalizing hint of spicy oak, opens with citrus and light herbal and peach blossom notes, those going on to litchis, pears and papaya, all coming in nicely and showing an appealing creamy note on the finish. Drink now. Score 88. **K**

YARDEN, VIOGNIER, 2006: Shows a thoroughly traditional Viognier personality. Following an aromatic and floral nose, flavors and aromas of ripe Anjou pears, peaches, spring flowers and minerals along with hints of citrus. Lively, clean, fresh and long. Drink now. Score 91. **K**

YARDEN, VIOGNIER, 2005: Aged partly in *barriques*, partly in stainless steel and reflecting a gentle hand with spicy wood. Lively gold in color, full-bodied, with nectarines, peaches, kiwis and hints of citrus that play nicely on the palate together with aromas and flavors of spring flowers. Drink up. Score 90. **K**

YARDEN, GEWURZTRAMINER, 2008: The color of freshly dampened straw, showing medium-bodied with traditional Gewurztraminer spices, litchis and floral notes. In the background, ripe peaches and a note of citrus peel, and finishing with notes of rose petals and minerals. Even though categorized as off-dry, there is but a bare hint of sweetness here, that tantalizing and refreshing. Drink now–2011. Score 90. **K**

YARDEN, GEWURZTRAMINER, 2007: Golden straw in color, off-dry, medium-bodied, with appealing spicy and floral notes running through, those including white pepper, anise and cinnamon. A lovely wine with tempting summer and litchi fruits. On the long finish, hints of rose petals and grapefruit peel. Drink now. Score 89. **K**

YARDEN, GEWURZTRAMINER, 2006: A medium-dry, medium-bodied white with just enough acidity to keep it lively. Floral and spicy aromas and flavors matched nicely by apricot, grapefruit and litchi fruits, all highlighted by an appealing hint of petrol. Drink now. Score 88. **K**

YARDEN, MOUNT HERMON WHITE, 2008: A pleasant enough entry-level wine, with peach, citrus and pineapple fruits. Drink now. Score 84. **K**

YARDEN, MOUNT HERMON WHITE, 2007: Nothing complex here, but appealing summer fruits and pineapple to make a good entry-level wine. Drink up. Score 84. **K**

YARDEN, NOBLE SEMILLON, BOTRYTIS, 2004: Golden in color, with fine concentration and balance, and developing deep honeyed botrytis-impacted spices and funkiness. On the nose and palate dried apricots, orange peel, toasty oak, and tropical fruits that come in toward the long, caressing finish. Drink now–2018. Score 92. **K**

YARDEN, NOBLE SEMILLON, BOTRYTIS, 2003: Deep and rich, with a concentrated personality of citrus peel, honeyed peaches, botrytis spice. Generously sweet, with fine balancing acidity and a long, sweet and caressing finish on which tropical fruits and butterscotch arise. Drink now–2015. Score 91. **K**

YARDEN, NOBLE SEMILLON, BOTRYTIS, 2002: Golden toward subdued orange in color, medium- to full-bodied and showing generous botrytis influence. Honeyed sweetness complemented nicely by aromas and flavors of orange peel and apricots. Soft, round and creamy on the palate, with good balancing acidity and hints of heather and white pepper on the moderately long finish. Drink now–2015. Score 90. **K**

YARDEN, NOBLE SEMILLON, BOTRYTIS, 2001: This lively, golden, medium-bodied dessert white offers up unabashed honeyed sweetness along with aromas and flavors of orange marmalade, pineapple and ripe apricots that meld comfortably into a soft, almost creamy texture. Plenty of balancing natural acidity and a medium-long finish boasting hints of spring flowers and spices. Promises to darken and attain greater complexity and depth in the future. Drink now–2012. Score 90. **K**

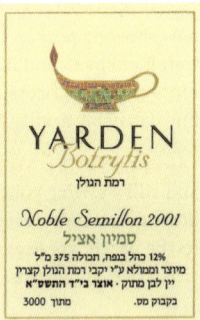

YARDEN, HEIGHTSWINE, 2006: This dessert wine is made entirely from Gewurztraminer grapes treated to sub-freezing temperatures at the winery. Showing varietal typicity with litchis, apricots and tropical fruits, all on a spicy background. Now starting to develop the floral and honeyed characteristics of an ice wine. Drink now–2012. Score 90. **K**

YARDEN, HEIGHTSWINE, 2005: Made entirely from Gewurztraminer grapes frozen at the winery. Pale gold in color, with a complex nose and palate that offers up pineapple, citrus, litchi, orange peel and floral aromas and flavors, those with a light hint of sea water that adds to the wine's charm and complexity. Drink now–2012. Score 91. **K**

YARDEN, HEIGHTSWINE, 2004: Generous sweetness set off by lively acidity. Elegant and rich, deep gold with a bronze overlay, with apricots, peaches and spices on the nose and palate set to a honeyed and floral background. Drink now. Score 90. **K**

YARDEN, HEIGHTSWINE, 2003: A tantalizing dessert wine, light- to medium-bodied with delicate honeyed apricot and peach aromas and flavors, good balancing acidity and an elegant, lingering finish. Drink now. Score 90. **K**

YARDEN, HEIGHTSWINE, 2002: Light gold in color, medium-bodied, with excellent balance. Plenty of natural acidity to back up the sweetness and keep it lively while allowing the peach, apricot and quince fruits to make themselves nicely felt. Honeyed and floral, generous and round. Drink now. Score 90. **K**

YARDEN, HEIGHTSWINE, 2001: Well balanced, generous and elegant, this honeyed dessert wine has a lively golden color and offers up a generous array of yellow peaches, apricots, melon, orange marmalade and quince, all on a floral and just-spicy-enough background. Drink now. Score 91. **K**

YARDEN, HEIGHTSWINE, 2000: A deliciously honeyed dessert wine, now showing pear and quince fruits together with traditional Gewurztraminer spices and litchis. As the wine develops in the glass look for hints of ripe apricots and white peaches. Generously sweet but with fine balancing acidity to keep it lively. Drink now. Score 92. **K**

YARDEN, HEIGHTSWINE, 1999: The first ice wine made by the winery and still showing youth and grace. Sweet, with generous mineral and floral overtones, now showing lightly honeyed tones and in addition to the peach, apple and tropical fruits of its youth appealing hints of citrus peel and litchis. Drink up. Score 89. **K**

YARDEN, MUSCAT DESSERT WINE, 2006: With a light brandy reinforcement, a light- to medium-bodied, generously sweet wine with good balancing acidity and showing dried summer fruits with a gentle honeyed touch. Somewhat one-dimensional. Drink now. Score 86. **K**

YARDEN, MUSCAT DESSERT WINE, 2005: Light straw in color, this medium-bodied, brandy-reinforced wine shows appealing dried apricot and peach fruits, those with a citrus honey overlay and finely balanced acidity to keep the wine lively. Drink up. Score 88. **K**

YARDEN, SPARKLING ROSÉ, 2008: A sparkling rosé made in the Champenoise method. A blend of 70% Chardonnay and 30% Pinot Noir, at this early stage showing dark pink and medium- to full-bodied. Brut in its level of dryness, displaying a complex set of aromas and flavors, those including citrus, blueberries, raspberries, dough and flowers on a light mineral background. Don't count on seeing this on the market for 4–5 years, and by then it will have lightened somewhat in color, will have maintained its freshness and fruits, but will show somewhat more dense and creamy. I'd even be willing to wager that this one will offer up a hint of walnuts on its finish as it continues to develop. Long, sophisticated and elegant. Drink from release. Score 91. **K**

YARDEN, BLANC DE BLANCS, 2001: The best Blanc de Blancs to date from the winery. Made from Chardonnay grapes by the traditional *methode Champenoise*, this medium-bodied sparkling wine shows just the right balance between yeasty sourdough bread, peaches, citrus and minerals. With a generous mousse and sharp, well-focused bubbles that go on and on, this crisp and sophisticated wine goes on to a long, mouth-filling finish. Drink now–2012. Score 92. **K**

YARDEN, BLANC DE BLANCS, 2000: A tempting sparkling wine showing appealing summer fruits, citrus and kiwis, those on a background of minerals and just a hint of yeast. A somewhat short mousse but sharp bubbles that linger nicely. Drink now. Score 89. **K**

YARDEN, BLANC DE BLANCS, 1999: Made by the traditional *methode Champenoise*, just yeasty enough to enchant, with rich citrus, peach and nectarine fruits and hints of spring flowers. Mineral-rich crispness, sharp, well-focused bubbles, a long mousse and a long and tempting near-creamy finish. Drink now. Score 90. **K**

YARDEN, BLANC DE BLANCS, 1998: Ripe and vibrant with crisp apple and citrus aromas and flavors along with hints of vanilla, toasted white bread and nuts. The mousse is somewhat short, but the bubbles are long-lasting and the nutty-grapefruit finish lingers nicely. Fully mature. Drink up. Score 90. **K**

Gamla

GAMLA, CABERNET SAUVIGNON, 2007: Reflecting light smoky wood and vanilla notes from the oak in which it aged, a soft, round and simultaneously spicy wine opening to show currants, purple plums and blackberry fruits. Just enough complexity to enchant. Drink now–2012. Score 88. **K**

GAMLA, CABERNET SAUVIGNON, 2006: Oak-aged for 12 months, medium-bodied, with soft tannins and light notes of spicy wood integrated nicely to show black cherry and blackberry fruits on a background that hints of freshly roasted coffee. Drink now–2012. Score 88. **K**

GAMLA, CABERNET SAUVIGNON, 2005: Medium- to full-bodied, dark garnet, a traditional Bordeaux blend showing soft, gently mouth-coating tannins and opening to reveal blackcurrant, wild berry and light Mediterranean herbal notes. Fine balance between oak, tannins, acidity and fruit and a generous, just-spicy-enough finish. Drink now. Score 88. **K**

GAMLA, CABERNET SAUVIGNON, 2004: Oak-aged for 12 months, showing good balance between soft tannins, spicy oak and berry, cherry and currant fruits, those matched nicely by hints of white pepper and anise on the moderately long finish. Drink now. Score 89. **K**

GAMLA, MERLOT, 2005: Garnet-red, medium- to full-bodied, with silky tannins and showing an appealing array of berry, black cherry and cassis fruits on a lightly spicy background, and reflecting its development in *barriques* with light overlays of spices and white chocolate. Drink now–2011. Score 88. **K**

GAMLA, MERLOT, 2004: Reflecting 12 months in French oak with spices and fresh herbs. Medium- to full-bodied, this dark ruby-toward-garnet wine has soft, integrated tannins and appealing berry, black cherry and cassis fruits backed up by a light hint of espresso coffee that comes in on the finish. Round and generous. Drink now. Score 88. K

GAMLA, MERLOT, 2003: Deep garnet, medium- to full-bodied, with still-firm tannins but with balance and structure that bode well for the future. Generous berry, currant and plum fruits here, with overlays of sweet cedar, hints of milk chocolate and an appealing herbaceous overlay. Drink now. Score 89. K

GAMLA, PINOT NOIR, 2005: Ruby toward garnet, medium-bodied, with soft tannins integrating nicely and showing appealing hints of spicy and vanilla-rich wood. Opens to show blackberry, blueberry and black cherry fruits with a hint of lemon-cola on the finish. Round and easy to enjoy. Drink now. Score 88. K

GAMLA, PINOT NOIR, 2004: Cherry red, medium-bodied, lightly oaked with berry, black cherry and floral aromas. Soft, round tannins and good balancing acidity lead to a medium-long and generously fruity finish. Drink up. Score 87. K

GAMLA, SANGIOVESE, 2007: Dark ruby toward garnet, medium-bodied, with caressing tannins, a smooth, round wine with raspberry and blackberry aromas and flavors on a chocolate and mocha-scented background, all lasting through the long and easy-going finish. Drink from release–2012. Tentative Score 88–90. K

GAMLA, SANGIOVESE, 2006: Showing more developed but fully consistent with an earlier tasting. Aromas and flavors of raspberries, strawberries and cassis, those on a medium-bodied frame with soft tannins, and showing appealing hints of spicy oak and sawdust, all leading to a fresh finish. Drink from release. Score 87. K

GAMLA, SANGIOVESE, 2005: Medium- to full-bodied, with chewy but gentle tannins coming together to show an appealing array of berry, minted chocolate and spiced tea. Long and caressing. Drink now. Score 90. K

GAMLA, CHARDONNAY, 2008: Light, with melon and apple notes, but falls somewhat buttery and flat on the palate. Drink now. Score 84. K

GAMLA, CHARDONNAY, 2007: Light gold, light- to medium-bodied, with citrus, peach and melon fruits on a pleasing light mineral background. Crisp, clean and delightful. Drink now. Score 88. K

GAMLA, CHARDONNAY, 2006: Golden straw in color, with light hints of spicy wood highlighting peach, citrus and tropical fruits. Drink now. Score 87. K

GAMLA, SAUVIGNON BLANC, 2008: The color of damp straw, medium-bodied, with fine acidity, a lively wine showing appealing citrus, green apples and passion fruits on a lightly spicy background. Drink now or in the next year or so. Score 87. K

GAMLA, SAUVIGNON BLANC, 2007: Light straw colored, light- to medium-bodied, with generous acidity, showing traditional green apple, citrus and passion fruits. Plenty of spices and acidity to keep the wine lively. Drink now. Score 87. K

GAMLA, WHITE RIESLING, 2008: Light golden straw in color, showing appealing floral, ginger and white peach aromas and flavors, those on a near creamy and lightly oily background. Lingers nicely on the palate. Drink now. Score 87. K

GAMLA, WHITE RIESLING, 2007: Light gold in color, medium-bodied, with citrus fruits overlaid with ripe pear and peach flavors. A somewhat short finish but that with a very appealing mineral overlay. Drink now. Score 86. K

GAMLA, BRUT, N.V.: Made by the *methode Champenoise*, a light- to medium-bodied, light golden straw blend of 50% each Pinot Noir and Chardonnay. A generous mousse when poured, sharp long-lasting bubbles and clean aromas and flavors, opening with citrus and apples and going on to hints of cherries. With crisp acidity to keep it lively, a good but not overly complex bubbly. Score 88. K

Golan

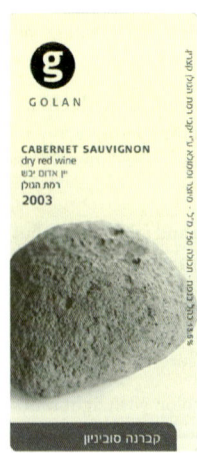

GOLAN, CABERNET SAUVIGNON, 2008: Soft and round, lightly tannic and showing blackberry and black cherry fruits, those supported comfortably by hints of black pepper and licorice. A good quaffing wine. Drink now. Score 86. K

GOLAN, CABERNET SAUVIGNON, 2007: With soft tannins and just a bare hint of vanilla from the American oak in which the wine developed for six months, showing wild berry and black cherry fruits on a lightly spicy background. Drink now. Score 86. K

GOLAN, CABERNET SAUVIGNON, 2006: Medium-bodied, with caressing tannins, a gentle hint of vanilla from the oak in which it developed for six months and appealing berry, currant and black cherry fruits. Round and generous, a good entry-level wine. Drink now. Score 86. **K**

GOLAN, CABERNET SAUVIGNON, 2005: Ruby toward garnet, medium-bodied, with soft tannins. Showing wild berry and blackcurrant fruits and reflecting its six months in American oak with light spiciness and vanilla. Soft, round and easy to drink. Drink up. Score 85. **K**

GOLAN, MERLOT, 2007: Lightly oak-aged, dark garnet toward royal purple, a medium-bodied, gently tannic wine with generous currant, berry and spicy notes. An easy-to-drink wine. Drink now. Score 87. **K**

GOLAN, MERLOT, 2006: Oak-aged for five months, dark garnet, medium-bodied and with soft tannins, a smooth and round wine with appealing wild berry, vanilla and light spicy notes. Not complex but a very pleasant quaffer. Score 86. **K**

GOLAN, GAMAY NOUVEAU, 2008: Made, as are the wines of Beaujolais, by the process of carbonic maceration and entirely from Gamay grapes, this super-young wine, released only weeks after the harvest, offers up a generous dose of raspberry, wild strawberry and grapey aromas and flavors. Dark black cherry toward purple, light, round, super-fruity and fun. Not to be taken with the least bit of seriousness but great fun to drink, especially when well chilled and consumed in large gulps. Drink up. Score 86. **K**

GOLAN, CHARDONNAY, 2007: Light gold in color, light, bright and refreshing, showing crisply dry with citrus and tropical fruits with an appealing flinty-mineral overlay. Drink now. Score 86. **K**

GOLAN, CHARDONNAY, 2006: Light straw in color, light- to medium-bodied, with clean, refreshing aromas and flavors of citrus, citrus peel, pineapples and minerals. As always, a good quaffer. Drink up. Score 85. **K**

GOLAN, MOSCATO, 2008: Made in the style of Moscato d'Asti entirely from Muscat Canelli grapes, with generous sweetness set off nicely by lively acidity and a light fizzy nature. Nothing complex here, but delightful aromas and flavors of wild flowers, green apples, peaches and passion fruit and minerals. Light- to medium-bodied, low in alcohol (6%) and remarkably refreshing, as good as an aperitif as a dessert wine with fruit-based pies, tarts and mousses. An ebullient wine to drink as well chilled as you would a Champagne. Drink now. Score 87. **K**

GOLAN, MOSCATO, 2007: Barely *frizzante* and not as successful as in previous years. Shows summer and tropical fruits but fails to satisfy because there is not nearly enough acidity to balance the more-than-generous sweetness. Drink up. Score 81. **K**

GOLAN, SION CREEK, WHITE, 2007: A semi-sweet blend of Sauvignon Blanc, Gewurztraminer, Riesling and Muscat. A few citrus and tropical fruits here, but lacking any kind of sophistication. Drink up. Score 79. **K**

Greenberg ✱✱✱

Located in Herzliya, not far from Tel Aviv, this micro-winery owned by Motti Greenberg is now producing about 2,000 bottles annually. First wines were released from the 2003 vintage, using Cabernet Sauvignon, Merlot and Shiraz grapes from the Karmei Yosef vineyards at the foothills of the Jerusalem Mountains.

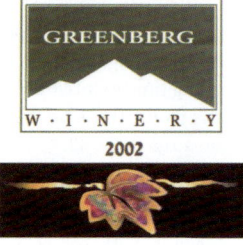

GREENBERG, CABERNET SAUVIGNON, 2006: Dark garnet toward royal purple, lithe and open-textured. Soft tannins and spicy wood integrating nicely to show currant and blackberry fruits, those with hints of espresso coffee and eucalyptus on the long finish. Drink now–2011. Score 88.

GREENBERG, CABERNET SAUVIGNON, 2005: Aged in oak for 12 months and racked four times before blending 85% Cabernet Sauvignon with 10% of Merlot and 5% Shiraz. Dark ruby toward garnet, medium- to full-bodied, with generous, soft tannins and light spicy wood opening to show blackcurrant, blackberry and spicy notes. On the finish a hint of eucalyptus. Drink now. Score 88.

GREENBERG, MERLOT, 2006: Dark, almost impenetrable garnet, a plush wine showing layers of raspberry, blackberry and fig aromas and flavors, those complemented by spices, minerals and a hint of lead pencil. Bodes for elegance. Drink now–2011. Score 89.

GREENBERG, MERLOT, 2005: Garnet toward royal purple, this medium- to full-bodied blend of 85% Merlot, 10% Cabernet Sauvignon and 5% Shiraz opens with generous, near-sweet tannins and spicy wood, those coming together nicely to show blackberry, black cherry and spicy aromas and flavors. Drink now. Score 87.

GREENBERG, SHIRAZ, 2006: Complex and supple, with layers of spices, wild berries, anise and leather, all coming together beautifully. A firm tannic grip here that carries through to the long finish. Drink now–2011. Score 91.

GREENBERG, SHIRAZ, 2005: Deep purple, with soft tannins and light spicy wood influences, this is a medium- to full-bodied blend of 85%

Shiraz, 10% Merlot and 5% Cabernet Sauvignon. On the nose and palate black fruits matched nicely by hints of saddle leather and earthiness. Generous and moderately long. Drink now. Score 89.

GREENBERG, ANIN, 2005: A blend of one-third each of Cabernet Sauvignon, Merlot and Shiraz, aged in oak separately for 12 months before blending. Medium- to full-bodied, dark garnet, with firm tannins needing time to integrate but already showing berry, black cherry and cassis fruits, those on a lightly earth and mineral background. Drink now–2012. Score 88.

GREENBERG, ANIN, 2004: A medium-bodied, dark garnet-toward-royal purple blend of 50% Merlot and 25% each Shiraz and Cabernet Sauvignon. Soft, well-integrated tannins highlight forward berry, black cherry and cassis aromas, those with an appealing spicy hint on the finish. Drink up. Score 87.

GREENBERG, APPOLONIA, 2005: A blend of 60% Shiraz and 20% each of Merlot and Cabernet Sauvignon, this medium- to full-bodied red opens with floral and tarry notes on the nose, those yielding in the glass to ample black fruits, spices and hints of cigar tobacco. Complex, generous and long. Drink now–2012. Score 89.

Gush Etzion ✦✦✦

Located at the Gush Etzion Junction near Jerusalem, the winery is owned largely by vintner Shraga Rozenberg and partly by the Tishbi family, and has its own vineyards in the Jerusalem Mountains providing Cabernet Sauvignon, Merlot, Pinot Noir, Shiraz, Cabernet Franc and Petit Verdot as well as Chardonnay, Viognier and Johannisberg Riesling grapes. First releases were in 1998 of 3,000 and the winery currently produces about 30,000 bottles annually. A new winery is now under construction with the potential for future production of up to 100,000 bottles.

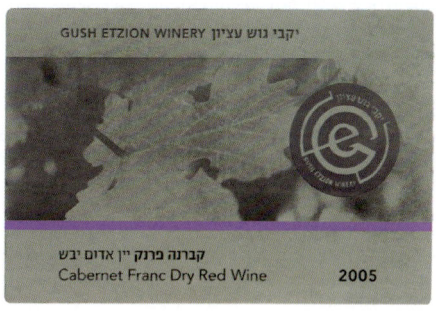

GUSH ETZION, NACHAL HAPIRIM, 2005: A medium- to full-bodied blend of Cabernet Sauvignon, Merlot, Cabernet Franc and Petit Verdot (60%, 25%, 10% and 5%, respectively). Reflecting oak-aging in new French oak for 12 months with lightly smoky cedar hints, showing soft tannins and opening to reveal currant and blackberry fruits, those on a light background of a fresh forest floor. Drink now. Score 87. **K**

GUSH ETZION, CABERNET SAUVIGNON, 2004: Garnet toward royal purple, medium- to full-bodied, with soft tannins and notes of smoke and vanilla from the *barriques* in which it aged. On the nose and palate an appealing array of blackcurrants, blackberries, dark chocolate and a note of licorice. Generous and mouth-filling. Drink now. Score 87. **K**

GUSH ETZION, CABERNET FRANC, 2005: Dark ruby toward garnet, medium- to full-bodied, with aromas and flavors of tar, bittersweet chocolate and spices overlaying blackberry and blackcurrant fruits. On the long finish, appealing hints of mint. Drink now–2011. Score 89. **K**

GUSH ETZION, CHARDONNAY, 2007: Light golden in color, medium-bodied, this unoaked white shows appealing citrus, peach and tropical fruits on a crisp mineral-rich background. Drink now. Score 86. **K**

GUSH ETZION, CHARDONNAY, ORGANIC VINEYARD, 2007: The color of damp straw, medium-bodied, showing lemon, pear and peach-pit aromas and flavors all with light hints of anise and earthy minerals. Drink now. Score 87. **K**

GUSH ETZION, SAUVIGNON BLANC, ORGANIC VINEYARD, 2007: Light straw with green tints, light- to medium-bodied, with refreshing lemon, peach and light earthy flavors and aromas. Crisp and clean, a good summertime quaffer. Drink now. Score 86. **K**

GUSH ETZION, CHARDONNAY, DESSERT WINE, 2006: The color of damp straw, reflecting its five months in oak with hints of spices that come together with not-at-all cloying sweetness. On the nose and palate appealing ripe peach and apricot fruits and vanilla. Drink now. Score 88. **K**

GUSH ETZION, CHARDONNAY, DESSERT WINE, ORGANIC VINE-YARD, 2006: Oak-aged for five months, golden toward apricot in color, medium- to full-bodied with moderate sweetness balanced by fresh acidity, and showing an appealing array of lightly honeyed tropical and summer fruits. Drink now. Score 87. **K**

Gustavo & Jo ★★★★

Located in the village of Kfar Vradim in the Western Galilee, and drawing on grapes from the Golan Heights and the Upper Galilee, this small winery was founded in 1995 by Gideon Boinjeau and produced only Cabernet Sauvignon wines until the release of a first white in 2005. Production of two series, Premium and Gustavo & Jo, averages 3,000 bottles annually.

Premium

PREMIUM, CABERNET SAUVIGNON, 2005: Full-bodied and aromatic with still gripping tannins and generous spicy wood needing time to settle down. Opens to reveal currant, blackberry, blueberry and chocolate-covered citrus peel, those yielding to notes of freshly hung tobacco. Long and generous. Drink now–2014. Score 91.

PREMIUM, CABERNET SAUVIGNON, 2004: Deep ruby toward garnet, medium- to full-bodied, with firm tannins that need time to integrate but already showing fine balance and structure. Aromas and flavors of blackberries, currants, near-sweet cedarwood and white pepper lead to a long tobacco and chocolate-rich finish. Drink now–2012. Score 91.

PREMIUM, CABERNET SAUVIGNON, 2003: Dark garnet toward black, full-bodied, with firm tannins integrating nicely, those well balanced by spicy wood and blackcurrant, blackberry and cassis fruits all on a background of minty chocolate. Long and complex. Drink now. Score 90.

PREMIUM, CABERNET SAUVIGNON, 2002: Deep garnet toward black, full-bodied, with still-firm but well-integrating tannins. Excellent balance between wood, tannins and an appealing array of black and red fruits, those yielding to spices, chocolate and mint. Long and complex but now maturing rapidly. Drink now. Score 90.

Gustavo & Jo

GUSTAVO & JO, CABERNET SAUVIGNON, 2005: Garnet toward royal purple, full-bodied with soft tannins and spicy oak. Showing a rich array of blackcurrant, blackberry and raspberry fruits on a background of spices and licorice. Drink now–2012. Score 90.

GUSTAVO & JO, CABERNET SAUVIGNON, UNFILTERED, INBAR, 2005: Inky-dark garnet in color, full-bodied, with fine balance between gently gripping tannins and spicy oak. On the nose and palate generous black fruits, those supported nicely by notes of bitter orange peel and spices. Long and generous. Drink now–2012. Score 91.

GUSTAVO & JO, CABERNET SAUVIGNON, 2004: Medium-dark garnet in color, with grapes primarily from the Upper Galilee, this spicy, generously oaked and tannic wine shows fine balance and structure and appealing black fruits. Hints of licorice and green olives come together nicely on a long and mouth-filling finish. Drink now–2012. Score 90.

GUSTAVO & JO, CABERNET SAUVIGNON, 2003: Dark garnet toward black, full-bodied, with still-firm tannins well balanced by spicy wood and blackcurrant, blackberry and cassis fruits all on a background of minty chocolate. Long and complex. Drink now. Score 89.

Gvaot ✳✳✳

Founded by Shivi Drori and Amnon Weiss on Shiloh in the Shomron region, with vineyards at an altitude of 700–900 meters above sea level, this boutique winery released its first wines from the 2005 vintage. Production in 2005 was for 5,000 bottles and current production is about 12,000 bottles annually, those of Cabernet Sauvignon, Merlot, Cabernet Franc and Chardonnay grapes. The winery is currently releasing wines in three series, Gofna Reserve, Masada and Herodion.

Gofna Reserve

GOFNA RESERVE, CABERNET SAUVIGNON, SINGLE VINEYARD, HAR'EL, 2007: New World Cabernet, full-bodied, with caressing tannins and forward blackberry and blackcurrant fruits, those supported by generous hints of spices and sweet Mediterranean herbs, all leading to a dark chocolate and tobacco finish. Drink now–2013. Tentative Score 89. K

GOFNA RESERVE, CABERNET SAUVIGNON, 2005: Generous spicy wood here after 24 months' development in French oak, but showing smooth and round. Almost inky-dark garnet in color, full-bodied, with concentrated black cherry and blackberry fruits. The tannins rise from mid-palate on and lead to a long and intense finish. Drink now. Score 87. K

GOFNA RESERVE, MERLOT, 2007: Medium- to full-bodied, opening with an enchanting sawdust and vanilla nose and then revealing currant and cherry fruits on an earthy and spicy background. A distinctive personality that needs time to soften. As this develops look for blueberry and chocolate notes. Drink now–2011. Score 89. K

GOFNA RESERVE, MERLOT, 2006: Dark garnet toward royal purple, medium- to full-bodied with gently mouth-coating tannins. Blended with 10% Cabernet Sauvignon and oak-aged for 14 months, opens to reveal blueberry and black cherry fruits on a background of roasted chestnuts and licorice. Long and generous. Drink now–2011. Score 89. K

GOFNA RESERVE, CABERNET FRANC, 2007: As predicted at an early tasting, the best yet from this winery. Medium- to full-bodied, opening with notes of freshly turned earth and loam, those parting to reveal black and blue berries along with spicy and toasty oak notes. Firm tannins but with fine balance and structure, a simultaneously muscular and elegant wine. Drink now–2012. Score 90. **K**

GOFNA RESERVE, CHARDONNAY-CABERNET, 2007: Medium- to full-bodied, a white wine with a hint of tannins, blend of 80% Chardonnay and 20% Cabernet Sauvignon, the red grapes with very short skin contact. Fine acidity balances those tannins and shows appealing citrus, pear and green apple fruits, those matched nicely by a hint of berries that plays on the palate. Call this one "unusual" or "odd" as you like, but an appealing and complex wine that will fascinate. Whether it will woo or not is another story altogether. Drink now. Score 87. **K**

Masada

MASADA, CABERNET SAUVIGNON, 2006: Made from grapes that had partly dried on the vines, cold-fermented before being transferred to oak barrels. Medium-bodied, with a vague hint of sweetness set off nicely by aromas and flavors of ripe berries and black cherries and, on the moderately long finish, a touch of eucalyptus. Drink now. Score 86. **K**

MASADA, MERLOT, 2006: Dark, almost impenetrable garnet in color, full-bodied, firm and concentrated, opening with peppery cedarwood, that yielding comfortably to blackberry and spicy and earthy aromas and flavors. A distinct personality and a long-lingering finish. Drink now–2012. Score 89. **K**

MASADA, MERLOT, 2005: Dark royal purple with orange reflections, this wine reflects its 18 months in *barriques* with spicy oak and mouth-coating near-sweet tannins in fine balance with minty, herb-scented cherry and berry flavors, those with overlays of milk chocolate and mint. Full-bodied, with fine tannins and a caressing finish. Drink now. Score 89. **K**

MASADA, CHARDONNAY-CABERNET SAUVIGNON, 2005: A blend of Chardonnay and Cabernet Sauvignon (75% and 25% respectively), the Cabernet with minimal skin contact yielding a rather unique *blanc de noirs*. Full-bodied, with a texture of cream and glycerin, showing a surprising but appealing array of citrus, pear and wild berry fruits. A complex and "interesting" wine but not for long cellaring. Drink up. Score 86. **K**

Herodion

HERODION, CABERNET SAUVIGNON, 2007: Reflecting its 12 months in *barriques* with gentle spicy oak, this medium- to full-bodied red has soft tannins and a round, fruity personality. On the nose and palate appealing black fruits, spices and hint of Oriental spices, all lingering nicely, the fruits and tannins rising on a long and mouth-filling finish Drink now–2011. Score 88. **K**

HERODION, CABERNET SAUVIGNON, 2006: Opens with a lightly funky aroma, that passing quickly. Reflecting its development in *barriques* with full body, firm tannins and generous spicy wood, those integrating nicely and showing appealing currant, blackberry, green olives and Mediterranean herbs. Drink now–2012. Score 88. **K**

HERODION, CABERNET SAUVIGNON, 2005: A blend of 85% Cabernet Sauvignon and 15% Merlot, reflecting sweet and spicy cedarwood from its 14 months' development in French oak, the wood in good balance with soft, gently mouth-coating tannins and fruits. Medium- to full-bodied, aromatic, and showing deep currant, black cherry and dark red fruits. Finishes with a touch of heat but that will integrate nicely in time. Drink now. Score 88. **K**

HERODION, MERLOT, 2007: Blended with 10% Cabernet Sauvignon, oak-aged for 12 months, medium- to full-bodied, with soft, caressing tannins and appealing blackcurrant and black cherry fruits, a generous and near-elegant wine with a long, licorice-hinted finish. Drink now–2011. Score 88. **K**

HERODION, CABERNET SAUVIGNON-MERLOT, 2006: Dark ruby toward garnet, aged for 14 months primarily in used French *barriques*, this blend of 60% Cabernet Sauvignon and 40% Merlot shows medium-bodied, with gently mouth-coating tannins. Round, soft and rich with appealing red berry and cassis notes, those on a lightly spicy background. Long and generous. Drink now. Score 88. **K**

HERODION, CABERNET SAUVIGNON-MERLOT, 2005: Dark garnet in color, medium-bodied, with soft tannins and gentle oak integrating nicely, this blend of 60% Cabernet Sauvignon and 40% Merlot was aged in French oak for 12 months. Aromatic, round and soft, with appealing aromas and flavors of blackberry and purple plum fruits, those supported by hints of spice and chocolate. Drink now. Score 87. **K**

Hakerem ✴

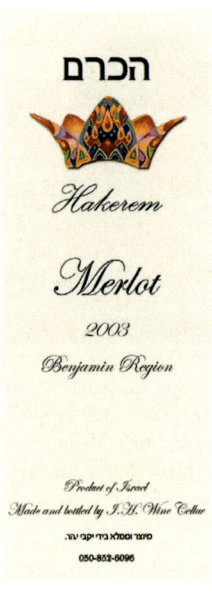

Founded in 2001 by Isaac Herskovitz and located in Beit-El, north of Jerusalem, this winery produces Cabernet Sauvignon and Merlot wines, drawing on grapes from various vineyards. The winery sometimes releases more than one wine under the same label. Annual production is currently about 6,000 bottles.

HAKEREM, CABERNET SAUVIGNON, KEDUSHAT SHVI'IT, 2008: The best wine to date from this small winery. Dark ruby toward garnet, medium- to full-bodied, with generous, softly caressing tannins and notes of spicy wood. On the nose and palate traditional Cabernet Sauvignon blackberry and blackcurrant fruits, those matched by generous hints of tobacco and earthy minerals. Drink now–2011. Score 88. **K**

HAKEREM, CABERNET SAUVIGNON 2005: Ruby toward cloudy garnet, aged in oak for 24 months, showing far-too-generous acidity and some barnyard aromas that tend to hide the black fruits here. Drink up. Score 76. **K**

HAKEREM, CABERNET SAUVIGNON, 2004: Deep ruby toward garnet, medium-bodied, with firm tannins and too-generous hints of spicy oak and earthiness with aromas and flavors of currants and black cherries. Drink up. Score 84. **K**

HAKEREM, CABERNET SAUVIGNON, 2003: Medium-bodied, with soft, nicely integrated tannins and plum, cherry, berry and spice notes, this smooth wine ends with an appealing fruity finish. Drink up. Score 86. **K**

HAKEREM, MERLOT, 2005: Medium-bodied, with somewhat coarse tannins and an overriding earthy note that tends to hide whatever fruits may be hidden. Drink up. Score 75. **K**

HAKEREM, DRY RED WINE, BATCH #17, 2006: An unlikely blend of undisclosed parts of Cabernet Sauvignon, Merlot, Pinot Noir, Malbec and Sangiovese, almost as if all of the "leftovers" were tossed together. Dull garnet in color, medium-bodied, with soft tannins and showing some red and black berries. A simple country-style wine. Drink up. Score 78. **K**

HAKEREM, MUSCAT, 2007: Dark bronzed-gold in color, thick, and even though categorized as half dry, so sweet that it is cloying. Comes in a bottle closed with a plastic screw-cap, one more appropriate for fruit juice than wine. Score 60. **K**

Hamasrek **

Established by brothers Nachum and Hanoch Greengrass in 1999 on Moshav Beit Meir in the Jerusalem Mountains, this kosher boutique winery draws on grapes from their own area as well as from Zichron Ya'akov and the Upper Galilee. In 2000 the winery released 5,000 bottles of Merlot and Chardonnay, and since then the winery has added Cabernet Sauvignon and Gewurztraminer to their line. Current production is about 20,000 bottles and wines are released in two series—The King's Blend and Hamasrek.

The King's Blend

HAMASREK, THE KING'S BLEND, JUDEAN HILLS, N.V.: A blend of Cabernet Sauvignon, Merlot and Zinfandel grapes (80%, 15% and 5% respectively) from the 2004 and 2005 vintages. Dark garnet, medium- to full-bodied, with soft tannins integrating nicely and showing generous berry, black cherry and herbal aromas and flavors. Lingers nicely. Drink now. Score 86. **K**

HAMASREK, THE KING'S BLEND, JUDEAN HILLS, N.V.: A blend of Cabernet Sauvignon, Merlot and Zinfandel grapes from the 2003 and 2004 vintages. Medium- to full-bodied, with chunky tannins, a strong influence of the wood and only bare hints of black fruits. Flat and one-dimensional. Drink up. Score 80. **K**

Hamasrek

HAMASREK, CABERNET SAUVIGNON, 2006: Oak-aged for ten months, garnet-red, showing chunky, country-style tannins and a moderate spicy oak influence. Appealing red fruits here when first poured but turns somewhat flat and flabby on the finish. Drink now. Score 82. **K**

HAMASREK, CABERNET SAUVIGNON, LIMITED EDITION, SINGLE VINEYARD, JUDEAN HILLS, 2005: Dark royal purple toward garnet in color, full-bodied and reflecting its time in *barriques* with near-sweet tannins and toasty oak. On the nose and palate, red and blackcurrants, raspberries and lightly pepper cedarwood notes, those leading to a long, espresso-coffee-rich finish. Drink now. Score 88. K

HAMASREK, CABERNET SAUVIGNON, 2005: Dark garnet, medium- to full-bodied, with near-sweet tannins and spicy wood well balanced by blackberry, currant and black cherry fruits. On the moderately long finish, hints of freshly turned earth and tobacco. Drink up. Score 84. K

HAMASREK, CHARDONNAY, 2006: Dark gold, medium-bodied, developed partly in oak and partly in stainless steel. Citrus peel, guava and tropical fruits here along with a hint of spices. Good balancing acidity. Drink now. Score 86. K

HAMASREK, CHARDONNAY, 2005: Golden straw with a green tint, medium-bodied, with hints of spices and vanilla from the oak in which it was partially aged. Citrus peel, guava and pear flavors. Drink up. Score 85. K

Hans Sternbach ✶✶

Founded by Gadi and Shula Sternbach in Moshav Givat Ye-shayahu in the Judean Hills, the Domaine Hans Sternbach's first release was of 1,800 bottles from the 2000 harvest. With a new winery located on the moshav and relying primarily on Cabernet Sauvignon grapes from its own nearby vineyards, production from the 2003 vintage was about 3,000 bottles and from 2004–2007 about 10,000 bottles annually. The winery produces four series: Janaba Reserve, Nachal Hakhlil, Socho Valley and Emek Ha'ella.

Janaba Reserve

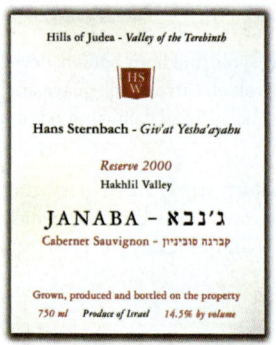

Hills of Judea - *Valley of the Terebinth*

HS
W

Hans Sternbach - *Giv'at Yesha'ayahu*

Reserve 2000
Hakhlil Valley

JANABA – ג'נבא
Cabernet Sauvignon – קברנה סוביניון

Grown, produced and bottled on the property
750 ml   *Produce of Israel*   14.5% by volume

JANABA RESERVE, CABERNET SAUVIGNON, HAKHLIL VALLEY, 2006: Made entirely from Cabernet Sauvignon grapes, oak-aged for 24 months, dark garnet toward royal purple, full-bodied with still-firm tannins holding back the fruits to some degree. Somewhat flat on the nose, but opens to reveal flavors of currant and blackberry fruits on a spicy and lightly herbal background. Drink now. Score 84.

JANABA RESERVE, CABERNET SAUVIGNON, HAKHLIL VALLEY, 2005: Youthful, dark royal purple, medium- to full-bodied, with firm tannins still controlling the wine but already showing blackcurrant, wild berry and spicy oak aromas and flavors. Drink up. Score 84.

Nachal Hakhlil

NACHAL HAKHLIL, 2006: Dark royal purple in color, this oak-aged blend of 70% Cabernet Sauvignon and 30% Merlot is showing medium- to full-bodied, with firm tannins opening to reveal generous currant, blackberry and Mediterranean herbs. Drink now. Score 84.

NACHAL HAKHLIL, CABERNET SAUVIGNON, 2005: An oak-aged blend of 80% Cabernet Sauvignon and 20% Merlot. Medium- to full-bodied, with somewhat coarse tannins not yet wanting to yield but showing appealing black fruits and a medium-long finish. Drink now. Score 85.

Socho Valley

SOCHO VALLEY, CABERNET SAUVIGNON, 2004: Made entirely of Cabernet Sauvignon grapes and aged in French oak for one year. Cloudy ruby toward purple in color, with black fruits almost completely buried beneath barnyard aromas. Drink up. Score 74.

Emek Ha'ella

EMEK HA'ELLA, 2005: An unoaked blend of 80% Cabernet Sauvignon and 20% Merlot. Light in body, with soft tannins and berry-cherry fruits. A simple quaffer. Drink up. Score 81.

Hatabor *

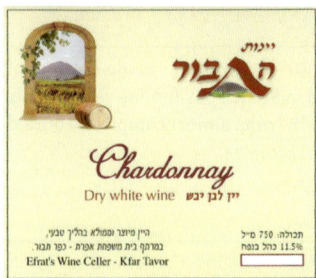

Located in the village of Kfar Tabor in the Lower Galilee, this winery was founded by Shimi Efrat in 1999 and released its first wines from the 2002 harvest. Grapes come primarily from nearby vineyards, and production is currently about 7,000 bottles annually.

HATABOR, CABERNET SAUVIGNON, 2006: Medium- to full-bodied, dark garnet in color, with firm tannins and generous spicy wood but opening slowly to reveal currant and blackberry fruits. One-dimensional. Drink up. Score 79.

HATABOR, CABERNET SAUVIGNON, 2005: Full-bodied, with almost searing tannins and far-too-generous wood hiding the fruits that struggle to make themselves felt. Drink up. Score 78.

HATABOR, MERLOT, 2005: Deep royal purple, medium- to full-bodied, with firm tannins yielding somewhat in the glass to reveal raspberry, cassis and herbal aromas and flavors. Drink up. Score 84.

HATABOR, MERLOT, 2004: Ruby toward garnet, medium-bodied, with chunky tannins and spicy wood. A country-style wine that opens to show plum and black cherry fruits on a herbal and black olive background. Starting to show age. Drink up. Score 80.

HATABOR, MERLOT-CABERNET SAUVIGNON, 2005: Medium-bodied, with soft tannins and a gentle wood influence. Showing appealing black and red berry as well as black cherry fruits. A good quaffer. Drink up. Score 85.

HATABOR, CHARDONNAY, 2006: Medium-bodied, with lively acidity and appealing citrus and tropical fruits. Simple but easy to drink. Drink up. Score 84.

Hevron Heights *

Located in Kiryat Arba, not far from the heart of the city of Hebron, this winery was founded in 2001 by a group of French investors and initially produced about 150,000 bottles per year, the target audience largely being observant Jews abroad. The winery reports current production of about 600,000 bottles annually, and produces a line of varietal and blended wines of Cabernet Sauvignon, Merlot, French Colombard, Sauvignon Blanc and Malbec grapes, drawing largely on grapes from the Judean Hills as well as vineyards near Hebron. The winery has a broad and somewhat confusing labeling system with a large number of series and brands including Hevron Heights, Noah, Hevron, Tevel, Efron's Cave, Shemesh, Pardess, Judea and Jerusalem Heights, some of which are also released as private labels.

Hevron Heights

HEVRON HEIGHTS, CABERNET SAUVIGNON, KIDRON, 2004: Dark garnet, this medium- to full-bodied wine reflects its 12 months' exposure to oak with spices and soft tannins. On the nose and palate black fruits and hints of pepper and star anise. Neither complex nor long but an acceptable entry-level wine. Drink up. Score 84. **K**

HEVRON HEIGHTS, CABERNET SAUVIGNON, GEDEON, 2004: Deep garnet toward purple, medium- to full-bodied, with firm and chunky country-style tannins. On the nose and palate blackberries, plums and a hint of orange peel. Turns almost sweet on the finish. Drink up. Score 83. **K**

HEVRON HEIGHTS, CABERNET SAUVIGNON, SDEH CALEV, 2003: Deep garnet, medium- to full-bodied, with soft tannins and currant and berry fruits matched by hints of spices and mint. Drink up. Score 84. **K**

HEVRON HEIGHTS, CABERNET SAUVIGNON, ISAAC'S RAM, 2003: Dark ruby toward garnet, medium-bodied, with soft tannins and notes of near-sweet cedarwood. Opens to reveal generous currant and blueberry notes on a lightly spicy background. Drink up. Score 85. **K**

HEVRON HEIGHTS, SYRAH, RESERVE, 2004: Dark royal purple, medium- to full-bodied, with firm tannins integrating nicely. On the nose and palate plums, blackberries and spices with a moderately long earthy-mineral finish. Drink up. 84. **K**

HEVRON HEIGHTS, ARMAGEDDON (MEGIDDO IN NORTH AMERICA), 2002: An unfiltered blend of 80% Cabernet Sauvignon, 15% Merlot and 5% Syrah, aged in new French oak for 24 months. To my palate, this wine has been so vastly different from tasting to tasting that it defies a firm description or consistent scoring. Overall, it continues to reflect generous sweet and smoky wood and gripping tannins. At this most recent tasting, the tannins and wood seem to finally be integrating, allowing the blackcurrant, red and black berries, and ripe red plum aromas and flavors to show. Drink up. Scores range from 79–84. **K**

HEVRON HEIGHTS, MAKHPELAH, 2002: A blend of 70% Cabernet Sauvignon, 26% Merlot and 4% Marsanne, oak-aged for more than 20 months. This dark garnet-going-to-adobe-brown wine is full-bodied, almost thick in texture, with chunky tannins and generous wood tending to hide the plum and blackberry fruits that never fully make their way to the surface. Drink up. Score 80. **K**

HEVRON HEIGHTS, SPECIAL RESERVE, 2002: Developed in French and American oak for 20 months, this blend of Cabernet Sauvignon, Merlot and Shiraz (65%, 25% and 10% respectively) shows full-bodied, with gripping tannins and generous spicy and smoky wood. Opens to reveal plum, wild berry and cassis fruits, those leading to a moderately long and generously peppery finish. Drink up. Score 83. **K**

HEVRON HEIGHTS, JERUSALEM HILLS, 2005: A medium-bodied blend of Petite Sirah, Merlot and Cabernet Sauvignon (60%, 30% and 10% respectively). Ruby toward garnet in color, with chunky tannins and black fruits. A country-style wine that ends on a somewhat bitter note. Drink up. Score 80. **K**

HEVRON HEIGHTS, CABERNET-MERLOT, JERUSALEM HEIGHTS, 2002: Perhaps the best yet from the winery. A full-bodied, softly tannic blend of 50% each of Cabernet Sauvignon and Merlot, opening to reveal juicy blackberry, raspberry and cassis fruits on a background of spices and leather. Lingers nicely. Drink up. Score 87. **K**

HEVRON HEIGHTS, TRIPLE RED, EFRON'S CAVE, 2003: Dark garnet, this medium-bodied, unoaked blend of one-third each Cabernet Sauvignon, Merlot and Syrah offers up soft tannins and forward berry-cherry fruits. Drink up. Score 79. **K**

HEVRON HEIGHTS, TRIPLE PLUM, EFRON'S CAVE, 2003: A light- to medium-bodied one-dimensional blend of Cabernet Sauvignon, Merlot and Syrah (35%, 35% and 30% respectively) with forward plum and black cherry fruits. Drink up. Score 78. **K**

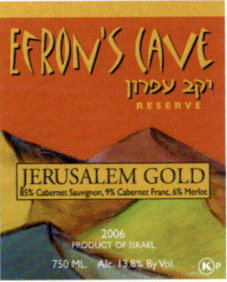

Noah

NOAH, CABERNET SAUVIGNON, 2006: Dark garnet, medium-bodied, with firm, chunky tannins. A hint of barnyard aromas that linger, and on the palate a note of mold that hides the skimpy berry fruits. Score 69. **K**

NOAH, CABERNET SAUVIGNON, TEVEL, 2005: Oak-aged for 18 months, dark ruby toward garnet, medium-bodied, with soft tannins and showing berry, cassis and cedarwood notes. A pleasant entry-level wine. Drink up. Score 84. **K**

NOAH, CABERNET SAUVIGNON, TEVEL, 2004: Medium-bodied, softly tannic, with black cherry, blackberry, cedar and bell pepper notes along with a smoky oak finish. Drink up. Score 80. **K**

NOAH, MERLOT, 2006: Garnet toward purple, medium- to full-bodied, with too-flabby tannins and somewhat muddy berry and cherry flavors. Drink up. Score 70. **K**

NOAH, MERLOT, TEVEL, 2005: Dark ruby toward garnet, oak-aged for 12 months, showing soft and round, with berry, black cherry and purple plums. Not complex but a good quaffer. Drink up. Score 84. **K**

NOAH, MERLOT, TEVEL, 2004: Medium-bodied, with soft tannins, hints of wood and generous berry, cherry and currant fruits. Drink up. Score 84. **K**

NOAH, PETITE SIRAH, GEDEON, 2005: Dark purple, medium-bodied, with chunky and somewhat coarse tannins, this distinct country-style wine shows skimpy berry and black cherry fruits, all with a not-entirely-wanted sweet aftertaste. Drink up. Score 78. **K**

NOAH, SHIRAZ-CABERNET SAUVIGNON, TEVEL, 2005: Aged in *barriques* for 12 months, a dark garnet blend of 60% Syrah and 40% Cabernet Sauvignon. Medium- to full-bodied, with blackberry, plum and black cherry fruits, those on a lightly spicy background. Not complex, an acceptable entry-level wine. Drink up. Score 80. **K**

NOAH, SHIRAZ-CABERNET SAUVIGNON, 2004: Garnet toward purple, medium-bodied, with soft tannins and gentle wood influences integrating nicely and showing appealing berry, black cherry and cassis fruits. Round and crisp. Drink up. Score 83. **K**

NOAH, EMERALD RIESLING, 2007: Straw-colored, light in body, with generous floral and citrus notes. Acidic, thin and cloyingly sweet. Score 68. **K**

NOAH, MUSCAT DESSERT, 2005: Golden-yellow in color, not so much full-bodied as it is thick. Unabashedly sweet and flowery, with apricot, peach and nutty aromas and flavors, but lacking balancing acidity. Drink up. Score 79. **K**

Kadesh Barnea **

This Negev Desert winery was established in 1999 by Alon Tzadok on Moshav Kadesh Barnea and has its own vineyards near the ruins of the Byzantine city of Nitzana, just north of the Egyptian border. Releases to date have included only Cabernet Sauvignon and Merlot-based wines, but the winery is now developing further vineyards containing Petit Verdot, Shiraz, Cabernet Franc, Sauvignon Blanc and Chardonnay grapes. Production for the 2004 and

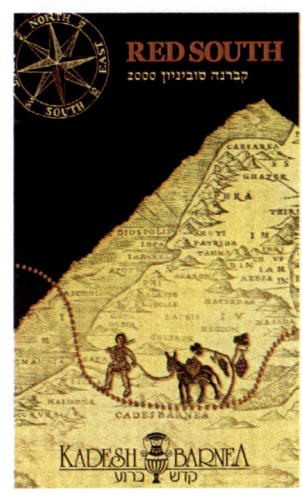

2005 vintages was about 5,000 bottles and in 2006 the winery made a major jump to 25,000 bottles. The wines have been kosher since the 2002 vintage.

The winery is one of the first in the country to be conducting experiments with making wines from vines irrigated by the brackish water that underlies much of the Negev desert, though these have not yet resulted in any releases.

KADESH BARNEA, CABERNET SAUVIGNON, 2006: Garnet toward royal purple, medium-bodied, with soft tannins and spicy oak. On the nose and palate forward berry, currant and black cherry fruits. Not complex but promises to be a good quaffer. Drink now. Score 82. **K**

KADESH BARNEA, CABERNET SAUVIGNON, ALON, 2005: Developing in American oak, this red is already showing generous wood balanced by soft, near-sweet tannins and good acidity. Aromatic, opening to reveal berry, cherry and cassis fruits, those matched by hints of bell peppers and chocolate. Drink up. Score 82. **K**

KADESH BARNEA, CABERNET SAUVIGNON, GILAD, 2005: A blend of Petit Verdot, Merlot and Shiraz. Medium-bodied, showing generous spicy wood and firm tannins that need time to integrate, this red opening slowly in the glass to reveal berry, black cherry and earthy-tobacco notes. Drink now. Score 85. **K**

KADESH BARNEA, CABERNET SAUVIGNON, 2004: Medium-dark garnet, medium-bodied, with chunky, country-style tannins. Blended with 15% Merlot, an easy-to-drink quaffer with berry and black cherry fruits. Drink up. Score 83. **K**

KADESH BARNEA, MERLOT, ALON, 2006: Dark royal purple, this medium- to full-bodied wine shows gripping, near-sweet tannins that yield slowly to reveal generous wild berry, currant and spices on first attack, those in turn opening to Mediterranean herbs and an appealing hint of black olives. Drink now. Score 83. **K**

KADESH BARNEA, MERLOT, ALON, 2005: Deep garnet toward royal purple, medium-bodied, opening with a light medicinal aroma, but that passes quickly to reveal aromas and flavors of berries, black cherries and plums. High acidity and chunky tannins make this a country-style wine, best for early drinking. Drink now. Score 83. **K**

KADESH BARNEA, MERLOT, GILAD, 2005: Blended with 15% Cabernet Sauvignon and aged in oak for ten months, this bright garnet, medium-bodied wine shows soft tannins, spicy oak and appealing plum, currant and tobacco. Somewhat acidic. Drink up. Score 83. **K**

KADESH BARNEA, GILAD, 2005: A blend of 80% Merlot and 10% each Shiraz and Petit Verdot. Dark garnet, medium- to full-bodied, with near-sweet tannins integrating nicely. Opens in the glass to reveal aromas and flavors of plums, blueberries and currants, those with overlays of white pepper and mint. Drink up. Score 83. **K**

Kadita ★★★★

Jonathan Goldman made wines at his home in Bikta Bekadita in the Upper Galilee for several years before he released his first commercial output of 600 bottles in 2001, a blend of Cabernet Sauvignon and Merlot. Grapes are currently drawn from the winery's own nearby vineyards and from Kerem Ben Zimra. Annual production is currently 4,000 bottles.

KADITA, CABERNET SAUVIGNON, 2007: Dark garnet, showing medium- to full-bodied with fine concentration, soft tannins and generous berry, black cherry and currant notes on a background of white pepper, green olives and eucalyptus. Fruits and tannins rise on the finish. Drink now–2012. Score 89.

KADITA, CABERNET SAUVIGNON, 2006: Full-bodied, intense and concentrated, showing deep, almost inky purple, with still-firm tannins and spicy wood in fine balance with natural acidity and fruits. Opens with aromas and flavors of raspberries and minty chocolate, those yielding to blackcurrants and red plums and finally to a long fruity finish with hints of white chocolate. Drink now–2013. Score 90.

KADITA, CABERNET SAUVIGNON, 2005: Deep royal purple, full-bodied, with firm tannins and spicy oak integrating nicely. On the nose and palate an array of blackberry, currant and black cherry fruits matched handsomely by hints of roasted herbs, green olives and, on the long finish, a hint of black licorice. Drink now–2011. Score 89.

KADITA, CABERNET SAUVIGNON, 2004: Youthful, deep royal purple, full-bodied, with generous soft tannins integrating nicely with concentrated black fruits, Mediterranean herbs, eucalyptus and hints of spicy cedarwood from the oak barrels. Long, concentrated and mouth-filling. Drink now. Score 90.

KADITA, CABERNET SAUVIGNON, 2003: A blend of grapes from two vineyards, one with volcanic soil, one with red soil, this still-youthful deep royal purple wine shows full body, firm tannins promising to integrate nicely and a tempting array of blackcurrant and wild berry fruits, those on a long, spicy tobacco and chocolate finish. Drink now. Score 89.

KADITA, MERLOT, 2006: Dark cherry red toward garnet, medium- to full-bodied, with soft, mouth-coating tannins and a gentle wood influence. Showing red and black berries, cassis and just the right hint of herbaceousness. Long and generous. Drink now–2012. Score 89.

KADITA, MERLOT, 2005: Full-bodied, deep and aromatic, with black pepper highlighting cherry, currant, chocolate and light licorice aromas and flavors, all lingering on the generous finish. Drink now–2012. Score 91.

KADITA, MERLOT, 2004: Full-bodied and aromatic, with firm but already well-integrating tannins, and showing a tempting array of blueberry, raspberry and purple plum fruits, those on a background of chocolate and Mediterranean herbs. Drink now. Score 89.

KADITA, SHIRAZ, 2004: Rich, ripe and generous, full-bodied, with liberal but refined tannins. On the nose and palate plum, blueberry, black cherry and gentle spices, all coming together with lively acidity. Powerful and graceful with flavors that linger on and on. Drink now. Score 91.

KADITA, CABERNET SAUVIGNON-MERLOT, 2005: Dark garnet, opening slowly to reveal a firm and remarkably concentrated wine with a complex set of aromas and flavors, those including cassis, blackberries, anise, tobacco, and espresso coffee, all still tightly wound. On the finish an unusual combination of super-firm tannins and an explosion of fruits. Drink now. Score 90.

KADITA, CABERNET-MERLOT, 2004: Deep garnet, medium- to full-bodied, with soft, caressing tannins and ripe blackberry, plum, currant and herbal aromas and flavors on first attack, those yielding very nicely to hints of coffee, tobacco and earthiness. Drink up. Score 87.

Kahanov ✶

Located in Gadera on the Central Plains, winemaker Yoav Kahanov is producing about 4,500 bottles annually, those based largely on Cabernet Sauvignon, Merlot and Petit Verdot grapes sourced from the Galilee and the Judean Mountains.

KAHANOV, CABERNET SAUVIGNON, 2005: Dark garnet, with chunky tannins giving the wine a distinct country style. Good blackberry fruits here but with earthy, weedy and dusty cedary oak more prominent than fruit. Somewhat coarse. Drink up. Score 78.

KAHANOV, MERLOT, 2004: Medium-bodied, a simple little country-style red with muted cherry fruits and showing too generous herbal notes. Loaded with volatile acidity. Drink up. Score 74.

KAHANOV, PETIT VERDOT, 2005: Full-bodied, with generous spicy wood and firm tannins and alcohol hanging on as if they do not want to yield. Some good black cherry fruits here, but that overpowered by gamey and tobacco notes. Perhaps best if used as a blending agent. Drink up. Score 77.

Karmei Yosef ✴✴✴✴

Founded in 2001 by Ben-Ami Bravdo and Oded Shosheyov, both professors of oenology at the Hebrew University of Jerusalem, the winery sits in the heart of the vineyards at Karmei Yosef on the western slopes of the Judean Mountains. The winery released 2,800 bottles of its first wine in 2001. Production from the 2007 vintages was of 24,000 bottles, and production for 2008 and 2009 is planned for 40,000 bottles annually. The winery relies largely on grapes grown in their own vineyards, among those Cabernet Sauvignon, Merlot, Shiraz and Chardonnay. The wines have been kosher since the 2007 vintage.

KARMEI YOSEF, CABERNET SAUVIGNON, BRAVDO, 2008: Full-bodied and with fine concentration and tight focus. Generous tannins here needing time to settle down but already showing the balance and structure to predict a fine future. Opens with spicy, almost sawdust oak on the nose, that going on to blackcurrants and blackberries, those on a background of bay leaves and dark chocolate. Promises to be a deep, long and complex wine. Best 2011–2016. Tentative Score 91–93. **K**

KARMEI YOSEF, CABERNET SAUVIGNON, BRAVDO, 2007: Deep garnet in color, full-bodied, with deep tannins and spicy wood, those opening to reveal a rich core of currant, wild berry, toasty oak and minted chocolate, all lingering nicely. Drink now–2012. Score 89. **K**

KARMEI YOSEF, CABERNET SAUVIGNON, BRAVDO, 2006: Dark garnet toward royal purple in color, medium- to full-bodied, and with overall good balance between still-firm tannins and spicy wood that allows the fruits to show nicely. On the nose and palate currants, wild berries and mint notes, those lingering nicely. Drink now–2012. Score 90.

KARMEI YOSEF, CABERNET SAUVIGNON, BRAVDO, 2005: Opens with a light medicinal aroma but that blows off quickly. Dark garnet toward royal purple, medium- to full-bodied, with soft tannins and gentle dusty cedar notes integrating nicely and showing forward ripe blackberries, currants, lead pencil and sweet herbal aromas and flavors. Intense, with tannins and near-sweet fruit rising on the finish. Drink now. Score 89.

KARMEI YOSEF, CABERNET SAUVIGNON, BRAVDO, 2004: Medium- to full-bodied with soft, near-sweet tannins and spicy wood well balanced by blackcurrant, wild berry and black cherry fruits. Round, generous and long. Drink now–2012. Score 91.

KARMEI YOSEF, CABERNET SAUVIGNON, BRAVDO, 2003: A well-balanced, well-structured blend of 80% Cabernet Sauvignon and 20% Merlot. Still young but already showing ripe, generous and mouth-filling aromas and flavors of plums, currants, black cherries and berries, with hints of minty spice and wood. Elegant and graceful wine. Drink now. Score 91.

KARMEI YOSEF, MERLOT, BRAVDO, 2008: Developing in new French *barriques*, still in its infancy but already showing dark garnet, medium-to full-bodied, with soft tannins and gentle wood parting to reveal generous black and red cherries, red currants, spices and minted chocolate notes. Rich and opulent, generous, long and mouth-filling. Best 2011–2015. Tentative Score 90–92. **K**

KARMEI YOSEF, MERLOT, BRAVDO, 2007: Dark garnet toward royal purple, medium- to full-bodied, with soft, near-sweet tannins and showing a generous array of blackberry, blueberry, spicy and earthy aromas and flavors. Drink now–2011. Score 89. **K**

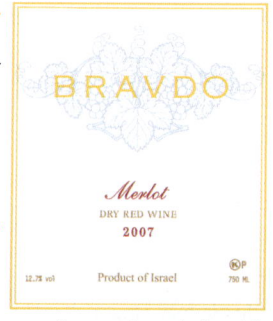

KARMEI YOSEF, MERLOT, BRAVDO, 2006: Blended with 15% of Cabernet Sauvignon, aged in *barriques* for 12 months, deep garnet toward royal purple in color, with once-gripping tannins now integrating nicely with spicy wood. Full-bodied, opens to reveal a core of plums, blackberries and blueberries, those on a background of exotic spices and hints of chocolate and mocha that linger nicely on the palate. Drink now–2012. Score 90.

KARMEI YOSEF, MERLOT, BRAVDO, 2005: After developing for 12 months in French and American oak, this dark ruby-toward-garnet wine is showing medium- to full-bodied, with near-sweet tannins and dusty wood highlighting intense currant, blackberry, black cherry and mocha aromas and flavors. A hint of unwanted sweetness creeping in on the finish. Drink now. Score 88.

KARMEI YOSEF, MERLOT, BRAVDO, 2004: Oak-aged for 12 months, with 10% of Cabernet Sauvignon blended in, this medium-bodied red shows appealing smoky oak and moderately firm tannins well balanced with cassis, blueberry and black cherry fruits. On the long finish, hints of anise, sweet cedar, sage and tobacco. Drink now. Score 90.

KARMEI YOSEF, SHIRAZ, BRAVDO, 2008: Dark royal purple in color, a dense, rich and aromatic wine made from intentionally late harvested grapes that yield sur-ripe berries, plums, and blueberry fruits. In the background cedary oak, spices and a generous dose of pepper. Best from 2012–2016, perhaps longer. Tentative Score 91–93. **K**

KARMEI YOSEF, SHIRAZ, BRAVDO, 2007: The first Shiraz release from the winery and a fine effort. Almost impenetrable dark garnet in color, an intense and spicy wine, offering wild berry and blackberry fruits, those with leathery overtones. Muscular but fine-grained tannins and a relatively high alcohol content (almost 16%) make this a near-blockbuster, but given time it will settle down nicely. Approachable and enjoyable now, but best starting in 2011. Score 91. **K**

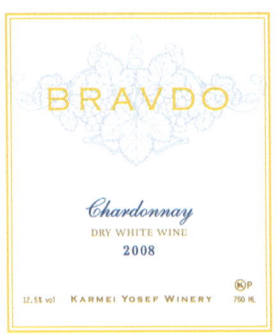

KARMEI YOSEF, CHARDONNAY, BRAVDO, 2008: Wisely developed in new oak *barriques* for just three months, showing tantalizing notes of spicy wood and toasted white bread, those parting comfortably to reveal generous nectarine, citrus and green apple notes, all leading to a finish hinting of sweet cream. Lively and easy to drink with just enough complexity to grab our attention. Drink now–2011. Score 89. **K**

KARMEI YOSEF, CHARDONNAY, BRAVDO, 2007: Made from 100% Chardonnay grapes, developed in oak for only three months to guard the aromas and freshness of the variety, this medium-bodied white shows forward pineapple, citrus and pear fruits, those with good acidity and a light mineral note keeping the wine lively. Lacks complexity but refreshing and easy to drink. Drink now. Score 87. **K**

KARMEI YOSEF, CHARDONNAY, BRAVDO, 2006: Fermented partly on its lees in new French and American oak and partly in stainless steel, this deeply golden white shows a green tint, and is bursting with layers of figs, apples, apricots, melon and light cedary oak. Rich, with mineral flavors that linger nicely on the finish. Drink up. Score 89.

KARMEI YOSEF, CHARDONNAY, BRAVDO, 2005: A bright and generous wine, light gold in color, medium- to full-bodied, with light hints of spice-tinted wood and layers of citrus, citrus peel, nectarine and melon fruits, all lingering nicely on the finish. Elegant. Drink up. Score 90.

Katlav ✳✳✳

KATLAV

Cabernet Sauvignon
2003

כשר 🔵 750 ml. 14.5 Alc.
Katlav Winery, Nes Harim 99885, Israel

Owner-winemaker Yossi Yittach founded this small winery on Moshav Nes Harim in the Jerusalem Mountains in 1996 and released his first wines from the 2000 vintage. The winery draws on Cabernet Sauvignon, Merlot and Syrah grapes from local vineyards. In addition to wines produced under the Katlav label, the winery also produces a series of wines under the Shemesh label, those destined primarily for export. Production for the 2007 vintage was about 18,000 bottles. Because of the *shnat shmita* (Sabbatical year for the vineyards), no wines were produced from the 2008 vintage.

KATLAV, CABERNET SAUVIGNON, 2007: Dark ruby in color, full-bodied, with near-sweet tannins and light spicy and cedar notes. Opens to reveal a tempting array of blackcurrant, blackberry and purple plum fruits, those complemented by hints of mocha and Mediterranean herbs, all lingering nicely. Drink now–2012. Score 89. **K**

KATLAV, CABERNET SAUVIGNON, 2006: Oak-aged for 24 months, dark ruby toward garnet, medium- to full-bodied, with soft tannins and light spicy oak coming together nicely with notes of red plums, cherries and raspberries. Faulted only by a light medicinal note that rises on the medium-long finish. Drink now. Score 85. **K**

KATLAV, CABERNET SAUVIGNON, RESERVE, 2005: Dark garnet, medium- to full-bodied, with soft tannins integrating nicely and showing generous hints of spicy oak. Blackcurrant and blackberry fruits, those well supported by hints of black pepper and Mediterranean herbs. Flawed only by a hint of volatile acidity that rises on the finish. Drink now. Score 86. **K**

KATLAV, CABERNET SAUVIGNON, 2005: Oak-aged for 18 months, garnet toward royal purple in color, with soft tannins and toasty wood.

Medium-bodied, with a basic berry, cherry and light spicy personality. Drink now. Score 85. **K**

KATLAV, MERLOT, 2007: Dark ruby toward garnet in color, medium-bodied, with soft tannins integrating nicely and showing black cherry, cola and nutmeg on toasty oak, those yielding on the finish to hints of mocha and sage. Deep and long enough to hold our interest. Drink now. Score 89. **K**

KATLAV, MERLOT, 2006: Garnet toward royal purple, medium- to full-bodied, with soft tannins promising to integrate nicely with light oak. Showing dried currants and berries, those overlaid with spices and mint and a tantalizing hint of earthy bitterness. Drink now. Score 86. **K**

KATLAV, MERLOT, SHEMESH, 2006: Dark royal purple, medium-to full-bodied, with gently caressing tannins. Opens to reveal a soft, round wine with a berry-cherry personality and a light overlay of dark chocolate. Drink up. Score 86. **K**

KATLAV, MERLOT, 2005: Medium-bodied, with soft tannins and reflecting its 18 months in French *barriques* with gently spicy wood, this round and easy-to-drink wine offers red and black berries and cherries backed up by hints of earthy minerals. Drink up. Score 84. **K**

KATLAV, SYRAH, 2005: Oak-aged for 22 months, medium- to full-bodied, with traditional Syrah leathery, meaty and spicy notes highlighting red plum, cherry and cassis fruits. Drink up. Score 87. **K**

KATLAV, PINOT NOIR, 2007: Light ruby in color, soft, round and easygoing, showing cherry, berry and spicy aromas and flavors. Light tannins and a gentle hand with the wood make this a good quaffer. Drink now. Score 85. **K**

KATLAV, PETIT VERDOT, 2007: Dark garnet in color, full-bodied, with tannins as intense as the acidity and fruits. Opens slowly to reveal blackcurrants, blackberries and black cherries, those complemented nicely by mocha and spicy oak notes. Potentially the best yet from the winery. Drink now. Score 88. **K**

KATLAV, WADI KATLAV, 2006: Medium- to full-bodied, dark garnet toward royal purple and oak-aged for 24 months, this blend of Cabernet Sauvignon, Merlot and Shiraz (60%, 30% and 10%, respectively) shows still-firm tannins integrating nicely with spicy wood and opening to reveal blackberry, black cherry and red currant fruits, those on a background of spices and earthy minerals. Drink now. Score 87. **K**

KATLAV, WADI KATLAV, 2005: A medium-bodied blend of 50% Cabernet Sauvignon, 40% Merlot and 10% Syrah, oak-aged for 24 months.

Dark garnet, with soft tannins integrating nicely with sweet cedar notes and currant, berry and black cherry fruits, those with an appealing light earthy-herbal overlay. Drink now. Score 86. K

KATLAV, CHARDONNAY, 2007: Blended with 10% Viognier and oak-aged in used barrels for 13 months, an unfiltered wine, medium- to full-bodied, with spicy oak and generous alcohol, but those in good balance with acidity and fruits. On the nose and palate grapefruit, tropical fruits and citrus peel, those matched by floral notes. Finishes with a light creamy texture. Drink now. Score 87. K

KATLAV, CABERNET SAUVIGNON, DESSERT WINE, 2006: Not Port-style, not Madeira- or Sherry-style, a rather unique dessert wine, super-dark garnet in color, full-bodied, with soft tannins yielding in the glass to generous sweetness, that balanced by natural acidity. On the nose and palate abundant ripe plums, berries and cassis, those with overlays of white pepper and chocolate, all leading to a fresh and long finish. A one-off, not to be repeated. Drink now–2012. Score 89. K

Katz *

Founded by Jossi Katz in 2001 and located on Moshav Mesilat Tzion in the foothills of the Judean Mountains, this small winery is currently producing about 7,000 bottles annually and plans to grow to an output of about 20,000.

KATZ, MESILAT TZION, 2004: A vaguely off-dry, distinctly alcoholic and far-too-generously oaked blend of Cabernet Sauvignon, Merlot and Petite Sirah. Lacks charm. Score 70.

KATZ, RENOIR, DRY RED RESERVE, 2004: Dark royal purple in color, this blend of Cabernet Sauvignon, Merlot and Petite Sirah (55%, 42% and 3% respectively) shows medium-bodied, with firm tannins and far too many sharp edges. An unwelcome medicinal hint hides the black fruits. Drink up. Score 74.

KATZ, RENOIR, DRY RED RESERVE, 2003: A country-style blend of 55% Cabernet Sauvignon, 45% Merlot and 5% Syrah, which was oak-aged for 24 months. Medium-bodied, with chunky tannins, a bit of coarseness, and only skimpy black fruits. Showing age. Drink up. Score 72.

KATZ, CABERNET SAUVIGNON-MERLOT, 2004: Categorized as semi-dry but with cloying sweetness and a distinct medicinal overlay. Score 60.

KATZ, MATISSE, 2004: Made with no sulfites or other chemical additives, this sweet blend of Cabernet Sauvignon, Merlot and Petite Sirah (50%, 41% and 9% respectively) shows some plum, raisin and caramel flavors and aromas. One-dimensional and far too alcoholic. Score 68.

KATZ, MATISSE, 2003: An off-dry and oxidized red blend that calls to mind nothing more than it does a kosher New York State Concord Grape wine. Score 55.

Kella David ✶

Founded in 1995 by Amos Barzilai on Moshav Givat Ye-shayahu in the Jerusalem Mountains, this small winery produces about 10,000 bottles of white wines annually, taking a break in production for 2005.

KELLA DAVID, DRY WHITE, 2008: Emerald Riesling and French Colombard grapes come together in what may be called a dry wine but has a distinct sweetness to it. Floral, with simple citrus and melon notes. Drink up. Score 79.

KELLA DAVID, DRY WHITE, 2007: A dry blend of French Colombard and Emerald Riesling, showing a floral and spicy nose and flavors of citrus and tropical fruits. Nothing complex here but an appealing entry-level quaffer. Drink up. Score 82.

KELLA DAVID, SEMI-DRY WHITE, 2007: Semi-dry as its label states, but with minimal fruit and the distinct kind of bitterness that one associates with overly roasted coffee or nuts and only minimal fruits. A blend of French Colombard and Emerald Riesling. Score 70.

Kfir ✷✷

Founded in 2003 by Meir Kfir in the village of Gan Yavne on the southern Coastal Plain, this small winery was originally known as Gefen Adderet and changed its name to Kfir in 2006. Although producing only about 8,000 bottles annually, it releases a large variety of labels, those from Cabernet Sauvignon, Merlot, Cabernet Franc, Sangiovese, Nebbiolo, Syrah, Petite Sirah, Zinfandel, Malbec, Viognier, Riesling, Gewurztraminer and Chardonnay grapes from the vineyards of Karmei Yosef, the Jerusalem Mountains and the Galilee.

KFIR, BARBERA, 2005: Opens with an iodine-medicinal aroma, but that blows off quickly. 86% Barbera with 14% Cabernet Sauvignon blended in to add backbone, this medium-bodied, oak-aged, dark ruby-toward-purple wine shows soft tannins integrating nicely with acidity, spicy wood and appealing berry and currant fruits. On the long and generous finish a hint of smoky tobacco. Drink now. Score 86.

KFIR, CABERNET FRANC, 2005: Made entirely from Cabernet Franc grapes and aged in *barriques* for 12 months, this medium-bodied and softly tannic wine is showing signs of premature aging. Opens with medicinal and barnyard aromas, the once youthful sweet cherry and currant fruits now taking on a stewed and oxidized note. Drink up. Score 76.

KFIR, SHIRAZ, BAR, 2005: Ruby toward garnet, medium-bodied, with chunky, near-sweet tannins. Showing basic plum and black cherry fruits, those with a hint of Oriental spices. Drink now. Score 84

KFIR, AVICHAI, 2006: Medium-garnet toward purple, an oak-aged blend of Merlot, Cabernet Sauvignon and Syrah, showing spicy and vanilla-rich wood, chunky, country-style tannins and black fruits. An appealing entry-level wine. Drink now. Score 84.

KFIR, GILAD, 2005: Dark garnet toward royal purple, this oak-aged blend of Sangiovese, Zinfandel, Nebbiolo, and Barbera grapes (64%,

26%, 8% and 2% respectively) has a distinctly Italian character. Medium-to full-bodied, with soft tannins integrating nicely, it shows appealing raspberry, cherry and red currant fruits overlaid with hints of black olives and anise, all with a light spicy oak overlay. Drink now. Score 86.

KFIR, SYRAH-PETITE SIRAH, 2006: Dark garnet toward royal purple in color, showing generous spicy wood and gripping tannins that need a bit of time to settle down and integrate with the blackberry, purple plum and black cherry fruits. Spicy, long and generous. Drink now. Score 86.

KFIR, SYRAH-PETITE SIRAH, 2005: Deep royal purple in color, this oak-aged blend of 58% Syrah and 42% Petite Sirah shows generous but not dominating spicy wood and tannins. Medium- to full-bodied, a round wine with plum, wild berry and black cherry fruits on a spicy background. Drink up. Score 87.

KFIR, ZOHARA, TEVA, 2006: A light- to medium-bodied blend of Syrah, Petite Sirah and Cabernet Franc. Medium-dark garnet, with soft tannins and forward blackberry and blueberry fruits. A pleasant and easy-to-drink entry-level wine. Drink now. Score 84.

KFIR, ZOHARA, TEVA, 2005: A medium-bodied and softly tannic blend of Cabernet Sauvignon, Merlot and Cabernet Franc. A basic berry-black cherry personality, those fruits with a distinct overlay of bitter orange peel. Drink up. Score 84.

KFIR, ZOHARA, TEVA, 2004: A somewhat clumsy blend of Sangiovese, Nebbiolo, Merlot, Cabernet Sauvignon, Cabernet Franc and Shiraz. Dark cherry red, medium- to full-bodied, with soft, near-sweet tannins and aromas and flavors of blackberries, currants and black cherries, matched nicely by hints of pepper, tar and light earthiness. Drink up. Score 84.

KFIR, ZOHARA, TEVA, 2003: Deep ruby toward garnet, this medium-bodied blend of Cabernet Sauvignon, Merlot and Argaman (68%, 22% and 10% respectively) shows light tannins and a fresh, lightly spicy berry-cherry personality. Drink up. Score 84.

KFIR, CABERNET FRANC, DESSERT WINE, 2004: Generously sweet, with good balancing acidity. Medium-full on the palate, maintaining the blackberry fruits and greenness typical to the variety. Appealing as an aperitif. Drink now. Score 86.

KFIR, CHARDONNAY, TEVA, 2006: Reflecting eight months of development in *barriques*, showing spicy wood and grapefruit aromas and flavors. Easy to drink but not at all complex. Drink up. Score 84.

KFIR, VIOGNIER, BAR, 2005: Light golden straw in color, with generous fresh acidity keeping it lively. Aromas and flavors of peaches, melon, citrus and freshly cut hay. Not representative of the variety but appealing and refreshing. Drink up. Score 84.

KFIR, GEWURZTRAMINER, WHITE NIGHTS, TEVA, 2007: Light golden straw in color, light- to medium-bodied, and with a bare hint of honeyed sweetness to an overall dry persona. Spicy apples and pears supported by lively acidity. Drink now. Score 85.

KFIR, WHITE NIGHTS, TEVA, 2005: An off-dry blend of 85% Gewurztraminer and 15% Riesling, showing mango, pineapple and citrus peel aromas and flavors. With good acidity to keep it lively and refreshing. A pleasant aperitif. Drink up. Score 84.

Kitron **

Founded by Maeir Bitoen and set on Kibbutz Ma'abarot, not far from the city of Hadera, and drawing on Cabernet Sauvignon, Shiraz and Merlot grapes from the Upper Galilee and the Judean Hills, this boutique winery released its first wines from the 2006 vintage, when production was about 14,000 bottles. Production from 2007 and 2008 is estimated at about 26,000 bottles for each year. Wines are released only in a reserve series.

KITRON, CABERNET SAUVIGNON, RESERVE, 2008: Tasted from stainless steel just before transfer to French oak *barriques*, still in embryonic form but already showing fine extraction, deep garnet color and generous tannins. Shows traditional black fruits and spices. Promising. Drink from release–2012. Tentative Score 86–88. **K**

KITRON, CABERNET SAUVIGNON, RESERVE, 2007: Dark garnet in color, full-bodied, with somewhat generous spicy and smoky wood and chunky, country-style tannins. Opens in the glass to show black fruits, those on a somewhat muddled background of cloves, cinnamon and chocolate. Drink now. Score 84. **K**

KITRON, CABERNET SAUVIGNON, RESERVE, 2006: Medium- to full-bodied, with gently gripping tannins and notes of spicy oak in fine balance with red currant and spice aromas yielding to black cherry, roasted herbs and espresso flavors. Tannins and fruits rise on the finish. Drink now–2011. Score 88. **K**

KITRON, MERLOT, RESERVE, 2007: Deep and dark, medium- to full-bodied, with firm tannins and spicy wood integrating nicely with purple plum, blueberry and cassis fruits. Not complex but a good quaffer. Drink from release. Tentative Score 84–86. **K**

KITRON, MERLOT, RESERVE, 2006: Dark ruby toward garnet, medium- to full-bodied, smooth and spicy with ripe berry, black cherry and chocolate flavors, with tannins and hints of sweet cedarwood rising on the finish. Drink now–2011. Score 87. **K**

KITRON, SHIRAZ, RESERVE, 2007: Dark garnet toward royal purple, with what is now far too generous wood and too coarse tannins that tend to hide whatever fruits are trying to make themselves felt. Drink from release. Tentative Score 82–84. **K**

KITRON, CABERNET SAUVIGNON-SHIRAZ, RESERVE, 2007: A blend of equal parts of Cabernet Sauvignon and Shiraz, showing dark garnet in color, medium- to full-bodied, with somewhat chunky tannins that give the wine a countrified quality. Opens to reveal generous currant, plum and blackberry fruits, those on a lightly spicy background, spicy oak and tannins rising on the finish. Drink from release. Tentative Score 86–88. **K**

Kleins *

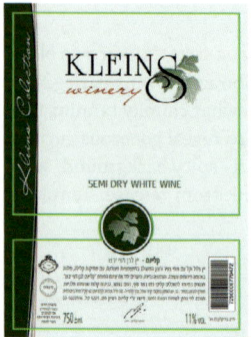

Founded in 2004 by Yom-Tov Klein, this winery is set in the old city of Hebron, and is producing wines from Merlot, Cabernet Sauvignon, Chardonnay, Sauvignon Blanc and other grapes, though none of them indicate either the grape variety or the vintage year on their labels. Production is reported at about 110,000 bottles annually.

KLEINS, DRY RED, N.V.: Dark garnet, with hints of browning, and distinctly barnyard aromas that hide whatever fruits may be trying to make themselves felt. Score 60. **K**

KLEINS, SEMI-DRY WHITE, N.V.: Crisply floral on the nose, but on the palate overly sweet, without balancing acidity and only the skimpiest of lemon and lime aromas and flavors. Score 68. **K**

KLEINS, YASMIN DESSERT, RED, N.V.: Super-sweet, coarse, alcoholic, oxidized and caramelized. Score 55. **K**

KLEINS, YASMIN DESSERT, WHITE, N.V.: Golden straw in color, heavy on the palate and cloyingly sweet with overripe peach fruits. Score 60. **K**

KLEINS, PORT WINE, ANATOT, N.V.: Pale ruby in color, medium-bodied and with burned rubber and muddy aromas and flavors. Score 55. **K**

La Terra Promessa ✳✳✳

Parma-born Sandro Pelligrini comes from a family of wine-makers, and he and his wife Irit founded this small winery in 1998 at their home on Moshav Shachar on the fringes of the northern Negev Desert. The winery relies on Cabernet Sauvignon and Merlot grapes from the Upper Galilee and Ramat Arad, as well as from a vineyard near the winery with Shiraz, Zinfandel, Sangiovese and Petite Sirah. The winery is currently producing about 4,500 bottles annually, in four series: the premium Rubino and La Crime Riserva and the regular La Crime and La Terra Promessa. As this book goes to press, the winery is considering moving to a new and more modern facility.

Rubino Riserva

RUBINO RISERVA, 2005: Full-bodied, with generous wood and firm tannins opening slowly to reveal black fruits on a licorice and earthy background. Drink now. Score 85.

RUBINO RISERVA, 2004: Dark garnet toward royal purple, full-bodied, with generous caressing tannins in fine balance with wood, natural acidity and fruits. On the nose and palate blackcurrants, blackberries and ripe plums, all with a hint of black truffles that makes itself felt on the finish. Drink now. Score 87.

RUBINO RISERVA, 2003: Reflecting its 24 months in *barriques* with generous spicy oak. Full-bodied, softly tannic and well balanced, this blend of 60% Cabernet Sauvignon and 40% Merlot offers up aromas and flavors of blackcurrants, plums and black cherries matched nicely by hints of cocoa and mint on the moderately long finish. Showing first signs of aging. Drink up. Score 85.

La Crime Riserva

LA CRIME RISERVA, 2005: Medium- to full-bodied, dark garnet toward royal purple, a blend of 45% Sangiovese, 45% Shiraz and 10% Cabernet Franc. Oak-aged for 24 months, opens with dusty cedarwood aromas that hang on and interfere with the black fruit flavors. Drink now. Score 85.

LA CRIME RISERVA, 2004: A dark garnet, medium- to full-bodied of 45% each Sangiovese and Cabernet Sauvignon and 10% Cabernet Franc. Reflecting 24 months in *barriques* with generous dusty oak and tannins, those yielding slowly in the glass to reveal an appealing array of plums, blackberries and a light leathery note. Drink now. Score 87.

La Crime

LA CRIME, 2006: A blend of Syrah, Sangiovese and Cabernet Franc. Garnet toward royal purple, medium-bodied, with soft tannins and forward ripe berry, black cherry and currant fruits. Somewhat one-dimensional but a good quaffer. Drink now. Score 84.

LA CRIME, 2005: Showing medium-bodied, with generous black fruit, tobacco and chocolate. Long, round and well-balanced. Drink up. Score 86.

La Terra Promessa

LA TERRA PROMESSA, CABERNET SAUVIGNON, 2006: Medium-bodied, with somewhat chunky tannins opening slowly to show black fruits on a light earthy-herbal background. A pleasant country-style wine. Drink now. Score 84.

LA TERRA PROMESSA, CABERNET SAUVIGNON, 2005: Garnet-red, medium-bodied, with soft tannins and an appealing hint of sweet herbs backing up plum and currant fruits. Lacking complexity. Drink up. Score 86.

LA TERRA PROMESSA, MERLOT, 2006: Dark garnet, medium-bodied, with soft tannins and hints of spicy wood, showing straightforward black fruits and hints of Mediterranean herbs. Drink up. Score 84.

LA TERRA PROMESSA, SYRAH, 2005: Medium-dark garnet, medium- to full-bodied, with appealing smoky oak and earthiness opening to reveal tempting black fruits and minerals. Generous and long. Drink up. Score 87.

LA TERRA PROMESSA, SYRAH, 2004: Deep inky purple and medium-to full-bodied, reflecting 16 months in oak with firm tannins and generous smoky wood, those in fine balance with plums, red berries and spices, all leading to a long, smoked-meat finish. Drink up. Score 88.

LA TERRA PROMESSA, PRIMITIVO, 2005: Made entirely from Primitivo grapes and aged for 12 months in 400 liter oak casks, this bright garnet wine shows soft, near-sweet tannins, spicy oak and ripe raspberry, cassis and cherry aromas and flavors. Drink now. Score 86.

LA TERRA PROMESSA, DESERT ROSE, NEGEV, 2005: Dark ruby toward garnet, medium-bodied, a blend of Sangiovese, Cabernet Sauvignon and Syrah (70%, 20% and 10% respectively). Developed in *barriques* for 14 months, showing appealing spicy cedar notes that complement red currants, plum and red berry notes. Just enough complexity to get attention. Drink now. Score 86.

LA TERRA PROMESSA, EMERALD RIESLING, 2008: The color of damp straw, light- to medium-bodied with aromas and flavors of citrus and pineapple. A bit of unwanted volatile acidity here. Drink up. Score 76.

Lachish **

Established on Moshav Lachish on the Central Plain by Oded Yakobson, Oscar Meisels and Gai Rosenfeld, this small winery relies entirely on Cabernet Sauvignon, Merlot and Shiraz grapes from their own vineyards. Current production is about 3,000 bottles annually.

LACHISH, CABERNET SAUVIGNON, 2006: Medium-bodied, with chunky tannins and ripe berry, black cherry and spices on the nose and palate. A simple but appealing country-style wine. Drink now. Score 83.

LACHISH, CABERNET SAUVIGNON, 2005: Garnet toward royal purple, medium- to full-bodied, a somewhat coarse but pleasing country-style wine with generous black fruits, spices and hints of Mediterranean herbs. Drink now. Score 84.

LACHISH, CABERNET SAUVIGNON, 2004: Medium- to full-bodied, with chunky, firm tannins that yield slowly in the glass to show ripe blackberry and currant fruits. Drink up. Score 84.

LACHISH, SHIRAZ, 2004: Medium- to full-bodied, with soft, mouth-coating tannins and spicy wood yielding in the glass to reveal plum, berry and citrus peel aromas and flavors. Drink up. Score 84.

Latroun *

Located in an idyllic setting at the foothills of the Judean Mountains midway between Jerusalem and the coast, the Trappist monks at this monastery have been producing wine since their arrival from France in the 1890s. For many years before the onset of the local wine revolution, weekend outings to the monastery to purchase wines were an important part of the social life of many. With over 400 dunams of land adjoining the monastery planted in grapes, the winery was the first to introduce Gewurztraminer, Riesling, Pinot Noir and Pinot Blanc grapes to the country and is currently producing about 300,000 bottles annually from twenty varieties of grapes. The winemaker is Father René.

LATROUN, CABERNET SAUVIGNON, 2008: Royal purple, medium-bodied, with chunky, country-style tannins and berry-cherry fruits. Alas, enough Brett here to give the wine a musty, barnyard personality. Drink up. Score 70.

LATROUN, CABERNET SAUVIGNON, 2007: Light- to medium-bodied, with soft, almost flabby tannins and a basic berry-cherry personality. A simple country-style wine. Drink now. Score 79.

LATROUN, CABERNET SAUVIGNON, 2006: Medium-bodied, with soft tannins and forward black fruits. Drink now. Score 83.

LATROUN, MERLOT, 2008: A somewhat coarse medium-bodied wine, its black fruits almost hidden by aromas of wet fur. Score 70.

LATROUN, MERLOT, 2007: As many of the wines of Latroun, a simple, somewhat coarse country-style wine. Generous blackberry and plum notes make this an easy-to-drink quaffer. Drink now. Score 80.

LATROUN MERLOT, 2006: Ruby toward garnet, medium-bodied, with soft tannins, this is a pleasant, country-style wine with berry and black cherry fruits. Drink up. Score 80.

LATROUN, PINOT NOIR, 2007: Ruby toward garnet in color, medium-bodied, a pleasant but simple little wine showing berry, cherry and light spicy notes. Drink now. Score 82.

LATROUN, PINOT NOIR, 2006: Light garnet in color, light- to medium-bodied, with soft, almost unfelt tannins, and with its berry and cherry aromas spoiled by a too-heavy Brett influence. Drink up. Score 76.

LATROUN, CHARDONNAY, 2008: Dark, almost bronzed gold, showing a bit of caramelization despite its youth, that hiding its citrus and tropical fruits. Drink up. Score 75.

LATROUN, CHARDONNAY, 2007: Light in color and in body, showing too-generous grapefruit and pineapple fruits. Drink up. Score 78.

LATROUN, SAUVIGNON BLANC, 2007: A simple little white, light- to medium-bodied with tropical fruits and a somewhat strong earthy note. Drink up. Score 74.

Lavie **

Located in the community of Ephrata not far from Jerusalem, the first wine of Asher Bentolila and Yo'av Guez was from the 2002 vintage. Drawing largely on grapes from the Jerusalem Mountains, the winery is currently producing about 3,000 bottles annually.

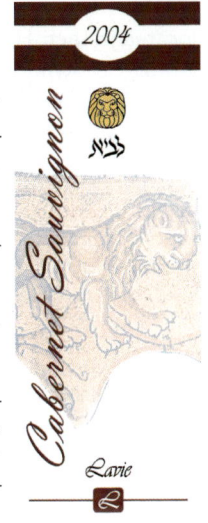

LAVIE, CABERNET SAUVIGNON, 2007: Garnet toward royal purple, medium-bodied, with chunky tannins and a heavy hint of spicy wood that somewhat hides the currant and blackberry fruits. Drink now. Score 80.

LAVIE, CABERNET SAUVIGNON, 2006: Medium-dark garnet, medium-bodied, with soft tannins and hints of spicy wood. Opens to show blackberry and purple plum fruits. A good quaffer. Drink up. Score 82. K

Levron ✶✶

Established by Segal and Yehuda Levron, with the winery located in their Haifa home, first releases are from the 2004 vintage. Drawing on Merlot and Cabernet Sauvignon grapes from Kerem Ben Zimra and the Gush Chalav area in the Galilee, the winery is currently producing 4,000 bottles annually and plans to expand to 6,000.

LEVRON, CABERNET SAUVIGNON, 2007: Garnet red, medium-bodied, with soft tannins and showing aromas and flavors of currants, blackberries and black cherries. On the finish notes of spices and bitter orange peel. Drink now. Score 84.

LEVRON, CABERNET SAUVIGNON, 2006: Ruby toward garnet, medium-bodied, with softly mouth-coating tannins and opening to show wild berry, black cherry and currant notes, all on a light background of earthy minerals. Finishes with an appealing spicy note. Drink up. Score 85.

LEVRON, MERLOT, 2007: Medium-bodied, dark garnet in color, with good balance between near-sweet tannins, spicy wood and black fruits. Not complex but a good quaffer. Drink now. Score 85.

LEVRON, MERLOT, 2006: Medium-bodied, with hints of spicy oak and vanilla accompanied by soft tannins. Opens in the glass to reveal berry, purple plum and light herbaceous notes. Drink up. Score 84.

LEVRON, MERLOT, 2005: Dark ruby, medium-bodied, with soft tannins and appealing berry, cherry and spicy notes. Past its peak. Drink up. Score 85.

Maccabim ✴✴

Founded in 2002 by Eytan Rosenthal, Gari Hochwald, Yo'av Heller and Ami Dotan in the community of Maccabim, at the foothills of the Jerusalem Mountains, and drawing grapes from that area as well as from the Galilee and the Ella Valley, this start-up winery's first release was of 1,200 bottles in 2002. Now producing Cabernet Sauvignon and Merlot wines, the winery releases about 5,000 bottles annually.

MACCABIM, CABERNET SAUVIGNON, 2006: Dark garnet toward royal purple, medium- to full-bodied, with notes of sweet cedar. Straightforward currant and berry fruits make for a good quaffer. Drink now. Score 84. **K**

MACCABIM, CABERNET SAUVIGNON, 2005: Medium- to full-bodied, with soft, near-sweet tannins and spicy wood integrating nicely. On the nose and palate currant, red berry and spices all leading to a medium-long finish. Drink up. Score 85. **K**

MACCABIM, CABERNET SAUVIGNON, 2004: Deep garnet, medium- to full-bodied, with spicy oak and soft tannins highlighting currant, black cherry and plum fruits. Drink now. Score 85. **K**

MACCABIM, MERLOT, 2006: Medium-bodied, a simple but pleasant little country-style wine with chunky tannins. Spicy oak and a berry-cherry personality. Drink now. Score 84. **K**

MACCABIM, MERLOT, 2005: Dark royal purple, medium- to full-bodied, with firm tannins and spicy wood along with blackberry, currant and plum fruits. Drink up. Score 85. **K**

Maor ✦✦✦

Established by Danny and Tal Maor on Moshav Ramot on the Golan Heights, the winery's first release was of 3,200 bottles from the 2003 vintage. Current production is 6,000–8,000 bottles annually, drawing on grapes from the Golan Heights and the Upper Galilee, those including Cabernet Sauvignon, Merlot, Syrah and Cabernet Franc.

MAOR, CABERNET SAUVIGNON, 2006: Dark garnet toward royal purple, with a nose rich with chocolate and licorice, opening to reveal medium- to full-bodied, with soft tannins integrating nicely. On the nose and palate blackcurrants, wild berries, and hints of freshly roasted herbs and espresso. Drink now–2011. Score 88.

MAOR, CABERNET SAUVIGNON, 2005: Blended with 15% Merlot and 3% Cabernet Franc, this generously oaked, dark garnet wine shows aromatic and tempting. Soft tannins give the wine a round, well-balanced personality, that flushed out by traditional currant, berry, black cherry and light herbal aromas and flavors. On the long finish a hint of freshly roasted coffee. Drink now–2011. Score 89.

MAOR, CABERNET SAUVIGNON, CLASSIC, 2004: Blended with 20% of Merlot, this deep ruby-toward-garnet wine is medium-bodied, with soft tannins integrating nicely with spicy wood. Look for aromas and flavors of raspberries, red plums and cranberries, those supported nicely by hints of freshly turned earth and green olives. Drink now. Score 88.

MAOR, CABERNET SAUVIGNON, 2004: Dark garnet, medium- to full-bodied, with generous but not dominating wood and firm tannins well balanced by fruits and acidity. On the nose and palate currants, wild berries and vanilla, all lingering nicely. Drink now. Score 87.

MAOR, SYRAH, 2006: Dark garnet toward royal purple in color, with generous but soft tannins and hints of spicy wood. Well balanced and showing appealing red plum, cassis, herbal and chocolate aromas and flavors, all leading to a generous and mouth-coating finish. Drink now–2011. Score 88.

MAOR, SYRAH, 2005: Dark garnet in color, with solid but yielding tannins and spicy oak, those in fine balance with fruits and acidity. Opens to show plum, currant, tar, tobacco and mineral notes, leading to a long and chocolate-tinted finish. Best yet from the winery. Drink now. Score 89.

MAOR, CABERNET SAUVIGNON-MERLOT, 2006: Dark ruby toward garnet, medium- to full-bodied, with soft tannins, fine concentration and a complex array of black and red fruits, those complemented by generous hints of Mediterranean herbs and, on the long finish, an appealing hint of freshly unearthed mushrooms. Drink now–2011. Score 88.

MAOR, SYRAH-MERLOT, 2006: Deep purple toward inky black in color, firm and well focused and capturing the traditional herbaceousness of Merlot and the minty, berry and meaty flavors of Syrah. Concentrated but soft and round. Drink now–2011. Score 88.

Margalit ✶✶✶✶✶

Among the first boutique wineries in the country, and the first to capture the imagination of sophisticated wine lovers. Founded in 1989, the winery was first located on Moshav Kfar Bilu near the town of Rehovot, and since 1994 has been set near the town of Hadera, at the foothills of Mount Carmel. Father and son team Ya'ir and Assaf Margalit are most renowned for their Bordeaux-style reds that are released in both a regular and a reserve series. In his role as a physical chemist, Ya'ir Margalit has published several well-known textbooks. Assaf, who studied in the agriculture faculty of Hebrew University at Rehovot, also trained in California.

Margalit's earliest release, in 1989, was of 900 bottles of Cabernet Sauvignon. More recent releases, including Cabernet, Merlot, Petite Sirah and Syrah, are made primarily of grapes from their own vineyards in Kadita in the Upper Galilee, while the Cabernet Franc is grown in their Binyamina vineyard. The winery offers three series, the top of the line Special Reserve and Margalit, and, starting with the 2003 harvest, Enigma, a Bordeaux-style blend. All of Margalit's wines are meant for cellaring. Production varies at between 17,000–21,000 bottles annually.

Special Reserve

SPECIAL RESERVE, CABERNET SAUVIGNON, 2007: Intense and concentrated, so firmly tannic at this stage that you might think it searing. No fear, however, for those tannins are in fine balance with wood and fruit, the wine shows an enviable structure, and all that is required for this one to show its glory is time. Destined to always be muscular, those muscles with an elegant and not at all showy note. As the wine develops look for currant, black cherry and blackberry fruits, those with hints of black pepper, nutmeg and licorice, all leading to a long, generous finish. Best 2011 or 2012–2020. Score 94.

SPECIAL RESERVE, CABERNET SAUVIGNON, 2006: Cabernet Sauvignon blended with about 13% of Margalit's Petite Sirah. Full-bodied, dense and intense, but at the same time round and yielding, offering up chocolate-covered cherries, cassis, wild berry and kirsch, those balanced nicely by spicy-cedary oak. Long, complex and destined for elegance. Drink now–2017. Score 93.

SPECIAL RESERVE, CABERNET SAUVIGNON, 2005: A blend of 85% Cabernet Sauvignon and 15% of Margalit's special Petite Sirah. Deep garnet toward inky black, remarkably concentrated and intense; still-firmly tannic at this stage but with fine balance and structure. Now starting to show a glorious array of currant, blackberry and plums on the first attack, those melding into hints of coffee, dusky spices and smoky notes. On the super-long finish, the tannins recede to let the fruits and a hint of espresso coffee rise to the surface. Potentially Margalit's longest-lived wine. Drink now–2022. Score 94.

SPECIAL RESERVE, CABERNET SAUVIGNON, 2004: A limited edition of 600 bottles, this full-bodied blend of 86% Cabernet Sauvignon and 14% Petite Sirah shows fine balance between tannins that are now integrating nicely, hints of sweet oak and generous but subdued blackcurrant, plum and chocolate aromas and flavors. Drink now–2014. Score 93.

SPECIAL RESERVE, CABERNET SAUVIGNON, 2003: Rich, ripe and concentrated, with layer after layer of dark plum, currant, anise, mocha, black cherries and sage. An oak-aged blend of Cabernet Sauvignon and Petite Sirah (87% and 13% respectively), this distinctly Old World wine has excellent balance between wood, lively acidity and well-integrated tannins. Complex and long. Drink now–2013. Score 93.

SPECIAL RESERVE, CABERNET SAUVIGNON, 2002: Coming into its own now, the once almost unbearable intensity now residing and letting the wine show its elegance. This almost impenetrable garnet-toward-inky-black blend of 80% Cabernet Sauvignon, 12% Petite Sirah and 8% Cabernet Franc remains remarkably concentrated and heavy enough to chew, but through its muscles shows great finesse. Ripe currants, purple plums, wild berries, spices and cedar flavors on a complex licorice and tobacco core and a long, intense finish. Drink now–2014. Score 93.

SPECIAL RESERVE, CABERNET SAUVIGNON, 2001: Dense and concentrated, with its once gripping tannins now settled in nicely. A full-bodied and rich blend of 85% Cabernet Sauvignon and 15% of

Margalit's very special Petite Sirah now showing layer after layer of currants, wild berries, plums and black cherries along with toasty oak, minerals and just the right hints of earthiness and sage on the very long finish. Drink now–2012. Score 91.

SPECIAL RESERVE, CABERNET SAUVIGNON, 2000: Showing every bit as elegant and luxurious as during its youth. A blend of 80% Cabernet Sauvignon, 15% Petite Sirah and 5% Merlot, opens with an earthy-mineral nose, that going to spring flowers and then on to aromas and flavors of blackcurrants, wild berries, black cherries and cigar box notes. On the long finish hints of dark chocolate and cigar tobacco. Drink now–2011. Score 92.

SPECIAL RESERVE, CABERNET SAUVIGNON, 1999: Harmonious, dense and tannic, this full-bodied and elegant blend of 87% Cabernet Sauvignon and 13% Carignan offers tempting spices and ripe fruit aromas and flavors of currants, plums, chocolate and coffee. Mature but showing great elegance. Drink now–2012. Score 93.

Margalit

MARGALIT, CABERNET SAUVIGNON, 2007: Made from intentionally early-harvested grapes, full-bodied, green and tannic, with brambly undertones and black licorice on first attack, those yielding to blackcurrant, tobacco and espresso coffee aromas and flavors. As the wine develops, look as well for notes of olives and truffles. Still quite solid but showing fine balance and structure and already starting to open to reveal an underlying finesse. Best 2011–2017. Score 92.

MARGALIT, CABERNET SAUVIGNON, 2006: Almost inky-black in color, offering a generous mouthful of currant, cherry, blackberry and blueberry fruits, those matched by layers of sweet spices. Big, broad and intense but yielding on the palate to show grace and elegance, and closing with a long, fruity finish. Drink now–2016. Score 92.

MARGALIT, CABERNET SAUVIGNON, 2005: Deep garnet toward royal purple, medium- to full-bodied, with soft but gripping tannins and fine balance and structure. Opens with red currant, raspberry and red plum fruits, those yielding to blueberries and appealing earthy-herbal overtones with gentle spicy wood on the long finish. Drink now–2015. Score 93.

MARGALIT, CABERNET SAUVIGNON, 2004: Dark garnet toward royal purple with orange reflections, this well-balanced, medium- to full-bodied wine is showing generous currant and berry fruits, those matched nicely by spicy wood, dark chocolate and espresso coffee. Long and luxurious. Drink now–2012. Score 92.

MARGALIT, CABERNET SAUVIGNON, 2003: Drinking beautifully, this blend of 88% Cabernet Sauvignon and 12% Cabernet Franc, both from the Kadita vineyard in the Upper Galilee is showing full-bodied, remarkably rich and with fine balance and structure. Opens as it did in its youth with earthy currants and black cherry fruits, and then goes on to reveal notes of raspberries, mocha and chocolate. Generous tannins here but those now gently caressing, giving the wine both roundness and elegance, all leading to a super-long finish on which one finds at one moment a note of anise and another a hint of saddle leather. At its best now, but this one will hold its peak comfortably until 2015. Score 94.

MARGALIT, CABERNET SAUVIGNON, 2002: This full-bodied blend of 85% Cabernet Sauvignon, 8% Merlot and 7% Cabernet Franc, its once firm tannins softening now, is showing aromas and flavors of blackcurrants, berries and game meat, together with a long finish. Complex and sophisticated, but not for much longer cellaring. Drink now. Score 92.

MARGALIT, CABERNET SAUVIGNON, 2001: This dark, dense and richly flavored oak-aged blend of 90% Cabernet Sauvignon and 10% Merlot offers generous currant, blackberry, sage and mineral aromas and flavors. Still-firm tannins, those integrating nicely now, and a long finish with tempting coffee, dark chocolate and hints of licorice and mint. Drink now–2012. Score 91.

MARGALIT, CABERNET SAUVIGNON, LOT 37, 2001: Vastly different in style from every other Margalit wine released, this wine was aged in *barriques* for two years, in contrast to all of Margalit's other wines, aged for only one. The blackcurrants that typify so many of this winery's wines have been replaced here by plums, and the oft-searing tannins that sometimes take years to integrate are already soft and now showing a sweet and dusty nature. Drink now–2012. Score 92.

MARGALIT, CABERNET SAUVIGNON, 2000: This full-bodied, still-tannic blend of 88% Cabernet Sauvignon and 12% Merlot had some rough edges in its youth but has now come fully into its own. Look for an abundance of raspberry, black cherry, sage, and spicy aromas and flavors, all with delicious leathery, cedarwood overtones. Drink now. Score 91.

MARGALIT, MERLOT, 2007: Anything but one of those rather boring internationalized Merlots that we have come to dread! Medium- to full-bodied, earthy, with big but velvety tannins and ripe purple plum, currant and blackberry fruits. Long and soft on the palate, with a finish that goes on and on. Drink now–2017. Score 93.

MARGALIT, MERLOT, 2005: Inky purple in color, offers up generous near-sweet oak, black cherries, blackberries and currants on first attack, those yielding to red plums and jammy raspberries. Dark and brooding at this time, with the tannins rising on the long finish. Drink now–2014. Score 93.

MARGALIT, MERLOT, 2004: Fresh, ripe and generous, with appealing blackberry, plum, cassis, mocha and vanilla aromas and flavors finishing with a hint of grilled herbs. Medium- to full-bodied, with soft tannins, a gently spicy wine that lingers nicely. Drink now. Score 90.

MARGALIT, MERLOT, 2002: Full-bodied, deep purple toward inky black in color and blended with 10% Cabernet Sauvignon to add backbone, this ripe, bold and delicious wine shows well-integrated tannins that give it a welcome softness, those matched nicely by aromas and flavors of plums, currants and black cherries, and a long spicy and cedar-flavored finish. Drink now–2012. Score 92.

MARGALIT, MERLOT, 2001: This complex, intense and well-balanced 85% Merlot and 15% Cabernet Sauvignon blend has abundant soft tannins and plenty of earthy and mineral notes overlaying spicy currant, wild berry and coffee aromas and flavors. Look for a long, lingering finish with an array of hazelnuts, coffee and anise. Drink now. Score 91.

MARGALIT, MERLOT, 2000: Remarkably tannic for a Merlot, this full-bodied wine which also contains 10% of Cabernet Sauvignon grapes is rich, ripe and concentrated, with layer after layer of currants, plums and black cherries, all with generous hints of tobacco, smoky oak and vanilla. Drink now. Score 92.

MARGALIT, MERLOT, 1999: With smooth tannins and rich flavors that fill the mouth and then linger nicely, this well-balanced, full-bodied, bold, ripe and delicious wine shows layer after layer of plum, currant, and black cherry flavors as well as a long finish on which you will find nice herbal overtones. Drink now. Score 90.

MARGALIT, CARIGNAN, 1999: A surprise when it was released, the one and only varietal Carignan released by Margalit. Blended with 5% Cabernet Sauvignon grapes, the wine was remarkably tight and closed during its youth but even then showing fine balance and structure.

Full-bodied, with a still-young garnet-toward-royal purple color, but with tannins that have subsided and now fully complement red berry, chocolate and notes of licorice all leading to a round and mouth-filling finish. Drink now. Score 90.

MARGALIT, CABERNET FRANC, 2007: Still a baby and because of that not yet showing its full charms, but already revealing remarkable promise. Full-bodied, with gently mouth-coating tannins, opens to reveal traditional Cabernet Franc "greenness," that yielding comfortably to blackberry, blueberry and cassis fruits, those complemented by notes of sweet peppers, green olives and an appealing note of *garrigue*. Give this one time to show its elegance. Best 2011–2018. Score 93.

MARGALIT, CABERNET FRANC, 2006: Dark garnet toward royal purple, medium- to full-bodied. Blended with 5% of Cabernet Sauvignon and showing rich blackcurrant, cherry and blackberry fruits matched nicely by floral and light earthy aromas and flavors, all coming to a long, round and caressing finish. Drink now–2015. Score 92.

MARGALIT, CABERNET FRANC, 2005: Dark cherry toward garnet and full-bodied, this round and polished wine shows abundant blackberry, currant and black cherry fruits, those matched nicely by hints of spices and cedarwood, all leading to a long, generously tannic finish. Elegant and faithful to the variety. Drink now–2013. Score 92.

MARGALIT, CABERNET FRANC, 2004: Deeply fragrant, this full-bodied wine was blended with 12% Cabernet Sauvignon. Silky-smooth tannins, black and red fruits, hints of tobacco and chocolate come together on a long, mouth-filling finish with an appealing hint of freshly turned earth. Drink now–2011. Score 90.

MARGALIT, CABERNET FRANC, 2003: Almost impenetrable deep purple, full-bodied, with excellent balance between soft, luxurious tannins and a tempting array of dark plum, wild berry and herbal aromas and flavors. Oak-aged, with the addition of 10% Cabernet Sauvignon, the wine is mouth-filling and long, showing a tantalizing hint of mint on the finish. Drink now–2012. Score 90.

MARGALIT, CABERNET FRANC, 2002: This deep royal purple, full-bodied, concentrated Cabernet Franc with 12% Cabernet Sauvignon blended in, shows aromas and flavors of spicy plums and earthiness on first attack that yield to an array of currant, anise, chocolate and sweet cedar, all coming together in a long mouth-filling finish. The wine has soft tannins, generous oak, plenty of acidity and overall good balance. Drink now. Score 92.

Enigma

2003

ENIGMA

Red Table Wine
C. Sauvignon 70% / Merlot 18% / C. Franc 12%
Galilee Mountains / Product of Israel

ENIGMA, 2007: Full-bodied, with soft tannins that coat the mouth gently, and opening to reveal a complex array of wild berries, black and red cherries and currants, those complemented by an intriguing melange of freshly roasted herbs and a touch of fresh-forest floor. Approachable and enjoyable now, but best 2011–2017. Score 92.

ENIGMA, 2006: Full-bodied, subtle and round, a softly tannic blend of 60% Cabernet Sauvignon, 23% Cabernet Franc and 17% Merlot. Opens with red currants and red plums, goes to black cherries and a pleasing light spiciness, and closing with a long, fruity and persistent finish. Drink now–2015. Score 93.

ENIGMA, 2005: This medium- to full-bodied blend of Cabernet Sauvignon, Cabernet Franc and Merlot (60%, 22% and 18% respectively) shows generous cassis, raspberry and cherry fruits, those matched nicely by caressingly soft tannins, lightly spicy oak and chocolate, all coming together elegantly on a long and mouth-filling finish. Drink now–2013. Score 93.

ENIGMA, 2004: A blend of 60% Cabernet Sauvignon, 21% Cabernet Franc and 19% Merlot. A Bordeaux blend with the clear Margalit signature, showing generous but near-sweet soft tannins and a moderate hand with the wood. On the nose and palate dark purple plum and currant fruits, those matched nicely by spices and a hint of red licorice that creeps in on the long finish. Drink now–2012. Score 93.

ENIGMA, 2003: Fully living up to its earlier promise, this Bordeaux blend of 70% Cabernet Sauvignon, 18% Merlot and 12% Cabernet Franc is showing remarkably rich, ripe and polished. Dark garnet, round and approachable, with a complex array of currant, plum and wild berry aromas and flavors, those well focused and long, and matched by a gentle spiciness and a hint of freshly roasted coffee that run through to the long finish. Drink now–2011. Score 92.

Meishar ★★★

Founded in 1991 by Ze'ev and Chaya Smilansky on Moshav Meishar in the southern coastal plains, this small winery relies entirely on its own vineyards of Cabernet Sauvignon, Merlot, Shiraz and Muscat grapes, and currently produces about 10,000 bottles annually of red wines in a Reserve and a Meishar series.

Reserve

RESERVE, 730, CABERNET SAUVIGNON, 2005: Dark royal purple in color, full-bodied, with softly caressing tannins and notes of sweet and spicy cedarwood, opening to reveal blackcurrants, blackberries and cherry fruits, those supported nicely by notes of bittersweet chocolate, and, on the moderately long finish, a hint of smoke. Drink now–2011. Score 87.

RESERVE 730, CABERNET SAUVIGNON, 2004: Full-bodied, this red reflects its 18 months in oak with firm tannins and sweet cedar notes, those integrating nicely with black cherries, ripe currants and light chocolate mousse flavors that sneak in quietly on the finish. Drink now. Score 89.

RESERVE, 730, MERLOT, 2005: Showing dark and spicy, with an enchanting earthy character that highlights cherry, blackberry and spice aromas and flavors. Long and mouth-filling. Drink now. Score 89.

RESERVE, 730, MERLOT, 2004: Made entirely from Merlot grapes, showing medium- to full-bodied along with a gentle hand with the oak and generous earthy-herbal overtones, those in fine balance with ripe currant and blackberry fruits. On the long finish, hints of Oriental spices and grilled meat. Drink now. Score 89.

Meishar

MEISHAR, CABERNET SAUVIGNON, 2005: Dark garnet toward royal purple, medium- to full-bodied, with fine balance between still-firm but already integrating tannins, spicy wood and well-focused currant, dark plum and black cherry fruits. Hints of ground pepper and anise that linger nicely. Drink now. Score 90.

MEISHAR, CABERNET SAUVIGNON, 2004: Dark garnet, medium- to full-bodied, with generous but soft tannins and smoky oak opening nicely to reveal aromas and flavors of blackcurrants, purple plums, white chocolate and spices. Long and mouth-filling. Drink now. Score 89.

MEISHAR, MERLOT, 2005: Medium-dark garnet, medium-bodied and with silky tannins allowing raspberry, blackberry and cassis fruits to show through nicely, those complemented by generous hints of cocoa and a light earthy-graphite sensation that lingers nicely. Drink now. Score 88.

MEISHAR, MERLOT, 2004: Dark royal purple in color, this gently oak-aged medium-bodied wine was blended with 15% of Cabernet Sauvignon. Long, soft and round with plum and blackberry fruits backed up by hints of Mediterranean herbs, chocolate and freshly turned earth. Drink now. Score 87.

MEISHAR, SHIRAZ-CABERNET SAUVIGNON-MERLOT, #41, 2005: A blend of 40% each Shiraz and Merlot and 20% Cabernet Sauvignon. Light ruby in color, light- to medium-bodied, with soft tannins and forward berry, cherry and cassis notes. One-dimensional and somewhat dilute. An acceptable quaffer. Drink up. Score 83.

MEISHAR, SHIRAZ-MERLOT-CABERNET SAUVIGNON, #41, 2004: Dark garnet, medium-bodied, with gentle sweet cedar and spicy oak overtones highlighting blackberries, black cherries and an array of herbs and spices. Look for hints of minerals and anise on the crisp finish. Drink now. Score 89.

MEISHAR, SHIRAZ-MERLOT-CABERNET SAUVIGNON, #41, 2003: A blend of 40% each of Shiraz and Merlot and 20% Cabernet Sauvignon. Aged in oak for eight months, medium-bodied, showing good balance between near-sweet tannins, spicy oak and fruits. On the nose and palate ripe plums, blackcurrants and blackberries matched by hints of earthiness and tobacco. Long and generous. Drink now. Score 90.

MEISHAR, TACSUM, 2003: Perhaps the winemakers were in a playful mood when they named this wine by spelling "Muscat" backward. Made from Muscat Canelli grapes that were sun-dried and then frozen before pressing, this is a wine as much in the Italian *appasimento* style as it is an ice wine. Not so much full-bodied as it is "thick," the wine shows unabashed sweetness and a dark, burnished bronze color. Good balancing acidity and flavors of apricots, ripe peaches and honeydew melon keep it lively. Drink now. Score 88.

Meister ✳

Founded by Ya'akov Meister in Rosh Pina in the upper Galilee and drawing on Cabernet Sauvignon, Merlot, Shiraz and Carignan grapes from his own and other Galilee vineyards, this small winery released its first wines to the market with 2,000 bottles in 2003. Current production is about 6,000 bottles annually.

MEISTER, CABERNET SAUVIGNON, 2007: Dark garnet, full-bodied and spoiled by far too many medicinal, moldy and sour notes that hide whatever fruits may be lurking here. Score 60.

MEISTER, CABERNET SAUVIGNON, 2006: A funky, muddy wine, with charred herbs, tar and searing tannins that end with a chalky aftertaste. Score 65.

MEISTER, MERLOT, 2007: Dark but not perfectly clear garnet and medium- to full-bodied. Dominated by unclean barnyard aromas that make the wine unappealing. Score 60.

MEISTER, MERLOT, 2006: Dry and bitter, with green earthy and tobacco ash aromas and flavors. Score 60.

MEISTER, SHIRAZ, 2006: Medium-bodied, with barnyard aromas and flavors of slightly sour stewed plums and cherries that lead to an earthy and balsamico finish. Tentative Score 55–57.

MEISTER, CARIGNAN, 2006: Medium-bodied, with spicy oak, weedy and vegetable aromas and flavors that hide the black fruits struggling without much success to make themselves felt. Tentative Score 68–70.

Miles **

Founded by vintner Eyal Miles in 2001 on Moshav Kerem Ben Zimra in the Upper Galilee, with its own vineyards containing Cabernet Sauvignon, Merlot, Sauvignon Blanc and Gewurztraminer, this winery is currently producing about 8,000 bottles annually.

MILES, CABERNET SAUVIGNON, RESERVE, 2006: Dark garnet, full-bodied, reflecting its 20 months in partly new, partly used French and American oak with generous spicy wood and somewhat chunky country-style tannins. Opens in the glass to show traditional blackcurrant and blackberry fruits, those supported by hints of spices and Mediterranean herbs. Drink now. Score 84.

MILES, CABERNET SAUVIGNON, RESERVE, 2005: Reflecting 18 months of oak-aging with generous smoky wood and gripping tannins only now starting to integrate. Opens to reveal currant, blueberry and plum fruits, those on a light background of earthy minerals. Drink now. Score 85.

MILES, CABERNET SAUVIGNON, 2005: Oak-aged for 15 months, deep ruby toward garnet, medium- to full-bodied, with chunky, country-style tannins with black fruits and a light earthy-mineral finish. Drink up. Score 84.

MILES, MERLOT, 2005: Deep garnet, medium-bodied with soft, mouth-coating tannins and near-sweet oak. A blend of 88% Merlot and 12% Cabernet Sauvignon opening to reveal blackberry, blueberry and currant fruits, all on a lightly spicy background. Drink now. Score 85.

MILES, CABERNET SAUVIGNON-MERLOT, 2005: A blend of 60% Cabernet Sauvignon and 40% Merlot, oak-aged for 18 months and showing soft tannins and dusty wood along with black fruits and hints of mint. Marred somewhat by a medicinal aroma. Drink now. Score 84.

MILES, SAUVIGNON BLANC, 2006: Light gold with a green tint, medium-bodied, showing citrus, guava and pineapple fruits. A hint of sweetness here but refreshing and lively. Drink up. Score 85.

Miller ✴

Established in 2003 by Dan Ashkenazi in the community of Sha'arei Tikva on the western slopes of the Samarian Mountains, this small winery is currently producing 7,000 bottles annually, relying primarily on Cabernet Sauvignon and Merlot grapes from local vineyards and vineyards in the Galilee.

MILLER, CABERNET SAUVIGNON, 2006: Garnet toward purple, medium-bodied, soft and round, with straightforward red berry, cherry and cassis fruits. Drink now. Score 80. K

MILLER, CABERNET SAUVIGNON, 2005: This dark cherry red wine is unoaked and medium-bodied, with soft tannins and simple but pleasant raspberry and cherry aromas and flavors. Already showing signs of age. Drink up. Score 78. K

MILLER, MERLOT, 2006: Unoaked, light- toward medium-bodied, with soft tannins and forward berry and cherry fruits on a lightly spicy background.A simple quaffer. Drink now. Score 84. K

MILLER, MERLOT, 2005: Ruby toward garnet, this medium-bodied, unoaked country-style wine has appealing berry, black cherry and cassis aromas and flavors. Drink up. Score 80. K

Mond ✳✳✳

Located in a pastoral setting on Moshav Mishmeret, not far from Kfar Saba, this boutique winery was founded by Moshe Keren, and the first wines were released from the 2004 vintage. The winery relies on Cabernet Sauvignon and Merlot grapes from the Ella Valley and from the Upper Galilee. Current production is about 7,000 bottles annually.

MOND, CABERNET SAUVIGNON, OLYMPIA, 2006: Oak-aged in *barriques* for 16 months, showing dark garnet, full-bodied and with generous wood and firm tannins starting to integrate with blackcurrant and wild berry fruits, those on a background of spices and licorice. Best 2010–2012. Score 87. **K**

MOND, CABERNET SAUVIGNON, OLYMPIA, 2005: Deep royal purple, medium- to full-bodied, reflecting its 18 months in oak with firm tannins and a generous spicy overlay. Opens to reveal currant, berry and red plum fruits along with notes of bittersweet chocolate and tobacco. Drink now. Score 86. **K**

MOND, CABERNET SAUVIGNON, OLYMPIA, 2004: Garnet to royal purple, medium-bodied, with soft tannins and notes of spicy and smoky oak from its 18 months in *barriques*. On the nose and palate traditional Cabernet blackcurrant and blackberry fruits, those matched nicely by hints of minted chocolate. Round, soft and generous. Drink up. Score 85. **K**

MOND, MERLOT, OLYMPIA, 2006: Dark ruby toward garnet, medium- to full-bodied, with gently mouth-coating tannins and generous hints of dusty oak. Opens in the glass to reveal blackberry and black cherry fruits, those matched nicely by hints of chocolate and eucalyptus. Drink now. Score 85. **K**

MOND, MERLOT, OLYMPIA, 2005: Dark garnet, medium-bodied, with silky tannins and showing a generous array of red and black berries and cassis. Marred somewhat by a too-generous oak impact. Drink up. Score 84. **K**

Mony **

Located in the foothills of the Jerusalem Mountains on the grounds of the Dir Rafat Monastery, the winery was operated for many years by the resident monks. About seven years ago, control of the vineyards and winery passed to the Ertul family, long-time vintners for the monastery. Grapes in the vineyards include Cabernet Sauvignon, Cabernet Franc, Merlot, Zinfandel, Shiraz, Carignan, Argaman, Petite Sirah, Chardonnay, Semillon, Emerald Riesling and other varieties. Annual production is about 22,000 bottles. The winery is currently producing wines in two series, the upper-level Reserve and the regular Mony, and from the 2005 vintage, the wines have been kosher.

Reserve

RESERVE, CABERNET SAUVIGNON, 2006: Dark but not perfectly clear garnet, with sharp and chunky tannins and perhaps too-generous spicy wood. Opens slowly to reveal stingy currant and berry fruits. Drink now. Score 80. **K**

RESERVE, CABERNET SAUVIGNON, 2005: Dark ruby toward brick-red, medium- to full-bodied, with a hint of barnyard aromas along with firm tannins and generous spicy wood that seem not to want to yield and hide the black fruits that are underneath. Drink up. Score 78. **K**

RESERVE, MERLOT, 2006: Garnet toward royal purple, medium-bodied, with firm tannins and generous smoky wood. Opens to show primarily red fruits on a background of Mediterranean herbs. Drink up. Score 82. **K**

RESERVE, MERLOT, 2005: Dark ruby toward garnet in color, medium- to full-bodied, showing spicy wood and a somewhat medicinal aroma.

Cherry and raspberry fruits struggle to make themselves felt through very generous earthy-herbal and tobacco notes. Drink up. Score 81. **K**

RESERVE, SHIRAZ, 2005: Showing softer and less tannic than at earlier tastings. Dark royal purple in color, soft and with round tannins, but with only skimpy red fruits and a not appealing barnyard aroma that lingers from first attack to finish. Drink up. Score 78. **K**

RESERVE, TALTALIM, 2005: A full-bodied, dark garnet blend of 60% Cabernet Sauvignon and 40% Merlot, reflecting generous smoky oak and firm, vanilla-tinged tannins from its 16 months in *barriques*. Opens to reveal blackberry, currant and purple plum fruits, those with appealing spicy overtones. Drink now. Score 86. **K**

RESERVE, CHARDONNAY, 2007: Damp straw in color, light- to medium-bodied with pineapple and citrus fruits spoiled somewhat by a rather heavy overlay of Brett. Drink up. Score 79. **K**

RESERVE, CHARDONNAY, 2006: Light golden straw in color, medium-bodied, with crisp acidity and straightforward pineapple, citrus and apple notes. Drink up. Score 82. **K**

Mony

MONY, CABERNET SAUVIGNON, 2007: Garnet toward purple in color, light- to medium-bodied, with soft tannins and a few red fruits. A simple country-style wine with a detracting hint of barnyard aromas. Drink up. Score 79. **K**

MONY, CABERNET SAUVIGNON, 2006: Ruby toward garnet, medium-bodied, with soft tannins and straightforward berry and black cherry fruits. A simple entry-level wine. Drink up. Score 80. **K**

MONY, CABERNET SAUVIGNON, 2005: Lightly oaked, this deep ruby wine is medium-bodied, with soft tannins and appealing red fruits. An entry-level wine already showing signs of aging. Drink up. Score 81. **K**

MONY, MERLOT, 2007: Dark ruby, medium-bodied, with soft, somewhat flabby tannins and skimpy berry and black cherry fruits. A simple country-style wine. Drink up. Score 80. **K**

MONY, MERLOT, 2006: Garnet toward royal purple, full-bodied, with soft, mouth-coating tannins and an array of berry, cherry and citrus peel aromas and flavors. One-dimensional but an acceptable quaffer. Drink up. Score 84. **K**

MONY, MERLOT, 2005: Ruby red, light- to medium-bodied, with soft tannins and a few currant and berry fruits. Drink up. Score 78. **K**

MONY, SYRAH, 2006: Medium-bodied, with firm tannins. Austere, with only a narrow band of wild berry fruits and a too-skimpy hint of spices. Drink now. Score 82. **K**

MONY, CHARDONNAY, 2005: Light straw in color and medium-bodied, this lightly oak-aged white shows some apple and pineapple aromas but leaves a sensation of flatness on the palate. Drink up. Score 79. **K**

MONY, MUSCAT DESSERT WINE, 2007: Without complexities but pleasant and aromatic. Generously sweet with good balancing acidity and basic citrus and tropical fruits. Drink now. Score 84. **K**

MONY, SEMILLON-CHARDONNAY, 2007: A blend of 70% Semillon and 30% Chardonnay. Light golden straw in color, light- to medium-bodied, the label stating dry but with a generous hint of sweetness of grapefruit and tropical fruits. A simple entry-level wine. Drink now. Score 81. **K**

MONY, MUSCAT DESSERT WINE, 2006: Golden yellow in color, with floral and citrus aromas and flavors. Medium-bodied, but somewhat clumsy, with its generous sweetness lacking balancing acidity. Drink now. Score 82. **K**

Na'aman★★★

Founded by Rami and Bettina Na'aman on Moshav Ramot Naftaly in the Upper Galilee, this small winery released their first wines from the 2004 vintage. With their own vineyards containing Cabernet Sauvignon, Merlot, Cabernet Franc, Malbec, Petit Verdot and Shiraz grapes, releases from 2004 were just under 1,000 bottles, in 2006 and 2007 about 3,500 bottles and releases for 2008 and 2009 were for 6,000 bottles.

NA'AMAN, CABERNET SAUVIGNON, 2007: Garnet toward royal purple, medium- to full-bodied, with chunky tannins and generous spicy oak. On the nose and palate berry, black cherry and Mediterranean herbs. An appealing country-style wine. Drink now–2011. Score 86.

NA'AMAN, CABERNET SAUVIGNON, 2006: Dark garnet in color, full-bodied, with firm tannins and a gentle hand with spicy oak. Opens with red plum and berry notes, those yielding to currant and orange peel, and goes on to a tannic finish with appealing herbal overtones. Drink now. Score 88.

NA'AMAN, CABERNET SAUVIGNON, 2005: Blended with 8% of Merlot, dark garnet toward royal purple, medium- to full-bodied, with still-firm tannins and generous wood, but those integrating nicely. Showing blackcurrant, blackberry and briar aromas and flavors with hints of roasted coffee in the background. Drink now. Score 85.

NA'AMAN, MERLOT, RAMIM RIDGE, 2005: Medium-bodied, with coarse tannins. Indeed deep purple in color, but with little charm beyond that, as medicinal and barnyard aromas and coarse tannins cover whatever fruits may be hiding here. Starting to show age. Drink up. Score 74.

NA'AMAN, CABERNET FRANC, 2006: Dark ruby toward garnet, medium- to full-bodied, with firm tannins, showing an array of blackberry, huckleberry, currant, black licorice and Mediterranean herbs, all lingering nicely. Drink now. Score 86.

NA'AMAN, DEEP PURPLE, 2006: Oak-aged for 13 months, a blend of Cabernet Sauvignon, Cabernet Franc, Merlot and Petit Verdot (40%, 30%, 20% and 10% respectively). Dark royal purple in color, medium- to full-bodied with still-firm tannins needing time to integrate. Opens to reveal blackberry, purple plum and cassis fruits along with generous hints of saddle leather and earthy minerals. Drink now. Score 86.

NA'AMAN, DEEP PURPLE, 2005: Cabernet Sauvignon, Cabernet Franc and Merlot in a traditional Bordeaux blend. Dark garnet, full-bodied, with tannins and wood settling in nicely and opening to show blackberry, blackcurrant and orange peel notes on a background of spices and minerals. Drink now. Score 87.

NA'AMAN, KING CRIMSON, 2006: A blend of Cabernet Sauvignon and Merlot. Dark garnet, full-bodied, with still-firm tannins starting to integrate with spicy wood. Showing an appealing array of currant, berry and black cherry fruits, those with hints of earthy minerals and spices. Lingers nicely. Drink now. Score 86.

NA'AMAN, CABERNET SAUVIGNON-MERLOT, KING CRIMSON, 2005: A medium-bodied, softly tannic, oak-aged blend of 75% Cabernet and 25% Merlot, this wine shows spicy wood, cherry and red currant aromas and flavors, those with appealing light bitter and herbal undertones. Drink up. Score 84.

NA'AMAN, PINK FLOYD, 2007: A rosé wine, dark rose-petal pink with hints of orange, this light- to medium-bodied blend of 60% Cabernet Sauvignon, 30% Cabernet Franc and 10% Petit Verdot shows appealing berry, cherry and light cassis notes, all with an appealing spicy background and good acidity to keep it lively. Drink up. Score 86.

Nachshon ✳✳✳

Founded in 1996 on Kibbutz Nachshon in the Ayalon Valley at the foot of the Jerusalem Hills, the winery raises its own Cabernet Sauvignon, Merlot, Shiraz, Cabernet Franc and Argaman grapes and produces about 20,000 bottles annually. The winery releases wines in four series, Ayalon, Sela, Pushkin and Nachshon.

Ayalon

AYALON, CABERNET SAUVIGNON, 2004: Dark garnet, full-bodied, with firm tannins and sweet cedarwood integrating nicely to show blackcurrant and berry fruits on a light herbal background. On the finish a hint of dark chocolate. Drink up. Score 86.

AYALON, CABERNET SAUVIGNON, 2003: Made entirely from Cabernet Sauvignon grapes, this deep-garnet wine was aged first for 25 months in new *barriques* and then for an additional 12 months in old ones. Medium- to full-bodied, and showing near-sweet tannins and hints of sweet cedarwood complemented nicely by spicy berry and currant fruits. Drink up. Score 87.

AYALON, MERLOT, 2004: Deep cherry-ruby red, medium-bodied, with soft tannins, aromas and flavors of raspberries and cherries, the wine is gently oaked, well rounded and nicely balanced. Drink up. Score 86.

AYALON, SYRAH, 2006: Garnet toward royal purple in color, this round and generous blend of 90% Syrah and 10% Cabernet Sauvignon is medium-bodied, with soft tannins, and shows raspberry, leathery and meaty aromas and flavors. Drink up. Score 85.

AYALON, SYRAH, 2005: Blended with 15% Cabernet Sauvignon, this dark royal purple, oak-aged wine opens with a light but tantalizing herbal nose and goes on to show black cherries, cassis and blackberries, those backed up nicely by hints of tobacco and licorice. Drink up. Score 86.

AYALON, CABERNET FRANC, 2006: Dark garnet, this medium- to full-bodied softly tannic blend of 90% Cabernet Franc and 10% Cabernet Sauvignon shows complex currant, plum, cedarwood and tobacco aromas and flavors. Well balanced and round, with an appealing finish highlighted by spicy oak and orange peel. Drink now. Score 86.

AYALON, CABERNET FRANC, 2005: Cabernet Franc, blended with 7–8% each of Merlot and Petit Verdot. Oak-aged partly in French, partly in American barrels, the wine opens with a light, somewhat pungent, aroma but that passes in a few moments to reveal plum, currant and citrus peel. Full-bodied, with firm tannins needing time to settle down. Drink now. Score 86.

Sela

SELA, FRENCH BLEND, 2006: Dark royal purple in color, this oak-aged blend of 57% Syrah, 20% Merlot, 13% Cabernet Franc and 10% Cabernet Sauvignon opens with a slightly musky aroma which passes quickly to reveal soft tannins integrating nicely and an array of berry, black cherry and cassis fruits, those on a lightly meaty background. Drink now. Score 85.

SELA, FRENCH BLEND, 2005: Medium-dark garnet with silky tannins, this blend of Syrah, Cabernet Sauvignon, Cabernet Franc and Petit Verdot (41%, 33%, 16% and 10% respectively) shows an appealing array of wild berries, currants and plums, those on a gently spicy background. Rich, round and moderately long. Drink up. Score 87.

Pushkin

PUSHKIN, 2006: A deep garnet, oak-aged blend of 60% Merlot, 30% Cabernet Franc and 10% Cabernet Sauvignon. Medium- to full-bodied, with firm tannins that yield in the glass to reveal appealing aromas and flavors of blackberries, currants and spices. Develops an odd acetic aroma in the glass. Drink up. Score 82.

PUSHKIN, 2005: This blend of Cabernet Sauvignon, Merlot, Cabernet Franc and Syrah (43%, 42%, 11% and 4% respectively) was aged partly in French *barriques* for six to eight months and partly in stainless steel tanks. Medium-bodied, with soft tannins and aromas of spicy wood, raspberries and cassis. Drink up. Score 83.

Nachshon

NACHSHON, CABERNET SAUVIGNON, 2006: Made entirely from Cabernet Sauvignon grapes, oak-aged for 18 months, showing medium- to full-bodied. Nothing complex here but a soft, round and generous little wine with an appealing berry, black cherry personality. Drink now. Score 85.

NACHSON, ALPHA, 2006: A lightly oaked blend of 60% Shiraz and 40% Cabernet Sauvignon, showing soft tannins and a simple but appealing wild berry and black cherry personality. Soft and round, an entry-level wine. Drink now. Score 84.

NACHSHON, SHIRAZ-CABERNET SAUVIGNON, SHANI, 2005: Oak-aged for 24 months, this medium- to full-bodied blend of 60% Shiraz and 40% Cabernet Sauvignon shows chunky, country-style tannins and a few red and black fruits. One-dimensional and short. Drink up. Score 82.

Nahal Amud ⋆

Established by Avi Abu in 1998 and located on Moshav Kfar Shamai near Safed in the Upper Galilee, the winery draws on grapes from its own vineyards, those including Cabernet Sauvignon, Cabernet Franc, Merlot and Petite Sirah. Current production is about 5,000 bottles annually.

NAHAL AMUD, CABERNET SAUVIGNON, 2006: Dark garnet, full-bodied, with sharp-edged tannins and too-generous acidity that make the black fruits seem almost sour. Drink up. Score 70. **K**

NAHAL AMUD, CABERNET SAUVIGNON, 2005: Garnet toward purple, medium-bodied, with chunky, somewhat coarse tannins, minimal fruits and an excessive earthy overlay. Drink up. Score 72. **K**

NAHAL AMUD, CABERNET SAUVIGNON, 2004: Medium-bodied, with coarse tannins and far-too-generous and not entirely clean earthy overlays and only the skimpiest of black fruits. Showing first signs of aging. Drink up. Score 75. **K**

NAHAL AMUD, MERLOT, 2006: Dark royal purple in color with chunky, country-style tannins. On the nose a strong herbaceousness and a near-sweetness hide whatever fruits may be here. Drink up. Score 70. **K**

NAHAL AMUD, MERLOT, 2005: Dark garnet with a hint of browning, medium-bodied, with firm tannins and an underlying sweetness to stewed red fruits. Drink up. Score 70. **K**

NAHAL AMUD, MERLOT, 2003: Dark but not fully clear royal purple, medium-bodied, with searing tannins and aromas and flavors that call to mind cherry liqueur. Score 68. **K**

NAHAL AMUD, CABERNET SAUVIGNON-MERLOT-SHIRAZ, 2003: Dark garnet, medium- to full-bodied, firmly tannic, with plum and currant fruits pushed into the background by unwanted medicinal and earthy aromas and flavors. Drink up. Score 79. **K**

Nashashibi ✶

Founded in 2001 by brothers Munir and Nashashibi Nashashibi, the winery is located in the village of Ibelin in the southwestern reaches of the lower Galilee, and set on a site where wine has been made since Roman times. Current production is about 15,000 bottles annually, that of Cabernet Sauvignon, Merlot and Chardonnay in two series, Special Reserve and Nashashibi. Grapes come from the Upper Galilee as well as from the winery's own vineyards at the foothills of the Carmel Mountains.

Special Reserve

SPECIAL RESERVE, CABERNET SAUVIGNON, 2005: Dark garnet and medium-bodied, with firm tannins starting to integrate. Showing generous smoke and spices from the wood casks in which it aged. On the nose and palate currants and berries. Starting to develop a barnyard aroma. Drink up. Score 80.

SPECIAL RESERVE, CABERNET SAUVIGNON, 2004: Garnet toward purple, medium-bodied, with firm tannins and spicy oak. An overlay of moldy barnyard aromas hides the fruits. Score 60.

SPECIAL RESERVE, CABERNET SAUVIGNON, 2003: Dark ruby toward garnet, medium- to full-bodied, with stale, moldy, barnyard aromas and flavors that hide the fruits. Score 60.

SPECIAL RESERVE, MERLOT, 2004: Medium-bodied, with almost unfelt tannins, this dark cherry red-toward-purple wine reflects its fourteen months of aging with generous smoky oak. Not much in the way of fruits here. Drink up. Score 78.

Nashashibi

NASHASHIBI, CABERNET SAUVIGNON, 2005: Medium- to full-bodied, dark garnet in color, this country-style wine is somewhat chunky on the palate but showing appealing black fruits and spices. Drink up. Score 84.

NASHASHIBI, CABERNET SAUVIGNON, 2004: Medium-dark garnet, medium-bodied, with chunky tannins. The once appealing aromas and flavors of spicy oak, cassis and blackberries now turning musky, with hints of barnyard. Drink up. Score 70.

NASHASHIBI, CABERNET SAUVIGNON, 2003: Garnet-red but browning at the rim, with unyielding tannins and only skimpy black fruits. Drink up. Score 74.

Natuf ✶✶

Shiraz
2006

משק יין כפר טרומן
Natuf Winery
750 Ml. 13.6% Alc.

Founded by Meir Akel and Ze'ev Cinamon on Moshav Kfar Truman in the Central Plains, not far from Ben Gurion Airport, this winery draws on grapes from the Ayalon Valley, and its releases have been primarily of Cabernet Sauvignon. Current production is about 4,500 bottles annually.

NATUF, CABERNET SAUVIGNON, 2006: Dark ruby toward garnet, full-bodied and reflecting its 14 months in *barriques* with firm tannins and spicy wood, those integrating to show ripe berry and black cherry fruits. Drink now. Score 84.

Cabernet
Sauvignon
2007

משק יין כפר טרומן
Natuf Winery
750 Ml. 14.3% Alc.

NATUF, CABERNET SAUVIGNON, 2005: Deep garnet and medium- to full-bodied, with near-sweet tannins and spicy oak in good balance with currant, blackberry and blueberry fruits. On the moderately long finish an appealing hint of freshly picked mushrooms. Drink now. Score 86.

NATUF, MERLOT, 2006: Dark royal purple, medium- to full-bodied, with somewhat chunky tannins and reflecting its ten months in French and American oak with generous spices and vanilla. Opens to show berry, cherry and pomegranate fruits on a somewhat overly acidic background. Drink now. Score 82.

NATUF, MERLOT, 2005: Dark ruby toward garnet, medium- to full-bodied, with firm tannins and spicy wood. Opens to reveal red fruits and Oriental spices on an earthy and licorice background. Drink now. Score 86.

NATUF, SHIRAZ, 2006: A blend of 85% Shiraz, 9% Cabernet Sauvignon and 6% Merlot. Medium- to full-bodied, with firm tannins and generous spicy wood parting to reveal plum, blackberry, licorice and meaty aromas and flavors. Drink now. Score 85.

Neot Smadar ✴

This small winery, the southern-most in the country, is located on an oasis on Kibbutz Neot Smadar in the Jordan Valley, 60 kilometers north of Eilat. The winery released its first wines from the 2001 vintage and since its inception has relied entirely on organically raised grapes of Cabernet Sauvignon, Merlot, Chardonnay, Sauvignon Blanc and Muscat Canelli, all grown in vineyards on the kibbutz. Due to the unique climate conditions, theirs is invariably the earliest harvest in the country. The winery is currently producing about 4,000 bottles annually.

קברנה סוביניון
Cabernet Sauvignon
2002

יין אורגני אדום יבש
Organic Dry Red Wine

13% Alc. By Vol. 750 ml.
Prod. & bot. By Neot Semadar Wine Cellars

נאות סמדר
אורגני מן המדבר

NEOT SMADAR, CABERNET SAUVIGNON, 2007: Ruby toward garnet, with soft, almost unfelt tannins and hints of spicy wood. Opens to show berry, currant and black cherry aromas. A simple but pleasant quaffer. Drink now. Score 84.

NEOT SMADAR, CABERNET SAUVIGNON, 2006: Medium-bodied, with soft tannins, hints of spicy wood and appealing currant and berry fruits. A simple quaffer. Drink up. Score 80.

NEOT SMADAR, MERLOT, 2007: Light garnet, medium-bodied, with chunky tannins and with a basic berry-cherry personality. A simple country-style wine. Drink up. Score 79.

NEOT SMADAR, MERLOT, 2006: Ruby toward garnet, medium-bodied, with soft tannins and gentle spicy wood notes. On the nose and palate appealing berry, currant and black cherry fruits. Drink now. Score 84.

NEOT SMADAR, MERLOT, 2005: Light- to medium-bodied, somewhat diluted on both nose and palate and with only skimpy black fruits. Drink up. Score 76.

NEOT SMADAR, CHARDONNAY, 2007: The color of damp straw, medium-bodied, with good balancing acidity to highlight citrus, apple and tropical fruits. Drink up. Score 82.

NEOT SMADAR, SAUVIGNON BLANC FUMÉ, 2006: Light golden straw, light- to medium-bodied, with spicy peach and citrus fruits. Drink up. Score 80.

NEOT SMADAR, MUSCAT DESSERT WINE, 2004: Light- to medium-bodied, generously sweet, with good balancing acidity and appealing dried apricot, apple and peach fruits. Drink up. Score 85.

Noga *

Owned by the Harari family and located between Gedera and Moshav Kidron on the Southern Plains, the winery's first release was of 2,000 bottles from the 2004 vintage. Current production is about 5,000 bottles annually and those under two labels, Noga and Tom, both blends of Cabernet Sauvignon and Merlot.

NOGA, 2007: Ruby toward garnet, a medium-bodied, softly tannic blend of Merlot and Cabernet Sauvignon. Opens to show berry, black cherry and licorice notes. A pleasant quaffer. Drink now. Score 84.

NOGA, 2006: An oak-aged blend of 80% Merlot and 20% Cabernet Sauvignon. Medium-bodied, with soft tannins, a round and easy-to-drink wine with currant, berry and black cherry fruits on a lightly spicy background. Drink now. Score 83.

NOGA, 2005: This blend reflects its oak-aging with spicy and vanilla-rich overtones and soft tannins. On the nose and palate black cherry and berry fruits. One-dimensional and short. Drink up. Score 79.

TOM, 2007: Light spicy and toasted white bread notes from its oak-aging, medium-bodied, with black fruits and an overlay of vanilla. A simple country-style wine. Drink now. Score 83.

TOM, 2006: A dark garnet, medium-bodied blend of 80% Cabernet Sauvignon and 20% Merlot, reflecting its oak-aging with spices and vanilla and showing appealing currant and black cherry fruits. Drink up. Score 85.

TOM, 2005: Garnet-red, this oak-aged blend of Cabernet Sauvignon and Merlot shows medium-bodied, with soft tannins and spicy oak yielding to reveal wild berry fruits. Drink up. Score 83.

Odem Mountain ✳✳✳

Founded by the Alfasi family in 2003, the winery is situated in a modern facility on Moshav Odem in the northern Golan Heights. It relies primarily on grapes grown in its own vineyards—one of which is organic—supplemented by grapes from other vineyards on the Golan, in the Upper Galilee, and in the Judean Hills. Currently producing wines based on Cabernet Sauvignon, Merlot, Shiraz and Cabernet Franc, the winery is considering future releases of Sauvignon Blanc and Pinot Noir. Production for 2003 was 6,500 bottles, and for 2004, 2005, 2006 and 2007 about 30,000 bottles. The wines will be kosher starting with the 2007 vintage, and production from that year is anticipated at 50,000 bottles.

The top-of-the-line series are Alfasi and Reserve, the mid-range series are Nimrod and Odem Mountain, and there is a special label, Volcanic, for wines made from organic grapes.

Alfasi

ALFASI, CABERNET-MERLOT, 2005: An oak-aged blend, this year of 70% Cabernet Sauvignon and 30% Merlot. Medium- to full-bodied, with soft tannins integrating nicely and unfolding on the palate to show a generous array of currant and berry fruits, those supported by hints of sweet herbs and green olives. Drink now–2011. Score 88.

ALFASI, CABERNET-MERLOT, 2004: This oak-aged blend of 60% Cabernet Sauvignon and 40% Merlot shows fine balance between still-firm tannins and spicy wood, those yielding in the glass to reveal black fruits, sweet herbs and, on the long finish, hints of green olives and anise. Drink now–2011. Score 91.

Reserve

RESERVE, CABERNET SAUVIGNON, 2006: Dark garnet toward royal purple in color, made entirely from Cabernet Sauvignon grapes, medium- to full-bodied, and oak-aged for 15 months. Opens with a low but appealing fruity and floral nose. Goes on to show blackcurrants and purple plums, those matched nicely by hints of spicy and vanilla-rich wood. Tannins and alcohol rise together on the finish, but given a bit more bottle time this may well vanish and give way to hints of raspberries and cranberries. Drink now–2011. Score 88.

RESERVE, CABERNET SAUVIGNON, 2005: Deep garnet toward royal purple, medium- to full-bodied, with generous, soft tannins and spicy wood in good balance with blackberry, currant and cassis fruits. On the moderately long finish, hints of cedar and freshly cut herbs. Drink now. Score 90.

RESERVE, CABERNET SAUVIGNON, 2004: Dark garnet toward inky black, full-bodied, with soft tannins and a moderate oak influence in fine balance with blackcurrant and blackberry fruits, those supported by hints of herbs and sweet cedar. Drink now. Score 89.

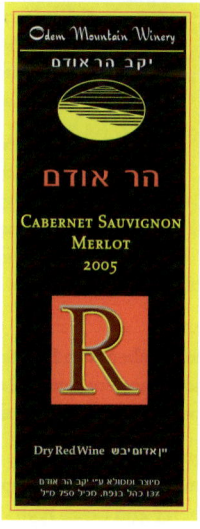

RESERVE, MERLOT, 2006: Aged in new French *barriques* for 15 months, dark ruby toward garnet, showing blueberries and black cherries on first attack, those yielding comfortably to notes of licorice and near-sweet tobacco. Long and generous. Drink now–2011. Score 89.

RESERVE, MERLOT, 2005: Garnet toward purple, reflecting ten months in oak with spicy and vanilla overlays and showing appealing berry and cassis fruits. Medium-bodied, with soft tannins integrating nicely and with a moderately long finish. Drink now. Score 87.

RESERVE, MERLOT, 2004: Oak-aged for 15 months, this almost inky-dark purple wine is medium- to full-bodied, with abundant but not dominating spicy wood. Opens to show wild berries, cassis, black cherries and appealing hints of chocolate that linger nicely. Generous and mouth-filling. Drink now. Score 88.

RESERVE, CABERNET SAUVIGNON-MERLOT, 2006: Oak-aged for 15 months, this blend of 60% Cabernet Sauvignon and 40% Merlot shows generous but gentle spicy wood in fine balance with soft tannins and acidity. Opens to reveal currant, berry and black cherry fruits on a background of chocolate, sweet spices and tarry notes. Long and generous. Drink now–2011. Score 89.

RESERVE, CABERNET SAUVIGNON-MERLOT, 2005: Deep ruby toward garnet, medium-bodied, with soft tannins integrating nicely with spicy and vanilla-rich wood. On the nose and palate, berry, black cherry and cassis, those backed up by sweet herbs and a hint of anise. Moderately long and complex. Drink now. Score 89.

Nimrod

NIMROD, CABERNET SAUVIGNON, 2006: Oak-aged for ten months, showing gentle layers of spicy wood and vanilla, this medium- to full-bodied, garnet-colored wine shows near-sweet tannins integrating nicely and opening to reveal berry, currant and sweet herbs. A light medicinal aroma on pouring blows off quickly. Generous and moderately long. Drink now. Score 88.

NIMROD, CABERNET SAUVIGNON, 2005: Medium- to full-bodied, this dark cherry red-toward-garnet wine is reflecting its ten months in oak with soft, mouth-coating tannins and hints of smoke. On the nose and palate blackcurrants, blackberries and black cherries, all lingering nicely. Drink now. Score 87.

NIMROD, MERLOT, 2006: Dark garnet with purple reflections and full-bodied with firm tannins that need a bit of time to integrate. Opens to show generous red currant, cherry and raspberry fruits, those supported by hints of Mediterranean herbs. Drink now–2011. Score 87.

NIMROD, MERLOT, 2005: Garnet toward purple, reflecting ten months in oak with spicy and vanilla overlays and showing appealing berry and cassis fruits. Medium-bodied, with soft tannins integrating nicely and with a moderately long finish. Drink up. Score 85.

Odem Mountain

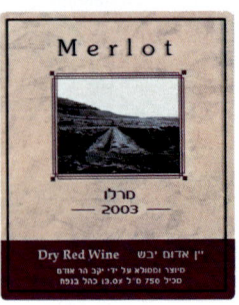

ODEM MOUNTAIN, CABERNET SAUVIGNON, 2006: Opens with a bit of bottle-stink, but that blows off quickly to reveal a medium- to full-bodied, softly tannic wine with generous blackcurrant and purple plum fruits, those matched nicely by hints of mocha and vanilla. Ripe, round and moderately long. Drink now. Score 86.

ODEM MOUNTAIN, CABERNET SAUVIGNON, 2005: Dark ruby toward garnet, medium-bodied, with soft tannins integrating nicely and well balanced by spicy oak. On the tangy nose and palate, traditional Cabernet blackcurrant and wild berry fruits. Drink up. Score 86.

ODEM MOUNTAIN, MERLOT, 2006: Medium-dark garnet, medium- to full-bodied, with soft, near-sweet tannins. Showing generous berry and black cherry fruits matched nicely by hints of cigar tobacco, tar and bittersweet chocolate. Drink now. Score 85.

ODEM MOUNTAIN, MERLOT, 2005: Dark ruby toward garnet, medium-bodied, with soft tannins and gentle spicy oak influences. Look for aromas and flavors of blueberries, cranberries and cassis. Not complex but a good quaffer. Drink now–2009. Score 85.

ODEM MOUNTAIN, CABERNET SAUVIGNON-SYRAH, 2006: This blend of 70% Cabernet and 30% Syrah is showing spicy, floral and earthy aromas and flavors on first attack, those opening to reveal currant, berry and black cherry fruits. Finishing with appealing leathery and cigar-box hints. Drink now. Score 85.

Volcanic

VOLCANIC, CABERNET SAUVIGNON, 2005: Garnet-red, medium-bodied, softly tannic and generously fruity, this unoaked blend of 87% Cabernet Sauvignon and 13% Merlot was made from organically grown grapes. On the nose and palate blackberry and currant fruits, a hint of wood and abundant acidity that makes the wine refreshing but somewhat one-dimensional. Drink now. Score 85.

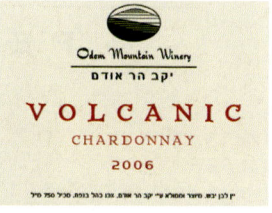

VOLCANIC, CABERNET SAUVIGNON, 2004: Fermented partly in stainless steel and then allowed to undergo malolactic fermentation in French oak *barriques*, this medium- to full-bodied deep-garnet blend of Cabernet Sauvignon and Merlot shows primarily herbal aromas and flavors when first poured, but then opens nicely in the glass to reveal currant and purple plum fruits. Drink up. Score 86.

VOLCANIC, CABERNET SAUVIGNON-MERLOT, 2007: Medium- to full-bodied, dark garnet, with generous wood and rustic, chunky tannins, opens in the glass to show blackberry, plum and spicy notes. An appealing country-style wine. Drink now. Score 87. **K**

VOLCANIC, CHARDONNAY, 2006: Aged for five months in new French oak, this light-gold wine shows an aromatic nose and light wood influences. Opens in the glass to reveal citrus, pineapple and ripe melon fruits, those supported nicely by hints of flinty minerals. Drink up. Score 87.

Pelter ★★★★★

Established in 2002 on Kibbutz Ein Zivan on the Golan Heights by Tal Pelter, who studied oenology and worked at several wineries in Australia, the winery plans to move soon to nearby Kibbutz Merom Golan. Drawing on Cabernet Sauvignon, Merlot, Cabernet Franc, Shiraz, Petit Verdot, Grenache, Semillon, Sauvignon Blanc, Gewurztraminer and Chardonnay grapes from the Golan, the Upper Galilee and the Jerusalem Mountains, the winery, one of only four in the country to produce a sparkling wine, releases wines in two series: T-Selection and Pelter. Production from the 2002 vintage was about 4,000 bottles. Growth has been well planned, and current production is about 80,000 bottles annually.

T-Selection

T-SELECTION, CABERNET SAUVIGNON, 2007: Still in its infancy but already showing smooth and generous. Full-bodied, deep and long with currant, berry and purple plum fruits supported nicely by hints of anise, raisins and earthy minerals. Ripe and supple, appropriate for aging. Best 2012–2017. Tentative Score 90–92.

T-SELECTION, CABERNET SAUVIGNON, 2006: With 20 months in new French *barriques*, a generously oaked wine, near-sweet because of its 15% alcohol content. Dark garnet in color, with generous velvety tannins that match the oak. Opens in the glass to reveal blackcurrants and black cherries, those along with tarry and spicy notes, and, rising on the very long finish, notes of sweet chewing tobacco. A California-style blockbuster but yielding in the glass to show its own kind of muscular elegance. Drink now–2015. Score 93.

T-SELECTION, CABERNET SAUVIGNON, 2004: Dark, dense and concentrated, this spicy and complex red shows muscular and earthy currants and blackberries, backed up by herbal and spicy oak, all with a generous dose of firm tannins. Turns smooth and polished as it opens to reveal tempting mineral, sage and cedar flavors. Long and generous, with a promise for true elegance. Drink now–2012. Score 92.

T-SELECTION, MERLOT, 2004: Big and bold, full-bodied, with firm tannins that take time to recede in the glass and then open to reveal blackberry, cassis and smoky oak on a generously spicy background that takes on depth and richness toward the long finish, on which a burst of fruit makes itself felt. Drink now. Score 90.

T-SELECTION, SHIRAZ, 2008: Medium- to full-bodied, already showing finely-grained tannins. Rich blackberry and plum fruits complemented nicely by pepper and mineral overtones, all with a fine sense of harmony and balance. Promises true elegance. Best 2012–2018. Tentative Score 92–94.

T-SELECTION, SHIRAZ, 2006: Oak-aged for 18 months, dark ruby, full-bodied but with such fine balance between tannins, oak, acidity and fruits that it seems to almost float on the palate. On first attack generous near-jammy blackberry and currant fruits, those yielding comfortably to plum, licorice and spices, all of which carry on to a long and generous finish. Drink now–2013. Score 91.

T-SELECTION, SHIRAZ, 2005: Dark crimson in color, opening with lightly sweet vanilla notes on the nose, this full-bodied, round and elegant wine shows a generous array of plum and currant fruits, freshly tanned leather and an appealing light earthy-herbaceousness. The soft but gripping tannins linger well into the long finish. Look as well for an appealing hint of bittersweet chocolate developing. Drink now–2012. Score 91.

T-SELECTION, SHIRAZ, 2004: Developed for 18 months in French oak, and showing fine balance and structure. Full-bodied, deeply tannic and concentrated enough to be thought of as chewy, but under that, red currants, plums and red berries along with black pepper, rosemary, thyme and a very appealing hint of peppermint. Fruits rise nicely on the long finish. Might easily be taken for a fine Australian Shiraz. Drink now–2012. Score 91.

T-SELECTION, PINOT NOIR, 2008: Still in its infancy and opening from moment to moment in the glass, at each step along the way revealing further charms. Medium- to full-bodied, with caressing tannins a concentrated and polished wine, with well-focused red berry and cherry fruits on first attack, those yielding to blueberries and notes of cinnamon and white pepper. As the wine continues to develop, look as well for notes of freshly turned earth and cloves. Best 2011–2016. Tentative Score 92–94.

T-SELECTION, PINOT NOIR, 2006: Dark cherry red toward garnet, medium- to full-bodied, with a generous 14.5% alcohol content, but don't let that throw you off because all is here in fine balance and with enviable structure. Ripe and distinctive in flavor, with blackberry, currant, raspberry and floral aromas and flavors supported by minerals and a hint of raw beef all coming together beautifully with delicate spices. A multi-layered and complex wine. Drink now–2013. Score 92.

T-SELECTION, CABERNET FRANC, 2008: Youthful royal purple in color, a firm, chewy and full-bodied wine showing a generous array of cedarwood, cigar tobacco and herbal elements to support currant and blueberry notes. Finishes with a generous mineral overlay. Best 2011–2016. Tentative Score 91–93.

T-SELECTION, CABERNET FRANC, 2007: Medium- to full-bodied, showing generous but not overpowering oak and firm chewy tannins that need time to settle in. On the nose and palate blueberries, raspberries and fresh herbs, and, in the background an appealing floral note. Long and generous. Best 2011–2014. Score 92.

T-SELECTION, CABERNET FRANC, 2006: Ruby toward royal purple in color, full-bodied, with silky tannins and a gentle hand with the oak. Showing gorgeous plum, blackberry and floral aromas and flavors on a background of sweet spices and, coming in on the finish, a tempting hint of semi-sweet chocolate. Long and generous. Drink now–2012. Score 92.

T-SELECTION, CABERNET FRANC, 2005: This full-bodied wine reflects its 14 months in new French oak with spicy wood and mouth-coating tannins, both integrating nicely. A generous array of black fruits on first attack, those opening to reveal overlays of fresh Mediterranean herbs, and finally, on the long finish, espresso coffee, dark chocolate and the barest but tantalizing hint of crushed raspberries. Drink now–2013. Score 92.

T-SELECTION, CABERNET FRANC, 2004: Deep, almost impenetrable in color, lush and elegant with a rich array of ripe raspberry, cassis and berry fruits, those matched nicely by herbal and bittersweet chocolate aromas and flavors. Firm tannins, especially on the finish, but with just the right levels of French oak influence and both balance and structure that bode well for the future. Drink now–2012. Score 91.

T-SELECTION, CABERNET FRANC, 2003: Oak-aged for 14 months in new French *barriques*. Smooth, rich and supple, with ripe plum, currant and berry fruits together with an array of mocha, tobacco and espresso coffee, all complemented nicely by a hint of vanilla-scented oak. Tannins and fruits rise on the finish. Showing its elegance nicely. Drink now–2012. Score 90.

T-SELECTION, PETIT VERDOT, 2006: A luxurious wine, deeply concentrated, thick, tannic and complex, showing wild berries, cassis, blackberry and pomegranate fruits, those complemented nicely by notes of cola and ginger, all with a light and tantalizing bitter citrus peel note that runs through to the super-long finish. Unique, expressive and cellar-worthy. Approachable and enjoyable now but best 2011–2017. Score 93.

T-SELECTION, SHIRAZ-GRENACHE, 2006: Deep garnet toward royal purple, medium- to full-bodied, with silky tannins and reflecting its 14 months in oak with a gentle spicy touch. Supple and graceful, showing cherry, blueberry and pomegranate fruits all on a background of white pepper and a hint of star anise. Drink now–2012. Score 93.

T-SELECTION, SHIRAZ-GRENACHE, 2005: Deep, almost inky-garnet in color, full-bodied, with firm tannins integrating nicely. Reflecting its 14 months in French *barriques* with spicy cedar, this blend of 60% Shiraz and 40% Grenache shows concentrated purple plum, blackberry and citrus peel notes on a background of sweet herbs and red licorice. Drink now–2014. Score 92.

T-SELECTION, SHIRAZ-GRENACHE, 2004: Medium-dark garnet toward purple, full-bodied, with generous tannins well balanced by the influence of aging in French oak casks for 14 months. Distinctive, ripe and luxurious, with near-sweet plum, blueberry and citrus peel intertwined beautifully with spicy, herbal and pomegranate aromas and flavors. Drink now–2012. Score 91.

T-SELECTION, SHIRAZ-GRENACHE, 2003: Dense purple in color, this rich, big and juicy wine is absolutely loaded with blackberry and plum fruits, those set off nicely by hints of cloves, coffee, citrus peel and black pepper, all on super-soft tannins. Harmonious, generous, long and mouth-coating. Drink now–2012. Score 91.

Pelter

PELTER, CABERNET SAUVIGNON-SHIRAZ, 2006: Oak-aged for 18 months in 30% new oak, dark garnet in color, with generous spicy oak opening on the nose, but that residing nicely to show an appealing array of cherry, raspberry, currant and peppery notes, the soft tannins caressing as the full-bodied wine fills the mouth. With fine balance and structure, showing elegance and length. Drink now–2013, perhaps longer. Score 92.

PELTER, CABERNET SAUVIGNON-SHIRAZ, 2005: Deep ruby toward garnet, full-bodied, with a generous backbone of wood and tannins, those integrating nicely and in fine balance with fruits. On the nose and palate blackcurrants, blackberries, raspberries and black cherries, all supported by appealing earthy and herbal undercurrents. Deep, long and smooth. Drink now–2012. Score 91.

PELTER, CABERNET SAUVIGNON-SHIRAZ, 2004: Aged in American oak for 18 months, this blend of 50% each of Cabernet Sauvignon and Shiraz shows a medium-dark garnet color, a strong acidic backbone and appealing spices and vanilla from the wood, none of which hold back layers of blackberry, cherry, herbal and earthy aromas and flavors. Good concentration, ripeness and smoothness lead to a long and generous finish, on which one will find appealing hints of minted bittersweet chocolate. Drink now–2012. Score 91.

PELTER, CABERNET SAUVIGNON-SHIRAZ, 2003: Deep ruby toward garnet, full-bodied, with gently caressing tannins, and on the nose and palate blackberry and blackcurrant fruits, those supported nicely by hints of espresso coffee and dark chocolate. Tannins and wood rise on the finish. Still drinking very nicely but showing signs of full maturity. Drink now or in the next year or so. Score 89.

PELTER, CABERNET SAUVIGNON-SHIRAZ, 2002: Medium-bodied, dark garnet in color, this oak-aged blend of 65% Cabernet Sauvignon and 35% Shiraz shows appealing herbal and leathery overlays, those nicely highlighting blackcurrant, plum and spicy oak aromas and flavors. Not for further cellaring. Drink up. Score 87.

PELTER, SHIRAZ-CARIGNAN, 2006: A blend of 60% Shiraz and 40% Carignan, reflecting gentle oak influences from its 14 months in older barrels. Dark garnet, with soft tannins and generous acidity integrating nicely, opening to show plum, wild berry and dark chocolate. Drink now–2012. Score 89.

PELTER, QUARTO, LIMITED EDITION, 2005: A rich Bordeaux blend of Cabernet Sauvignon, Merlot, Cabernet Franc and Petit Verdot. Deep royal purple, full-bodied, with still-firm tannins just starting to settle down. Opens to show berry and cassis fruits on a lightly spicy background, with a long red fruit finish. Drink now–2012. Score 90.

PELTER, TRIO, 2007: Dark cherry toward garnet in color, a blend of 70% Cabernet Sauvignon and 15% each of Merlot and Cabernet Franc. Reflecting its 14 months in used *barriques*, shows a gentle influence of spicy wood and soft, gently mouth-coating tannins that highlight red currant, raspberry and red cherry notes. Soft, round and generous, a medium-bodied wine with a hint of eucalyptus on the moderately long finish. As good with grilled fish or seafood as with small cuts of beef, pork or lamb. Drink now–2011. Score 90.

PELTER, TRIO, 2006: A blend of 70% Cabernet Sauvignon and 15% each of Merlot and Cabernet Franc. Dark ruby toward garnet, medium- to full-bodied, showing gentle spicy oak and soft tannins that yield to show currant, red and black berries and cherries on a lightly earthy-mineral background. Long and mouth-filling. Drink now. Score 91.

PELTER, TRIO, 2005: A blend of 80% Cabernet Sauvignon and 10% each Merlot and Cabernet Franc, this medium- to full-bodied wine reflects its 14 months in oak with moderate smoky, almost musky aromas and soft tannins integrating nicely. Opens to show a tempting array of cassis, berry and black cherry fruits, those leading to a long, spicy finish with a welcome light hint of bitterness coming in at the end. Drink now. Score 91.

PELTER, TRIO, 2004: A blend of 90% Cabernet Sauvignon with 5% each of Merlot and Cabernet Franc. Deep ruby toward garnet, medium- to full-bodied, showing a rich core of berry and currant flavors, those with herbal and cedar overlays, all on a background of supple tannins. Long and generous. Drink now. Score 91.

PELTER, CABERNET SAUVIGNON-MERLOT-CABERNET FRANC, 2003: My most recent tasting note holds firmly: Medium- to full-bodied, round and generous with silky soft tannins allowing us to focus on blueberry, plum, cola and light herbal-spicy notes, all leading to a long and satisfying finish. Drink now. Score 90.

PELTER, CHARDONNAY, 2008: Unoaked to show off the wine's rich mineral, summer fruits, kiwis and peach pits. Medium-bodied, with good balancing acidity. Perhaps not as lively as one expects of an un-oaked Chardonnay, but showing a generous share of elegance. Drink now. Score 90.

PELTER, CHARDONNAY, 2007: Golden straw in color, light- to medium-bodied and unoaked, opens with grapefruit and pineapple notes, those going on to citrus, green apples and pears. Stylish, juicy and long, finishing on a light flinty-mineral note. Drink now. Score 90.

PELTER, SAUVIGNON BLANC, 2008: Medium-bodied, light, bright straw in color, unoaked and with generous lively acidity to show off tropical fruits, red grapefruit and notes of grapefruit peel, all on a mineral-rich background. Drink now. Score 89.

PELTER, SAUVIGNON BLANC, 2007: Light, bright and lively, with pears and passion fruit at its core, those opening to show grapefruit, floral and light mineral notes in the background. Unoaked, a fresh and thoroughly appealing wine finishing with an elegant note. Drink now. Score 89.

PELTER, GEWURZTRAMINER, 2008: The first wine in the country to use a glass stopper instead of a cork. Full-bodied, with fine balancing acidity and generous yeasty white bread notes, opens on the palate to reveal a charming array of pineapple, litchi and grapefruit, those supported nicely by Oriental spices that come in from mid-palate and then linger long and comfortably. Lovely as an aperitif, with goose liver dishes or as an accompaniment to fruit-based desserts. Drink now–2011. Score 90.

PELTER, GEWURZTRAMINER, 2007: Medium-bodied, showing traditional Gewurztraminer aromas and flavors of rose petals, ginger, litchi and peppermint on first attack, those opening to show generous pineapple fruits, and those going to dried apricots. Spicy, just barely off-dry and long, a generous and delightful mouthful. Drink now. Score 90.

PELTER, SEMILLON, 2007: Light, tasty and tangy, with green pineapple, grapefruit and white peach fruits supported nicely by spring flowers and a tantalizing light hint of honey. Long and elegant. Capable of some age. Drink now. Score 91.

PELTER, SEMILLON, 2006: Fermented partly in stainless steel and partly in *barriques* for three months, this straw-colored wine opens with citrus peel and pear aromas and flavors, those going to melon and green apples, all with an appealing spicy overlay. Drink now. Score 90.

PELTER, BLANC DE BLANC, BRUT, N.V.: Even though this sparkling wine is categorized as non-vintage, it was made entirely from Chardonnay grapes from the 2005 vintage. With sharp bubbles that go on and on, a fresh and aromatic wine, showing gentle notes of yeasty white bread that highlight notes of lime and grapefruit, those complemented by hints of Oriental spices. On the long finish look as well for hints of roasted nuts. Score 91.

Poizner ✳✳✳

Located in Zichron Ya'akov and founded by Yoav Poizner in 2002, the winery released about 2,500 bottles from each of the 2005, 2006 and 2007 vintages. Releases from 2008 are anticipated at about 3,500 bottles. The winery relies on Cabernet Sauvignon, Merlot, Syrah, Carignan and Malbec, from their own vineyards. Mourvedre and Petit Verdot will be coming on line shortly, and all of the wines are aged for at least 12 months in French oak.

POIZNER, CABERNET SAUVIGNON, 2007: Ripe and near-sweet, with fig, plum, raspberry and espresso coffee notes. Medium-bodied with soft tannins; a round and generous wine. Drink from release. Tentative Score 86–88.

POIZNER, CABERNET SAUVIGNON, SINGLE VINEYARD, KFAR YUVAL, 2006: Dark garnet in color, medium- to full-bodied, with soft tannins integrating nicely and reflecting its 14 months in French oak with gentle spicy and vanilla overlays. Opens to reveal traditional Cabernet aromas and blackcurrant and blackberry fruits, those with an appealing hint of minted chocolate, black licorice and a note of red cherries on the long finish. Drink now–2011. Score 90.

POIZNER, CABERNET SAUVIGNON, 2005: Oak-aged in French *barriques* for 14 months, this blend of 85% Cabernet Sauvignon and 15% Merlot shows fine balance between soft, gently mouth-coating tannins, a light hand with spicy wood and an array of traditional Cabernet, blackcurrant and blackberry fruits. In the background generous hints of lead pencil and green olives. Drink now. Score 88.

POIZNER, MERLOT, 2007: Tasted from components and already showing deep garnet in color, medium-bodied with soft tannins integrating nicely to show a lightly spicy berry-cherry personality. Drink now. Score 86.

POIZNER, MERLOT, SINGLE VINEYARD, ZICHRON YA'AKOV, 2006: Blended with 4% of Carignan, oak-aged in French *barriques* for 15 months and showing medium- to full-bodied. Dark garnet in color with nicely integrating soft tannins and spicy wood supporting aromas and flavors of blackberries, cassis and bitter orange peel. Long, round and generous. Drink now–2011. Score 88.

POIZNER, MERLOT, 2005: Full-bodied, dark ruby toward garnet, opening with firm tannins and generous wood influence from its 12 months in French oak, but those integrating well with raspberry and plum fruits, and those backed up nicely by spicy and toasty hints on the finish. Drink up. Score 87.

POIZNER, SYRAH, 2007: Medium-bodied, with soft tannins, gently spicy wood and generous blackberry and spice notes. Generously fruity with a clean, round finish. Drink now–2011. Score 87.

POIZNER, CARIGNAN, OLD VINES, 2006: Showing much, as at barrel-tastings. Dark garnet with purple and orange reflections, full-bodied and firm. Made from grapes from 35-year-old vines, reflects its 16 months in French oak with light spicy and dusty wood, that highlighting aromas and flavors of red cherries, red currants, raspberries and spice. On the lingering finish generous hints of cocoa and vanilla. Drink now. Score 88.

POIZNER, SYRAH-SHIRAZ-CARIGNAN, 2006: Dark ruby toward garnet, oak-aged for 16 months, this blend of French and Australian clones of Syrah and Shiraz and Carignan (50% Syrah and 25% of Shiraz and Carignan) shows full-bodied, with soft tannins integrating nicely. Reflecting the oak with vanilla and white pepper, those parting to reveal raspberry, red plum and cassis notes along with a generous note of Mediterranean herbs. Drink now. Score 87.

Psagot ✳✳✳

Located in the northern Jerusalem Mountains, overlooking Wadi Kelt (Nachal Prat), the winery was founded by Na'ama and Ya'akov Berg, who planted their first vineyards in 1998. The oak *barriques* used by the winery are stored in a cave containing ancient pressing facilities, which maintains 90% humidity and temperatures up to 18 degrees Celsius. Relying on Cabernet Sauvignon, Merlot, Cabernet Franc, Viognier and Chardonnay grapes, the winery's top-of-the-line wine is a Bordeaux blend named Edom. Regular varietal wines are produced in the Psagot series and there is also a Port-style wine. Production from the 2007 and 2008 vintages was of about 65,000 bottles annually and anticipated production for 2009 is for 80,000 bottles.

Edom

EDOM, 2007: A Bordeaux blend of 57% Cabernet Sauvignon, 19% Merlot, 12% each of Cabernet Franc and Petit Verdot, showing still-firm tannins and generous acidity, those needing a bit of time to settle down. Dark garnet in color, opens with black fruits and spicy wood, yields to red fruits and hints of Mediterranean herbs, all leading to a generous finish. Drink now–2013. Score 89. K

EDOM, 2006: A blend of 57% Cabernet Sauvignon and 33% Merlot, with the remainder made up of Petit Verdot and Cabernet Franc. Medium- to full-bodied, generously but not aggressively oaked, with firm tannins just now starting to settle in. Opens with red currants and raspberries, those parting to make way for plums and black fruits on an earthy-herbal background, all with a light bitter streak that some will find appealing and others not. Drink now. Score 86. K

EDOM, 2005: Deep garnet in color, this blend of Cabernet Sauvignon and Merlot (75% and 25% respectively) opens with a rich vanilla and white chocolate nose, then settles down in the glass to reveal aromas and flavors of black cherries, plums and currants. Medium- to full-bodied, with soft but mouth-coating tannins, a good touch of spicy cedarwood, and, on the finish, an appealing earthy minerality. Drink now. Score 88. **K**

EDOM, 2004: This blend of 75% Cabernet Sauvignon and 25% Merlot reflects its 14 months in *barriques* with firm but nicely integrating tannins, spicy and vanilla-rich oak, and on the nose and palate, black-berries, currants and an appealing hint of freshly turned earth. A solid effort, with a long berry-rich finish. Drinking nicely but not for much longer cellaring. Drink now. Score 87. **K**

Psagot

PSAGOT, CABERNET SAUVIGNON, SINGLE VINE-YARD, 2007: Almost impenetrable inky-dark garnet in color, full-bodied, and with generous oak waiting to settle down and reflect the wine's inherent good balance. On the nose and palate ripe currant, black-berry and citrus peel notes, those complemented by notes of sweetened chewing tobacco and mocha. Drink now–2013, perhaps longer. Score 90. **K**

PSAGOT, CABERNET SAUVIGNON, 2007: Deep garnet toward royal purple, oak-aged for 13 months, full-bodied, with firm tannins and smoky wood set-tling in nicely now and showing rich and generous with well-focused red and blackcurrant fruits overlaid with hints of cocoa and cedarwood. Drink now–2011. Score 88. **K**

PSAGOT, CABERNET SAUVIGNON, 2006: Garnet toward royal purple in color, with firm but yielding tannins, and at this stage showing medium- to full-bodied. On the nose and palate traditional Cabernet blackberry and blackcurrant fruits, those comple-mented by spices and hints of Mediterranean herbs. Drink now. Score 86. **K**

PSAGOT, CABERNET SAUVIGNON, 2005: Dark, almost impenetrable garnet with green and purple reflections, this medium- to full-bodied wine reflects its 13 months in French *barriques* with a moderate touch of spicy oak and firm tannins that are in fine balance with blackberry, black cherry and cassis fruits. On the moderately long finish look for appealing hints of sweet herbs and tobacco. Drink up. Score 88. **K**

PSAGOT, MERLOT, 2007: Aromatic, medium-, perhaps medium- to full-bodied, with plum, raspberry and a hint of spicy licorice. Soft, gently gripping tannins lead to a round finish. Drink now–2011. Score 87. **K**

PSAGOT, MERLOT, 2006: Dark garnet in color, with generous oak and gripping tannins receding nicely and showing good balance and structure. Fine spices and vanilla here to highlight plum, currant and orange peel notes that go on to a medium-long finish. Drink now. Score 88. **K**

PSAGOT, CABERNET FRANC, 2007: Aromatic, opening with a nose of eucalyptus, tar and spicy wood. Medium- to full-bodied, showing a hint of muscle going on to reveal dark plum, currant, tobacco and mocha notes, those on an appealing background of freshly cut herbs. A solid effort. Drink now–2013. Score 90. **K**

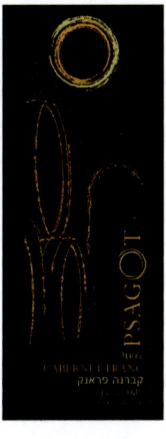

PSAGOT, CABERNET FRANC, 2006: Medium-dark ruby toward garnet in color, medium-bodied, with soft, gently caressing tannins and appealing spicy oak. Showing pleasant red currant and raspberry fruits on a background of earthy minerals and herbs and saddle leather. Drink now. Score 88. **K**

PSAGOT, CHARDONNAY, 2007: Light golden with orange reflections, medium-bodied, and showing fresh peach, apricot and citrus fruits, those complemented nicely by hints of celery and vanilla. More a "fun" wine than one to be taken with too much seriousness. Drink up. Score 86. **K**

PSAGOT, VIOGNIER, 2007: Light golden straw in color, medium-bodied, with fragrant pear, citrus and spice flavors. Hints of oak that play nicely with crisp balancing acidity. Drink up. Score 86. **K**

Ra'anan **

Established by Ra'anan Margalit in 1994 on Moshav Ganei Yochanan in the Southern Plains, the winery utilizes Cabernet Sauvignon, Merlot and Chardonnay grapes from its own vineyards, located nearby at Karmei Yosef. Current production is about 8,000 bottles annually.

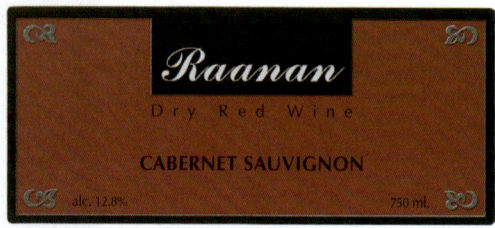

RA'ANAN, CABERNET SAUVIGNON, RESERVE, 2006: Garnet toward royal purple, medium- to full-bodied, with gently mouth-coating tannins and spicy, toasty oak. Opens to show appealing blackcurrant and berry fruits. Drink now. Score 84.

RA'ANAN, CABERNET SAUVIGNON, RESERVE, 2005: Dark garnet, medium-bodied, with gripping tannins, generous sweet cedarwood and black fruits. Drink up. Score 80.

RA'ANAN, CABERNET SAUVIGNON, RESERVE, 2004: With its chunky and somewhat coarse tannins, this is a country-style wine but one with charm, showing currant, plum and wild berry aromas and flavors. Showing age. Drink up. Score 82.

RA'ANAN, MERLOT, 2006: Medium-bodied, with soft tannins, spicy oak and black fruits. Not complex but a good quaffer. Drink now. Score 84.

RA'ANAN, MERLOT, 2005: Garnet to purple, medium-bodied, with soft, near-sweet tannins and hints of spices, licorice and earthy minerals supporting berry and cassis aromas and flavors. Drink up. Score 84.

Ramim *

Founded in 1999 on Moshav Shachar in the Southern Plains by Nitzan Eliyahu and producing its first wines from the 2000 harvest, the winery draws grapes from three self-owned vineyards, in Kfar Yuval and Safsufa, both on the Lebanese border, and on Moshav Shachar. Red varieties include Cabernet Sauvignon, Merlot, Sangiovese, Cabernet Franc, Syrah from France and Shiraz from Australia, as well as early plantings of Barbera, and Nebbiolo. White varieties include Zinfandel, Chardonnay, Gewurztraminer, Riesling, Semillon and Muscat.

The winery, which relies on Hungarian, French and American oak barrels, releases wines in a variety of series and under a large number of labels, some released only periodically. Among the series are Special Reserve, Art Reserve, Reserve and Ramim. Production in 2002 was 22,000 bottles, in 2003, 55,000 bottles, and in 2005 and 2006 jumped to about 70,000 bottles. Current production is not known. The wines have been kosher since the 2003 vintage.

Special Reserve

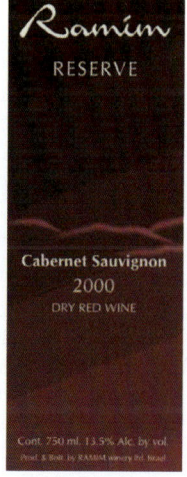

SPECIAL RESERVE, CABERNET SAUVIGNON, 2003: Dark garnet, medium- to full-bodied, with firm tannins and generous spicy wood influences, those somewhat holding back the currant and blueberry fruits that are here. One-dimensional, short and past its peak. Drink up. Score 79. K

Art Reserve

ART RESERVE, CABERNET SAUVIGNON, 2006: Dark garnet in color, medium-to full-bodied, with tight tannins that seem not to want to integrate. On the nose and palate skimpy black fruits and a too-generous green note that lingers on the finish. Drink now. Score 82. K

ART RESERVE, CABERNET SAUVIGNON, 2005: Medium-bodied, with chunky, country-style tannins and showing generous herbal, green olive and cherry aromas and flavors. Lacks complexity but an easy-to-drink quaffer. Drink now. Score 84. **K**

ART RESERVE, MERLOT, 2005: Oak-aged for 18 months, dark ruby toward garnet, medium-bodied, showing black cherry, toasty oak and nutmeg notes, and, on the tannic finish, hints of mocha and sage. Drink up. Score 80. **K**

ART RESERVE, SHIRAZ, 2005: Medium- to full-bodied, with gently mouth-coating tannins and showing appealing spicy rhubarb, herbal, earthy and mineral accents, with drying tannins rising on the moderately long finish. Drink now. Score 86. **K**

ART RESERVE, CABERNET FRANC, 2005: Garnet-red, medium-bodied, with chunky tannins and a few cherry-berry fruits, those marred by barnyard and Bretty aromas and flavors. Drink up. Score 78. **K**

ART RESERVE, CABERNET SAUVIGNON-MERLOT, 2005: Medium- to full-bodied, with soft tannins and spicy wood. Opens to reveal straightforward plum and berry fruits on a spicy and toasty oak background. Drink up. Score 82. **K**

Ramim

RAMIM, CABERNET SAUVIGNON, SHACHAR, 2007: Medium- to full-bodied, with chunky and tight tannins and spicy cedar notes that tend to hide the blackberry and currant flavors that are barely felt. Drink now. Score 84. **K**

RAMIM, CABERNET SAUVIGNON, SHACHAR, 2005: A medium-bodied, modest wine with spicy wood and ripe and earthy plum, herb and sage notes, those fading somewhat on the finish. Drink now. Score 85. **K**

RAMIM, CABERNET SAUVIGNON, SHACHAR, 2004: Dark garnet, medium- to full-bodied, with chunky, somewhat country-style tannins this oak-aged red shows generous spicy wood on first attack but that yielding to blackberry and currant fruits. Somewhat one-dimensional and short. Drink now. Score 84. **K**

RAMIM, MERLOT, 2006: An easygoing wine with spicy cherry, cola and plum fruits. Medium-bodied with soft tannins. A good entry-level wine. Drink up. Score 83. **K**

RAMIM, MERLOT, SHACHAR, 2005: Deep garnet, medium- to full-bodied, with firm tannins, perhaps too-generous smoky oak, and only skimpy berry-cherry aromas and flavors Drink up. Score 82. **K**

RAMIM, CABERNET FRANC, 2004: Deep ruby toward garnet, with gripping tannins settling in nicely, and with aromas and flavors of plums, wild berries and wood-inspired spices and vanilla. Showing signs of age. Drink up. Score 80. **K**

RAMIM, MOSAIC, 2005: A somewhat odd blend of Cabernet Sauvignon, Merlot, Pinot Noir and Shiraz (54%, 31%, 8% and 7% respectively) aged in Hungarian and American oak for six months. Light- to medium-bodied, with almost unfelt tannins and a berry-cherry personality. A simple quaffing wine. Drink up. Score 80.

RAMIM, CABERNET SAUVIGNON-MERLOT, 2005: Medium-bodied, with mineral and cedar notes complementing berry and cherry flavors. A simple quaffer. Drink up. Score 82. **K**

RAMIM, GEWURZTRAMINER, 2007: Pleasant enough, although not at all typical of the varietal, showing soft peach, tangerine and nutmeg aromas and flavors. Drink up. Score 82. **K**

RAMIM, CHARDONNAY, DESSERT ICE, 2003: Showing dramatically better than at an earlier tasting, almost as if my palate were discerning two different wines. Medium-bodied, dark golden in color, with generously sweet kiwi, pineapple and citrus fruits backed up by gentle acidity. At its best served icy-cold. Drink up. Score 84. **K**

Ramot Naftaly ✳✳✳

אזור קדש
kedesh valley

קברנה סוביניון

Cabernet Sauvignon
D r y   r e d   w i n e

2 0 0 5

בקבוק מס' 0001 מתוך 3800

750 ml   Ramot Naftaly Winery   14% vol

Founded on Moshav Ramot Naftaly in the Upper Galilee in 2003 by vintner Yitzhak Cohen working with winemaker Tal Pelter, this small winery owns vineyards planted with Cabernet Sauvignon, Merlot, Shiraz, Petit Verdot and Malbec. Production from the 2007 vintage was about 9,000 bottles.

RAMOT NAFTALY, CABERNET SAUVIGNON, RESERVE, 2006: Full-bodied, with soft, round tannins. Oak-aged for 18 months, opening to show a tempting array of blackberry, raspberry and licorice notes all lingering nicely. An appealing fruit-forward wine. Drink now–2011. Score 88.

RAMOT NAFTALY, CABERNET SAUVIGNON, 2006: Made entirely from Cabernet Sauvignon grapes, this garnet-toward-purple, medium-to full-bodied red is showing soft tannins and generous berry, black cherry and currant fruits and, on the background, hints of spices and earthiness that linger nicely. Drink now. Score 86.

RAMOT NAFTALY, CABERNET SAUVIGNON, RESERVE, 2005: Full-bodied and firm, with generous spicy wood reflecting its 20 months in oak. Opens slowly on the palate to reveal fine balance between tannins, wood and fruits. On first attack primarily red fruits, those yielding to black (currants and berries), all accompanied by overtones of Mediterranean herbs and licorice. Drink now. Score 90.

RAMOT NAFTALY, MERLOT, 2006: Dark garnet with orange reflections, medium- to full-bodied, with gentle wood influences and soft tannins nicely balanced with aromas and flavors of dark plums and currants, grilled herbs and toasty notes. Drink now. Score 85.

RAMOT NAFTALY, BARBERA, 2006: Dark cherry red, medium-bodied, with soft tannins and gentle wood. On the nose and palate red berries, cherries and hints of spices, vanilla and minerals leading to a mouth-filling fruity finish. Drink now. Score 86.

RAMOT NAFTALY, BARBERA, 2005: Ruby toward garnet, medium-bodied, reflecting its ten months in French oak with polished tannins and opening to reveal blackberries, minerals and a hint of licorice. Finishes round and with a light toasty oak character. Drink up. Score 86.

RAMOT NAFTALY, DUET, 2006: Aged in oak for ten months, this garnet-red blend of Merlot and Cabernet Sauvignon (60% and 40% respectively) shows good balance between soft tannins, spicy wood and fruits. Generous red currant and raspberry notes on first attack, those shifting comfortably to cassis, chocolate and Oriental spices. Drink now. Score 86.

RAMOT NAFTALY, DUET, 2005: This lightly oak-aged blend of Merlot and Cabernet Sauvignon (65% and 35% respectively) is medium-bodied, with soft tannins and hints of sweet cedarwood highlighting youthful berry and black cherry fruits. Not complex but appealing. Drink up. Score 86.

Recanati ★★★★

Established in 2000, this modern winery located in the Hefer Valley in the north part of the Sharon region relies on grapes from their own as well as contract vineyards, primarily in the Upper Galilee. The winery is currently seeking land either in the Upper Galilee or the Judean Hills, in order to build a new winery and to expand its production.

From its founding until late 2007, the senior winemaker of the winery was Lewis Pasco, who has now moved on and been replaced by the equally talented Gil Shatzberg, formerly of Amphorae. The winery produces wines in several series: the top-of-the-line age-worthy Special Reserve wines, which are often blends of Cabernet Sauvignon and Merlot; and two varietal series, Reserve and Recanati, which now include Cabernet Sauvignon, Merlot, Syrah, Petite Sirah-Zinfandel, Chardonnay and most recently Sauvignon Blanc. The winery also has a popularly priced series named Yasmine. Production is currently about 750,000 bottles annually and the winery is moving toward 800–850,000.

Special Reserve

SPECIAL RESERVE, 2008: Super-dark, almost inky garnet in color, developing in 60% new oak *barriques*, already showing remarkably supple and well balanced, a big wine that even in its youth shows rich, ripe and intense with well-focused currant, blueberry and blackberry fruits, all on a background of sweet spices. Still fairly tannic but destined to be a seamless and deftly balanced wine. Best 2011–2016, perhaps longer. Tentative Score 91–93. **K**

SPECIAL RESERVE, 2007: Dark, almost impenetrable garnet in color, full-bodied, with still gripping tannins starting to settle in nicely and showing fine balance with spicy and lightly smoky wood. Opens with a fruity nose and then goes on to reveal aromas and flavors of currants, cherries and wild berries, those complemented by notes of sweet cedarwood and chocolate. Drink now–2014. Score 90. **K**

SPECIAL RESERVE, 2006: A blend of 97% Cabernet Sauvignon and 3% Merlot. Full-bodied, with firm tannins integrating nicely and showing currant, blackberry and cherry liqueur aromas and flavors. Generous toasty oak here at this stage, but that, with the tannins, are settling in nicely to show a simultaneously intense but round and elegant wine. Drink now–2013. Score 90. **K**

SPECIAL RESERVE, 2005: Deep royal purple, full-bodied, with firm, still rough-edged tannins, those integrating nicely with light spicy wood and fruits to show fine balance and structure. A blend of 84% Cabernet Sauvignon and 16% Merlot, this is a big, rich and bold wine, with concentrated layers of currant, blackberry, anise and cedary oak flavors. Drink now–2013. Score 93. **K**

SPECIAL RESERVE, 2004: A blend of 92% Cabernet Sauvignon and 8% Merlot, with generous but not exaggerated toasty oak and soft tannins, those integrating nicely and opening to reveal a rich array of currant, blackberry and black cherry fruits, with gentle overlays of mint and chocolate. As the wine develops look for a hint of cigar tobacco on the long finish. Drink now–2012. Score 93. **K**

SPECIAL RESERVE, 2003: This deep, broad, gently tannic blend of 72% Cabernet Sauvignon and 28% Merlot combines Cabernet currants, cassis and spicy-herbal overtones with typical Merlot softness. Good balance between wood, tannins and fruits, and a long finish. Drink now–2012. Score 92. **K**

SPECIAL RESERVE, 2001: As in its youth, deep garnet toward royal purple, full-bodied, with fine balance between well-integrated soft tannins, spicy and mocha-rich oak, and currant, blackberry and ripe red plum fruits. Some variation between bottles but that primarily in fruit intensity. Drink now. Score 90. **K**

Reserve

RESERVE, CABERNET SAUVIGNON, 2008: Developing in 20% new oak and partly in one- and two-year-old *barriques*, showing a traditional Cabernet profile, with currants and raspberries supported nicely by dried spices. Full-bodied, with soft tannins integrating nicely, good concentration and a long finish. Best 2011–2014, perhaps longer. Tentative Score 88–90. **K**

RESERVE, CABERNET SAUVIGNON, 2007: Dark, full-bodied, loaded with chocolate, spices and licorice, opening to reveal a generous array of currants, black cherries and blueberries, all of which linger through a long and supple finish. Drink now–2015. Score 90. **K**

RESERVE, CABERNET SAUVIGNON, 2006: Dark garnet toward royal purple, medium- to full-bodied (leaning more toward the full), with generous near-sweet tannins, and on the nose and palate a generous array of blackcurrant, blackberry, spice and mocha notes. Juicy and long. Drink now–2011. Score 90. **K**

RESERVE, CABERNET SAUVIGNON, 2005: Dark garnet, medium- to full-bodied, with softly caressing tannins and showing a generous array of blackcurrant, wild berry and purple plum fruits, those supported nicely by hints of sweet herbs and reflecting its 18 months in *barriques* with lightly toasty oak. Rich, round and generous. Drink now–2011. Score 90. **K**

RESERVE, CABERNET SAUVIGNON, 2004: Dark garnet with orange and purple reflections, this medium- to full-bodied wine shows soft, gently yielding tannins. Shows generous but well-balanced and a measured hand with spicy wood. Opens to reveal currant, plum and blackberry fruits, those well supported by light hints of herbs and cedarwood. Drink now. Score 91. **K**

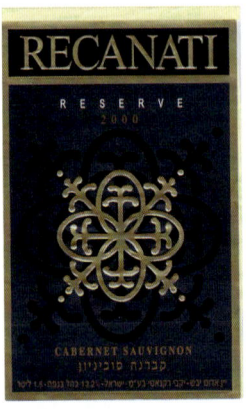

RESERVE, CABERNET SAUVIGNON, 2003: Super-dark garnet in color, ripe and rich, now showing full-bodied with soft tannins integrating nicely. On the nose and palate an appealing array of currant and berry fruits, those complemented by hints of Oriental spices and toasty oak. Generous. Drink now. Score 90. **K**

RESERVE, MERLOT, 2008: Developing in *barriques*, showing deep garnet, with near-sweet soft tannins. Ripe tannins part comfortably to reveal black cherry, currant and black olive notes, those supported by notes of mocha and freshly turned earth. Very nice indeed. Drink now–2014, perhaps longer. Tentative Score 89–91. **K**

RESERVE, MERLOT, 2006: Full-bodied, firm in texture, with its tannins integrating nicely and showing appealing blackberry, blueberry and currant fruits, those supported by a hint of mocha. Chewy, round and long. Drink now–2012. Score 90. K

RESERVE, MERLOT, 2005: A single vineyard wine, made entirely with grapes from the Manara Vineyard. Smooth, round and generous, rich and spicy, with a core of raspberry, cherry and creamy oak backed up by hints of minted chocolate that linger nicely. Good balance between fresh acidity, wood and fruits, and a long finish. Drink now–2011. Score 90. K

RESERVE, MERLOT, 2004: Dark garnet, medium- to full-bodied, with firm tannins and near-sweet oak integrating well. On the nose and palate black cherries, berries and currants on a tantalizing earthy-herbal background. On the long finish, hints of chocolate. Drink now. Score 90. K

RESERVE, SYRAH, 2006: Dark garnet in color, with still-firm tannins needing time to settle in but showing fine balance and structure. On the nose and palate black cherry and blackcurrant fruits, those matched by hints of grilled beef, herbal and green olive notes. Drink now–2011. Score 89. K

RESERVE, SYRAH, 2005: Aged for 14 months in French and American oak. Medium-dark garnet in color, with well-focused tannins and moderate spicy wood in fine balance with black cherry, wild berry and cassis fruits, those with just a hint of smoked meat in the background. At this stage the still-firm tannins hold the wine back a bit. Drink now. Score 89. K

RESERVE, SHIRAZ, 2004: Dark cherry red toward garnet, full-bodied, supple and round, with blackberry, black cherry, herbal and beefy aromas and flavors, those coming together with firm tannins and sweet cedarwood. On the long tannic finish, toasted bread and mocha. Drink now. Score 89. K

RESERVE, CABERNET FRANC, 2008: Smooth and velvety, with tannins that grip just right and stand up nicely to light toasty wood. Notes of rose petals, cherries and raspberries on first attack, those yielding nicely to notes of black cherries, tar and toasted rye bread. Culminates in an impressively persistent finish on which the oak takes on an appealing sweetish note. Drink from release–2014. Tentative Score 90–92. **K**

RESERVE, CABERNET FRANC, 2006: With its once firm tannins now integrating nicely, showing medium-dark garnet, full-bodied, and reflecting its 14 months in oak with generous but not imposing sweet cedar. Dark berry, black cherry and plum fruits highlighted by notes of tobacco, bell peppers and bittersweet chocolate, all lingering nicely on the finish. Drink now–2012. Score 91. **K**

RESERVE, PETITE SIRAH-ZINFANDEL, 2008: Developing in two-year-old *barriques*, showing soft tannins, light spicy notes and opening to reveal appealing ripe plum and berry fruits. With good balance between acidity and fruits, showing round and easy to drink. Drink now–2011. Score 90. **K**

RESERVE, PETITE SIRAH-ZINFANDEL, 2007: Medium-to full-bodied, dark, almost impenetrable garnet, opens with black fruits and a gentle note of spicy wood. Goes on in the glass to reveal red berry and light leathery and peppermint notes. Drink now–2012. Score 90. **K**

RESERVE, PETITE SIRAH-ZINFANDEL, 2006: Reflecting its eight months in oak with gently smoky and spicy wood and softly caressing tannins, a blend of 80% Petite Sirah and 20% Zinfandel. Youthful royal purple, opens to reveal blackberry, pomegranate, mocha and sage notes. Drink now–2012. Score 90. **K**

RESERVE, PETITE SIRAH-SHIRAZ, SPECIAL EDITION, 2007: A blend this year of 60% Petite Sirah and 40% Shiraz, dark royal purple in color, medium-bodied, showing soft, well-integrated tannins and just the right note of dusty oak. On the nose and palate blackberries, blueberries and cassis, those matched nicely by notes of chocolate and mocha. Simultaneously "fun" and elegant. Drink now–2011. Score 90. **K**

RESERVE, CHARDONNAY, 2008: An appealing note of spicy oak to show off fine citrus and summer fruits, those with light hints of pepper and juniper berries, and, on the generous finish, a tantalizing note of bitter citrus peel. Drink now–2012. Score 89. **K**

RESERVE, CHARDONNAY, 2006: Developed *sur lie*, partly in new, partly in used oak *barriques*, this medium- to full-bodied white shows an appealing buttery nature to highlight green apple, pineapple and nutty flavors and aromas. Complex but lively and with good length. Drink up. Score 90. **K**

RESERVE, SAUVIGNON BLANC, 2008: Light straw colored, with lively lemon, grapefruit and gooseberry fruits along with chalky minerals. Light, lively and refreshing. Drink now. Score 87. **K**

RESERVE, SAUVIGNON BLANC, 2007: Light straw in color, light- to medium-bodied, showing appealing red grapefruit, passion fruit and kiwi fruit, those with hints of spices and grassiness. Good acidity keeps the wine lively and refreshing. Drink up. Score 88. **K**

Recanati

RECANATI, CABERNET SAUVIGNON, 2008: Aging in older barrels and showing a gentle spicy wood influence along with soft, gently mouth-coating tannins. Opens to reveal red currant, berry and orange peel notes, those supported nicely by notes of freshly cut Mediterranean herbs and earthy minerals. Drink now–2012. Score 90. **K**

RECANATI, CABERNET SAUVIGNON, 2007: Garnet with purple and orange reflections, opens with a rich, fruity nose. Medium- to full-bodied, with soft tannins and a gentle spicy overlay from the wood, and an overall currant and black cherry personality. Smooth, rich and concentrated for the vintage, with tannins rising on the finish. Drink now. Score 89. **K**

RECANATI, CABERNET SAUVIGNON, 2006: Ruby toward garnet in color, medium- to full-bodied with soft tannins integrating nicely, and traditional Cabernet Sauvignon aromas and flavors of berries and currants on a lightly spicy background. Drink now. Score 87. **K**

RECANATI, CABERNET SAUVIGNON, 2005: Dark garnet with orange and purple reflections, this medium- to full-bodied wine shows soft tannins and Mediterranean herbs balanced nicely by generous currant, plum and berry. Rich, round and soft. Drink up. Score 88. **K**

RECANATI, MERLOT, 2008: Garnet in color, medium-bodied, with silky, near-sweet tannins. On the nose and palate generous black fruits, cocoa and mocha. Showing soft and round with good grip and length. Drink now–2011. Score 89. **K**

RECANATI, MERLOT, 2007: Ripe and rich, garnet-colored, reflecting its four months in oak with gentle spices and a tantalizing hint of cedar, those matched by soft tannins and showing black cherry, plum and currant fruits along with light hints of minerals and mocha. Drink now. Score 88. **K**

RECANATI, MERLOT, 2006: Dark garnet in color, medium- to full-bodied, with somewhat gripping tannins and generous spices and smoke from the wood in which it aged, those and a touch of Brett holding back the berry and cherry fruits that lie underneath. Drink now. Score 85. **K**

RECANATI, MERLOT, 2005: Garnet-red, medium- to full-bodied, with generous soft tannins nicely balanced by hints of cedarwood. Firm but lively, with appealing aromas and flavors of red berries, spices and tobacco that linger nicely. Drink up. Score 87. **K**

RECANATI, SHIRAZ, 2008: Developing partly in stainless steel vats, partly in *barriques*, showing good color and fruit extraction. Medium-bodied, opening with a floral nose and going on to show purple plum, blackberry and leathery notes, those on a background of violets and spring flowers. Appealing but not meant for aging. Drink from release. Tentative Score 86–88. **K**

RECANATI, SHIRAZ, 2007: Medium-bodied, with soft tannins but a crisp texture and showing juicy raspberry and red plum fruits, those finishing on a light note of licorice. Drink now–2011. Score 87. **K**

RECANATI, SHIRAZ, 2006: Garnet with orange reflections, medium- to full-bodied, showing light spicy and vanilla-rich oak along with soft tannins, that part nicely to show black and red berry fruits along with hints of cassis and orange peel, and on the moderately long finish a nice hint of licorice. Drink now. Score 88. **K**

RECANATI, BARBERA, 2006: Light garnet toward purple in color, medium-bodied, with soft tannins and generous acidity. Reflects its eight and a half months in *barriques* with light spicy notes and appealing crushed blackberry and cherry and chocolate notes, all leading to a light peppery finish. Drink now. Score 88. **K**

RECANATI, BARBERA, 2005: Deep royal purple in color, blended with 10% Zinfandel, showing medium-bodied, with soft tannins, light spicy oak and pleasing acidity. On the nose and palate cherry, blueberry, blackberry and cassis notes. Aromatic and lightly spicy, and, on the finish, a hint of chocolate. Drink up. Score 88. **K**

RECANATI, PETITE SIRAH-SHIRAZ, SPECIAL EDITION, 2006: Dark garnet enough to be thought of as brooding, with a nearly explosive nose packed with raspberries and chocolate. Medium-bodied, with soft, caressing tannins that part comfortably to reveal a generous array of blackberries and blueberries, cassis, tobacco and dark chocolate, all of which linger long and comfortably. Drink now–2011 Score 92. **K**

RECANATI, ROSÉ, 2008: Somewhere between rose-petal pink and the color of strawberry juice, a blend of 80% Barbera and 20% Merlot, those with minimal skin contact. Fresh, firm and crisply dry with appealing notes of strawberries, berries and dried cherries followed by hints of white pepper and red licorice on the finish. Sits easily on the palate. Drink now. Score 88. **K**

RECANATI, ROSÉ, 2007: A blend of Cabernet Franc and Merlot in equal parts. Rose-petal pink with an orange tint, light- to medium-bodied, with appealing strawberry, raspberry and red currant fruits that sit comfortably on the palate. Well crafted, with good balancing acidity. Drink up. Score 88. **K**

RECANATI, CHARDONNAY, 2008: Reflecting its several months in oak with gentle hints of spices, a medium- to full-bodied white showing an appealing array of peach, pear and citrus fruits, those backed up nicely by lively acidity. Fresh and with an appealing note of complexity. Drink now–2011. Score 88. **K**

RECANATI, CHARDONNAY, 2007: With its notes of melon, lemon, lemon peel and light hints of fresh sea air and minerality, calls to mind a Petit Chablis. Developed *sur lie* for several months, showing fine crispness and liveliness, a very good bet for summertime drinking. Drink up. Score 88. **K**

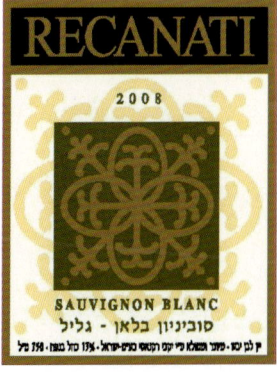

RECANATI, SAUVIGNON BLANC, 2008: Light gold in color, a lively unoaked white showing pineapple, citrus and citrus peel notes, those supported by a nice hint of Mediterranean herbs. Fresh and lively, with just enough complexity to catch our attention. Drink now. Score 87. **K**

RECANATI, SAUVIGNON BLANC, 2007: Light gold, with green and orange tints, an unoaked white showing appealing citrus, melon and pear fruits on a background of freshly mown grass. Drink up. Score 86. **K**

Yasmine

YASMINE, RED, 2008: A medium-bodied, softly tannic blend primarily of Caberent Sauvignon and Merlot, with a bit each of Carignan and Petite Sirah. Made partly by carbonic maceration, deep purple in color, showing appealing wild berry, black cherry and currant fruits with notes of orange peel and a hint of white pepper. Round and soft, a comfortable quaffer. Drink now. Score 86. **K**

YASMINE, RED, 2007: Light- to medium-bodied, with soft, almost unfelt tannins and a basic berry-black cherry personality. An entry-level quaffer. Drink up. Score 84. **K**

YASMINE, WHITE, 2008: A blend of Sauvignon Blanc, Emerald Riesling and French Colombard. Light golden straw in color, unoaked and aromatic, showing tropical and citrus fruits, those with a bare hint of sweetness and an appealing floral note, an easy to drink entry-level wine, the best in the series to date. Drink now. Score 85. **K**

Red Poetry **

Established in 2001 by Dubi Tal on Havat Tal on the western slopes of the Judean Mountains, the winery has its own vineyards with Cabernet Sauvignon, Merlot, Cabernet Franc, Petit Verdot, Shiraz, Petite Sirah, Sangiovese, Riesling and Gewurztraminer grapes. The winery releases wines in two series, Reserve and Red Poetry. Current production is about 10,000 bottles annually.

Reserve

RESERVE, CABERNET SAUVIGNON, 2005: Medium- to full-bodied, showing good balance between soft tannins, spicy cedarwood and black fruits. A soft, round wine with a medium-long finish. Drink now. Score 85.

RESERVE, CABERNET SAUVIGNON, 2004: Dark garnet, medium-bodied, with soft tannins. Opens with barnyard aromas but those blow off quickly to reveal appealing blackberry and black cherry fruits. Somewhat short and one-dimensional. Drink up. Score 84.

Red Poetry

RED POETRY, CABERNET SAUVIGNON, 2006: Dark garnet, medium- to full-bodied and developed in *barriques* for 14 months, a blend of 85% Cabernet Sauvignon and the balance of Cabernet Franc and Merlot. Showing soft, near-sweet tannins, spicy and vanilla-rich wood that open to show blackcurrant, blackberry and blueberry fruits. Not complex but generous. Drink now. Score 85.

RED POETRY, CABERNET SAUVIGNON, 2005: Ruby toward garnet, medium- to full-bodied, with soft tannins integrating nicely and showing generous plum, currant and wild berry fruits. Moderately long. Drink now. Score 85.

RED POETRY, MERLOT, 2006: Flushed out with 10% of Cabernet Sauvignon and aged for 12 months in oak. Medium- to full-bodied, with soft, albeit somewhat chunky tannins, opening to reveal appealing red and black fruits on a lightly spicy and earthy-herbal background. Drink now. Score 85.

RED POETRY, MERLOT, 2005: Dark ruby in color, medium-bodied, with soft, near-sweet tannins and spices from the oak in which it aged.

On the nose and palate appealing red berry and red currant fruits leading to a lightly herbal and green olive finish. Drink up. Score 85.

RED POETRY, SHIRAZ-CABERNET SAUVIGNON, 2005: Deep royal purple in color, medium- to full-bodied, with soft, near-sweet tannins and hints of smoky oak. A blend of 80% Shiraz and 20% Cabernet Sauvignon, developed in new French oak for 12 months and showing forward plum, wild berry and currant fruits on a background of earthy-herbaceousness. Drink now. Score 86.

RED POETRY, SHARONA, 2005: A blend of 60% Merlot and 40% Cabernet Sauvignon, oak-aged for 12 months. Garnet-red in color, medium-bodied, with firm tannins and too generous spicy wood that hold back the black fruits that struggle to make themselves felt. Drink up. Score 79.

RED POETRY, EHRLICH, 2005: Dark garnet toward royal purple, a medium- to full-bodied blend of 40% Merlot, 40% Shiraz and 20% Cabernet Sauvignon. Reflects its 12 months in oak with soft, lightly spicy tannins and a note of vanilla, those parting to reveal wild berries, plums and blackcurrants. In the background an appealing hint of freshly tanned leather. Drink now. Score 86.

RED POETRY, EHRLICH, 2004: Dark garnet, a medium- to full-bodied blend of 40% each Merlot and Shiraz and 10% each of Cabernet Sauvignon and Petite Sirah. Soft tannins integrating nicely with spicy wood and natural acidity. On the nose and palate berries, black cherries, purple plums and hints of cola and leather, all leading to a long finish. Drink now. Score 87.

RED POETRY, CHARDONNAY, 2007: Dark gold toward burnished copper in color, full-bodied, far too generously oaked, with precious few fruits hidden by too heavy and smoky vanilla notes. Well past its peak. Drink up. Score 74.

Rosh Pina *

Set near the village of Rosh Pina in the Galilee, this small winery was founded by Ya'akov Blum in 2001 and released its first wines in 2002. Grapes are drawn from the Galilee, those including Cabernet Sauvignon, Shiraz and Carignan. No wines were released from the 2005 vintage due to damages done to the winery during the 2006 war between Israel and the Hezbollah forces of Lebanon. The winery is currently releasing about 4,000 bottles annually.

ROSH PINA, CABERNET SAUVIGNON, 2004: Medium-bodied, dark brick-red in color, with chunky tannins, this is a simple country-style wine with a few raspberry and plum flavors. Drink up. Score 78.

ROSH PINA, MERLOT, 2004: Garnet-red, medium-bodied, with a few cherry and wild berry fruits but those overpowered by earthy, musty aromas and flavors. Drink up. Score 74.

ROSH PINA, MERLOT, 2003: Coarse enough to be thought of as vulgar, with chunky tannins, far too much acidity, and earthy and only bare hints of wild berry fruits. Drink up. Score 70.

ROSH PINA, SHIRAZ, 2003: Dark, but not fully clear garnet in color, with chunky country-style tannins and a bit of coarseness. On the nose and palate black cherry and cassis fruits, those with a somewhat exaggerated earthy character. Showing age. Drink up. Score 74.

ROSH PINA, CARIGNAN, TEVA, 2004: A few raspberry fruits, but those struggling to be felt against too-dominant horsy, leathery and herbal aromas and flavors. Score 70.

ROSH PINA, CABERNET SAUVIGNON-MERLOT, 2004: Opens with powerful aromas of tobacco, stingy black fruits and an oddly sour cedarwood note and finishes with a distinct barnyard stink. Score 65.

ROSH PINA, CABERNET SAUVIGNON-SHIRAZ, 2003: This blend of 60% Cabernet and 40% Shiraz is light ruby toward brick-red, light- to medium-bodied, far too acidic and with chunky country-style tannins. A few berry and black cherry fruits. Showing age. Drink up. Score 75.

Rota ✷✷✷

Founded by Erez Rota on the Negev Heights, this artisanal winery released its first wines in 2002. The winery and its beautifully planted and tended vineyards are set on an isolated farm, surrounded by magnificent desert mountains. Grapes under cultivation are Cabernet Sauvignon, Merlot, Shiraz and Muscat of Alexandria. In addition, the winery also receives grapes from the Ella Valley.

First releases in 2002 were of 1,000 bottles. Production from the 2006 vintage was of 3,000 bottles and plans for the 2009 harvest are for 12,000 bottles.

ROTA, CABERNET SAUVIGNON, 2007: Dark garnet, medium- to full-bodied, with gripping tannins and spicy wood yielding to black fruits, spices and notes of candied citrus peel. Drink now–2012. Score 85.

ROTA, CABERNET SAUVIGNON, 2006: Garnet toward royal purple, medium-bodied, with somewhat chunky tannins and generous wood, those parting slowly to make way for berry and blackcurrant fruits. Drink now. Score 85.

ROTA, CABERNET SAUVIGNON, 2005: Dark garnet with violet reflections, medium- to full-bodied, with gently mouth-coating tannins and near-sweet cedar notes. Opens to reveal currant, blackberry and blueberry fruits along with a hint of the peel of bitter oranges. Drink up. Score 87.

ROTA, MERLOT, 2006: Deep garnet, medium- to full-bodied, with firm tannins and spicy French oak integrating nicely. Opens on the palate to show abundant red currant and raspberry fruits, those matched by hints of white pepper and green olives. Generous and long. Drink now–2011. Score 87.

ROTA, MERLOT, 2004: Dark garnet in color with orange and green reflections, this deeply extracted wine shows mouth-coating tannins and a judicious hand with spicy oak. Opens with a bit of bottle stink but that passes quickly to reveal a deeply aromatic wine with an array of red and black berries, currants, Oriental spices and chocolate, all lingering comfortably on a long, fruity finish. Drink up. Score 88.

ROTA, CABERNET SAUVIGNON-MERLOT, 2006: Deeply aromatic, this dark garnet, medium- to full-bodied wine is showing soft, mouth-coating tannins and a moderate hand with spicy oak. On the nose and palate berry, black cherry and cassis fruits, those complemented by hints of pepper, anise and light earthiness. Drink now–2011. Score 87.

Rozenbaum ✶

Founded by Avi Rozenbaum in 1998, this small winery is located on Kibbutz Malkiya in the Upper Galilee near the Lebanese border. Grapes, including Cabernet Sauvignon, Merlot, Sangiovese, Chardonnay and Muscat of Alexandria, come from the Kadesh Valley. Production in 2003 was of 7,000 bottles, no wines were produced in 2004 and, with a new partner, 5,000 bottles were produced from the 2005, 2006 and 2007 harvests.

ROZENBAUM, CABERNET SAUVIGNON, 2006: Ruby toward garnet, medium-bodied with chunky country-style tannins and a distinct note of Brett that makes the wine unapproachable. Score 60.

ROZENBAUM, CABERNET SAUVIGNON, 2005: Dark garnet, with coarse tannins and a medicinal overlay that hides whatever fruits may be hiding here. Score 68.

ROZENBAUM, BLEND, 2006: Somewhat muddied garnet red, with flabby tannins and a simple berry-cherry personality, the fruits hidden by a bit of bottle stink that fails to fade away. Score 60.

ROZENBAUM, BLEND, 2005: A coarse, alcoholic and hot blend of Cabernet Sauvignon and Merlot. Lacks charm. Score 70.

Ruth ✶✶✶

Founded by Tal Ma'or and located in Kfar Ruth, adjoining the city of Modi'in, this family-owned winery produced several hundred bottles of wine from the 2002 vintage and current production is 4,000 bottles annually. Grapes, including Cabernet Sauvignon, Merlot and Shiraz, are harvested from vineyards on the central plain and in the hills of Jerusalem.

Reserve

RESERVE, CABERNET SAUVIGNON, 2004: Reflecting its prolonged development (30 months) in *barriques* with generous spicy wood along with hints of sawdust, a full-bodied wine showing poached red plums and cherry-pudding notes, those on a background of licorice and Mediterranean herbs, all with a rather sweet overlay. Drink now. Score 80. **K**

RESERVE, CABERNET SAUVIGNON, 2003: Oak-aged for 30 months, medium-bodied, with generous spicy wood and mouth-coating tannins. Shows red cherry and red berry fruits, those on a background of red licorice and roasted herbs. Drink now. Score 85. **K**

Ruth

RUTH, CABERNET SAUVIGNON, 2005: Medium-bodied, with soft tannins integrating nicely. Showing appealing blackberry and grape flavors supported nicely by bramble, spice and tobacco notes. Drink now. Score 86. **K**

RUTH, CABERNET SAUVIGNON, 2004: This dark-garnet, medium-bodied wine offers up straightforward cherry, berry and raspberry fruits with hints of spices, licorice and roasted herbs that run throughout. Drink up. Score 84. **K**

RUTH, MERLOT, 2005: Its youthful rough edges now smoothing out nicely, blended with 5% Cabernet Sauvignon and aged for 24 months in *barriques*, this medium- to full-bodied red shows spicy wood and firm tannins, those in fine balance with blackcurrant,

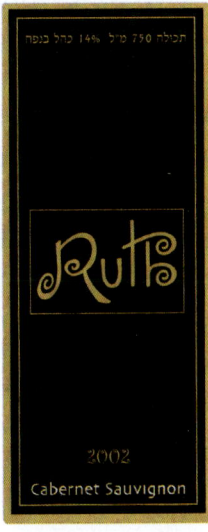

plum and berry fruits all on a light licorice background. Drink now–2011. Score 87. **K**

RUTH, MERLOT, 2004: Medium-bodied with chunky tannins, but those well balanced by smoky wood and appealing aromas and flavors of black fruits. Lacking complexity but appealing. Drink up. Score 84. **K**

RUTH, CABERNET SAUVIGNON-MERLOT, 2006: A blend of 60% Cabernet Sauvignon and 40% Merlot, developed in oak for 12 months, showing medium- to full-bodied, soft and round with blackberry, currant and black cherry fruits highlighted by notes of bittersweet chocolate and tobacco. Drink now. Score 88. **K**

RUTH, CABERNET SAUVIGNON-MERLOT, 2005: A blend of 60% Cabernet Sauvignon and 40% Merlot, aged in *barriques* for 14 months. Dark garnet, medium- to full-bodied, with spicy wood and soft tannins integrating nicely and showing appealing currant and berry fruits on a light licorice background. Drink up. Score 85. **K**

RUTH, CABERNET SAUVIGNON-MERLOT, 2004: Medium-dark garnet in color, with soft tannins and medium body. On the nose and palate, clean blackcurrant and berry aromas as well as a hint of spices. Drink up. Score 85. **K**

RUTH, SHIRAZ-MERLOT, 2006: Medium- to full-bodied, a dark garnet blend of equal parts of Shiraz and Merlot, aged in new oak for 15 months. A country-style wine showing generous oak and chunky tannins, but do not take that as negative for the wine opens beautifully on the palate to show red plums and raspberries on a peppery background. Drink now. Score 88. **K**

Safed *

Founded by Moshe Alon in 2002 and located in the heart of the old city of Safed, this winery relies largely on grapes from the Upper Galilee. Production is about 10,000 bottles annually, the wines from Cabernet Sauvignon, Merlot, Cabernet Franc and Gewurztraminer grapes.

SAFED, CABERNET SAUVIGNON, RESERVE, 2006: Blended with Merlot and Cabernet Franc grapes, aged in new *barriques* for 16 months, showing dusty, not-clear garnet in color, opening with a strong barnyard whiff and going on to show a few red fruits, those alas overlaid with soggy cardboard and, rising on the finish, a most unwanted note of vegetal and animal decay. Score 55. **K**

SAFED, CABERNET SAUVIGNON, 2006: Developed in oak for nine months. Dark garnet, medium-bodied, dominated by earthy, compost pile and barnyard aromas that make it impossible to find whatever fruits may be hiding. Score 55. **K**

SAFED, CABERNET SAUVIGNON, RESERVE, 2005: Marked by searing tannins, burning alcohol and aromas that call to mind the sewers of Paris. Score 50. **K**

SAFED, CABERNET SAUVIGNON, 2004: Stale, with aromas of dirty barnyard and flavors and stewed prunes. Score 55. **K**

SAFED, MERLOT, RESERVE, 2006: Developed in *barriques* for 15 months, showing dark garnet in color, medium- to full-bodied with generous raspberry, cherry and cassis fruits. Lacks complexity but a good quaffer. Drink now. Score 82. **K**

SAFED, MERLOT, 2006: Dark ruby with a hint of off-brown, medium-bodied, with chunky tannins. Aged in used French and Bulgarian oak for 15 months, showing somewhat muddled red fruits and a too-deep earthy-herbal overlay. Drink up. Score 72. **K**

SAFED, CHARDONNAY, 2006: Despite its youth this bronze-colored wine has gone toward vinegar, that with a distinct aroma of sewage. Score 50. **K**

SAFED, SAUVIGNON BLANC, 2007: Acidic enough to be thought of as puckering and sour, with a strong petrol-like aroma that one cannot shake. Score 50. **K**

SAFED, GEWURZTRAMINER, 2007: Damp straw colored, light- to medium-bodied, with stewed apricot and peach fruits but those hidden under a far too acidic and tart note. Noted on the bottle as having an 11.5% alcohol content but alcoholic on the nose and hot on the finish. Score 65. **K**

Salomon **

Located on Moshav Amikam in the Ramot Menashe forest not far from Zichron Ya'akov, this winery was founded in 1997 by Itamar Salomon. For several years the winery made only small quantities of wine for home consumption, and the first commercial release was from the 2002 vintage. Grapes are currently drawn from the Golan Heights, but the winery is planting its own vineyards with Cabernet Sauvignon, Merlot, Cabernet  Franc and Shiraz grapes in the Upper Galilee. Production in 2004 was about 2,500 bottles, 5,000 in 2005, 2006 and 2007, and 8,000 bottles in 2008.

SALOMON, CABERNET SAUVIGNON, 2006: Medium- to full-bodied, with chunky, country-style tannins and notes of spicy wood that open to show currant and wild berry fruits. A pleasant little country-style wine. Drink now. Score 84.

SALOMON, CABERNET SAUVIGNON, 2005: Despite its youth, showing signs of premature aging. Medium-bodied, with tannins more gripping than at an earlier tasting, with its once clean cherry, plum and sandalwood aromas and flavors now taking on a hint of barnyard. Drink up. Score 78.

SALOMON, MERLOT, 2006: Deep royal purple in color, medium-bodied, with soft tannins integrating nicely and showing black fruits, espresso coffee and a hint of Mediterranean herbs. Not complex but a good quaffer. Drink now. Score 84.

SALOMON, MERLOT, 2005: Medium-bodied, soft and round, with black cherry, grape and light hints of herbs and cocoa. Look for a hint of toasted bread on the finish. Drink up. Score 85.

SALOMON, SHIRAZ, 2005: Dark garnet toward royal purple, medium- to full-bodied, with silky tannins and showing generous plum, berry and licorice notes all leading to a moderately long finish. Drink now. Score 85.

SALOMON, STAV (AUTUMN), 2005: An oak-aged blend of Cabernet Franc, Cabernet Sauvignon and Shiraz (60%, 30% and 10% respectively), showing garnet toward royal purple in color, medium-bodied, soft and round. On the nose and palate, black and red berries matched by notes of Mediterranean herbs, cigar tobacco and licorice. Appealing but somewhat short on the finish. Drink now. Score 85.

Saslove ✶✶✶✶

Established by Barry Saslove in 1998 on Kibbutz Eyal in the Sharon region, this boutique winery has vineyards in the Upper Galilee currently planted with Cabernet Sauvignon, Merlot, Syrah and Sauvignon Blanc grapes, and plans to grow Cabernet Franc, Petit Verdot and Gewurztraminer grapes in the future. The winery recently opened a new facility primarily for receiving and fermenting grapes in the Upper Galilee, not far from its vineyards. The barrel room and visitors' center remain on Kibbutz Eyal.

Current production of red wines is in three series: Reserved, Adom and Aviv. The winery occasionally produces white wines as well. Production has grown steadily, from 35,000 bottles in 2002 to about 100,000 bottles from the 2007 and 2008 vintages.

Under the label "K by Saslove," the winery released kosher wines from the 2003, 2004 and 2005 vintages, but that line has been discontinued. Saslove is now producing a kosher wine, Sagol, at the facility of Asif.

Reserved

RESERVED, CABERNET SAUVIGNON, 2006: Showing full-bodied, with generous oak and still firm tannins integrating nicely and showing fine balance with fruits and acidity. Promises to soften with time but destined to be deep, dark and concentrated while simultaneously rich and elegant. On the nose and palate dried and fresh currants, blackberries and raspberries, those in sharp focus and supported by notes of spices and Mediterranean herbs. Drink now–2015. Score 91.

RESERVED, CABERNET SAUVIGNON, 2005: Made from organically raised Cabernet Sauvignon grapes from the Kadita vineyard, oak-aged for 24 months in

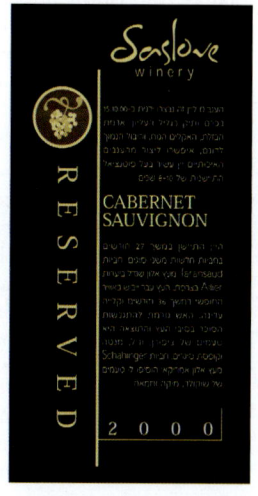

French and American oak, full-bodied with firm but gently mouth-coating tannins parting nicely to reveal traditional Cabernet aromas and flavors of blackcurrants and blackberries. The fruits supported nicely by complex notes of mocha, bittersweet chocolate, Oriental spices and Mediterranean herbs, all of which play nicely on the palate and lead to a long and generous finish. Drink now–2012, perhaps longer. Score 91.

RESERVED, CABERNET SAUVIGNON, 2004: Reflecting 27 months in French oak with generous sweet-and-spicy oak, that well balanced by soft, mouth-coating tannins, acidity and fruits. Opens with currants and berries, those yielding to earthy, herbal and tobacco notes and, on the long finish, a hint of mint. Round, generous and long. Drink now–2013. Score 92.

RESERVED, CABERNET SAUVIGNON, 2003: This oak-aged blend of 88% Cabernet Sauvignon and 12% Merlot is dark garnet and medium- to full-bodied. Showing generous sweet-and-spicy wood and tannins in fine balance with currant, black cherry and blackberry fruits and a complex array of herbs and spices. On the long finish a hint of raspberry liqueur. An elegant wine. Drink now. Score 91.

RESERVED, MERLOT, 2003: Medium-dark garnet with orange reflections, this medium- to full-bodied wine shows generous but well-integrating tannins set off nicely by vanilla and spice notes from the wood, and appealing black cherry, plum and berry fruits. Long and mouth-filling. Drink now. Score 89.

RESERVED, SYRAH, 2005: Already showing the potential for a plum and spice-rich nose along with flavors of ripe black fruits and smoked meat, those supported throughout by hints of freshly tanned leather. Drink from release–2011. Tentative Score 90–92.

Adom

ADOM, CABERNET SAUVIGNON, 2007: Tasted from components but already showing dark garnet in color, full-bodied, with generous near-sweet tannins and ripe black cherry, purple plum and currant fruit that promise to be pure and well focused. On the background, light toasty oak and finishing with notes of mocha and spices. Best from release–2016. Tentative Score 89–91.

ADOM, CABERNET SAUVIGNON, 2006: Full-bodied, rich, smooth and complex, with firm tannins integrating nicely with spicy wood and opening to reveal currant and berry fruits, those complemented by notes of sage and minerals, and, on the long finish, light sweet cedar and blackberries. Tasted from components but already showing simultaneously concentrated and elegant. Drink now–2015. Score 90.

ADOM, CABERNET SAUVIGNON, 2005: Well-crafted. Full-bodied, reflecting its 20 months in oak with firm tannins integrating nicely with spicy and vanilla-rich cedar. Opens with blackcurrants and wild berry fruits, those yielding to notes of plums, black cherries, orange peel, and, on the long, generous finish, an appealing hint of bittersweet chocolate. As the wine develops, look as well for notes of sweet spices and herbs coming in nicely. Drink now–2012. Score 91.

ADOM, CABERNET SAUVIGNON, 2004: Medium- to full-bodied, with soft, mouth-coating tannins in fine balance with spicy and smoky wood and acidity. On the nose and palate traditional Cabernet blackcurrant and blackberry fruits, those matched nicely by light tobacco and chocolate-coated orange peel on the long finish. Drink now. Score 89.

ADOM, MERLOT, 2007: Dark garnet toward royal purple, medium- to full-bodied, with caressing tannins, a rich, soft and round wine, showing blackberry, espresso coffee and black olive notes all on a lightly spicy background. On the long finish a surprising but appealing note of citrus peel. Tasted from components. Drink from release. Tentative Score 88–90.

ADOM, MERLOT, 2006: Full-bodied and generously tannic but lean and crisp on the palate, opening to show an enchanting array of raspberry, blackberry, cranberry, tobacco and sage notes, those supported by generous but not overpowering spicy wood. On the long finish notes of espresso coffee and a hint of saddle leather. Drink now–2013. Score 89.

ADOM, MERLOT, 2005: Medium- to full-bodied with fine concentration, yet soft and supple with generous but not imposing wood after 20 months in French and American oak. Opens with bold aromas and flavors of toasty oak and freshly roasted coffee, those yielding nicely to a generous array of cassis, purple plum and black cherry fruits, and those complemented nicely by hints of bittersweet chocolate and spices. Drink now–2011. Score 90.

ADOM, SHIRAZ-CABERNET SAUVIGNON, 2006: A full-bodied, deep royal purple blend of ⅔ Cabernet and ⅓ Shiraz, in which both varieties make themselves felt nicely. Developed in *barriques* for 22 months, its elements already coming together nicely and showing opulence. On the nose and palate a tempting array of currants, plum, blueberries and black pepper, those on a light tarry background. Delicious now, but with its best still in front of it. Best 2011–2015. Score 91.

ADOM, SHIRAZ-CABERNET SAUVIGNON, 2005: Developed in oak for 20 months, this blend of 60% Shiraz and 40% Cabernet Sauvignon will remind many of the Mollydooker wines of Australia. Dark garnet, full-bodied, with firm tannins and peppery wood notes, those given a racy feeling by generous currant, cherry and raspberry fruits. On the background, tantalizing hints of pepper and tar, all culminating in a long, mouth-filling finish. Drink now–2012. Score 91.

ADOM, MARRIAGE, 2004: Dark, almost impenetrable garnet, this medium-bodied, smooth and round blend of Cabernet Sauvignon, Merlot and Shiraz opens with generous spicy-dusty oak on the nose but that yielding nicely to black and red currants, crushed berries and appealing hints of licorice. Drink now. Score 90.

ADOM, MARRIAGE, 2003: Aged in a variety of oak barrels, fermented with different yeasts, this full-bodied blend of Cabernet Sauvignon, Merlot and Syrah is one of Saslove's best efforts to date. Full-bodied and tannic but simultaneously soft, round and elegant, on the nose and palate a basic blackcurrant personality but that matched by a generous array of berry, black cherry and spices, all lingering nicely on the finish. Drink now. Score 90.

Aviv

AVIV, CABERNET SAUVIGNON, 2007: A near-twin to the 2006 edition. Blue-black in color, medium- to full-bodied with firm tannins and smoky wood integrating nicely now and showing fine balance to highlight blackberry, purple plum and currant fruits, those complemented by hints of spices, cloves and espresso coffee. Drink now. Score 88.

AVIV, CABERNET SAUVIGNON, 2006: Almost blue-black in color, medium- to full-bodied with firm tannins and smoky wood integrating nicely now and showing fine balance to highlight blackberry, purple plum and currant fruits, those complemented by hints of spices, cloves and espresso coffee. Drink now. Score 89.

AVIV, CABERNET SAUVIGNON, 2005: Dark garnet, medium- to full-bodied with firm tannins integrated nicely with a generous array of blackcurrant and blackberry fruits, those with an appealing spicy overlay. Drink now. Score 89.

AVIV, CABERNET SAUVIGNON, 2004: Dark garnet-red, medium- to full-bodied, with soft, mouth-coating tannins. Good balance here and a tempting array of currant, plum and spices, those backed up by hints of vanilla and green olives. Drink up. Score 88.

AVIV, MERLOT, 2007: Made in stainless steel vats with oak chips, as are all of the wines in the Aviv series. Medium-bodied, with soft tannins and appealing notes of spicy and vanilla-rich oak, opening to show wild berry, currant and purple plums, those highlighted by light notes of sage and chocolate. Finishes round and smooth and moderately long with fruits rising. Drink now–2011. Score 88.

AVIV, MERLOT, 2006: Soft and round, medium- to full-bodied, this blend of 85% Merlot and 15% Cabernet Sauvignon offers up a generous and well-balanced array of cassis and berry fruits, those on a background of Mediterranean herbs. Long and satisfying. Drink now. Score 89.

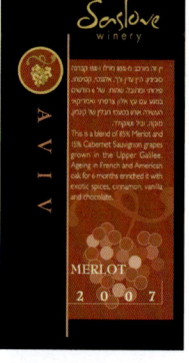

AVIV, MERLOT, 2005: Medium-bodied, with caressing, near-sweet tannins and a generous array of black fruits backed up nicely by earthy, herbal and chocolate aromas and flavors that linger nicely on the palate. Drink now. Score 90.

AVIV, MARRIAGE, 2007: A medium-bodied, soft and round blend of 25% Merlot, 65% Cabernet Sauvignon and 10% Shiraz opening to show appealing red currant, raspberry and blueberry notes, those supported by notes of spices and, as traditional to this wine, red licorice. Drink now. Score 88.

AVIV, MARRIAGE, 2006: Deep garnet toward royal purple, medium- to full-bodied, with silky tannins. A blend of 60% Merlot, 33% Cabernet Sauvignon and 7% Petite Sirah, showing black fruits, spices and hints of red licorice on the finish. Drink now. Score 89.

AVIV, MARRIAGE, 2005: A medium- to full-bodied blend of Merlot, Cabernet Sauvignon and Syrah (60%, 32% and 8% respectively), showing good balance between soft tannins, wood and fruits. On the nose and palate dark plums, cassis and berries that come together nicely. Soft and caressing. Drink now. Score 88.

Sagol

SAGOL, CABERNET SAUVIGNON, SINGLE VINEYARD, 2007: Although Barry Saslove's name appears nowhere on this wine, it carries his wine-maker's signature in every way. Oak-aged for six months, and reflecting gentle spicy wood and soft tannins, a soft but concentrated wine showing generous black fruits, those balanced well by hints of spices and tobacco, all coming to a long finish on which you will find notes of dark chocolate and anise creeping comfortably in. Drink now–2012. Score 90. **K**

Sassy ✳

Sasson Bar-Gig established this small winery in 2000 in the town of Bat Yam on the outskirts of Tel Aviv. The winery draws on grapes from Gush Etzion and the Golan Heights, and is currently producing about 8,000 bottles annually, the reds aged in oak for about 12 months.

SASSY, CABERNET SAUVIGNON, 2006: Medium-bodied, with firm tannins and dusty wood that tend to hide the black fruits that struggle to make themselves felt. Drink up. Score 77.

SASSY, CABERNET SAUVIGNON, 2005: Ruby toward garnet, medium-bodied, with firm tannins that open slowly to show currant and berry fruits. A simple country-style wine. Drink up. Score 80.

SASSY, CABERNET SAUVIGNON, 2004: A country-style wine, medium-bodied, with an herbal edge to currant and cherry fruits. Well past its peak. Score 70.

SASSY, MERLOT, 2005: Dark garnet but, despite its youth, showing clearing at the edges. Somewhat coarse tannins hold back the black fruits that fail to make themselves fully felt. Drink up. Score 77.

SASSY, MERLOT, 2004: Garnet-red but already showing its maturity with hints of browning. Medium-bodied, still showing some red fruits but now starting to caramelize. Past its peak. Score 75.

Savion ✳✳✳

Founded by Ashi Salmon and Eli Pardess and set on Moshav Mesilat Tzion in the Jerusalem Mountains, this micro-winery released its first wine from the 2000 vintage and is currently producing about 2,500 bottles annually. Grapes come primarily from Ramat Dalton and other vineyards in the Upper Galilee, but the winery has new vineyards in which it is raising its own Cabernet Sauvignon, Merlot and Shiraz grapes.

SAVION, CABERNET SAUVIGNON, 2006: Deep royal purple, firm, concentrated and intense, this medium- to full-bodied wine shows generous soft tannins and complex blackberry, currant, tobacco and anise aromas and flavors. Already revealing sharp focus and tannins that firm up on the long, fruity finish. Drink now–2012. Score 89.

SAVION, CABERNET SAUVIGNON, 2005: Blended with 15% of Merlot and developed partly in American and partly in French oak, medium- to full-bodied, with now softened tannins and vanilla-rich wood. Opens to reveal currant, blackberry, black cherry, spicy cedar and hints of sage. On the long finish, cherry and berry fruits rise. Drink now–2011. Score 90.

SAVION, CABERNET SAUVIGNON, 2004: Blended with 10% of Merlot and aged for 12 months in primarily French oak. Garnet toward royal purple, medium- to full-bodied, with firm tannins and spicy wood integrating nicely with fruits and acidity. On the nose and palate black-currants and berries complemented by herbal and tobacco notes and, on the long finish, a hint of white chocolate. Drink now–2011. Score 89.

SAVION, CABERNET SAUVIGNON, 2003: Intensely deep royal purple, medium- to full-bodied, with gripping tannins well balanced by spicy wood and acidity. On the nose and palate red and blackcurrants and berries, those with appealing hints of sweet herbs and, on the generous finish, a tempting overlay of bittersweet chocolate. Drink up. Score 90.

Sde Boker ✴✴✴

Located on Kibbutz Sde Boker in the heart of the Negev Desert, this small winery was founded in 1998 by former Californian Zvi Remick who studied winemaking at California's Napa Valley College. Relying on Cabernet Sauvignon, Merlot, Carignan and Zinfandel grapes grown in the desert, production currently varies between 3,000–5,000 bottles annually.

SDE BOKER, CABERNET SAUVIGNON, 2005: Dark garnet toward inky purple, medium- to full-bodied, with soft tannins integrating nicely and showing generous but not imposing spicy cedarwood. Look for aromas and flavors of black fruits, Oriental spices and green olives, all lingering nicely. Drink now. Score 87.

SDE BOKER, CABERNET SAUVIGNON, 2004: Showing dark garnet toward purple, medium- to full-bodied, with soft tannins integrating nicely. On the nose and palate traditional Cabernet blackcurrant, blackberry and spices, with hints of smoky wood and vanilla rising on the finish. Drink now. Score 88.

SDE BOKER, CABERNET SAUVIGNON, 2003: Medium- to full-bodied, with good balance between wood, soft tannins and tempting blackcurrant, cherry and spicy aromas and flavors. Long and generous. Drink up. Score 88.

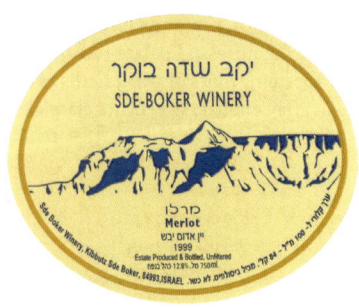

SDE BOKER, MERLOT, 2005: Bright ruby toward garnet, with soft, gently mouth-coating tannins. Showing a moderate wood influence. On the nose and palate plum, berry and black cherry fruits, those complemented by hints of sweet herbs. Drink now. Score 86.

SDE BOKER, MERLOT, 2004: Garnet-red, medium-bodied, with firm tannins integrating nicely with spicy wood and aromas and flavors of black fruits, Mediterranean herbs and a hint of tar. Drink up. Score 85.

SDE BOKER, CABERNET SAUVIGNON-MERLOT, 2006: Deep garnet-red, medium- to full-bodied, with spicy aromas and flavors of currants, cherries, anise, herbs and pepper. Well balanced and well focused, with tangy red fruits and smoky oak on the finish. Drink now. Score 88.

Sea Horse ✶✶✶✶

This boutique winery was established in 2000 on Moshav Bar Giora in the Jerusalem Mountains. Ze'ev Dunie has his own vineyards planted in Syrah and Zinfandel, and draws on Cabernet Sauvignon and other red grapes from the Upper Galilee. Mourvedre, Grenache and Petite Sirah are planted as well, coming on line with the 2010 vintage.

The winery's initial production, from the 2001 vintage, was of 1,800 bottles. Production in 2007 was about 18,000 bottles, and predicted production for 2010 is for about 15,000 bottles. Current releases include two Cabernet Sauvignon-based wines, Elul and Fellini; a Zinfandel-based wine, Lennon; a Syrah-based wine, Antoine; and in selected years, Munch, which is made entirely from Petite Sirah grapes. There is also one blend, Gaudi, and in barrels from the 2006 vintage are Primitivo and Petit Verdot. The winery's first white wine, a Chenin Blanc, was released from the 2007 vintage.

Elul

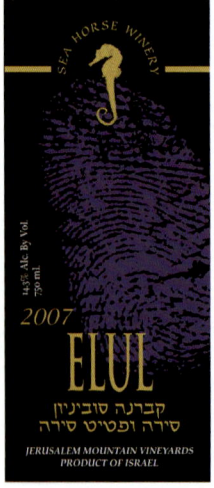

ELUL, 2007: An early tentative blend, showing dark garnet toward royal purple, with gently gripping tannins and wood in good balance with blackberries and purple plums yielding to currants, a potpourri of spices and a note of tobacco. Promising. Drink from release–2013. Tentative Score 89–91.

ELUL, 2006: Full-bodied, with generous firm tannins and cigar-box notes in fine balance with fruits. A blend of Cabernet Sauvignon, Syrah and Petite Sirah (75%, 20% and 5%, respectively). On first attack blackberry and blackcurrant fruits, those opening to reveal notes of Oriental spices, mocha and cigar tobacco. Look for a long, tantalizing near-sweet finish on which tannins and fruits rise nicely. Drink now–2012, perhaps longer. Score 91.

ELUL, 2005: A blend of 73% Cabernet Sauvignon, 18% Syrah and 9% Petite Sirah, developed for 20 months in French and American oak, and showing dark, youthful royal purple, medium- to full-bodied with firm, near-sweet tannins. Opens with currant, kirsch and black cherry fruits, those yielding to hints of licorice, spices and berries, all leading to a long and complex finish. Drink now. Score 91.

ELUL, 2004: A blend of 75% Cabernet Sauvignon, 20% Syrah and 5% Petite Sirah. Deep, almost impenetrable garnet, full-bodied, with firm tannins complemented by spicy oak. On first attack currants and plums, those yielding to red and black berries, a hint of iron, and finally to bittersweet chocolate and Mediterranean herbs, all lingering comfortably. Ripe, round and mouth-filling. Drink now. Score 92.

ELUL, 2003: This well-balanced blend of Cabernet Sauvignon, Syrah and Petite Sirah (85%, 10% and 5% respectively) was developed for 20 months in *barriques*. Ripe black cherry, currant and berry fruits overlaid nicely by hints of anise, spicy oak and light earthiness, all culminating in a long and generous finish. Rich and elegant. Drink now. Score 92.

ELUL, 2002: Deep garnet toward royal purple, a full-bodied blend of 85% Cabernet Sauvignon, 9% Merlot and 6% Syrah. Generous but soft and well-integrating tannins and jammy currant and berry aromas and flavors set off by spices and toast, all showing appealing overtones of Mediterranean herbs. Plush and elegant, with a long finish that yields bittersweet chocolate. Showing first signs of age. Drink up. Score 88.

Fellini

FELLINI, 2007: Dark garnet with green and orange reflections, a blend of 55% Syrah and 45% Cabernet Sauvignon, now showing heady, near-sweet tannins and near-sweet cedarwood in good balance with fruit and natural acidity. On the nose and palate generous black fruits complemented by notes of bittersweet chocolate, freshly cured cigar tobacco and, on the long finish, a hint of red licorice. Drink now–2015, perhaps longer. Score 91.

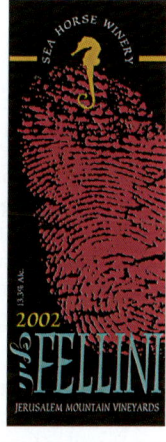

FELLINI, 2006: A medium-bodied, soft and round blend of 55% Syrah and 45% Cabernet Sauvignon, those oak-aged for 18 months. Showing soft and round, with silky tannins and a gentle hand with the oak. Opens to show plums, raspberries and cassis, those with notes of vanilla and licorice that linger nicely. Drink now–2012. Score 90.

FELLINI, 2005: A blend of 46% each Cabernet Sauvignon and Syrah, those complemented by 8% of Petit Verdot. Developed in French and American oak for 16 months, this medium- to full-bodied wine shows silky tannins along with cherry, raspberry and licorice aromas and flavors, those opening to reveal tempting hints of Mediterranean herbs and bittersweet chocolate on the finish. Drink now–2011. Score 90.

FELLINI, 2004: Super-dark amber toward inky-black in color, this blend of equal parts Cabernet Sauvignon and Syrah developed in oak for 16 months and shows gentle cedar and cigar-box hints that run throughout. On the nose and palate wild berries, currants and a generous hint of citrus peel, those complemented nicely by light earthy and leathery overtones. Mouth-filling, long and generous. Drink up. Score 90.

Lennon

LENNON, TÊTE DE CUVÉE, 2007: Still showing a distinct country style, with its tannins somewhat chunky and its wood rather pronounced, but those in fine balance and merely needing time to integrate. As this one develops, look for generous plum, berry and licorice aromas, the tannins destined to be always muscular but parting on the finish to reveal notes of raspberries, black pepper and sage. Drink now–2015. Score 91.

LENNON, 2004: Aged in oak for 14 months, this medium- to full-bodied blend of 95% low-yield Zinfandel vines and 5% Petite Sirah, the wine shows good balance between wood, tannins and alcohol. Opens to reveal generous raspberry, plum and cassis fruits, those matched nicely by light peppery, vanilla and minty overtones. Firm and concentrated, lingering nicely on the palate. Drink now. Score 90.

LENNON, TÊTE DE CUVÉE, 2004: Made from low-yield organically raised Zinfandel grapes and blended with 5% Petite Sirah, the wine is full-bodied, fruity and with a whopping 15.6% alcohol, but has the balance and structure to carry it. Tightly focused currants, plums and wild berries matched nicely by pepper and mocha from the oak. Drink now. Score 91.

LENNON, 2003: A medium- to full-bodied blend of 95% Zinfandel and 5% Petite Sirah. With 14 months in American oak, this generously tannic wine shows good concentration of ripe, juicy cherry and wild berry flavors as well as an appealing pepper and anise edge. Drink now. Score 90.

Take Two

TAKE TWO, 2006: This oak-aged blend of Primitivo, Zinfandel and Petite Sirah shows deep and dark, with fine intensity and generous firm tannins backing up plum, cherry and chocolate aromas and flavors, those on a medium- to full-bodied frame, all leading to a long fruity finish. Drink now. Score 88.

TAKE TWO, 2005: A medium-bodied, softly tannic blend of 85% Zinfandel, 10% Petite Sirah and 5% Carignan that was aged for eight months in primarily American oak. With light peppery and chocolate overtones highlighting plum, raspberry and wild berry fruits, those with hints of anise and minerals. Ripe, round and generous. Drink now. Score 89.

TAKE TWO, 2004: Dark garnet, aged in oak for eight months, this blend of 88% Zinfandel, 10% Petite Sirah and 2% Cabernet Sauvignon shows light meaty and leathery notes. Smooth and round, with wild berry and cassis fruits that make themselves felt nicely. Drink now. Score 90.

Camus

CAMUS, 2006: Firm and gripping tannins opening to reveal dense blackcurrant and blackberry fruits, those backed up by aromas and flavors of minerals, black pepper and cigar box. At this stage massive, but with balance and structure that bode well for future elegance. Drink now–2012. Score 90.

CAMUS, 2005: This almost inky-garnet, full-bodied blend of 92% Syrah and 8% Petite Sirah reflects its 12 months in French oak with a gentle layer of spicy wood, that well balanced by generous but yielding tannins and on the nose and palate smoky blackberries and currants, Oriental spices and hints of game meat. Soft, round and well focused with the tannins rising on the long, supple finish along with appealing hints of leather and black pepper. Drink now–2011. Score 90.

CAMUS, 2004: Dark garnet, medium-bodied, and with soft, caressing tannins, this blend of 94% Syrah and 6% Petite Sirah reflects its 12 months in oak with refreshing acidity, and spicy-toasty oak. On the nose and palate blackcurrant, blackberry, tobacco, and a hint of freshly tanned leather, with white pepper and cigar tobacco rising on the long finish. Drink now. Score 90.

CAMUS, 2003: Shiraz, showing inky-dark garnet, full-bodied with its firm tannins in fine balance with wood and fruits. On the nose primarily black fruits, and on the palate wild berry, black and red cherries, and an appealing leathery note on the finish. Rich and complex and clearly at its peak now. Drink now. Score 90.

Antoine

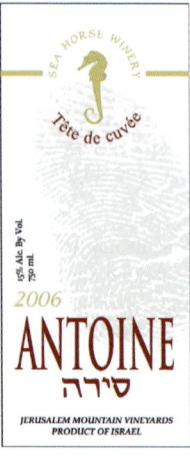

ANTOINE, TÊTE DE CUVÉE, 2007: A medium- to full-bodied blend of 72% Syrah and 14% each of Grenache and Mourvedre, showing firm tannins and generous wood, those in fine balance with fruits. Opens with blackberries, raspberries and mint. As the wine develops in the glass, it shows full-bodied, dense and chewy, the still firm tannins integrating nicely and yielding to huckleberries and blueberries, all with tannins and a light tobacco note rising on the long finish. Drink from release–2015. Tentative Score 90–92.

ANTOINE, TÊTE DE CUVÉE, 2006: Full-bodied, with still gripping tannins waiting to settle in. Reflecting its oak-aging for 18 months with generous but soft and spicy cedar notes, showing tempting bittersweet chocolate and a cigar tobacco note that underlie red berry, blueberry and currant fruits. A blend of 74% Syrah and 13% each of Grenache and Mourvedre, with an appealing herbal hint rising on the long and so-far muscular finish. Drink now–2015. Score 91.

ANTOINE, TÊTE DE CUVÉE, 2005: Made entirely from Syrah grapes, this full-bodied wine spent 16 months in used French barrels and now shows deep garnet-toward-royal purple color with gripping tannins in fine balance with gentle oak. Opens on plummy and leathery notes that yield to blackberries, spices and red licorice. A long, generous finish with a tantalizing bitter note. Drink now–2011. Score 90.

ANTOINE, 2005: Made entirely from Syrah grapes, this full-bodied wine spent 16 months in used French barrels. Shows dark garnet in color, with once gripping tannins now integrated nicely and in fine balance with spicy oak. On the nose and palate plums, blackberries, spices and red licorice. Long and generous. Drink now–2011. Score 90.

ANTOINE, 2004: Medium- to full-bodied, with its once firm tannins now integrating nicely with wood and fruits. Revealing traditional Syrah aromas and flavors of plums, blackberries and licorice, those supported nicely by near-sweet oak and a hint of spiced meat on the long and satisfying finish. Drink now. Score 91.

Munch

MUNCH, 2007: Dark, almost impenetrable royal purple in color, full-bodied and with still muscular tannins waiting to settle down. On first attack a strong whiff of blackberries and notes of dusty and spicy wood, those parting to reveal notes of *garrigue* and roasted herbs. Destined to be both muscular and elegant. Drink from release. Tentative Score 90–92.

MUNCH, 2006: Petite Sirah at its best. Dark, almost impenetrably inky garnet in color, full-bodied, concentrated and intense, showing generous wood and mouth-coating tannins, those in fine balance with red plum, blueberry and currant fruits. Give this one time and it will prove supple, ripe and rich. Drink now–2012. Score 91.

MUNCH, 2005: Made entirely from Petite Sirah grapes from a dry-farmed vineyard. Dark, almost inky teeth-staining purple, with firm, brooding tannins waiting to settle down, and full-bodied enough to be thought of as chewy, but with all of that in fine balance with blackberries, currants, ripe plums and hints of citrus peel and tobacco all on a spicy and near-leathery background. Intense rather than elegant, recalls some of the most interesting wines of this variety from California. Drink now–2013. Score 91.

Gaudi

GAUDI, 2007: A blend of 60% Carignan and 20% each of Cabernet Sauvignon and Syrah. Medium- to full-bodied, with gentle spicy oak and comfortably gripping tannins. Developed in *barriques* for six months, opens to reveal red and blackcurrants, those going on to generous wild berry and peppery notes. Soft, round, generous and moderately long. Drink now–2011. Score 89.

GAUDI, 2006: Dark royal purple, medium-bodied, with soft but mouth-coating tannins, this is a "wild" wine in that it seems to almost burst forth on the nose and palate, at first with raspberry and cassis notes and then, with a second burst, tobacco and spices. Happily, all of these integrate nicely and lead to a long, simultaneously tannic and fruity finish. A blend of 50% Carignan, 33% Syrah and 17% Cabernet Sauvignon. Drink now. Score 88.

GAUDI, 2005: Garnet toward purple, this blend of Carignan, Petite Sirah and Cabernet Sauvignon (30%, 30% and 40% respectively) reflects its eight months in oak with medium body, soft tannins and a personality best described as round. Easy to drink, but with just enough complexities to make it interesting . On the nose and palate plum, currant and wild berries along with hints of spices and licorice. Drink now. Score 88.

Sea Horse

SEA HORSE, GRENACHE, ROMAINE, 2008: A medium- to full-bodied (leaning to the full) blend of 50% Grenache and 25% each Syrah and Mourvedre. Dark cherry red toward garnet in color, with generous but gently caressing tannins. Smooth, round and ripe. On the nose and palate blackberry, cherry, blueberry and exotic spices, those lingering long and comfortably. Drink from release–2013. Tentative Score 90–92.

SEA HORSE, GRENACHE, ROMAINE, 2007: Dark garnet in color, medium- to full-bodied, showing an appealing bitter-sweet streak that parts to reveal blackberry, red cherry, pomegranate and sweet red pepper flavors, those supported nicely by notes of rose petals and tobacco. A blend of 60% Grenache and 40% Syrah, needing time for its elements to come together but already showing fine balance and structure. Drink from release–2013. Tentative Score 89–91.

SEA HORSE, PETIT VERDOT PLUS, 2005: A blend of 66% Petit Verdot and 34% Cabernet Sauvignon, aged in American oak *barriques* for 20 months. Medium- to full-bodied, with velvety smooth tannins, generous oak and an abundance of currant, blackberry, pomegranate, cola, ginger and black pepper aromas and flavors. Drink now. Score 89.

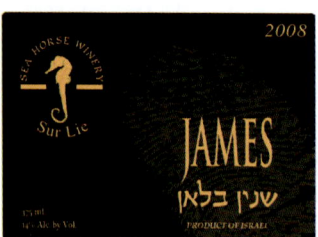

SEA HORSE, CHENIN BLANC, JAMES, 2008: A surprisingly full-bodied Chenin Blanc, but what a happy surprise, for this rich and stylish wine is on its way to showing a tempting array of fig, white peach, almond, mineral and cardamom notes, all on a background of heather and minerals. If Sea Horse's 2007 Chenin Blanc might have called to mind the better dry wines of this varietal from South Africa, this one would make a fine competitor to a well made Vouvray. Drinking nicely now but best from mid–2010–2014. Score 91.

SEA HORSE, CHENIN BLANC, JAMES, 2007: Made from 32-year-old vine Chenin Blanc, with drastic cutting back to concentrate the crop, and fermented and developed *sur lie* in three-year-old *barriques*. Rich, crisply dry and well focused, with tangy mineral, chamomile, grapefruit, white peach and nectarine aromas and flavors, those supported very nicely by hints of figs and ginger. At the same time tangy, lively and elegant. Drink now. Score 89.

Segal ★★★★

Established in the 1950s as Ashkelon Wines and later taking on the name of the family that owned it, in 2001 the company was bought out by Barkan Wineries, but kept its name. Under winemaker Avi Feldstein, with quality vineyards in several regions of the Upper Galilee, and operating now in Barkan's state-of-the-art facilities at Kibbutz Hulda, the winery is now producing several excellent wines, including Single Vineyard and Unfiltered wines, both from Cabernet Sauvignon grapes. Other series are Ben Ami, Marom Galil (including those wines labeled *Single* and *Fusion*), Rechasim, the single-vineyard Dovev varietal wines, Batzir and the popular-priced, entry-level Shel Segal series. The winery relies on Cabernet Sauvignon, Merlot, Argaman, Chardonnay, Sauvignon Blanc, Emerald Riesling and French Colombard grapes, and current production is about 1.5 million bottles annually, of which nearly one million are in the Shel Segal series.

Single Vineyard

SINGLE VINEYARD, CABERNET SAUVIGNON, DISHON, 2006: Garnet toward purple, medium- to full-bodied, already showing a rather generous hand with smoky wood that tends to hold back the fruits and herbal notes here. Drink from release. Tentative Score 86–88. **K**

SINGLE VINEYARD, CABERNET SAUVIGNON, DISHON, 2005: Dark, almost inky-garnet in color, concentrated and intense. Full-bodied and tannic enough to be thought of as chewy, the tannins integrating nicely and showing fine balance with the wood in which the wine was aged. Generous black fruits here, but not so much a fruity wine as a spicy one, led by aromas and flavors of smoked bacon, licorice and espresso coffee. Drink now–2012. Score 90. **K**

SINGLE VINEYARD, CABERNET SAUVIGNON, DISHON, 2003: Full-bodied, with generous, near-sweet tannins and smoky wood now integrated nicely and opening to reveal red currant, wild berry, vanilla and hints of tar, all lingering nicely. Drink up. Score 90. ᴋ

SINGLE VINEYARD, MERLOT, DOVEV, 2004: Dark garnet toward royal purple, this medium- to full-bodied wine was super-generous with its tannins in its youth, so waiting to release this one was a wise move on the part of the winery. With those tanninins now integrating nicely, spicy and showing well-tuned balance and structure. Aromas and flavors of black cherries, blackberries and purple plums, those matched nicely by spicy oak accents and, on the long finish, hints of espresso and dark chocolate. Drink now–2012. Score 90. ᴋ

SINGLE VINEYARD, MERLOT, DOVEV, 2003: Developed in French and American *barriques* for 19 months, this wine is showing full-bodied, with firm tannins and spicy wood integrating well and opulent blueberry, currant and plum flavors, those with spicy and floral notes with hints of licorice in the background. Long, smooth, round and polished. Drink now. Score 91. ᴋ

Unfiltered

UNFILTERED, CABERNET SAUVIGNON, 2006: Full-bodied, concentrated, deeply tannic and with generous wood even at this early stage, the tannins and wood holding back the black fruits and Oriental spices that are trying to make themselves felt. Perhaps better with time. Drink from release. Tentative Score 86–88. ᴋ

UNFILTERED, CABERNET SAUVIGNON, 2005: Blended with 10% Merlot, aged partially in partly new, partly used French and American oak for 30 months, showing full-bodied with generous but gently mouth-coating tannins, the wood and the tannins in fine balance with the fruits. With almost liqueur-like notes of kirsch and cassis, those yielding comfortably to notes of purple plums and pepper. Long and generous. Drink now–2011. Score 90. ᴋ

UNFILTERED, CABERNET SAUVIGNON, 2004: Blended with 10% of Merlot and oak-aged in French and American *barriques* for 22 months, showing dark, firm and intense. Full-bodied, with still gripping tannins and generous but not dominating oak with good balance between those and the red and blackcurrants, black cherries, sage and spicy cedarwood on the nose and palate. On the long finish, a generous overlay of minerals and an appealing hint of bitterness. Drink now. Score 90. **K**

Rechasim

RECHASIM, CABERNET SAUVIGNON, DISHON, 2005: Garnet toward royal purple, medium- to full-bodied with fine concentration. Generous spicy wood and soft tannins part to reveal blackberry, purple plum and currant fruits, those with appealing spicy and herbal notes lingering comfortably on the finish. Drink now–2011. Score 89. **K**

RECHASIM, CABERNET SAUVIGNON, DISHON, 2004: Dark, youthful royal purple in color, intense and concentrated, with a rich array of currant, tobacco, sage and cedarwood aromas and flavors. Fine balance between wood, tannins and acidity yield a ripe and supple Cabernet. Drink now. Score 90. **K**

RECHASIM, MERLOT, DOVEV, 2007: Garnet toward royal purple in color, medium- to full-bodied, with soft, fairly flabby tannins still holding the wine back somewhat. As it does open, the wine shows a basic blackberry-black cherry personality, the fruits overlaid with freshly cut Mediterranean herbal aromas and flavors. Drink from release. Tentative Score 85–87. **K**

RECHASIM, MERLOT, DOVEV, 2006: Dark garnet toward royal purple, full-bodied, with firm tannins just now starting to settle down. With generous spicy wood and crisp acidity, opens to reveal an array of near-sweet black fruits. Needs time for its elements to come together. Drink now. Score 87. **K**

RECHASIM, MERLOT, DOVEV, 2005: Deeply aromatic, full-bodied with chewy tannins needing time to settle in but showing good balance and structure. Opens to reveal spicy oak along with black cherry and raspberry fruits, goes on to reveal a tempting herbaceousness and, on the finish, a hint of eucalyptus. Drink now–2011. Score 89. **K**

RECHASIM, MERLOT, DOVEV, 2004: Dark garnet, this medium- to full-bodied, herbal, spicy and generously tannic wine shows fine balance and structure. Aromas and flavors of black cherries, blackberries and currants matched nicely by spicy oak accents and, on the long finish, hints of espresso and dark chocolate. Drink now–2011. Score 90. **K**

Ben Ami

BEN AMI, CABERNET SAUVIGNON, 2006: Medium-bodied, with soft, near-sweet tannins, notes of toasted oak and aromas and flavors of wild berries and currants. An entry-level wine. Drink up. Score 84. **K**

BEN AMI, CABERNET SAUVIGNON, 2005: Dark royal purple, medium-bodied with generous near-sweet tannins and equally generous smoky wood. Aromas and flavors of currants, blackberries and herbs. Drink up. Score 84. **K**

Marom Galil

MAROM GALIL, CABERNET SAUVIGNON, SINGLE, 2005: Dark garnet with orange and green reflections, medium- to full-bodied and showing soft tannins, generous oak and forward blackberry, black cherry and currant fruits on a background of minted chocolate. Generous and long. Drink now–2011. Score 89. **K**

MAROM GALIL, CABERNET SAUVIGNON, SINGLE, 2004: Made entirely from Cabernet Sauvignon grapes from several Galilee vineyards. Dark garnet in color, with generous spicy and dusty wood influence reflecting 19 months in oak, showing currants, blackberries, bittersweet chocolate and stony minerals on a lightly spicy background. Drink now. Score 88. **K**

MAROM GALIL, MERLOT, SINGLE, 2006: Garnet toward royal purple, medium- to full-bodied, with soft tannins integrating nicely. On the nose and palate, appealing spicy oak parts to reveal a blackberry, black cherry personality, the fruits showing an earthy-mineral overlay. Drink now. Score 87. **K**

MAROM GALIL, MERLOT, SINGLE, 2005: A blend of 85% Merlot and 15% Cabernet Sauvignon and oak-aged for 14 months. Medium- to full-bodied, with soft tannins integrating nicely and showing appealing blackberry, blueberry and violet notes, the fruits and tannins rising on the finish. Drink now. Score 87. **K**

MAROM GALIL, SYRAH, SINGLE, 2005: Blended with 6% of Cabernet Sauvignon, medium- to full-bodied, with soft tannins integrating nicely and showing spicy red and black fruits, those complemented by near-sweet tobacco and meaty notes on the finish. Drink now. Score 88. **K**

MAROM GALIL, RED, FUSION, 2005: A dark ruby toward garnet, medium-bodied and gently tannic blend of Merlot, Cabernet Sauvignon and Cabernet Franc. Soft, round and smooth with aromas and flavors of spicy currants and berries. Drink up. Score 85. **K**

MAROM GALIL, CHARDONNAY, 2007: Medium-bodied, golden straw in color, showing hints of smoky oak, with a note of mint overlaying pineapple, lemon and lime fruits. Drink up. Score 85. **K**

MAROM GALIL, CHARDONNAY, 2006: Light golden in color, with a light buttery note from the wood in which part of the wine was aged for six months, showing medium-bodied, with lively acidity and appealing citrus and pineapple notes. Drink up. Score 86. **K**

MAROM GALIL, MUSCAT DESSERT, 2006: Unabashedly sweet, lacking balancing acidity to add liveliness, and not so much fruity as it offers up a mouthful of honeyed herbs. Drink up. Score 84. **K**

Shel Segal

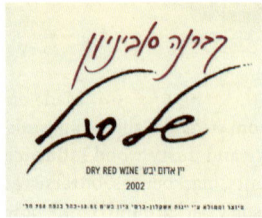

SHEL SEGAL, CABERNET SAUVIGNON, 2007: Medium-bodied with soft tannins, an easy-to-drink entry-level wine with spicy red fruits. Drink up. Score 84. **K**

SHEL SEGAL, CABERNET SAUVIGNON, 2006: Garnet in color, medium-bodied, with soft tannins and forward red fruits. An entry-level wine. Drink up. Score 84. **K**

SHEL SEGAL, DRY RED, 2007: Garnet toward royal purple, medium-bodied with soft tannins. Round, with generous red fruits, a good entry-level wine. Drink up. Score 84. **K**

SHEL SEGAL, DRY RED, 2006: The winery's annual best seller. An entry-level wine showing light- to medium-bodied, with soft tannins, royal purple color and easy-to-take red fruits. A blend of 75% Argaman, about 20% Merlot and the balance of other various grapes. Simple but honest. Drink up. Score 84. **K**

Shdema *

Set on Kibbutz Revivim in the Negev Dessert, this small winery released its first wines from the 2004 vintage. Relying on Cabernet Sauvignon and Merlot grapes from their own vineyards and with Shiraz and Petit Verdot soon coming on line, winemaker Omri Kaluski is currently producing about 2,500 bottles annually.

SHDEMA, CABERNET SAUVIGNON, 2006: Garnet toward purple, medium- to full-bodied, with firm, astringent tannins and acidity that hide the fruits that are lurking here. Drink now. Score 74.

SHDEMA, CABERNET SAUVIGNON, 2005: Dark purple, medium-bodied, with high acidity and coarse, almost stinging tannins, and minimal berry and black cherry fruits that struggle to make themselves felt. Drink up. Score 73.

SHDEMA, CABERNET SAUVIGNON, SDE BOKER, 2005: Dull, somewhat cloudy garnet, medium-bodied, with soft tannins. Showing muddy and bitter with only stingy black fruits. Score 70.

SHDEMA, MERLOT, 2006: Dark purple in color, medium-bodied, with coarse tannins and muddy aromas and flavors. Score 65.

SHDEMA, MERLOT, 2005: Dull garnet, medium-bodied, with barnyard aromas and showing somewhat watery. Score 70.

SHDEMA, MERLOT, SDE BOKER, 2005: Dark garnet, medium-bodied, with soft tannins, moderate wood influence and appealing currant and berry fruits accompanied by hints of pepper. Drink up. Score 83.

Shiloh ✶✶✶

Established in Shiloh in the Binyamin region of Judea and Samaria, this winery released its first wines from the 2005 vintage. Winemaker Amichai Lourie relies on Cabernet Sauvignon, Merlot, Cabernet Franc, Petit Verdot, Petite Sirah and Chardonnay grapes, those largely from the winery's own vineyards. Production in 2005 was of 20,000 bottles, in 2006 of 40,000 bottles, and in 2007 of 70,000 bottles. In addition to a flagship wine named Mosaic, wines are released under three labels—Sod Reserve (Secret Reserve), Shor (Bull) and Shiloh.

SHILOH, MOSAIC, 2006: Deep garnet with purple reflections, full-bodied, with generous but not overpowering spicy wood and gently mouth-coating tannins. A blend of 60% Merlot and 20% Cabernet Franc, those flushed out with Cabernet Sauvignon, Petite Sirah and Petit Verdot, opens to show a generous berry and chocolate personality, and on the long finish notes of dried herbs. Medium- to full-bodied, with good concentration and finishing on a velvety note. Drink now–2014. Score 91. **K**

SHILOH, CABERNET SAUVIGNON, RESERVE, SOD, 2007: Aging in 400 liter barrels and tasted as a component, showing deeply tannic and with generous wood, waiting to find its balance if that balance is there. Drink from release. Tentative Score 83–85. **K**

SHILOH, CABERNET SAUVIGNON, RESERVE, SOD, 2006: Developed for 16 months in new and older French *barriques*, medium- to full-bodied, with soft tannins and notes of sweet cedarwood. An aromatic wine, opening to reveal blackcurrants and black cherries, those matched by notes of citrus peel, chocolate and freshly roasted herbs. Fine balance and a long and generous finish on which the tannins and fruits rise nicely. Drink now–2012. Score 89. **K**

SHILOH, CABERNET SAUVIGNON, SHOR, 2006: Dark garnet toward royal purple, medium- to full-bodied, with soft tannins integrating nicely and a gentle hand with spicy wood. On the nose and palate lightly spicy blackcurrant, black cherry and blackberry fruits, those on a background of mint-tinged vanilla. Drink now. Score 87. **K**

SHILOH, CABERNET SAUVIGNON-MERLOT, SHOR, 2006: A dark ruby toward garnet, medium-bodied blend of 50% Cabernet Sauvignon, 47% Merlot and 3% of Petite Sirah with soft tannins. Reflecting oak-aging for 12 months with notes of vanilla and crème caramel, opens in the glass to show currant, blackberry and purple plum fruits, those matched by notes of roasted herbs and freshly roasted coffee beans. Drink now–2011. Score 87. K

SHILOH, MERLOT-SHIRAZ, SHOR, 2006: Showing generous vanilla and smoky notes from its 14 months in American oak, but that balanced by good fruits and lively acidity. Medium- to full-bodied, opens slowly in the glass to reveal gently gripping tannins, generous black fruits and notes of chocolate. Round and generous. Drink now–2011. Score 86. **K**

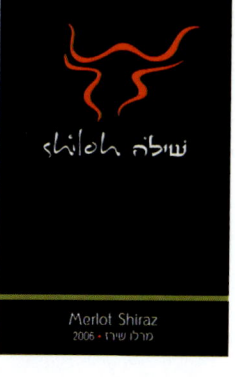

SHILOH, MERLOT-SHIRAZ, 2005: Dark garnet, medium- to full-bodied, reflecting its 14 months in French oak with generous but not overpowering spicy oak in good balance with soft, well-integrating tannins. On the nose and palate red currant and raspberry fruits, Mediterranean herbs and a hint of licorice. Long, round and generous. Drink now. Score 87. **K**

SHILOH, ROSÉ, 2007: Somewhere in color between rose-petal pink and cherry red, a crisply dry rosé. A blend of Barbera and Cabernet Franc, those allowed only short skin contact, showing appealing raspberry, strawberry and blueberry fruits. A pleasant medium-bodied quaffer. Drink up. Score 87. **K**

SHILOH, CHARDONNAY, 2007: Light golden straw, medium-bodied, with citrus and summer fruits on a background of spicy oak. A good quaffer. Drink up. Score 86. **K**

Sifsaf *

Founded by Arik Elbaz on Moshav Safsufa in the Upper Galilee, the winery's own vineyards contain Cabernet Sauvignon, Merlot, Cabernet Franc, Barbera, Nebbiolo, Sangiovese, Syrah, Chardonnay, Viognier and Sauvignon Blanc grapes. Production is about 15,000 bottles annually. Although the labels on the Sifsaf bottles state a given vintage year, the owner/winemaker acknowledges that because labels are expensive, he may at times use the same label for more than one year, which makes it impossible to know precisely which wine one is tasting or purchasing.

SIFSAF, CABERNET SAUVIGNON, 2006: Not so much a fruity wine as it is one dominated by aromas and flavors of sawdust, dill and apple vinegar. Score 50. **K**

SIFSAF, CABERNET SAUVIGNON, 2005: Medium-bodied, with dusty wood and sour pickle aromas and flavors overpowering whatever fruits might be here. Score 55. **K**

SIFSAF, SYRAH, 2005: With odors of iodine and burning rubber and flavors of vinegar, many will consider this an undrinkable wine. Score 50. **K**

SIFSAF, CHARDONNAY, 2005: Dark gold toward bronze, acidic enough to pucker the lips and with apple vinegar aromas. Score 50. **K**

SIFSAF, CHARDONNAY, 2004: Medicinal, musty, pungent and unclean aromas and flavors. Score 50. **K**

SIFSAF, SAUVIGNON BLANC, 2004: Musty, bitter, with distinct iodine aromas and flavors that coat the mouth. Score 50. **K**

Smadar ✶✶✶

Established by Moty Sela in 1998 and located in Zichron Ya'akov, this winery draws on grapes from nearby vineyards owned by the family, those containing Cabernet Sauvignon, Merlot, Cabernet Franc and Carignan grapes. Production is currently about 4,000 bottles annually.

SMADAR, CABERNET SAUVIGNON, 2007: Somewhat astringent at this stage of its development, but showing overall balance and structure that should make this an easy-drinking Cabernet with black cherry and blackberry notes on a background of green olives. Drink from release. Tentative Score 84–86.

SMADAR, CABERNET SAUVIGNON, 2006: Firm and ripe, medium- to full-bodied with an appealing earthy-mineral streak that runs through berry, cherry and anise aromas and flavors. Drink now. Score 85.

SMADAR, CABERNET SAUVIGNON, 2005: Dark garnet in color, full-bodied with firm tannins that seem not to want to yield, and generous wood that somewhat hide the black fruits, citrus peel and chocolate that try hard to make themselves felt. Drink up. Score 85.

SMADAR, MERLOT, 2007: Almost inky-black at this stage of its development, showing gripping tannins and spicy wood needing time to settle in. Good black fruits here but a chocolate, licorice and spice-rich wine. Drink now–2011. Score 87.

SMADAR, MERLOT, 2006: Dark royal purple in color, medium-bodied, with soft tannins. A round wine opening to show a gentle hand with spicy wood and appealing black fruits. On the finish look for hints of chocolate and vanilla that play nicely on the palate. Drink now. Score 86.

SMADAR, MERLOT, 2005: Deep garnet toward inky-purple, medium- to full-bodied, with soft, mouth-coating tannins and gentle spicy wood in fine balance with plum, blackberry and currant fruits all on a background of exotic spices. A long finish on which tannins and fruits rise together. Drink up. Score 86.

SMADAR, CARIGNAN, 2007: Medium- to full-bodied, dark garnet in color, with firm tannins and generous acidity needing time to integrate but already showing appealing red fruits, spices and earthy minerals, all with a hint of black pepper on the finish. Drink from release–2011. Tentative Score 86–88.

SMADAR, CARIGNAN, 2006: Medium- to full-bodied, with concentrated aromas and flavors of black cherries, raspberries, minerals and spices, all backed up by just-firm-enough tannins and peppery oak. Drink now. Score 85.

SMADAR, CABERNET FRANC, 2007: Dark royal purple, medium-bodied with still-tight tannins. On the nose and palate dried cherries and cranberries along with generous overlays of sage and green olives. Drink from release. Tentative Score 82–84.

SMADAR, CABERNET FRANC, 2006: A modest wine, medium-bodied, ruby toward garnet in color, with herbal and cedar notes opening to reveal black cherries and hints of tobacco. Drink now. Score 85.

Snir **

Founded in 2002 by Danny Stein and located on Kibbutz Snir in the Upper Galilee, the winery relies on Cabernet Sauvignon and Merlot grapes from the Sha'al vineyards. Initial production was of 1,200 bottles and current production is about 5,000 bottles annually. The winery releases wines in two series, Nimrod and Snir.

Nimrod

NIMROD, CABERNET SAUVIGNON, 2005: Dark ruby toward purple, medium-bodied, with soft tannins integrating nicely with gently spicy wood. On the nose and palate red currants, wild berries and spices. Flawed by a note of volatile acidity. Drink up. Score 82.

NIMROD, CABERNET SAUVIGNON, 2004: Dark, but not fully clear royal purple, aged in oak for one year, medium-bodied, with soft, well-integrating tannins and plum and blackberry fruits on a lightly spicy background. Drink up. Score 80.

NIMROD, CABERNET SAUVIGNON-MERLOT, 2006: Garnet toward royal purple, medium-bodied with somewhat chunky tannins, a pleasant little country-style wine with red and black berry, cherry and cassis fruits. A good quaffer. Drink now. Score 84.

NIMROD, CABERNET SAUVIGNON-MERLOT, 2005: Ruby toward garnet in color, medium-bodied, an oak-aged blend of 66% Cabernet Sauvignon and 34% Merlot showing red berries and cassis on a light background of minerals. Not complex but a good quaffer. Drink up. Score 84.

Snir

SNIR, CABERNET SAUVIGNON, 2006: Dark ruby toward garnet, medium- to full-bodied with near-sweet tannins, a round, soft and easy-to-drink wine with generous black fruits. Drink now. Score 84.

SNIR, CABERNET SAUVIGNON, 2005: Dark royal purple, medium-bodied, with soft tannins and lightly spicy wood. Shows currant, blackberry and raspberry fruits with a light spicy note that runs through to the finish. Drink now. Score 85.

SNIR, MERLOT, 2006: Ruby red, medium-bodied, with soft tannins and forward berry, black cherry and currant fruits. A pleasant but somewhat internationalized Merlot. Drink up. Score 84.

SNIR, MERLOT, 2005: Garnet toward purple, medium-bodied, with soft tannins and an appealing array of spicy berries and black cherries. Not complex but a good quaffer. Drink up. Score 84.

Somek ✶✶✶

Established by Australian-trained winemaker Hilla Ben Gera and vintner Barak Dahan in Zichron Ya'akov, the winery released its first wines from the 2003 vintage with 1,500 bottles. The winery is currently releasing about 7,000 bottles annually and relies on its own vineyards, those with Merlot, Syrah, Carignan, Petite Sirah and Chardonnay grapes. Coming on line in the near future will be Cabernet Franc, Malbec, Mourvedre and Petit Verdot grapes. The winery produces wines in a reserve and regular series.

Reserve

RESERVE, BIKAT HANADIV, 2005: Dark, almost inky-garnet in color, medium- to full-bodied, this 24-months oak-aged blend of Cabernet Sauvignon, Merlot, Carignan and Petite Sirah (40%, 40%, 15% and 5% respectively) opens with a rich crushed berry and spicy nose. Firmly tannic at this stage of its development, but with gently mouth-coating tannins and spicy wood integrating nicely, the wine opens to reveal blackberry and cassis fruits, those with overlays of tobacco and chocolate. Drink now–2012. Score 90.

RESERVE, BIKAT HANADIV, 2004: A generously oak-aged blend of 60% Cabernet Sauvignon, 35% Merlot and 5% Petite Sirah, showing good balance between spicy wood, firm tannins and fruits. On first attack purple plums and blueberries, those yielding to black fruits, chocolate and hints of espresso coffee all lingering nicely on the palate. Drink now. Score 88.

Somek

SOMEK, MERLOT, 2004: Deep ruby toward garnet, medium-bodied, with gently mouth-coating tannins. Showing spices and vanilla from its oak-aging, those parting to reveal a generous array of currant and wild berry fruits and, on the moderately long finish, an appealing hint of Mediterranean herbs. Drink up. Score 87.

SOMEK, SYRAH, 2005: Dark garnet, medium- to full-bodied, reflecting its development in French oak for 20 months with a generous overlay of spicy and dusty wood and gripping tannins. Needs time in the glass to open and reveal the near-sweet black fruits, chocolate and peppery notes. Drink now–2011. Score 88.

SOMEK, SYRAH, 2004: Mediterranean Syrah, with peppery wild berry, black cherry and plum aromas and flavors, those matched nicely by chewy but yielding tannins, intimations of spicy wood and a beefy hint on the finish. Medium- to full-bodied, with the clear potential for elegance. Drink now. Score 89.

SOMEK, CARIGNAN, 2004: Oak-aged for 20 months in French *barriques*, medium-bodied, with generous black fruits, spicy oak and vanilla, a softly tannic wine that opens nicely on the palate. Plenty of spicy wood here, but that well integrated and, on the long finish, hints of orange peel and chocolate. Drink up. Score 88.

SOMEK, HANADIV VALLEY, 2004: A blend of Cabernet Sauvignon, Merlot and Petite Sirah (60%, 35% and 5% respectively). Garnet toward royal purple, with good balance between spicy wood, gently mouth-coating tannins, wild berries and black fruits, all with hints of tobacco and licorice that make themselves felt. Drink up. Score 86.

SOMEK, CHARDONNAY, 2005: Light golden in color, medium- to full-bodied, developed *sur lie* for 12 months in French oak. Buttery and lively at the same time, showing generous white peach, citrus and apple notes, those supported nicely by hints of spices that toy on the palate. Drink up. Score 88.

Soreq ✦✦✦

Founded in 1994 on Moshav Tal Shachar and situated at the foot of the Jerusalem Mountains, with Nir Shacham as winemaker, this boutique winery relies entirely on Cabernet Sauvignon and Merlot grapes grown in its own vineyards, and releases wines in Special Reserve and regular editions. Current production is about 5,000 bottles annually.

Special Reserve

SPECIAL RESERVE, CABERNET SAUVIGNON, 2004: Dark garnet toward royal purple, full-bodied, with generous, somewhat chunky tannins and dusty wood giving the wine a countrified personality. Generous currant, berry and black cherry fruits on a background of spicy oak and Mediterranean herbs. Drink now–2011. Score 87.

Soreq

SOREQ, CABERNET SAUVIGNON, TAL SHACHAR, 2006: Dark garnet toward purple in color, full-bodied, with firm tannins that need time to integrate but already showing appealing cassis, berry and black cherry fruits leading to a long minty finish. Drink now. Score 86.

SOREQ, CABERNET SAUVIGNON, KEREM YOSEF, 2004: Impenetrably dark garnet, full-bodied and concentrated, with near-sweet tannins and vanilla from the *barriques* in which it developed. On the nose and palate plums, berries and hints of somewhat astringent red licorice. Drink now. Score 87.

SOREQ, MERLOT, TAL SHACHAR, 2005: Made entirely from Merlot grapes, showing soft tannins and spicy wood integrating nicely to reveal generous cedary blackberry and wild berries, those on a background of sage and minerals. Drink now. Score 89.

SOREQ, MERLOT, KEREM YOSEF, 2005: Blended with 14% of Cabernet Sauvignon and aged in oak for 18 months, this dark-garnet full-bodied red shows a narrow band of blackberry and game aromas and flavors. Somewhat awkward. Drink up. Score 83.

SOREQ, MERLOT, TAL SHACHAR, 2004: Dark garnet toward royal purple, full-bodied, with softly mouth-coating tannins and hints of vanilla and cinnamon. Opens to reveal currant and berry fruits, those on a lightly spicy background. Long and generous. Drink now. Score 88.

Sraya ✲✲

Founded in 2002 by Sraya Ofer and set in the Jordan Valley, this small winery receives Cabernet Sauvignon, Merlot and Shiraz grapes from vineyards in Karmei Yosef and the Ella Valley. First releases were of under 1,000 bottles and currently the winery is releasing about 3,500 bottles annually.

SRAYA, CABERNET SAUVIGNON, 2005: Dark ruby, medium-bodied, with softly mouth-coating tannins and appealing currant, blackberry and blueberry fruits on a lightly spicy background. Drink now. Score 85.

SRAYA, CABERNET SAUVIGNON, 2004: Ruby toward garnet, medium-bodied, with soft tannins integrating nicely and showing red currant and cherry fruits on a spicy, herbal background. On the finish a hint of saddle leather. An appealing quaffer. Drink now. Score 85.

SRAYA, MERLOT, 2005: Ruby toward garnet, medium-bodied, a soft, round wine with appealing wild berry, cherry and spicy notes. A good quaffer. Drink now. Score 84.

SRAYA, MERLOT, 2004: A round, smooth and easy-going wine, medium-bodied, with soft tannins and forward berry, black cherry and spicy notes. Drink up. Score 85.

Srigim **

Founded by Uriel Harari and Moti Mordechai on Moshav Srigim in the Ella Valley in 2000, this small winery released its first wines from the 2002 harvest. Drawing on grapes from the Judean Mountains, the Ella Valley and Gush Etzion, current production is about 3,000 bottles annually.

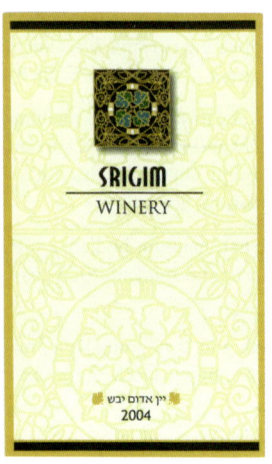

SRIGIM, CABERNET SAUVIGNON, BARRIQUE, 2006: Blended with 5% Cabernet Franc, dark garnet in color and reflecting its 18 months in oak with spices and smoke. Once firm tannins now integrating nicely and opening to reveal a generous black-fruit nose, and on the palate blackcurrants, black cherries and mint. On the finish an appealing hint of baking chocolate. Drink now. Score 87.

SRIGIM, CABERNET SAUVIGNON, BARRIQUE, 2005: Dark royal purple, a medium-bodied blend of 85% Cabernet Sauvignon and 7.5% each of Cabernet Franc and Petit Verdot. Aged in *barriques* for 14 months, showing spicy and dusty oak, firm tannins and a few blackberry and currant fruits. Somewhat alcoholic on the nose. Drink now. Score 82.

SRIGIM, CABERNET FRANC, 2006: Youthful royal purple in color, medium-bodied, with aromatic oak and chocolate on the nose and showing forward black fruits. Round, soft and caressing. Drink now. Score 86.

SRIGIM, CABERNET FRANC, BARRIQUE PREMIUM, 2005: Dark garnet, a medium- to full-bodied blend of 85% Cabernet Franc with 7.5% each of Cabernet Sauvignon and Petit Verdot. Showing spices and vanilla from the oak, opening with blueberries and currants, those going to notes of purple plums, all on a background of eucalyptus and licorice. Smooth, round and moderately long. Drink now. Score 86.

SRIGIM, CABERNET FRANC, 2005: A dark royal purple, medium- to full-bodied blend of 85% Cabernet Franc and 7.5% each of Cabernet Sauvignon and Petit Verdot. Oak-aged for 14 months, showing black fruits on an appealing earthy-mineral background. Tannins and a hint of unwanted acidity rise on the finish. Drink now. Score 84.

SRIGIM, PETIT VERDOT, 2006: A blend of 85% Petit Verdot with 7.5% each of Cabernet Franc and Cabernet Sauvignon. Dark, bold and tannic, with aromas and flavors of blackberries, licorice and sweet cedar, all on a background of dusty wood. Drink now. Score 86.

SRIGIM, PETIT VERDOT, 2005: Dark garnet toward royal purple, medium- to full-bodied, this oak-aged blend of 85% Petit Verdot and 7.5% each Cabernet Sauvignon and Cabernet Franc shows fine balance between fruits, spicy wood and acidity. Aromatic, long and mouth-filling. Drink now. Score 86.

SRIGIM, CABERNET SAUVIGNON-MERLOT, 2005: A blend of 60% Cabernet Sauvignon and 40% Merlot, oak-aged for 13 months. Medium-bodied, soft and round with black fruits and gentle tannins. Lacks complexity. Drink up. Score 84.

Stern ✳✳✳

Founded by Johnny Stern on Kibbutz Gadot in the Upper Galilee, first production from the 2004 harvest was of 1,100 bottles, and current production is about 5,000 bottles annually. The winery currently relies on Cabernet Sauvignon, Merlot, Cabernet Franc, Shiraz and Petit Verdot grapes.

STERN, CABERNET SAUVIGNON, 2007: Showing full body, soft but mouth-coating tannins and traditional Cabernet aromas and flavors of blackberries and blackcurrants, those on a spicy background. Look as well for hints of licorice and dark chocolate. Drink now–2011. Score 87.

STERN, CABERNET SAUVIGNON, 2006: Dark garnet toward royal purple, medium- to full-bodied, with soft, gently mouth-coating tannins and generous blackberry, currant and citrus peel notes supported nicely by hints of Mediterranean herbs. Lingers nicely. Drink now. Score 87.

STERN, CABERNET SAUVIGNON, 2005: Dark ruby toward garnet, medium-bodied, reflecting its 16 months in French oak with soft tannins and hints of spices. Blended with 10% of Shiraz, opens to reveal red currant and raspberry fruits on a light licorice background. Drink now. Score 85.

STERN, CABERNET SAUVIGNON, 2004: Oak-aged for 12 months, this garnet-red, medium-bodied wine shows soft, well-integrated tannins and an appealing array of currant, wild berry and floral aromas and flavors, and finishes moderately long with hints of Oriental spices. Drink up. Score 85.

STERN, SHIRAZ, 2006: Medium-dark garnet in color, medium- to full-bodied, with silky tannins and generous wild berry and purple plum fruits on a spicy and earthy background. Well focused. Drink now–2011. Score 86.

STERN, CABERNET FRANC, 2007: Youthful royal purple in color, full-bodied, with gripping tannins that need time to settle down but already showing good balance and structure. Opens to reveal earthy, almost loamy flavors with dense berry, spicy oak and toast flavors. Drink now. Score 86.

STERN, CABERNET FRANC, 2006: Made entirely from Cabernet Franc grapes, aged in new *barriques* for 14 months, showing dark garnet, medium- to full-bodied, with soft tannins and appealing black fruits on a lightly leathery and earthy mineral background. Drink now. Score 87.

STERN, OR, 2006: A blend of Merlot, Cabernet Sauvignon and Cabernet Franc (40%, 35% and 25% respectively). Developed in French oak for 13 months, dark garnet in color, with still-firm tannins but those integrating nicely and showing appealing red fruits, spices and a hint of tobacco on the finish. Drink up. Score 85.

STERN, ROTEM, 2006: The winery's second Bordeaux blend of Cabernet Sauvignon, Merlot and Cabernet Franc (in this case 65%, 22% and 13% respectively). Deep garnet toward royal purple in color, reflecting its 13 months in French oak with soft tannins and opening to reveal blackberry, blueberry and currant fruits, those highlighted by light earthy and herbal notes. Long and generous. Drink now. Score 88.

Tabor ✶✶✶✶

Founded in 1999 by several grape-growing families in the village of Kfar Tabor in the Lower Galilee, this modern winery draws on white grapes largely from their own vineyards near Mount Tabor and on red grapes from the Upper Galilee. Initial production was of 20,000 bottles and current production is close to 1,000,000 bottles annually. With 800 dunams (about 200 acres) of vineyards coming on line under long-term contracts, additional vineyards in the planning stage, a full-time agronomist now aboard, and the winery undergoing major physical expansion, long-term planning is to raise production to between 3–6 million bottles annually.

European-trained winemaker Arieh Nesher is currently releasing wines in three series. The top-of-the-line label is Mes'cha, a blend of Cabernet Sauvignon, Merlot and Shiraz. A second label, Adama, reflects the type of soils in the vineyards. In reading the labels it may be useful to know that *adama* translates into soil; *gir* is chalky soil; *terra rossa* is red earth; *charsit* is clay and *bazelet* refers to volcanic soil. There is also a more basic series released under the label Tabor.

Several years ago, the Central Bottling Corporation, which is the local producer of Coca-Cola, bought into Tabor and in 2005 increased its holdings in the winery to 51%. Wines continue to rise in quality as well as to offer excellent value for money.

Mes'cha

MES'CHA, 2007: Tasted from components, each a tentative blend of about 75% Cabernet Sauvignon, 15% Merlot and 10% Syrah, those aging in different French oak *barriques*. Already showing the potential to be intense and concentrated, full-bodied, firmly tannic in its youth but those settling down nicely to reveal currant, purple plum and blackberry fruits, those complemented by notes of bitter orange peel, tobacco and dark chocolate. The wine will be approachable and enjoyable on release but will show its best (with perhaps a note of toasted herbs coming in) from 2011–2016. Potentially the best wine to date from Tabor. Tentative Score 92–94. K

MES'CHA, 2005: Dark garnet with orange and purple reflections, full-bodied with once firm tannins and generous oak now settling in nicely and showing in fine moderation and in fine balance with fruits. A concentrated wine, opening in the glass to reveal red currants, wild berries and red licorice, those with light overlays of herbal and cigar tobacco. A blend of 75% Cabernet Sauvignon, 15% Shiraz and 10% Merlot, aged partly in 2000 liter casks and partly in 225 liter *barriques* for 18 months. Long, generous and elegant. Drink now–2014. Score 91. **K**

MES'CHA, 2003: A blend of Cabernet Sauvignon, Shiraz and Merlot (75%, 15% and 10% respectively), this deep-garnet, medium- to full-bodied wine reflects its 18 months in oak with tannins and spicy wood integrating and opening to reveal blackcurrant, berry and plum fruits on a background of spicy wood and Mediterranean herbs. Generous, well balanced and long. Drink now–2011. Score 90. **K**

MES'CHA, 2002: A blend of Cabernet Sauvignon and Merlot, this medium- to full-bodied red shows firm but well-integrated tannins with spicy oak and generous currant and blackberry fruits, those matched by hints of spices, earthiness and tobacco on the finish. Drink now. Score 90. **K**

MES'CHA, RED DESSERT WINE, 2005: Made from Cabernet Sauvignon grapes, medium- to full-bodied, with generous sweetness and showing jammy raspberry and plum fruits. A bit cloying, too literally "a sticky." Drink now. Score 83. **K**

Adama

ADAMA, CABERNET SAUVIGNON, BAZELET, 2007: Dark garnet toward royal purple, medium- to full-bodied, a rich, softly tannic wine showing dried currant, blackberry, sage and herbal notes and, on the finish, notes of minerals and dark chocolate. Drink now–2014. Score 90. **K**

ADAMA, CABERNET SAUVIGNON, BAZELET, 2005: Medium-dark garnet toward purple, this medium- to full-bodied blend of 87% Cabernet Sauvignon and 13% Merlot was developed in 2000 liter wood casks and shows generous blackcurrant, blackberry, citrus peel and earthy-mineral aromas and flavors. On the long finish hints of sweet cedar, tobacco and eucalyptus. Drink now–2012. Score 90. **K**

ADAMA, CABERNET SAUVIGNON, BAZELET, 2004: Dark garnet in color, with deep purple and orange reflections, this medium- to full-bodied wine shows good balance between smoky wood, acidity and fruits. On the nose and palate concentrated currant and blackberry fruits matched by espresso and vanilla. Seductive and elegant. Drink now. Score 90. **K**

ADAMA, CABERNET SAUVIGNON, TERRA ROSSA, 2007: Super-dark garnet in color, an aromatic wine, opening with spicy wood and wild berries on the nose. Full-bodied, showing still firm tannins that need a bit of time to settle in, but already revealing red currants, spices, licorice and notes of freshly roasted herbs. Drink now–2014. Score 90. **K**

ADAMA, CABERNET SAUVIGNON, TERRA ROSSA, 2006: Oak-aged for nine months, medium- to full-bodied, with soft tannins, hints of spicy wood and vanilla and mouth-coating tannins settling down nicely. Showing currant, blackberry and generous earthy minerals along with Mediterranean herbs. Round and generous. Drink now–2011. Score 89. **K**

ADAMA, CABERNET SAUVIGNON, TERRA ROSSA, 2005: Dark garnet toward royal purple, medium- to full-bodied, with firm, near-sweet tannins integrating nicely. Aromatic and flavorful, with red plums, raspberries and currants matched by minerals and light hints of herbaceousness. Round, long and generous. Drink now–2011. Score 89. **K**

ADAMA, CABERNET SAUVIGNON, TERRA ROSSA, 2004: Dark garnet, medium- to full-bodied, with spicy wood and soft tannins integrating nicely. Red currants, blackberries, raspberries and red plums on the nose and palate, those backed up by an appealing hint of earthiness that lingers nicely. Drink now. Score 88. **K**

ADAMA, MERLOT, BAZELET, 2007: Dark garnet, medium- to full-bodied with a sweet, almost jammy raspberry nose that goes on to show spicy plums, cherries and blackberries, those complemented nicely by spicy cedar notes, with fruits and tannins rising on the finish. Drink now–2012. Score 89. **K**

ADAMA, MERLOT, BAZELET, 2006: Garnet toward royal purple, with light spicy wood on near-sweet tannins and opening to reveal currant, purple plum and blackberry fruits, those on a background of milk chocolate and, on the finish, nice hints of mint and white pepper. Drink now. Score 89. **K**

ADAMA, MERLOT, BAZELET, 2005: Dark ruby toward garnet, medium-bodied and showing red and black berries, red currants, earthy minerals and hints of white chocolate, all on a lightly spicy and herbal background. Blended with 10% of Cabernet Sauvignon, round and generous. Drink now. Score 90. **K**

ADAMA, MERLOT, BAZELET, 2004: Medium- to full-bodied, reflecting its 12 months in *barriques* with gentle hints of spicy wood and well-integrated tannins, those in fine balance with blackcurrants, red plums and wild berries. Good length and with hints of mint and chocolate on the finish. Drink now. Score 89. **K**

ADAMA, MERLOT, GIR, 2007: Developed in mostly French oak for 12 months, intensely dark garnet in color, opening with a rich mineral and black fruit nose, going on to show firm but gently caressing tannins on a medium- to full-bodied frame. Opens in the glass to reveal currant, plum and licorice notes and finishes with a generous hint of espresso. Drink now–2013. Score 90. **K**

ADAMA, MERLOT, GIR, 2006: Garnet toward youthful royal purple, medium-bodied, with soft tannins integrating nicely and showing blackberry, blueberry and cassis notes, those supported by a generous green and herbal overlay that may not please all. Drink now. Score 87. **K**

ADAMA, MERLOT, GIR, 2005: Medium-dark ruby in color, with berries and blackcurrants backed up comfortably by near-sweet tannins and hints of spicy wood, all coming together beautifully. Drink now. Score 89. **K**

ADAMA, MERLOT, GIR, 2004: Medium-bodied, with gentle spicy oak influences and soft tannins integrating nicely, with raspberry, blackberry, cassis and light earthy overtones. A round, smooth and near-elegant wine. Drink up. Score 89. **K**

ADAMA, SHIRAZ, CHARSIT, 2004: Full-bodied, with soft tannins, good hints of smoky oak and sweet cedar, and generous black plums, berries and currants. Still young but promising to be a simultaneously complex and easy-to-drink wine. Drink now. Score 88. **K**

ADAMA, ROSÉ, CHARSIT, 2008: Ruby toward cherry red, medium-bodied, a lovely rosé, fresh, crisp and full of life, with the most positive kinds of tutti-frutti aromas and flavors, those including strawberries, raspberries, red currants and just a tantalizing hint of bubble-gum to tease our palates. Rosé as rosé should be. Drink now. Score 89. **K**

ADAMA, CABERNET FRANC, ROSÉ, CHARSIT, 2007: Cherry red in color, crisply dry, with a tempting array of raspberry, red and black cherries and watermelon fruits all on a crisply dry and tangy floral background. Round and refreshing. Drink up. Score 88.

ADAMA, SAUVIGNON BLANC, GIR, 2008: Unoaked, a lovely and lively wine, showing light golden straw in color, medium-bodied and with crisp balancing acidity to highlight aromas and flavors of minerals, grapefruit, lime, anise and oyster shell notes. Tangy citrus and a grassy hint linger nicely. Drink now. Score 89. **K**

ADAMA, SAUVIGNON BLANC, GIR, 2007: The color of light golden straw, showing apple, melon and peach fruits, those supported nicely by crisp acidity, stony minerals and a light hint of freshly mown grass. Lightly *frizzante* when served well chilled. Drink now. Score 88. **K**

ADAMA, GEWURZTRAMINER, GIR, 2007: Light golden straw in color and medium-bodied, so sweet and lacking balancing acidity that one cannot distinguish any of the traditional fruits or spices of the Gewurztraminer grape. For reasons not fully clear, more than a bit *frizzante*. Drink up. Score 75. **K**

Tabor

TABOR, CABERNET SAUVIGNON, 2007: Garnet toward royal purple, with soft tannins integrating nicely with a light overlay of cedar (the wine was developed in stainless steel tanks with oak staves). Opens with an appealing note of mint on the nose, that yielding to red currants, red berries and citrus. If the wine is faulted at all it is only by somewhat too generous acidity. Drink now. Score 87. **K**

TABOR, CABERNET SAUVIGNON, 2006: Ruby toward garnet in color, medium-bodied, with soft tannins. A soft, round and fruity red showing blackcurrants and blackberries on a lightly spicy background. Not complex but quite appealing Drink now. Score 86. **K**

TABOR, CABERNET SAUVIGNON, 2005: Medium-bodied, with soft tannins integrating nicely, this unoaked red shows appealing blackberries, currants and spices, all filling the mouth comfortably. Easy to drink and with just enough complexity to hold our attention. Drink up. Score 85. **K**

TABOR, MERLOT, 2007: Garnet toward royal purple, medium-bodied, with light spicy and vanilla notes added by aging with oak staves. With soft tannins integrated well, a soft, round and fruit-forward wine showing raspberry and milk chocolate notes, all lingering nicely. Easy to drink. Drink now. Score 87. **K**

TABOR, MERLOT, 2006: Soft, smooth and round, with gently mouth-coating tannins and appealing berry, black cherry and currant fruits showing appealing herbal overtones. Drink now. Score 86. **K**

TABOR, MERLOT, 2005: Ruby toward garnet and medium-bodied, with berry and cherry fruits, this unoaked, soft round wine makes for easy quaffing, although not all will appreciate the hint of sweetness it carries. Drink up. Score 85. **K**

TABOR, SHIRAZ, 2005: This dark garnet-red-toward-royal purple wine reflects its 12 months in oak with gentle spicy wood and tannins that, while still firm, show no sharp edges. On the nose and palate, plums and blackberries complemented by hints of earthy minerals and, rising on the finish, a hint of raspberries. Drink now. Score 88. **K**

TABOR, PNINIM (PEARLS), 2007: Dark black cherry toward royal purple in color, medium-bodied and made entirely from Merlot grapes. Three things surprise here—first that the wine reminds of nothing more than a fine Dolcetto d'Alba, second that it is lightly and enchantingly *frizzante*, and third that it is semi-sweet. Not a wine to be taken overly seriously, but with generous berry, plum, blackberry and dark chocolate, with well-integrated tannins. Serve well chilled. Drink up. Score 88. **K**

TABOR, CHARDONNAY, 2008: Light gold in color, medium-bodied, a fresh and lively unoaked Chardonnay with citrus, melon and Anjou pears on a crisp mineral background. Just complex enough to grab our attention. Drink now. Score 88. **K**

TABOR, CHARDONNAY, 2007: Sparkling, clear light gold in color, light- to medium-bodied, with appealing flinty and steely minerals and finely tuned acidity supporting appealing citrus, grapefruit and passion fruit aromas and flavors, a lovely unoaked white. Not overly complex but drinking beautifully. Drink up. Score 88. **K**

Tanya ✳✳✳

Located in the town of Ofra at the foot of the Hebron Mountains, this winery established by Yoram Cohen released its first wines in 2002. Drawing on Cabernet Sauvignon and Merlot grapes from Gush Etzion and the Golan Heights, the winery produced 6,500 bottles in 2004 and current production is about 30,000 bottles annually. The winery, showing marked quality improvement on a regular basis, produces three series, Enosh, Halel, and Reserve.

Enosh

ENOSH, CABERNET SAUVIGNON, 2005: Dark garnet toward royal purple, full-bodied, with soft, gently mouth-coating tannins and spicy wood in fine balance with blackcurrant, blackberry and plum fruits all leading to a long, spicy finish. Drink now. Score 89. **K**

Halel

HALEL, CABERNET SAUVIGNON, 2006: Dark garnet toward royal purple, full-bodied, with soft, gently mouth-coating tannins and a gentle hand with spicy wood. Opens to show traditional Cabernet blackcurrant and blackberry fruits, those yielding to show hints of orange peel. Drink now–2011. Score 88. **K**

HALEL, CABERNET SAUVIGNON, 2005: Deep and concentrated, almost impenetrable garnet in color and with firm tannins and generous wood still holding back the fruits here. No fear though, for this one shows fine balance and structure that bode well for the future. Oak-aged for 16 months, opening in the glass to reveal firm but elegant dried currants and blackberry aromas and flavors, those gaining complexity and depth on the long finish. Drink now–2012. Score 90. **K**

HALEL, MERLOT, 2006: With Tanya's signature of near-sweet tannins, a soft and generous medium- to full-bodied wine with a plush texture and its cherry, red berry fruits supported nicely by notes of tobacco, eucalytpus and smoke. Oak-aged for 14 months and with appealing spicy oak notes rising on the finish. Drink now–2011. Score 89. **K**

HALEL, CABERNET FRANC, 2006: Made entirely from Cabernet Franc grapes, developed in *barriques* for 14 months, dark, almost impenetrable garnet in color, a medium- to full-bodied, softly tannic wine. On first attack notes of plums, tar and bittersweet chocolate, those yielding to aromas and flavors of blackcurrants and espresso coffee, all with a comfortable overlay of black pepper. Long and generous. Drink now–2012. Score 90. **K**

HALEL, CHARDONAY, 2007: Light, bright golden in color, wisely oaked for only four months, that giving the wine a bare hint of creaminess but not at all hiding the tempting grapefruit, lemon and tropical fruits that make themselves felt nicely. Refreshing and complex enough to grab our attention. Drink now. Score 89. **K**

Reserve

RESERVE, CABERNET SAUVIGNON, ELIYA, 2006: Full and firm, almost muscular, with firm tannins that need time to integrate but already showing good balance and structure. Opens to reveal blackberry, currant and purple plum fruits, those with hints of mocha and black pepper. Drink now–2012. Score 88. **K**

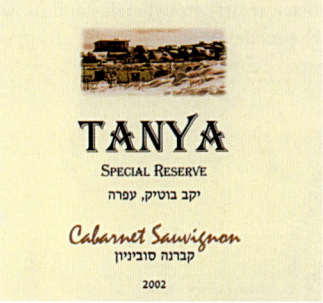

RESERVE, CABERNET SAUVIGNON, 2005: Dark ruby toward garnet, medium- to full-bodied, with firm tannins and spicy wood opening to reveal blackcurrant, blackberry and black cherry fruits, those with light overtones of fresh herbs. Drink now. Score 87. **K**

RESERVE, MERLOT, ELIYA, 2006: Deep ruby toward garnet, medium-bodied, with caressing soft tannins and hints of spices and vanilla from the *barriques* in which it developed. On first attack raspberries and cherries, those yielding to red plums and cassis, all on a light background of Mediterranean herbs. Drink now–2011. Score 88. **K**

RESERVE, MERLOT, 2005: Aromatic, deep garnet in color, medium- to full-bodied with soft, mouth-coating tannins and a gentle wood influence. On the nose and palate blackberries and cassis fruits supported nicely by hints of chocolate and mint. Drink now. Score 87. **K**

RESERVE, PINOT NOIR, 2007: Dark ruby in color, full-bodied and with near-chewy tannins waiting to settle down. Opens to reveal raspberry and cassis fruits on a generously herbal background. Drink from release. Tentative Score 86–88. **K**

RESERVE, CABERNET FRANC, 2007: Garnet toward royal purple, medium- to full-bodied, with mouth-coating tannins. Opens to reveal traditional black fruits on a background of spring flowers and dark chocolate. Drink from release. Tentative Score 86–88. **K**

RESERVE, CABERNET SAUVIGNON-MERLOT, ELIYA, 2006: A full-bodied blend of 70% Cabernet Sauvignon and 30% Merlot, the once-chunky tannins and generous wood now softening and falling into better balance. Still a somewhat country-style wine, but showing appealing black and red currants and berries, along with hints of licorice and chocolate. Drink now. Score 86. **K**

RESERVE, CABERNET SAUVIGNON-MERLOT, 2005: Developed in oak for ten months, now showing soft, round and generous with black fruits, strawberries and hints of bittersweet chocolate and, on the moderately long finish, an appealing hint of saddle leather. Drink now. Score 86. **K**

Teperberg ✦✦✦

Founded in 1870 by the Teperberg family in the Jewish quarter of the old city of Jerusalem, and then relocating outside of the walls, the winery moved to Motza, on the outskirts of the city, in 1964, and there took on the name of Efrat. For much of that time it produced primarily sacramental wines for the ultra-Orthodox community. During the 1990s it also started producing table wines. Starting in 2002, under the supervision of California-trained winemaker Shiki Rauchberger the winery began producing wines destined to appeal to a more sophisticated audience. Now relocated to their newly constructed winery on Kibbutz Tzora at the foothills of the Jerusalem Mountains, the winery has officially changed its name back to Teperberg.

More than a mere change in name and loction, the new winery, still partly under construction, now boasts fully modern equipment, a new and very impressive barrel room and increasing control over its vineyards, and is currently producing about 4 million bottles annually. Wines of interest are in the Reserve, Terra and Silver series. The Efrat label has not fully disappeared and may now be considered a sub-label of the winery that includes an Efrat and an Israeli series. With the exception of the wines in the Reserve and Terra series, all of the wines are *mevushal*. Target production within the next five years is 7 million bottles annually.

Reserve

RESERVE, CABERNET SAUVIGNON, 2007: A dark, full-bodied and intense wine with still-deep, almost searing tannins, but already showing balance and structure that bode well for the future. Big and broad-shouldered, with blackberry, blackcurrant, fig and mocha notes backed up by hints of lead pencil and cocoa. On the opening aroma and on the long finish a hint of licorice. Generous, with an appealing toasty sensation rising on the finish. Drink now–2013. The best to date from Teperberg. Score 91. **K**

RESERVE, CABERNET SAUVIGNON, 2006: Dark toward inky-garnet, full-bodied, reflecting its 15 months in oak with gentle spices and a hint of smoke, with once firm tannins now settling in and fine balance with wood and fruits. On the nose and palate an appealing array of spicy currant, blackberry, cedar and mineral notes, those with a light hint of anise on the long and generous finish. Holds back a bit when first poured but opens very nicely in the glass. Drink now–2012. Score 89. **K**

RESERVE, CABERNET SAUVIGNON, 2005: Dark garnet, medium- to full-bodied, with soft tannins and gentle smoky wood integrating nicely. Currant, blackberry and raspberry fruits complemented by hints of orange peel and light mocha aromas and flavors, all with a hint of Oriental spices rising on the finish. Drink now. Score 88. **K**

RESERVE, MERLOT, 2008: Almost inky black in color, full-bodied, with gripping tannins, a muscular Merlot opening slowly in the glass to reveal blackberries, cassis and dark chocolate. Long and mouth-filling. Drink from release. Tentative Score 88–90. **K**

RESERVE, MERLOT, 2007: Super-dark garnet, full-bodied, with generous tannins now settling in nicely to highlight abundant currant and blackberry fruits on first attack, those yielding to red berries and, on the long finish, hints of loamy earthy and sweet spices. Drink now–2013. Score 90. **K**

RESERVE, MERLOT, 2005: Dark garnet toward purple, medium-bodied, with soft tannins, rich earthiness and red fruits on the nose, those opening to show generous tangy blackcurrants, minerals and cocoa powder, all lingering nicely. Drink up. Score 88. **K**

RESERVE, SHIRAZ, 2008: Super-dark garnet, with a leathery and licorice nose, opening to show firm tannins that yield slowly to reveal black fruits on a minty, smoked meat background. Drink from release. Tentative Score 88–90. **K**

RESERVE, MERITAGE, 2006: A medium- to full-bodied blend of Cabernet Sauvignon, Merlot, Cabernet Franc and Petit Verdot, showing soft tannins and just the right notes of dusty oak, those in good balance with fruits. Opens with aromatic blueberries on the nose, goes on to aromas and flavors of currants, cherries and wild berries, those complemented by notes of tar and grilled beef. Drink now–2011. Score 87. **K**

Terra

TERRA, CABERNET SAUVIGNON, 2008:
Tasted from components. Deep and dark, with
ample mouth-coating tannins and a gentle
wood influence. Opens to reveal black fruits on
a floral and earthy-mineral background. Drink
from release. Tentative Score 88–90. **K**

TERRA, CABERNET SAUVIGNON, 2007: Traditional Cabernet. Super-dark garnet, with generous gripping tannins and spicy wood integrating
nicely to show off black fruits, those with hints
of mint and freshly roasted coffee. Drink now–
2012. Score 88. **K**

TERRA, CABERNET SAUVIGNON, 2006: Dark garnet, medium- to
full-bodied, and reflecting its 14 months in French oak. Hints of toasty
oak and moderately firm tannins, those in fine balance with acidity
and fruits. With raspberry, cherry and cassis fruits complemented by
notes of spices and a hint of what might be dried apricots, all leading
to a long, gentle and near-elegant finish. Drink now–2011. Score 88. **K**

TERRA, CABERNET SAUVIGNON, 2005: Dark garnet with purple and
orange reflections, this wine shows a gentle hand with spicy oak and
soft tannins. On the nose and palate traditional Cabernet blackcurrant and blackberry fruits, those with spice and orange peel overlays
and, on the moderately long finish, an appealing hint of cigar tobacco.
Drink now. Score 90. **K**

TERRA, MERLOT, 2007: Dark garnet, with nicely gripping tannins and
a gentle hand with the wood, those in fine balance with blackberries
and blueberries. In the background appealing hints of Oriental spices
and earthy minerals. Drink now–2011. Score 88. **K**

TERRA, MERLOT, 2006: Deep garnet toward royal purple, medium- to
full-bodied with caressing tannins, reflecting its 14 months in *barriques*
with sweet and dusty oak, gentle spices and a hint of smoke. On the
nose and palate currant, blackberry and cranberry fruits, those backed
up nicely by light earthy-herbal and dark chocolate overlays. Drink
now. Score 88. **K**

TERRA, MERLOT, 2005: Garnet toward royal purple, medium- to
full-bodied, with still gripping tannins in fine balance with wood, fruits
and acidity. On first attack black fruits and a light earthy overlay, those
yielding to raspberries, currants and minerals. On the mouth-filling

finish generous hints of bittersweet chocolate and licorice. Drink now. Score 90. **K**

TERRA, MALBEC, 2008: Still in embryonic form but already showing dark royal purple in color, medium- to full-bodied, generously aromatic and with red plums, black and red berries and notes of milk chocolate. Drink from release.Tentative Score 87–89. **K**

TERRA, MALBEC, 2007: Developed in new French and American oak *barriques* for 12 months, dark garnet in color, medium- to full-bodied, with firm tannins well balanced by notes of sweet toast and vanilla. On the nose and palate plums, black cherries and notes of cocoa. Not an Argentinean nor a Cahors Malbec, but one with a distinct Mediterranean personality. Drink now. Score 88. K

TERRA, PETIT VERDOT, 2007: Medium-bodied with spicy overtones and soft tannins. A supple, almost velvety wine with currant, tobacco and floral aromas and flavors, with both tannins and fruits rising comfortably on the finish. Drink now. Score 87. **K**

TERRA, CABERNET SAUVIGNON-MER-LOT, 2007: A dark garnet blend of Cabernet Sauvignon, Merlot, and Cabernet Franc (25%, 70% and 5% respectively). With light exposure to oak and showing medium-bodied, its once chunky tannins now settled in comfortably and opening to show a blackberry-cherry personality. A very pleasant quaffer. Drink now. Score 87. **K**

TERRA, CABERNET SAUVIGNON-MERLOT, 2006: Oak-aged for six months, this garnet-toward-royal purple blend of 70% Cabernet Sauvignon, 25% Merlot and 5% Cabernet Franc shows an appealing array of blackberry, black cherry and cassis fruits, those on a background of lightly spicy cedar. Round and generous. Drink now. Score 87. **K**

TERRA, SAUVIGNON BLANC, 2008: Light gold, fresh and refreshing, with tangy acidity to highlight citrus, pear and tropical fruits, those matched nicely by notes of oyster shells and lemongrass. Drink now–2011. Score 89. **K**

TERRA, EMERALD RIESLING, 2008: With not-at-all offensive off-dry sweetness, showing apple and rose petal notes. A floral wine, without complexities but fine for those who enjoy Emerald Riesling. Drink now. Score 84. **K**

Silver

SILVER, CABERNET SAUVIGNON, 2008: Deep garnet in color, medium- to full-bodied, with somewhat flabby tannins that dull the black fruits and spices that are here. Drink now–2011. Score 84. **K**

SILVER, CABERNET SAUVIGNON, 2007: Garnet toward royal purple, medium- to full-bodied, with silky tannins and a generous sense of spiciness. An appealing melange of black and red fruits along with light notes of tobacco and chocolate. Drink now. Score 86. **K**

SILVER, CABERNET SAUVIGNON, 2006: Showing a light spicy and smoky wood influence, medium- to full-bodied, with soft mouth-coating near-sweet tannins and a generous array of forward black fruits. Just enough complexity here to grab one's interest. Drink up. Score 87. **K**

SILVER, MERLOT, 2008: A classic style of Merlot, soft, round and supple, with plums and spices on a background of red currants, freshly ground coffee and an appealing hint of bitterness on the finish. Drink now–2012. Score 87. **K**

SILVER, MERLOT, 2007: Dark garnet, medium- to full-bodied, with gently mouth-coating tannins and light spicy and vanilla notes. Opens to show berry, black cherry and purple plum fruits on a lightly spicy background with a hint of black olives coming in on the finish. Drink now. Score 86. **K**

SILVER, MERLOT, 2006: Garnet toward purple, medium- to full-bodied, with dusty wood and soft tannins coming together nicely with blackberry and berry fruits. Medium-long and generously fruity on the finish. Drink up. Score 86. **K**

SILVER, SYRAH, 2008: Dark royal purple in color, medium- to full-bodied, showing soft tannins that highlight the forward and ripe plum and black cherry fruits. Finishes with notes of spice and cedar. Drink now–2011. Score 85. **K**

SILVER, SYRAH, 2007: Garnet-red, medium-bodied, with soft tannins and showing aromas and flavors of stewed plums and wild berries. Spicy but somewhat muddled. Drink up. Score 82. **K**

SILVER, SYRAH, 2006: Dark royal purple in color, reflecting its five months in oak with gentle spices and a hint of toasty wood. Medium-bodied, with soft but mouth-coating tannins opening to reveal purple plum and blackberry fruits, those complemented by a light and appealing earthiness that continues to a medium-long finish. Drink up. Score 88. **K**

SILVER, SANGIOVESE, 2007: True to the Sangiovese traits, showing a medium-dark garnet toward ruby, medium-bodied, with spice, anise and cedar notes highlighting currant and wild berry fruits. Not overly complex but flavorful and rich. Drink up. Score 87. **K**

SILVER, CABERNET SAUVIGNON-MERLOT, 2006: A medium-bodied blend of Cabernet Sauvignon, Merlot and Cabernet Franc (70%, 25% and 5% respectively). Dark garnet, showing spicy wood, soft tannins and an appealing hint of earthiness on the black fruits. Drink up. Score 88. **K**

SILVER, MERITAGE, 2006: A deep, almost inky-garnet, lightly-oaked blend of Cabernet Sauvignon, Merlot and Cabernet Franc (70%, 25% and 5% respectively). Medium-bodied, opens with wild berries and hints of orange peel, those yielding to gentle overtones of vanilla and espresso coffee. Drink up. Score 86. **K**

SILVER, CHARDONNAY, 2008: Treated to a half year of oaking, showing a nice hint of spicy wood on the nose, a bright and lively wine with good acidity, tropical, apple and lime fruits and, on the long finish, hints of melon and spices. Lingers nicely. Drink from release. Score 87. **K**

SILVER, WHITE RIESLING, LATE HARVEST, 2008: Light gold in color, with honeyed peach and nectarine fruits on first attack, those leading to an appealing note (one that makes you smile) of caramel apples on a stick. Generously sweet but with fine balancing acidity. Drink now–2013. Score 89. **K**

SILVER, WHITE RIESLING, LATE HARVEST, 2007: Shining gold in color, with moderate sweetness offset by natural acidity. Opens to show notes of honeysuckle, dried apricots and honeyed apples, those complemented nicely by hints of white pepper. Lively, fresh and complex, as good as an aperitif as a dessert wine. Drink now–2011. Score 88. **K**

Israeli

ISRAELI, CABERNET SAUVIGNON, 2006: Medium-bodied with soft tannins, this garnet-toward-purple, country-style blend of 85% Cabernet Sauvignon and Merlot shows simple aromas and flavors of berries, black cherries and spices. Drink now. Score 82. **K**

ISRAELI, CABERNET SAUVIGNON, 2005: Medium-bodied, soft and round with blackberry, currant and black cherry fruits. An entry-level quaffer. Drink up. Score 84. **K**

ISRAELI, MERLOT, 2007: Garnet toward royal purple, medium-bodied with soft tannins and appealing berry and cassis notes. Soft and round, the wine was blended with 10% Shiraz and 5% Cabernet Sauvignon. Drink up. Score 85. **K**

ISRAELI, MERLOT, 2006: Blended with 10% of Shiraz and 5% of Cabernet Sauvignon, a medium-bodied, country-style wine with straightforward berry and black cherry aromas and flavors. Drink up. Score 80. **K**

ISRAELI, SHIRAZ, 2006: Made entirely from Shiraz grapes and aged for five months in oak. Ruby toward garnet, medium-bodied, with soft but mouth-coating tannins and with a light earthy overlay on its black fruits. Drink up. Score 80. **K**

ISRAELI, MERLOT-PETITE SIRAH, 2006: Dark garnet, medium-bodied, with soft tannins, this is a clean, simple wine with blackberry and cherry fruits. Drink up. Score 79. **K**

ISRAELI, MERLOT-PETITE SIRAH, 2005: Medium-bodied, with soft tannins and hints of spicy wood. Aromas and flavors of currants and blackberries. Simple but appealing. Drink up. Score 85. **K**

ISRAELI, ZINFANDEL, BLUSH, 2008: A half-dry wine, with a lively pink color but with hardly perceptible fruits hidden by too-generous sweetness. Drink up. Score 75. **K**

ISRAELI, CHARDONNAY, 2008: Lightly oaked, and light- to medium-bodied, this lively straw-colored wine shows appealing citrus, peach and mineral aromas and flavors. Drink up. Score 85. **K**

ISRAELI, SAUVIGNON BLANC, 2008: Light- to medium-bodied, with citrus and tropical fruits balanced by notes of minerals and spices. A good entry-level white. Drink now. Score 84. **K**

ISRAELI, EMERALD RIESLING, 2008: Light, floral and packed with citrus and summer fruits. Off-dry, so drink quite well chilled. Drink up. Score 82. **K**

Efrat

EFRAT, CABERNET SAUVIGNON, 2007: Dark ruby toward garnet, medium-bodied, with chunky, country-style tannins. Opens to reveal appealing black fruits and hints of spices. A soft, round entry-level wine. Drink up. Score 83. **K**

EFRAT, CHARDONNAY, 2007: Medium-bodied, reflecting its three to four months in stainless steel with oak staves by a light hint of spicy wood. Fresh and aromatic, with appealing citrus, tropical fruits and pear fruits. Drink up. Score 85. **K**

Three Vines ✸✸✸

Located on Moshav Ramot Naftaly in the Upper Galilee, this small winery (formerly known as Ben Barak winery) draws on Cabernet Sauvignon, Merlot, Syrah, Cabernet Franc and Viognier grapes from its own vineyards. The winery is temporarily sharing facilities with the Ramot Naftaly winery, in which its founder Yossi Ben Barak was a former partner. Current releases are about 3,500 bottles annually.

THREE VINES, CABERNET SAUVIGNON, 2007: Full-bodied, with still-firm tannins waiting to integrate but already opening to reveal an attractive array of blackberries, blackcurrants and licorice, all leading to a long and mouth-filling finish. Drink now. Score 86.

THREE VINES, CABERNET SAUVIGNON, 2006: Deep royal purple, medium- to full-bodied, showing still-firm tannins and dusty cedar, but those yielding well to currant, blackberry and spices, all lingering nicely. Drink now. Score 86.

THREE VINES, CABERNET SAUVIGNON, 2005: Dark royal purple, medium- to full-bodied, with soft, mouth-coating tannins and a judicious hand with spicy wood. Flavors and aromas of currant, blackberry and wild cherry fruits, those supported nicely by hints of herbs and vanilla. On the medium-long finish a hint of green olives. Drink up. Score 85.

THREE VINES, MERLOT, 2007: Barrel tasting showed medium- to full-bodied, with soft, mouth-coating tannins and hints of spicy oak. Opens to show forward berry and black cherry fruits, those complemented nicely by hints of earthy minerals and spices. Drink now. Score 85.

THREE VINES, MERLOT, 2006: Dark garnet, medium- to full-bodied, with soft tannins integrating nicely and showing spicy red plum, raspberry and currant aromas and flavors. Drink up. Score 85.

THREE VINES, MERLOT, 2005: Ruby toward garnet, medium-bodied, with soft tannins and appealing red plum and raspberry fruits on a lightly spicy background. Not complex but a good quaffer. Drink up. Score 85.

THREE VINES, EMEK KADESH, 2006: A blend of Cabernet Sauvignon, Merlot and Shiraz (77%, 16% and 7% respectively). Garnet toward inky-black, medium- to full-bodied with firm tannins integrating nicely and showing spicy and near-sweet cedar. Opens to reveal a generous array of currant, berry and plum fruits, those lingering to a rich and long finish. Drink now. Score 87.

Tishbi ✳✳✳

Following the initiatives of Baron Edmond de Rothschild, the Tishbi family started to plant vineyards in 1882 on the slopes of Mount Carmel near the town of Zichron Ya'akov and continued to cultivate vines throughout the next hundred years. In 1985, Jonathan Tishbi, a fourth-generation member of the family, launched this family-owned winery in the nearby town of Binyamina, initially named Habaron as homage to Baron Rothschild, and later renamed Tishbi.

With Golan Tishbi serving as senior winemaker, the winery has made the leap from about 750,000 bottles to an output of nearly 1,000,000 annually. Drawing on grapes from their own nearby vineyards as well as from vineyards in the Jerusalem region and the Upper Galilee, the winery produces several series, the top-of-the-line being the age-worthy varietal Special Reserve wines, the varietal Estate and Vineyards, and the more popularly priced Tishbi. The lower-level Baron series was recently discontinued. The winery also occasionally produces a sparkling wine and a Port-style wine.

Special Reserve

SPECIAL RESERVE, CABERNET SAUVIGNON, BEN ZIMRA, 2002: Deep purple in color, ripe, bold and concentrated, the wine has solid and chewy tannins, those well balanced by oak. On the nose and palate spicy currant and berry fruits. Drink now. Score 90. **K**

SPECIAL RESERVE, CABERNET SAUVIGNON, GUSH ETZION, 2002: Medium- to full-bodied, oak-aged for 18 months, well balanced, with soft tannins and aromas and flavors of currant, cherry, plum and wild berry fruits, just the right hints of spicy wood and anise on the medium-long finish. Drink up. Score 88. **K**

SPECIAL RESERVE, CABERNET SAUVIGNON, BEN ZIMRA, 1999:
Ripe and harmonious, this well–balanced, now fully mature wine offers up fresh cherry, spice and plum flavors along with supple tannins, all overlaid by appealing hints of earthiness and herbs. Showing age. Drink up. Score 85. **K**

SPECIAL RESERVE, CABERNET SAUVIGNON, SDE BOKER, 1999:
Made from grapes grown in the Negev Desert, the wine is not so much earthy or herbal but instead is marked by distinct flavors of green olives and spices. Full-bodied, now fully mature, with well-integrated tannins, it shows ripe and well-focused black cherry and currant flavors along with an appealing, long finish. Drink up. Score 88. **K**

SPECIAL RESERVE, CABERNET SAUVIGNON, KFAR YUVAL, 1999:
With earthy currant and cherry flavors emerging through firm tannins, this rich and concentrated wine is now fully mature and showing the smooth and supple texture promised in its youth. Drink up. Score 88. **K**

SPECIAL RESERVE, 2004: Super-dark garnet in color, full-bodied, a blend of 50% Cabernet Sauvignon, 40% Merlot and 10% Cabernet Franc, the grapes all from Sde Boker in the Negev. Good balance between firm tannins, spicy wood and fruits, showing appealing blackcurrant, blackberry and tobacco notes. On the long finish a light minty note. Drink now–2010. Score 90. **K**

SPECIAL RESERVE, CHARDONNAY, 2007: Reflecting spicy and vanilla notes from its oak-aging, medium-bodied, with generous pineapple, citrus and pear notes leading to a long finish. Drink up. Score 88. **K**

SPECIAL RESERVE, CHARDONNAY, 2006: Aged in oak for six months, medium-bodied, this golden straw wine shows light spicy accents running through the appealing citrus, citrus peel and melon aromas and flavors. Lingers nicely. Drink up. Score 87. **K**

Estate

ESTATE, CABERNET SAUVIGNON, 2006: Ruby toward garnet, medium-bodied, with soft tannins and a gentle wood influence. On the nose and palate blackberry, blueberry and currant fruits complemented by notes of spices. Drink now–2011. Score 87. **K**

ESTATE, CABERNET SAUVIGNON, 2005: Deep garnet with violet and orange reflections, medium- to full-bodied, with still-firm tannins but those in fine balance with acidity, wood and fruits. A blend of 90% Cabernet Sauvignon, 7% Cabernet Franc and 3% Petit Verdot, oak-aged for about 13 months, showing an appealing layer of spiciness together with currant and blackberry fruits. Drink now. Score 88. **K**

ESTATE, MERLOT, 2006: Dark garnet with orange reflections, full-bodied, with soft, well-integrating tannins. Opens with blackberries and hints of spices, goes on to show ripe red berries and hints of chocolate. Long and generous. Drink now. Score 88. K

ESTATE, MERLOT, 2005: Deep ruby toward garnet, medium-bodied, with spicy cedar aromas and somewhat subdued red currants, black cherries and herbal notes. Shows good depth, with tannins rising on the crisp finish. Drink now. Score 85. K

ESTATE, SHIRAZ, 2006: A once strong whiff of alcohol now blowing off and letting the wine open. Medium- to full-bodied, with black cherry, blackcurrant and plums all with a somewhat earthy edge. Drink now. Score 84. K

ESTATE, SHIRAZ, 2005: Dark cherry toward garnet in color, medium- to full-bodied, with soft tannins integrating nicely. On the nose and palate cherry, raspberry and spicy aromas and flavors on a light earthy background. Drink now. Score 89. K

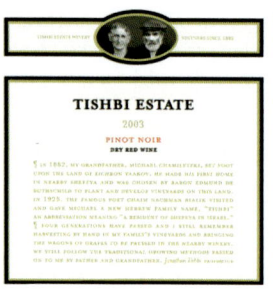

ESTATE, PINOT NOIR, 2006: Light- to medium-bodied, with a somewhat muddy garnet color, showing too much volatile acidity and, on the nose and palate, forward red berry and strawberry fruits, the kind that one expects from a red lollypop. Drink up. Score 80. K

ESTATE, PINOT NOIR, 2004: Light wood influences and soft tannins, this medium-bodied wine shows berry, plum and light earthy-mineral hints leading to a medium-long finish. Drink up. Score 84. K

ESTATE, CABERNET FRANC, 2006: Dark garnet in color, full-bodied and with chewy tannins, a well-focused wine, its spicy (almost peppery) wood settling down nicely to show a fine array of currant and blackberry fruits, those with an appealing leathery overtone. Long and satisfying. Drink now–2011. Score 89. K

ESTATE, CHARDONNAY, 2008: Blended with 10% of Viognier, golden straw in color, medium-bodied with green apple, summer fruits and melon note. Drink now. Score 86. K

ESTATE, CHARDONNAY, 2007: Developed in oak for two months, light golden straw in color, light- to medium-bodied, showing appealing green apple, grapefruit and mineral notes. Drink up. Score 86. K

ESTATE, SAUVIGNON BLANC, 2008: Unoaked, light- to medium-bodied, light straw colored, showing apple and citrus fruits on a light grassy background. Drink now. Score 85. K

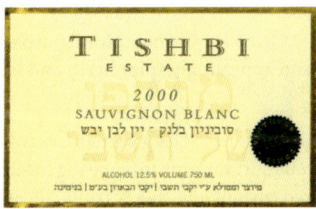

ESTATE, SAUVIGNON BLANC, 2007: Light and refreshing, with citrus, melon and guava fruits. Given a hint of sweetness by a light overlay of honeysuckle. Drink up. Score 86. K

ESTATE, LATE HARVEST RIESLING, 2005: Made from Emerald Riesling grapes, light- to medium-bodied, with generous sweetness and appealing floral and summer fruits. Best with fruit-based desserts. Drink up. Score 84. K

ESTATE, LATE HARVEST RIESLING, 2004: Made from Emerald Riesling grapes. Floral on the nose, with ripe peach and apricot fruits. Moderate sweetness set off nicely by acidity makes for a pleasant quaffer. Drink up. Score 85. K

Vineyards

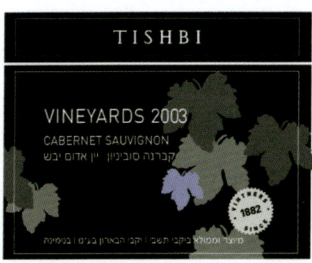

VINEYARDS, CABERNET SAUVIGNON, 2007: Ruby toward garnet, medium-bodied and with soft tannins that make it almost as round as a Pinot Noir. On the nose and palate an appealing berry and black cherry personality. A good quaffer. Drink now. Score 85. K

VINEYARDS, CABERNET SAUVIGNON, 2006: Medium-bodied, with soft tannins and forward berry, currant and cherry fruits. Not complex, but a good quaffer. Drink up. Score 85. K

VINEYARDS, MERLOT, 2007: Light garnet in color, medium-bodied and round, with ripe, juicy plum and black cherry and vanilla aromas and flavors on a lightly spicy background with tannins rising on the finish. Drink now. Score 85. **K**

VINEYARDS, MERLOT, 2006: Garnet toward purple, medium-bodied, with soft tannins and appealingly spicy berry and black cherry fruits. Drink up. Score 85. **K**

VINEYARDS, MERLOT, 2005: Deep garnet toward purple, medium-bodied, with generous soft tannins integrating nicely and showing appealing raspberry, red currant and cherry fruits, those on a lightly spicy and herbal background. Round and medium-long. Drink up. Score 85. **K**

VINEYARDS, SAUVIGNON BLANC, 2007: Medium-bodied, light straw in color, with citrus and green apple fruits complemented by notes of citrus peel and figs. A good quaffer. Drink now. Score 86. **K**

VINEYARDS, SAUVIGNON BLANC, 2006: Light- to medium-bodied, with hints of figs, grass, lime and sweet peas. Not complex but friendly, with a nice mineral-rich finish. Drink up. Score 86. **K**

VINEYARDS, WHITE RIESLING, 2006: Light and fresh, with apple, honeysuckle and citrus notes leading to a crisp finish. Drink up. Score 84. **K**

VINEYARDS, EMERALD RIESLING, 2006: Light in body, off-dry, with floral and citrus aromas and flavors. Good acidity to balance the light sweetness. Drink up. Score 84. **K**

VINEYARDS, FRENCH COLOMBARD, 2006: Light golden straw in color, light- to medium-bodied, with citrus and tropical fruits on a floral background. Drink up. Score 83. **K**

VINEYARDS, DRY MUSCAT, 2008: As light in color as in body, a sweet, floral nose and crispy dry green apple and citrus flavors come together to make a pleasant little quaffing wine. Drink up. Score 85. **K**

Tishbi

TISHBI, CABERNET SAUVIGNON-PETITE SIRAH, 2007: Garnet toward royal purple, with soft tannins and showing a basic berry-cherry personality, the fruits on a lightly earthy-herbal background. An entry-level wine. Drink now. Score 83. **K**

TISHBI, CABERNET SAUVIGNON-PETITE SIRAH, 2006: Deep garnet, with soft tannins, a round wine showing red and black berries and black cherries on a lightly spicy background. Easy to drink. Drink up. Score 85. **K**

TISHBI, FRENCH-RIESLING, 2008: Light golden straw in color, light- to medium-bodied, an off-dry blend of French Colombard and Emerald Riesling with fine acidity to show its citrus and tropical fruits. A pleasant quaffer. Drink now. Score 84. **K**

TISHBI, FRENCH-RIESLING, 2007: An off-dry blend with gentle sweetness set off by lively acidity and offering pineapple, citrus and green apple notes. Drink up. Score 84. **K**

TISHBI, MUSCAT OF ALEXANDRIA, 2007: The color of damp straw, light- to medium-bodied, deeply aromatic with jasmine and heather on the nose and showing moderately sweet. Simple citrus and tropical fruits. Drink now. Score 82. **K**

Trio ✦✦✦

Founded by Oran, Tal and Kobi Shaked, with Oran as winemaker and located in Ramat Gan, this small winery released its first wines from the 2006 vintage. The winery sources Cabernet Sauvignon, Shiraz and Merlot grapes from the Jerusalem Hills and from the Upper Galilee. Releases from 2006 were of 4,000 bottles, from 2007 of 9,500, and anticipated production for 2008 is for about 17,000 bottles.

TRIO, SECRET, 2008: Tasted from components, some developing in *barriques*, others in larger Gardellotto vats. A tentative, full-bodied blend of Cabernet Sauvignon and Syrah, showing savory cedarwood notes and generous but soft tannins just starting to find their balance with blackberry, cassis and red plum fruits, those matched nicely by hints of saddle leather and dark chocolate. Shows promise as simultaneously intense and elegant. Best 2011–2014. Tentative Score 89–91.

TRIO, SECRET, 2007: Medium- to full-bodied, reflecting its 12 months in *barriques* with notes of spicy and vanilla-rich wood. Silky tannins part to reveal a generous array of wild berry, currant and bitter citrus peel notes all in fine balance with spicy notes that run through the medium-long finish. Drink now–2013. Score 90.

TRIO, SECRET, 2006: Dark, almost impenetrable garnet in color, full-bodied, made entirely from Cabernet Sauvignon grapes, with firm tannins that yield and show just the right dose of spicy and vanilla-rich oak. On first attack blackberries, those yielding in the glass to red currants and raspberry fruits, all with appealing overlays of black pepper, cigar tobacco and a note of freshly turned truffles. Drink now–2011. Score 92.

TRIO, SPECIAL CUVÉE, 2007: Made entirely from Syrah grapes, developed in partly new and partly one-year-old *barriques* for 14 months, showing medium- to full-bodied (leaning toward the full), with gently gripping tannins settling in nicely with notes of spicy wood. Opens to reveal wild berry, blackberry and raspberry fruits. Still tight and needs a bit of time to show its zest, that matched by a long and persistent finish. Drink now–2013. Score 91.

TRIO, THE SPIRIT OF THE JERUSALEM HILLS, 2008: Developing in stainless steel tanks with oak staves, still a quite tentative blend of 86% Cabernet Sauvignon and 14% Merlot. Showing dark garnet in color, with soft tannins, medium- to full-bodied with appealing blackcurrant and wild berry fruits, those with light overlays of Oriental spices and bittersweet chocolate. Best from 2011. Tentative Score 88–90.

TRIO, THE SPIRIT OF THE JERUSALEM HILLS, 2007: A blend of 84% Cabernet Sauvignon, 14% Merlot and 2% Petit Verdot. Showing generous berry aromatics, medium- to full-bodied, developed with oak staves in stainless steel vats, with gently mouth-coating tannins and notes of spicy wood parting to reveal generous blackberry, cassis and blueberry fruits, those hinting nicely of fresh Mediterranean herbs. Drink now–2011. Score 88.

TRIO, THE SPIRIT OF THE JERUSALEM HILLS, 2006: Made entirely from Cabernet Sauvignon grapes, with a light hint of spicy wood and gently mouth-coating tannins integrating nicely and parting to show the fruits. Medium- to full-bodied, dark garnet in color and opening in the glass to reveal red currant, blackberry and raspberry fruits along with gentle hints of white chocolate, all of which linger nicely on the long finish. Simultaneously elegant and easy to drink. Drink now. Score 90.

Tulip ✳✳✳

Located on Kfar Tikva near the town of Kiryat Tivon, not far from Haifa, this winery is an effort of the Yitzhaki family. The winery currently draws on Cabernet Sauvignon and Syrah grapes from the Alma vineyard and other locations in the Upper Galilee, as well as Cabernet Sauvignon, Merlot, Cabernet Franc and Petit Verdot from the Karmei Yosef and Mata vineyards near Jerusalem. Currently in development are vineyards planted in red varieties near Mount Meron.

The winery is currently releasing about 80,000 bottles annually, those in four series: varietal Grand Reserve and Reserve; blended wines, Mostly; and single-variety wines, Just. The winery also occasionally releases Tulip, a white dessert wine, and a Port-style reinforced red wine.

Grand Reserve

GRAND RESERVE, 2004: This blend of Cabernet Sauvignon and Merlot reflects its 30 months in oak with notably heavy, somewhat sweetish wood and firm, chunky country-style tannins that seem to not want to integrate. Beneath those and making their way slowly to the surface are blackberry, kirsch and dark chocolate aromas and flavors. A good wine but lacking the fine-tuned balance or depth that might have made it more interesting. Drink now. Score 86.

GRAND RESERVE, CABERNET SAUVIGNON, 2003: Oak-aged for 30 months, but with the once-heavy wood now integrating with soft tannins and opening to reveal appealing blackcurrant and berry fruits, those with overlays of dark chocolate and sweet herbs. Drink now. Score 88.

Reserve

RESERVE, CABERNET SAUVIGNON, 2006: Blended with 5% Petit Verdot and oak-aged for 18 months in new French *barriques*, showing an abundance of spicy oak and a more than generous 15% alcohol content. Full-bodied, with firm tannins only now starting to integrate and opening slowly to reveal spicy blackcurrant and blackberry fruits on a background of cigar tobacco. Drink now–2011. Score 88.

RESERVE, CABERNET SAUVIGNON, 2005: Dark garnet, full-bodied, showing still-youthful firm tannins that need time to integrate. A blend of 90% Cabernet Sauvignon with equal parts of Petit Verdot and Cabernet Franc, aged in new French oak *barriques*, showing fine balance between spicy wood and fruits. Opens to reveal blackberry, currant and light leathery notes, all on a generously peppery and vanilla-rich background. Long and juicy. Drink now–2011. Score 88.

RESERVE, CABERNET SAUVIGNON, 2004: Dense royal purple toward black, full-bodied, deeply tannic, with generous wood influence but good balance and structure. On the nose and palate generous spices to highlight blackcurrant, chocolate and a light overlay of cigar tobacco. Drink up. Score 89.

RESERVE, SYRAH, 2006: Dark garnet with orange and violet reflections, this full-bodied red is lithe and well focused. Opens with a surprising but pleasing root beer note which holds through the long finish as a background to plum, blackberry and leathery notes. Well balanced, long and generous. Drink now–2011. Score 88.

RESERVE, SYRAH, 2005: Blended with 10% of Cabernet Sauvignon and oak-aged for 14 months, this medium- to full-bodied wine shows soft, near-sweet tannins integrating beautifully Fine balance here between spicy wood, black and red berries, plums and a generous hint of bittersweet chocolate. On the long finish light and appealing hints of earthiness and tobacco. Drink up. Score 90.

Mostly

MOSTLY, SHIRAZ, 2006: Dark garnet, medium- to full-bodied, a blend of 65% Shiraz, 30% Cabernet Sauvignon and 5% Petit Verdot. Firm tannins dominate when first poured, but those yield nicely in the glass to reveal generous currant and purple plum fruits, those supported nicely by hints of Oriental spices and saddle leather. Tannins and fruits rise simultaneously on the finish. Drink now–2011. Score 89.

MOSTLY, SHIRAZ, 2005: Dark garnet, this blend of 60% Shiraz, 20% each of Cabernet Sauvignon and Merlot shows medium-bodied, soft, round and well balanced, filling the mouth nicely. On the nose and palate blackberries, plums and gently spicy oak from its 14 months in *barriques*. Look for hints of Mediterranean herbs and freshly turned earth on the moderately long finish. Drink now. Score 87.

MOSTLY, CABERNET FRANC, 2006: A blend of 86% Cabernet Franc and 7% each of Merlot and Cabernet Sauvignon. Showing spicy oak and firm tannins now integrating well. Opens to show red and black berries, green pepper and earthy aromas and flavors. On the moderately long finish appealing hints of licorice and mint. Drink now–2012. Score 88.

MOSTLY, CABERNET FRANC, 2005: A gently oaked-aged blend of 80% Cabernet Franc, 15% Merlot and 5% Cabernet Sauvignon. Dark garnet toward purple, medium- to full-bodied, with soft tannins integrating nicely and showing generous plum, berry and light earthy aromas and flavors. Drink up. Score 87.

Just

JUST, CABERNET SAUVIGNON, 2006: Dark, almost impenetrable garnet, full-bodied and concentrated, with generous, soft tannins yet maintaining the roundness that has come to typify the Tulip wines. Opens slowly in the glass to reveal blackcurrant, wild berry and kirsch, those backed up by spicy wood and appealing hints of herbaceousness on the long finish. Drink now. Score 88.

JUST, CABERNET SAUVIGNON, 2005: Dark garnet, this medium-bodied wine's soft tannins are integrating nicely with hints of the oak in which it was aged for six months. On the nose and palate plums, cassis and berries along with intimations of vanilla and tobacco on a moderately long finish. Drink now. Score 88.

JUST, MERLOT, 2007: Medium-bodied, with somewhat chunky, country-style tannins. A subdued nose but with appealing flavors of blueberries, cherries, blackberries and currants on a background of spicy oak and minted chocolate. A pleasant country-style wine. Drink now. Score 85.

JUST, MERLOT, 2006: Medium-bodied, with gentle, near-sweet tannins, this soft, round aromatic red shows appealing berry, black cherry and currant fruits on a light background of spicy oak and eucalyptus. Drink now. Score 87.

JUST, MERLOT, 2005: Reflecting 12 months in oak with soft, slightly chunky tannins and hints of spices. Dark garnet, medium- to full-bodied, opening in the glass to show blueberries, black cherries and from mid-palate on hints of chocolate and a light earthiness. On the finish a pleasing herbaceousness. Drink up. Score 87.

JUST, SHIRAZ, 2005: Oak-aged for about 12 months, medium-bodied, with still-firm tannins, those in good balance with spicy wood and earthy, plum and spicy aromas and flavors. Drink up. Score 85.

Tulip

TULIP, BLACK TULIP, 2005: A Bordeaux blend of Cabernet Sauvignon, Merlot, Cabernet Franc and Petit Verdot (66%, 14%, 14% and 6%, respectively), that given a distinct California touch by being aged in new oak for somewhat over 24 months. Full-bodied, with firm tannins and reflecting generous vanilla, smoky and spicy oak, those parting slowly in the glass to reveal black fruits and notes of Oriental spices. Primarily for those who thrive on the flavor of oak. Drink now–2011. Score 86.

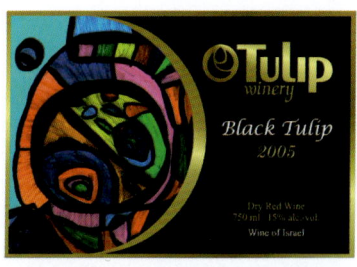

TULIP, WHITE TULIP, 2008: Containing 60% Gewurztraminer and 40% Sauvignon Blanc, a small portion of which was oak-aged. This is, to say the least, not at all a standard blend. Golden straw in color, medium-bodied and deeply aromatic. On the nose and palate a somewhat unusual combination of grassiness, litchis, grapefruit and peppermint. Interesting but perhaps not to everyone's taste. Drink now. Score 86.

TULIP, WHITE TULIP, 2007: A blend of 70% Gewurztraminer and 30% Sauvignon Blanc, medium-bodied, dry, but so highly aromatic and fruit-forward that you might think this was a sweet wine. On the nose and palate litchis, tropical fruits, ripe peaches and notes of peppermint, none of which seem to come together as a coherent whole. Drink up. Score 83.

Tzora Vineyards ✶✶✶✶

Set on Kibbutz Tzora at the foothills of the Jerusalem Mountains and overlooking the Soreq Valley, this formerly kibbutz-owned winery released its first 1,500 bottles from the 1993 vintage. Production is currently about 80,000 bottles annually.

The winery was founded as a one-man enterprise by Ronnie James, a visionary viticulturist who was dedicated to the influence of *terroir* on his wines. James, who earned a high level of respect throughout the local wine industry, passed away in 2008, but not before bringing aboard winemaker Eran Pick who had experience in California, Bordeaux and Australia. Pick has maintained the winery's devotion to *terroir* and is currently releasing five wines, three of those named after the single vineyards from which the grapes were harvested (Hachalukim, Shoresh and Neve Ilan), one a Judean Hills blend made from two vineyards, and Misty Hills, a flagship wine released only from selected vintages.

Private investment has added state-of-the-art equipment to the winery. The winery has full control over its own vineyards, those yielding Cabernet Sauvignon, Merlot, Syrah, Mourvedre, Sauvignon Blanc, Chardonnay and Gewurztraminer. The Tzora wines have been kosher since the 2002 vintage. Construction of a new winery in the Shoresh vineyards is currently in the planning stage.

TZORA VINEYARDS, CABERNET SAUVIGNON, GIVAT HACHALUKIM, 2008: Dark garnet in color, deeply aromatic, full-bodied and showing tannins that lurk quietly before making themselves felt in fine balance with the influence of the wood. Opens to show floral and veggie notes, those complementing and not at all hiding the blackcurrant, purple plum and blackberry fruits. Opens nicely on the palate. A wine with presence. Best 2011–2015. Tentative Score 89–91. **K**

TZORA VINEYARDS, CABERNET SAUVIGNON, GIVAT HACHALUKIM, 2007: Dark garnet in color, generously aromatic and opening to reveal a medium- to full-bodied red with soft tannins integrating nicely with spicy wood and fruits. On the nose and palate opens with raspberries, those going to blackberries, currants and hints of orange peel. Firm but yielding, generous and long. Drink from release–2012. Score 90. **K**

TZORA VINEYARDS, CABERNET SAUVIGNON, GIVAT HACHALUKIM, 2006: Made entirely from Cabernet Sauvignon grapes, with softly caressing tannins and reflecting a gentle hand with oak. Medium- to full-bodied, with generous currant and wild berry fruits, those matched nicely by hints of anise and white pepper. Finishes moderately long with a note of minted chocolate. Drink now. Score 88. **K**

TZORA VINEYARDS, CABERNET SAUVIGNON, SHORESH, 2008: Perhaps to be blended with a small amount of Syrah, at this stage full-bodied and concentrated but at the same time elegant and round. A spicy red, medium- to full-bodied, with gripping tannins in fine balance with spicy wood and fruits. On the nose and palate generous black fruits and notes of Oriental spices, those backed up by a comfortable hint of dark chocolate. As this one develops look as well for a note of mint that will creep in softly. Drink from release–2015. Tentative Score 90–92 **K**

TZORA VINEYARDS, CABERNET SAUVIGNON, SHORESH, 2007: Blended with 15% Syrah, opens with a deep nose of plums and freshly turned earth. Goes on to show spicy oak and gently caressing tannins in fine balance with peppery blackcurrants and blackberries, and on the long finish, with tannins rising comfortably, an appealing note of saddle leather. Drink now–2015. Score 90. **K**

TZORA VINEYARDS, CABERNET SAUVIGNON, SHORESH, 2006: Dark garnet, medium- to full-bodied, reflecting its 18 months in oak with a sweet cedar nose. Soft tannins integrating nicely with the oak and opens to show a tempting array of currants, wild berries and purple plums, those matched by notes of minerality and cocoa. Drink now–2014. Score 90. **K**

TZORA VINEYARDS, CABERNET SAUVIGNON, NEVE ILAN, 2005: Made entirely from Cabernet Sauvignon grapes, dark ruby toward garnet in color, full-bodied with tannins showing more gripping, and with somewhat earthy and herbal aromas and flavors rising, the fruits are more subdued than at an earlier tasting. Continuing to show black fruits and hints of licorice. Drink now. Score 87. **K**

TZORA VINEYARDS, CABERNET SAUVIGNON, GIVAT HACHALUKIM, 2005: Dark ruby toward garnet, medium- to full-bodied, with soft tannins and generous spicy wood. Opens to show generous red and black fruits, those supported nicely by hints of freshly turned earth and tobacco. Drink now. Score 90. **K**

TZORA VINEYARDS, MISTY HILLS, 2006: A blend of equal parts of Cabernet Sauvignon and Syrah, those aged for 18 months in *barriques*. Deep and youthful royal purple in color, full-bodied, concentrated and intense, showing generous mouth-coating tannins and a judicious hand with the oak, all in fine balance with fruits. On first attack strawberries and red currants, those going to black fruits on a background of earthy minerals and Oriental spices. As this one continues to develop look as well for notes of saddle leather and tobacco. Drink now–2015. Score 92. **K**

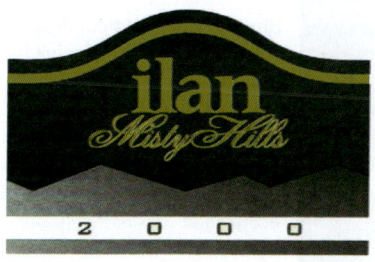

TZORA VINEYARDS, MERLOT, NEVE ILAN, 2006: Garnet-red with orange and purple reflections, this medium- to full-bodied wine shows

401

generous but near-sweet soft tannins integrating nicely, and already opening to reveal bountiful red fruits and an appealing spicy overlay. Tannins and steely minerals rise pleasantly on the finish to make this a very fine Merlot. Drink now–2011. Score 89. **K**

TZORA VINEYARDS, MERLOT, GIVAT HACHALUKIM, 2005: Ruby toward purple, medium-bodied, with soft, perhaps even flabby tannins and an unwanted hint of bitterness that interferes with the currant, berry and plum fruits. Drink now–2011. Score 85. **K**

TZORA VINEYARDS, MERLOT, SHORESH, 2005: Dark garnet toward royal purple, medium- to full-bodied, with soft, mouth-coating tannins and spicy wood integrating nicely. Opens to show a fine array of berry, black cherry and citrus peel, those leading to a moderately long finish. Drink now. Score 89. **K**

TZORA VINEYARDS, CABERNET SAUVIGNON-MERLOT, NEVE ILAN, 2008: A blend of equal parts of Cabernet Sauvignon and Merlot, dark garnet toward royal purple in color, opening soft, round and almost creamy with fine blackcurrant and wild berry notes, and then going on to show hints of hot pepper, freshly cured tobacco and Mediterranean herbs. A long, near-sweet finish. Drink now–2014. Score 90. **K**

TZORA VINEYARDS, CABERNET SAUVIGNON-MERLOT, NEVE ILAN, 2007: Tasted from components but already showing the potential for elegance. Dark garnet toward royal purple, medium- to full-bodied (perhaps destined in the end to be full-bodied) with generous mouth-coating tannins and spicy wood in fine balance with red currant and wild berry fruits, those on a background that hints nicely of tobacco

and freshly turned soil. Rich and firm but with the clear promise for elegance. Drink now–2013. Score 90. **K**

TZORA VINEYARDS, CABERNET SAUVIGNON-MERLOT, NEVE ILAN, 2006: Medium- to full-bodied, deep garnet toward royal purple, with tannins integrated with notes of spicy oak and fruits. A blend of 70% Cabernet Sauvignon and 30% Merlot opening with raspberries and red currants, those yielding to red plums, spices and earthy minerals. Soft, round and generous. Drink now–2012. Score 89. **K**

TZORA VINEYARDS, MERLOT-CABERNET SAUVIGNON, JUDEAN HILLS, 2006: Garnet toward royal purple, medium- to full-bodied, with soft tannins and reflecting its 12 months in oak with a gentle spiciness. A blend of 65% Merlot and 35% Cabernet Sauvignon with aromas and flavors of cassis, blackberries and an appealing hint of vanilla. Easy to drink but with just enough complexity to catch our attention. Drink now. Score 87. **K**

TZORA VINEYARDS, CABERNET SAUVIGNON-SYRAH, SHORESH, 2007: Dark, almost inky-garnet in color, full-bodied, with firm, still gripping but near-sweet tannins needing time to integrate, but already promising fine balance and structure. Opens with blackcurrants and purple plums, those coming together nicely with grilled herbs, cigar tobacco and, on the long finish, appealing hints of saddle leather and bitter orange peel. Drink now–2013. Score 89. **K**

TZORA VINEYARDS, SYRAH–CABERNET SAUVIGNON, MEUBANIM, 2006: Meubanim is a sub-section of the Shoresh vineyard, an area of particularly low yield and judged to be individual enough in personality that the grapes were separated for this special blend. Full-bodied, with firm, almost puckering tannins and leathery and gamey on the nose, but showing promise for integration and a muscular kind of elegance. Opens to reveal red currants, raspberries, chocolate and tobacco. Long, intense and mouth-filling. Drink now–2011. Score 90. **K**

TZORA VINEYARDS, ROSÉ, GIVAT HACHALUKIM, 2007: Made from Cabernet Sauvigon grapes, pale pink with an orange tint, light- to medium-bodied. Showing berry, cherry and watermelon notes, a dry wine with a hint of sweetness that creeps in. Drink up. Score 86. **K**

TZORA VINEYARDS, BLANC, NEVE ILAN, 2008: Made entirely from Chardonnay grapes, developing in French oak, 40% of which are new, already drinking quite nicely. Showing medium-bodied, with fine acidity and minerality setting off tropical and summer fruits, those on a lightly spicy background. Fresh and lively with just enough complexity to grab our attention. Drink now. Score 88. **K**

TZORA VINEYARDS, GEWURZTRAMINER, SHORESH BLANC, 2007: Bright golden in color, opening on the nose with what seem like sweet fruits but comes to the palate as completely dry, showing litchi, kiwi and peach fruits. Medium-bodied, soft, round and caressing, and ends with a light honeyed note that lingers nicely. Drink now. Score 88. **K**

TZORA VINEYARDS, GEWURZTRAMINER, DESSERT WINE, OR, 2006: Light, sweet and silky, almost calling to mind an ice wine, with distinct honeyed pineapple and pear fruits and a hint of kumquat marmalade on the finish. A low 8% alcohol content and good balancing acidity to make the wine both lively and tempting. Drink now. Score 89. **K**

Tzuba ★★★

Set on Kibbutz Tzuba in the Jerusalem Hills, the winery's first releases from the 2005 vintage were of 30,000 bottles. Founded by Moti Tzamir, who was largely responsible for the production of the wines of 2005 and 2006, and with South African-born vintner and winemaker Paul Dubb now firmly in charge, the winery currently issues wines in three series: the top-of-the-line Hametzuda that will be produced only in selected years; Tel Tzuba of varietal and blended wines, and the popularly priced Hama'ayan. The winery also produces a red dessert wine. The winery's grapes all come from the kibbutz's own vineyards, those containing Cabernet Sauvignon, Cabernet Franc, Merlot, Petit Verdot, Shiraz, Malbec and Pinot Noir grapes as well as white grapes Viognier, Chardonnay and Sauvignon Blanc.

Hametzuda

HAMETZUDA, 2006: Made entirely from Cabernet Sauvignon grapes, deep purple, medium- to full-bodied, with generous, soft tannins coming together with notes of spicy wood, and opening to show blackcurrants, red and black berries and notes of espresso coffee and green olives. Long and generous. Drink now–2013. Score 90. **K**

HAMETZUDA, 2005: A blend of 75% Merlot and 25% Cabernet Sauvignon, oak-aged for 24 months. Medium-dark garnet, full-bodied, with near-sweet tannins now integrating nicely to show an appealing array of blackberry, cherry and herbal notes. A gentle spicy wood influence and a hint of licorice on the long finish add to the charms of the wine. Drink now. Score 88. **K**

HAMETZUDA, CHARDONNAY, 2007: Oaked for only three and a half months, this medium-bodied, light gold wine shows a light green tint and opens to reveal generous summer and tropical fruits on a background of lively acidity. On the finish an appealing hit of green apples. Drink now. Score 88. **K**

Tel Tzuba

TEL TZUBA, CABERNET SAUVIGNON, 2007:
Medium- to full-bodied, with gently gripping tannins. Dark garnet with purple and orange reflections, opening with red berries, those yielding comfortably to currants and wild berries on a gently spicy background. Fruits and tannins rise on the finish. Drink now–2011. Score 89. **K**

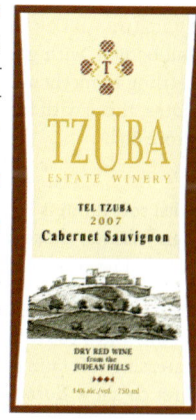

TEL TZUBA, CABERNET SAUVIGNON, 2006:
Reflecting spices and near-sweet tannins from its 14 months in French oak, a medium- to full-bodied red with good concentration, soft tannins and a gentle wood influence. On the nose and palate, starts off with blackcurrants and blackberries, those yielding to a pleasing red berry-cherry character and finally, on the long finish, notes of Mediterranean herbs. Drink now. Score 90. **K**

TEL TZUBA, CABERNET SAUVIGNON, 2005: A blend of 85% Cabernet Sauvignon, 9% Cabernet Franc and 6% Merlot, aged in French oak for 14 months. Ruby to purple, medium- to full-bodied, with soft tannins and gentle wood. Showing clean red fruits on a lightly spicy, moderately long finish. Drink now. Score 87. **K**

TEL TZUBA, MERLOT, 2007: Medium-deep garnet in color, generously aromatic, medium- to full-bodied and with soft tannins. On the nose and palate wild berries, red currants and spices, and on the moderately long finish a hint of espresso coffee. Marred somewhat by a slight bitter streak that runs through. Drink now–2011. Score 87. **K**

TEL TZUBA, MERLOT, 2006: Dark garnet with violet reflections, medium-bodied, with soft, gently mouth-coating tannins. Opens to reveal blackberry, currant and purple plum fruits, those supported nicely by hints of mint, licorice and, on the finish, a hint of bittersweet chocolate. Drink now. Score 88. **K**

TEL TZUBA, MERLOT, 2005: An oak-aged Merlot with the addition of 6% Pinot Noir. Ruby toward garnet, medium- to full-bodied, with gripping tannins and generous wood yielding slowly to reveal blackberry, currant and plum aromas and flavors. Drink up. Score 85. **K**

TEL TZUBA, SHIRAZ, 2007: Dark garnet toward royal purple, medium- to full-bodied, with generous but not overpowering spicy oak and vanilla, those parting to reveal raspberry, cherry and red plum fruits in fine harmony with spices and notes of leather. Polished, long and well focused. Drink now–2013. Score 89. **K**

TEL TZUBA, SHIRAZ, 2006: Garnet toward royal purple, medium- to full-bodied, with good concentration and balance. Firm tannins are settling in nicely now and part to reveal cherry, blueberry and cassis notes, those with hints of spices and saddle leather. Drink now–2012. Score 89. **K**

TEL TZUBA, SHIRAZ, 2005: Dark ruby toward purple, medium-bodied, with soft tannins integrating nicely and showing appealing plum and berry fruits, those supported by hints of spices and saddle leather. Drink now. Score 87. **K**

TEL TZUBA, PINOT NOIR, 2007: Pinot with a distinctly Burgundian flavor. Dark ruby in color, medium- to full-bodied, with generously caressing soft tannins. On first attack quite firm, but opens in the glass first to show floral, mineral and raspberry fruits and then to black cherries, green tea and notes of both Oriental spices and saddle leather. A multi-layered wine. Drink now–2012. Score 88. **K**

TEL TZUBA, SANGIOVESE, 2007: Dark cherry red toward garnet, medium-bodied, soft and round, with fine-grain tannins and floral, blackberry and black cherry fruits. Not a complex wine but an appealing one. Drink now. Score 86. **K**

TEL TZUBA, SANGIOVESE, 2006: A blend of 85% Sangiovese and 15% Nebbiolo, oak-aged for 14 months, showing medium- to full-bodied, with soft tannins integrating nicely. Generous raspberry and cherry fruits on first attack open to show blueberries and notes of spices. Round, soft and complex, although easy to drink. Drink now. Score 89. **K**

TEL TZUBA, CHARDONNAY, 2007: Lightly oaked, golden straw in color, medium-bodied, with citrus and citrus peel aromas and flavors supported by a hint of sweet cream. Drink up. Score 86. **K**

TEL TZUBA, VIOGNIER-SAUVIGNON BLANC, 2006: A light straw-to-golden-colored blend of 63% Viognier and 37% Sauvignon Blanc. Developed in French oak for four months, showing generous acidity and appealing grapefruit, citrus peel and green apple aromas and flavors. Not complex but lively and refreshing. Drink up. Score 85. **K**

TEL TZUBA, CHARDONNAY DESSERT WINE, N.V.: Intentionally harvested late, almost at the point where the grapes had raisined and then fortified to a 14.5% alcohol level. Generous sweetness balanced nicely by acidity makes this a lively wine, showing honeyed apricot and peach notes. Sweet and spicy but not at all syrupy, a comfortable and refined wine with a clear hint of Anjou pears coming in on the finish. Drink now. Score 89. **K**

Hama'ayan

HAMA'AYAN, SANGIOVESE, 2006: Not much in common with its Italian cousins made from the same grape. Medium-bodied, with somewhat chunky tannins and showing basic berry and red plum notes. Drink up. Score 84. **K**

HAMA'AYAN, SANGIOVESE, 2005: Made entirely from Sangiovese grapes, oak-aged for 14 months, this red is showing soft, well-integrating tannins, a moderate overlay of spicy wood and appealing berry, cherry and plum fruits. A good quaffer. Drink up. Score 85. **K**

HAMA'AYAN, BELMONT RED, 2006: A somewhat unusual blend of 55% Pinot Noir and 45% Merlot, those developed in new French *barriques* for 14 months. Medium-bodied, soft and round, opens with a generous red-fruit and flowery nose, goes on to show berries, red cherries, cassis and a hint of currants. Not overly complex but a very good quaffer and a fine accompaniment to food. Drink up. Score 88. **K**

HAMA'AYAN, SEMILLON, 2006: An unoaked blend of 88% Semillon and 12% Sauvignon Blanc, with grapefruit, mandarin orange and citrus peel aromas and flavors. Drink up. Score 82. **K**

HAMA'AYAN, BELMONT WHITE, 2007: A light gold, unoaked blend of 55% Sauvignon Blanc and 45% Semillon. Showing appealing pineapple and peach fruits, a fresh, round and lively wine that opens nicely on the palate. Drink up. Score 87. **K**

Vanhotzker ✷✷

Founded by Eli Vanhotzker in 2003 on Moshav Meron, the winery has its own vineyards with Cabernet Sauvignon and Merlot grapes on the slopes of Mount Meron in the Upper Galilee. Releases, entirely of Cabernet Sauvignon from the 2004 and 2005 vintages, were of 1,500 bottles, and production from the 2006 vintage was 3,000 bottles, that including the winery's first Merlot.

VANHOTZKER, CABERNET SAUVIGNON, 2006: Ruby toward garnet, medium-bodied, with gently mouth-coating tannins. On the nose and palate currant and berry fruits along with notes of dark chocolate and Mediterranean herbs. Drink now. Score 85. **K**

VANHOTZKER, CABERNET SAUVIGNON, 2005: Dark garnet, medium- to full-bodied, with firm tannins and ripe and juicy currant, black cherry and kirsch aromas and flavors. On the finish herbal and vanilla notes. Drink up. Score 84. **K**

VANHOTZKER, CABERNET SAUVIGNON, 2004: Medium- to full-bodied, with generous soft tannins and spicy oak already integrating nicely and showing good balance with blackcurrant, plum and blackberry fruits. Generous and moderately long. Drink up. Score 85. **K**

VANHOTZKER, MERLOT, 2006: Medium- to full-bodied, with still-firm tannins waiting to settle down. Opens in the glass to reveal purple plum and cassis notes. Drink now. Score 84. **K**

Villa Wilhelma ✷✷

Founded in 2003 by Motti Goldman and Amram Surasky and located on Moshav Bnei Atarot not far from Ben Gurion Airport on the central plain, the winery draws its red grapes from the vineyards of the Upper Galilee and from Karmei Yosef at the foothills of the Jerusalem Mountains. Wines are released in two series, Grand Reserve and Villa Wilhelma, and the winery has grown from production of 3,500 bottles from the 2003 vintage to 18,000 bottles in 2007.

Grand Reserve

GRAND RESERVE, CABERNET SAUVIGNON, 2006: Tasted as components and at this stage showing medium- to full-bodied, with so-far gentle oak influences and soft tannins. Opens to show traditional Cabernet blackcurrant and blackberry fruits along with hints of Mediterranean herbs. Drink from release. Tentative Score 84–86.

GRAND RESERVE, CABERNET SAUVIGNON, 2005: Generous toasty wood on this full-bodied and still-firmly tannic wine, but those in good balance with black fruits, spices and hints of licorice. Drink now. Score 85.

GRAND RESERVE, CABERNET SAUVIGNON, 2004: Bright garnet in color, full-bodied, with once searing tannins now settling down but still showing generous oak that reflects the wine's 30 months in oak. Beyond the wood, appealing raspberries, red currants and a hint of bitter baking chocolate that comes in on the finish. Drink up. Score 81.

GRAND RESERVE, MERLOT, 2006: Showing a super-generous dose of near-burned toasted white bread, chunky country-style tannins and a few fruits that struggle but never quite make their way to the fore. Drink up. Score 78.

GRAND RESERVE, MERLOT, 2005: Ruby toward garnet in color, medium-bodied, with soft, near-sweet tannins and showing appealing red fruits. A simple country-style wine. Drink up. Score 83.

GRAND RESERVE, MERLOT, 2004: Firm, ripe and smooth in its youth, but now its 30 months in oak taking its toll. The wine has taken on a rather flat personality, cedary and earthy notes now dominating the black fruits that are here. Drink up. Score 83.

GRAND RESERVE, MEDOCABERNET, 2005: Named after Bordeaux's Medoc wines, a medium- to full-bodied blend of 75% Cabernet Sauvignon and 25% Merlot. Oak-aged for 21 months in medium- to heavy-toasted oak and showing generous smoke and firm tannins, those parting slowly in the glass to reveal blackberry, raspberry and cassis fruits on a generously spicy background. Straightforward and lacking depth. Drink up. Score 84.

GRAND RESERVE, MEDOCABERNET, VERSION 1, 2004: This medium- to full-bodied blend of Cabernet Sauvignon and Merlot shows generous spicy and smoky wood after having spent 18 months in oak, along with aromas and flavors of wild berries, cassis and Mediterranean herbs. Drink up. Score 85.

GRAND RESERVE, MEDOCABERNET, VERSION 2, 2004: Dark garnet in color, full-bodied, with once searing tannins now receding but continuing to reflect its 30 months in oak with a far-too-smoky, nearly burned woody overlay that makes it difficult to find the fruits that lie underneath and never quite make themselves felt. Showing signs of age. Drink up. Score 76.

GRAND RESERVE, CHARDONNAY, 2006: Deep honeyed gold in color, full-bodied and buttery, already showing quite generous oak. Opens in the glass to show green melon and citrus on a lanolin-like background. Drink up. Score 82.

Villa Wilhelma

VILLA WILHELMA, CHARDONNAY, 2004: Dark golden, dominated by bitter almonds and wood, but now with the addition of a distinctly resinous aroma. Score 68.

VILLA WILHELMA, SAUVIGNON BLANC, 2005: Light straw in color, opening with strong sulphur and earthy aromas that linger on and interfere with whatever fruits may be here. Drink up. Score 72.

VILLA WILHELMA, EMERALD RIESLING, 2006: Categorized as semi-dry. Opens with a resinous nose and goes on to show pineapple and citrus fruits. Closes with barnyard aromas. Score 68.

VILLA WILHELMA, EMERALD RIESLING, 2005: Categorized as half-dry but lacking acidity and sweetness. Floral and medicinal on the nose, and with a distinct hint of sour pineapple juice on the palate. Score 60.

Vitkin ✶✶✶✶

Established by Doron and Sharona Belogolovsky on Moshav
Kfar Vitkin on the central Coastal Plain, this winery released
its first wines from the 2002 vintage. Bordeaux-trained winemaker Assaf Paz relies on Carignan, Cabernet Franc, Syrah,
Pinot Noir, Tempranillo, Petit Verdot, Petite Sirah, Viognier,
French Colombard, Johannisberg Riesling, Gewurztraminer
and Muscat grapes from vintners in the Jerusalem hills as
well as several other parts of the country. The winery, special-
izing in creative blends and producing several varietal wines,
is currently producing about 35,000 bottles annually. The
Vitkin series is of age-worthy wines, and the Israeli Journey
wines are meant for relatively early drinking.

Vitkin

VITKIN, PINOT NOIR, 2007: Made from low-yield vines and harvested
early, oaked for ten months, with silky tannins with just enough of a
grip to catch our attention. Dark in color for a Pinot but showing fine
varietal traits, opening with black cherry, red plums and raspberries,
those supported nicely by notes of spices, cedarwood and minerals.
Supple, fresh and rewarding. Drink now–2012. Score 90.

VITKIN, PINOT NOIR, 2006: Developed for ten months partly in new
and recycled 250 liter barrels formerly used with Viognier. Medium-
bodied, with soft tannins integrating nicely, showing gentle, spicy
mushroom forest-floor notes, those supporting cassis and fine red and
black berries. From mid-palate on, hints of roasted cashew nuts and
smoke along with an appealing hint of bitter almonds on the finish.
Drink now–2011. Score 89.

VITKIN, PINOT NOIR, 2005: Made from grapes harvested in the
Judean Hills and aged in new and used French oak for 15 months, this
medium-bodied wine has soft tannins that integrate well with raspberry, blackberry and cherry fruits, those on a background of persim-
mons and hazelnuts. Drink now. Score 87.

VITKIN, CARIGNAN, 2007: As with many of the Vitkin wines, reflecting the sensitive use of new and old oak with a gentle dose of spicy
and vanilla-rich wood, with tannins still firm but needing only a bit of
time to settle down. On the nose and palate raspberries, dark cherries,

minerals and spices. A long finish with tannins, fruits and notes of pepper rising. Best now–2012. Score 90.

VITKIN, CARIGNAN, 2006: Made entirely from Carignan grapes and developed in new 360 liter French oak casks for 15 months. Intensely dark garnet in color, full-bodied, with deep, firm tannins just starting to settle in, deep garnet in color and showing fine extraction. On first attack, shows primarily spicy black fruits, those yielding to 'let loose' notes of mint and freshly turned earth. Simultaneously concentrated and intense while warm and generous, with fruits and tannins rising on the long finish. Drink now–2013. Score 91.

VITKIN, CARIGNAN, 2005: Made from grapes of 30–40-year-old vines, this full-bodied red offers up generous oak and tannins, those integrating well and showing fine balance with purple plums, blackberries and spices. Light meaty and mineral overlays. Drink now–2011. Score 91.

VITKIN, CARIGNAN, 2004: Deep purple, medium- to full-bodied, with firm tannins that are now integrating nicely to reveal spicy wood, earthy minerals and blackberry and plum fruits, those overlaid nicely with a pleasing gamey sweetness that lingers on the long finish. Drink now. Score 90.

VITKIN, CABERNET FRANC, 2007: Cabernet Franc in all its dark purple glory. Deep but silky tannins, a light hand with the oak and full-bodied, opening to show aromas and flavors of blackberry and currant fruits, the aromas and flavors soaring and with a long, stylish finish. Drink from release–2013. Tentative Score 90–92.

VITKIN, CABERNET FRANC, 2006: Ripe and polished, a blend of 86% Cabernet Franc and 14% Petit Verdot. Aged in new French oak for 15 months and showing gentle near-sweet cedar notes along with soft tannins that are integrating nicely. On the nose and palate currants and black cherries, those parting to reveal notes of toasted white bread, figs and tobacco. On the long and mouth-filling finish floral and mocha hints. Drink now–2013. Score 91.

VITKIN, CABERNET FRANC, 2005: Deep garnet toward royal purple, oak-aged for 16 months and blended with 12% Petit Verdot, the wine offers up generous tannins integrating nicely with the wood. Already showing an abundant array of spicy black cherries and currants, those with overtones of Madagascar green peppercorns, herbs and smoked meat. Long and satisfying. Drink now–2011. Score 90.

VITKIN, CABERNET FRANC, 2004: Deep, almost impenetrable royal purple in color, this blend of 90% Cabernet Franc and 10% Petit Verdot shows fine balance between wood, moderately firm tannins and vegetal-fruity characteristics. On first attack pepper and spicy wood, that followed by blackcurrants, plum and blackberry fruits, all supported by hints of cloves, Oriental spices and, on the long and mouth-filling finish, Mediterranean herbs. Drink now–2011. Score 90.

VITKIN, PETITE SIRAH, 2007: Opens with the traditional rich huckleberry, boysenberry and blackberry notes that we have come to associate with the better wines of this variety. And then kick in minerals, chocolate-covered cherries and firm, somewhat chunky, country-style tannins that rise and linger very nicely on the long finish. Drink now–2012. Score 90.

VITKIN, PETITE SIRAH, 2006: Dark royal purple, medium- to full-bodied, with fine extraction and with lively notes of spices, white pepper, tobacco and cedarwood supporting generous blackberry and huckleberry fruits. Chewy tannins rise on the finish along with hints of hazelnuts and grilled beef. Drink now–2013. Score 90.

VITKIN, PETITE SIRAH, 2005: Made from old-vine grapes and oak-aged for 16 months. Full-bodied, impenetrably dark purple-black, with deep spicy overlays and firm tannins all coming together beautifully. On the nose and palate blackberry and blueberries, those matched nicely by notes of white pepper, peppermint, chocolate and cedarwood, and on the long finish enchanting hints of raspberry jam. Drink now–2012. Score 91.

VITKIN, PETITE SIRAH, 2004: Dark garnet in color, reflecting its 15 months in partly new French oak with fine balance between firm tannins, sweet cedar and spicy oak, all coming together nicely to reveal a broad array of plum, blackberry, meaty and herbal aromas and flavors. Long and complex, with hints of minerals and bittersweet chocolate rising on the finish. Drink now–2011. Score 91.

VITKIN, BLENDED RED, AS YET UNNAMED, 2006: Not only unnamed but unidentified, in that the winery is holding the blend close to its chest, not to be disclosed until the wine's release. Aged in new French oak for about 20 months, showing generous wood but that in fine balance with equally generous but gently mouth-coating tannins. Dark royal purple and full-bodied, opens with a burst of blueberry and purple plum notes, those yielding in the glass to black fruits that are simultaneously spicy and jammy and, on the remarkably long finish, notes of nutmeg and bittersweet chocolate. A wine headed for elegance. Approachable on release, but best 2011–2015. Score 93.

VITKIN, RED DESSERT WINE, N.V.: A medium- to full-bodied blend of Petite Sirah, Carignan, Cabernet Sauvignon and Petit Verdot, reinforced with white alcohol to 17% strength. On the nose candied fruits, strawberries, exotic spices and chocolate, its generous sweetness balanced nicely by good natural acidity. Drink now. Score 87.

VITKIN, GEWURZTRAMINER, LIMITED EDITION, 2007: Light- to medium-bodied, light golden in color, so crispy dry that if this were a Champagne you would categorize it as "extra brut." On first attack a floral (look especially for rose petals) and spicy nose, and on the palate litchis, peaches and peach pits, those supported nicely by a vague but tantalizing near-bitter overtone. Crisp, clean and refreshing. Drink up. Score 88.

VITKIN, JOHANNISBERG RIESLING, 2008: Combining the charms of Rhine and Alsace Riesling, light gold in color, medium-bodied, with fine balance between fruits and acidity. Opens on the nose to show white peach, grapefruit and white mulberries, those on a lightly spicy background. Give this one a bit of time and it may show a light petrol note. Drink now–2011. Score 90.

VITKIN, JOHANNISBERG RIESLING, 2007: Light golden with a green tint, showing a delicate floral nose, that hinting of petrol and then opening to aromas and flavors of lemon and lime, green apples and a tantalizing hint of white pepper. A delicate and elegant wine. Drink now–2011. Score 89.

VITKIN, JOHANNISBERG RIESLING, 2006: Light gold in color, opens with a floral nose and goes on to reveal apricot, grapefruit, bitter orange peel and notes of green apples. Since release has come to show traditional Riesling traits. Spicy and long, with the flowers of Alsace and the petrol note of the Rhine. Drink now–2012. Score 90.

VITKIN, RIESLING, LATE HARVEST, 2006: Based on 90% Johannisberg Riesling, with a bit of French Colombard and Viognier blended in, light golden, showing generous sweetness and concentration set off nicely by balancing acidity. Opens to show citrus and dried apricots, those lightly honeyed and on a background of heather and spring flowers. Good intensity and length. This will age nicely. Drink now–2012. Score 89.

VITKIN, RIESLING, LATE HARVEST, 2005: Pale gold, medium-bodied, with lightly honeyed summer and tropical fruits and an appealing floral-citrus finish. Drink now. Score 89.

VITKIN, RIESLING, LATE HARVEST, 2004: With about 20% of the grapes in this wine affected by botrytis, this lightly funky, bronzed-gold-colored wine shows unabashed near-honeyed sweetness, and on the nose and palate dried apricots, tropical fruits and wild spring flowers. Drink up. Score 88.

Israeli Journey

ISRAELI JOURNEY, RED 2007: Medium- to full-bodied with soft tannins and gentle wood influences, a round and generous deep garnet blend of Carignan, Syrah and Cabernet Franc. Opens with a light floral note, goes on to red plums, currants and berries on a light peppery and earthy-mineral background, all leading to a tempting near-sweet finish. Drink now. Score 87.

ISRAELI JOURNEY, RED, 2006: Garnet toward royal purple, aged in new and used French oak for ten months, showing good balance between lightly spicy wood, soft tannins and hints of vanilla and Mediterranean herbs, all of which support aromas and flavors of currant, plum and berry fruits, all leading to a generously peppery finish. Medium- to full-bodied, and well balanced, a blend of 45% each of Syrah and Carignan and 10% Cabernet Franc. Drink now. Score 86.

ISRAELI JOURNEY, PINK, 2008: Light cherry red, a rosé primarily of Carignan and Syrah with small amounts of Tempranillo and Cabernet Franc blended in. Crisply dry and generously fruity, shows a low nose but opens to appealing aromas and flavors of strawberries, raspberries and black cherries, those with floral and spicy overtones. Medium-bodied, crisply dry and refreshing, strong enough to stand up to chicken and veal dishes. Drink up. Score 88.

ISRAELI JOURNEY, PINK, 2007: Bright red enough that a glance might make you think this rosé wine was cherry or raspberry juice. Anything but! Light- to medium-bodied, a blend of Tempranillo, Carignan, Syrah and Cabernet Franc, showing raspberry and cassis fruits, those with an overlay of jam-like strawberries. Crisply dry, with lively acidity, a refreshing and "fun" wine. Drink up. Score 88.

ISRAELI JOURNEY, WHITE, 2008: A blend of 55% Viognier, 35% French Colombard and 10% Gewurztraminer, the Viognier aged in new French oak, the others *sur lie* in stainless steel tanks. Flowery on both the nose and palate, shows crisp and refreshing acidity, and opens to reveal generous ripe summer fruits. Lively and refreshing. Drink now. Score 88.

ISRAELI JOURNEY, WHITE, 2007: A blend of 60% Viognier, 30% old vine French Colombard and 10% Gewurztraminer, aged on its lees partly in stainless steel and partly in large oak casks. Light-to medium-bodied, freshly aromatic and showing red grapefruit, tropical fruit and white peaches on a lightly spicy background. Dry but with a very pleasant hint of sweetness. Finishes fresh and lively. Drink up. Score 88.

Yaffo ✳✳✳

Founded in Jaffa in 1998 by Moshe and Anne Celniker and today located in the basement of their home in the Tel Aviv suburb of Ramat Hachayal, this small winery is currently producing about 10,000 bottles annually. Grapes, primarily Cabernet Sauvignon and Merlot, come from Kibbutz Netiv Halamed Hey in the Jerusalem Hills and from the Golan Heights. The winery also produces a Port-style wine.

YAFFO, CABERNET SAUVIGNON, 2005: Medium-bodied, with supple tannins and spicy plum, wild berry and currant fruits, opening to reveal hints of incense and sage. Tannins rise on the finish along with a generous mineral hint. Drink now. Score 88.

YAFFO, CABERNET SAUVIGNON, 2004: Dark ruby toward garnet, medium-bodied, with chewy tannins integrating nicely with black fruits, spices and an appealing herbal overlay. Drink up. Score 86.

YAFFO, MERLOT, 2005: Medium- to full-bodied, with rich red currant and black cherry fruits complemented by mocha and vanilla from the oak barrels in which it was aged. Tannins and a hint of bitterness rise on the long finish. Drink now. Score 86.

YAFFO, MERLOT, 2004: Soft and round, deep garnet-red, reflecting its 12 months in *barriques* with hints of spices and vanilla and with soft tannins integrating nicely. On the nose and palate blueberry, blackberry and plum fruits. Moderately long, with a hint of milk chocolate on the finish. Drink up. Score 85.

YAFFO, HERITAGE, 2005: A Bordeaux blend of 78% Cabernet Sauvignon and 22% Merlot, but with a distinctly fruit-forward New World personality. Full-bodied, with generous plum and blackcurrant fruits supported very nicely indeed by hints of dark chocolate. Reflects its 18 months in French *barriques* with notes of spices and vanilla. Well-balanced and long, the best wine to date from this small winery. Drink now–2011. Score 89.

YAFFO, ROUGE, 2006: A blend of 50% Cabernet Sauvignon, 45% Merlot and 5% Shiraz, oak-aged for eight months and showing plum and berry fruits that are held back by still-searing tannins that show no sign of integrating. Drink now. Score 85.

YAFFO, ROUGE, 2005: A blend of 45% Merlot, 50% Cabernet Sauvignon and 5% Shiraz, dark garnet, with smoky oak and soft tannins, opens to show blackberries and currants on a spicy background. Satisfying and long. Drink now. Score 87.

Yatir ★★★★★

Set in a state-of-the-art winery near the archaeological digs of Tel Arad at the foot of the Judean Hills, this boutique winery draws its name from the Yatir Forest. Originally a joint venture of Carmel and the vintners of the Yatir region, the winery is now owned solely by Carmel but maintains complete autonomy under the supervision of Australian-trained winemaker Eran Goldwasser. The winery, which releases wines under the Yatir Forest and Yatir labels, cultivates their own vineyards, those with Cabernet Sauvignon, Merlot, Shiraz, Sauvignon Blanc, and Viognier grapes. Also currently under cultivation are Tempranillo, Malbec and Petit Verdot, those at this stage destined primarily as blending agents. The first wines were from the 2001 vintage, and current production is between 100,000–120,000 bottles annually. Growth over the next two to three years is estimated at about 150,000 bottles.

Yatir Forest

YATIR FOREST, 2006: Dark garnet in color, with orange and green reflections, full-bodied and showing soft, mouth-coating tannins and a moderate touch of spicy oak. A Bordeaux blend, opening to show tempting currant, blackberry and black cherry fruits, those on a background of exotic spices and an enchanting hint of bitter chocolate that comes in on the finish. Drink now–2014. Score 91. **K**

YATIR FOREST, 2005: A full-bodied Bordeaux blend of 77% Cabernet Sauvignon, 13% Petit Verdot and 10% Merlot. A third aged in new and two-thirds aged in old wood *barriques* for 15 months, this deep royal purple wine casts intense orange and green reflections. Soft tannins integrating beautifully and the intentionally gentle hand with the wood come together nicely to let the wine open with spicy berry and cassis aromas and flavors, those going on to show blackberries and an underlying and fascinating mélange of bitter herbs. Long, generous and elegant. Drink now–2014. Score 94. **K**

YATIR FOREST, 2004: Almost inky in its deep garnet color, this full-bodied blend of Cabernet Sauvignon, Merlot and Syrah (80%, 14% and 6% respectively) is showing elegant and solid, with soft tannins, smoky wood and vanilla, all in fine balance with ripe blueberry, blackcurrant and plum flavors. Look as well for an appealing, earthy undercurrent leading to a long, deep, broad and generous finish. Drink now–2014. Score 93. K

YATIR FOREST, 2003: This blend of 85% Cabernet Sauvignon and 15% Merlot reflects its 12 months in *barriques* with gentle spices and lightly dusty wood and is showing fine balance between tannins, wood and acidity. On the palate light herbal and white pepper traits underlying rich blueberry and blackcurrant fruits. Well focused, long and elegant. Drink now–2012. Score 93. K

YATIR FOREST, 2002: Made from 100% Cabernet Sauvignon grapes, this dark garnet-toward-purple, full-bodied wine is now showing still-firm tannins, gentle and well-integrated smoky oak and sweet cedar aromas, those coming together very nicely with aromas and flavors of ripe currant and purple plum fruits as well as generous hints of chocolate and mint. Throwing sediment and worth decanting. Drink now. Score 90. K

YATIR FOREST, 2001: Dark ruby toward garnet, this medium- to full-bodied blend of 85% Cabernet Sauvignon and 15% Merlot shows good balance between soft tannins and oak. Rich aromas and flavors of currants, wild berries and cherries integrating nicely with spicy oak and generous minerals. A luxurious and elegant wine. Worth decanting because some bottles are throwing sediment. Drink up. Score 91. K

Yatir

YATIR, CABERNET SAUVIGNON, 2008: Smooth, well focused and refined. On the nose chocolate-covered cherries, and then showing full-bodied, with near-sweet tannins, and just enough spice from the wood to tantalize. On first attack a red-fruit Cabernet, going on to show blackberries and black cherries. Long, generous and destined for elegance. Best 2011–2016. Tentative Score 92–94. K

YATIR, CABERNET SAUVIGNON, 2007: Impenetrably dark garnet in color, full-bodied, with firm tannins and gentle wood influence integrating nicely. On first attack black fruits and spices, those parting to show notes of fresh herbs, black olives and bittersweet chocolate. Best 2011–2014, perhaps longer. Score 91. K

YATIR, CABERNET SAUVIGNON, 2006: Rich and deeply extracted, with generous blackberry, currant, black cherry and wild berries that are highlighted by mocha, vanilla and cedarwood overtones. Long and elegant. Drink now–2015. Score 93. **K**

YATIR, CABERNET SAUVIGNON, 2005: Blended with 15% of Shiraz, this dark garnet with purple and orange reflections is showing fine balance between gentle spicy wood and mouth-coating tannins that are integrating nicely. On first attack blackberries and currants, those yielding to raspberries, spices and light overlays of earthiness and leather, all with a hint of what at one moment feels like lead pencil and the next like cigar box. Long, generous and destined for elegance. Drink now–2014. Score 92. **K**

YATIR, MERLOT, 2006: Dark and dense but even at this early stage showing admirable depth, length and complexity. On the nose and palate layer after layer of currants, black cherries, chocolate and mocha all backed up by tannins that are simultaneously soft and powerful. Drink now–2014. Score 92. **K**

Merlot-Shiraz-Cabernet
Judean Hills

YATIR, MERLOT, 2005: Medium- to full-bodied, with generous near-sweet tannins, this seductive wine is already showing delicious blueberry, blackberry, mocha and vanilla flavors. Plush and round, on the way to becoming a delicious, complex and concentrated wine. Drink now–2012. Score 90. **K**

YATIR, SHIRAZ, 2007: Deep garnet toward royal purple, full-bodied, with gripping tannins starting to integrate now. Opens with a burst of spicy purple plums and blackberries, those yielding comfortably to red fruits, tobacco and dark chocolate. Needs time to show its elegance. Best 2011–2016. Score 93. **K**

YATIR, SHIRAZ, 2006: Full-bodied and concentrated with still firm tannins that need time to settle in. Showing fine balance and structure, the tannins integrating nicely now with a gentle spicy wood influence and opening in the glass to show blackberry, black cherry and prune notes, those on a background that hints of grilled beef and dark chocolate. Drink now–2017. Score 93. **K**

YATIR, SHIRAZ, 2005: Dark, almost impenetrable garnet in color, intentionally aged in old oak *barriques* in order to highlight the typical characteristics of the variety but still showing generous wood, the wine opens with meaty and herbal aromas, those yielding nicely to cherry, red currant and berry fruits and finally, creeping in comfortably, an agreeable hint of saddle leather. Long, generous and destined for intense elegance. Drink now–2014. Score 93. **K**

YATIR, CABERNET FRANC, 2008: As many of the Yatir wines, deeply extracted and showing almost impenetrably dark royal purple in color. Supple and rich, packed with mulberry, raspberry and cassis, those complemented by hints of toasty oak, and finally, raspberry and cherry notes that rise on the long finish. Possibly destined for blending but if released as a varietal, best from release–2015. Tentative Score 90–92. **K**

YATIR, CABERNET FRANC, 2007: Probably destined to be a blending agent. Developed in large oak casks, showing super-dark royal purple. Full-bodied, with still gripping tannins, but those showing signs of integrating nicely and destined to be smooth and velvety. Offers up a generous mouthful of black cherry, strawberry, raspberry and white pepper aromas and flavors, those complemented by notes of white pepper, all lingering nicely. If released as a varietal, best release–2014. Tentative Score 88–90. **K**

YATIR, CABERNET FRANC, 2006: Deep royal purple, full-bodied, and showing faithful to the variety with complex black cherry, blackberry and cassis fruits accented by spices, cedarwood, coffee and hints of tar and vanilla. Drink now–2011. Score 90. **K**

YATIR, PETIT VERDOT, 2007: Inky dark and dense in color, with firm, still gripping tannins that need nothing more than time to show the wine's elegance. On the nose and palate a generous array of black cherries, red and blackcurrants along with notes of mint, chocolate and tar, all coming together in a long and generous finish. Drink from release–2014. Tentative Score 89–91. **K**

YATIR, PETIT VERDOT, 2006: Deep purple, a powerful wine with intense tannins, concentration and complexity. On the nose and palate layers of plum, blackberry, pomegranate, coffee and earth, those already showing hints of smoky oak. An outstanding example of a variety that is not often bottled on its own. Drink now–2013. Score 92. **K**

YATIR, BLENDED RED, 2005: A blend of Merlot, Shiraz, Cabernet Franc and Petit Verdot (37%, 36%, 15% and 12% respectively). Aged in oak for 12 months, this still-young wine shows firm tannins nicely balanced with lightly spicy wood. Starts with a rich blackberry nose and then goes on to aromas and flavors of wild berries, currants and anise, all on a gently herbal background. Drink now–2012. Score 90. **K**

YATIR, CABERNET SAUVIGNON-MERLOT-SHIRAZ, 2004: A blend of 40% each Cabernet Sauvignon and Merlot and 20% Shiraz, this full-bodied red shows depth and concentration but never loses sight of elegance. Deep royal purple in color, with near-sweet tannins and appealing smoky and light vegetable overlays highlighting aromas and flavors of ripe plums, blackberries, cherry and licorice. On the long finish a tantalizing hint of spicy oak. Drink now–2012. Score 91. **K**

YATIR, CABERNET SAUVIGNON-MERLOT-SHIRAZ, 2003: A blend of 56% Cabernet Sauvignon, 33% Merlot and 11% Shiraz. Aged in oak for one year, this medium- to full-bodied wine shows ripe berry, cherry and currant fruits, those with just a hint of toasted oak, all backed up with vanilla and spicy aromas and flavors. Long and caressing. Drink now–2011. Score 90. **K**

YATIR, SAUVIGNON BLANC, 2008: Light golden straw with a green tint, developed primarily in stainless steel and partly in older *barriques* for 3–4 months. Fresh and crisp, with citrus, kiwi and gooseberry fruits all with a light hint of oyster shells and sea water. Drink now. Score 89. **K**

YATIR, SAUVIGNON BLANC, 2007: Showing elegance and subtlety with citrus, passion fruit, green apple and grapefruit aromas and flavors on a grassy and stony-mineral background. Well crafted. Drink up. Score 90. **K**

YATIR, SAUVIGNON BLANC, 2006: Fermented in stainless steel and then transferred to used oak for only three months in order to keep the crisp fruitiness of the wine intact, this light golden straw, medium-bodied wine sits gently on the palate, its fresh acidity highlighting pineapple, citrus and light grassy overtones. Easy to drink yet with a distinct touch of elegance. Drink up. Score 90. **K**

Sauvignon Blanc
Negev

YATIR, VIOGNIER, 2008: Unoaked, a juicy wine, showing pear, peach and greengage plum fruits, those supported by notes of fennel seed and peach pits, all coming together in a long, harmonious and near-creamy finish. Drink now–2011. Score 91. **K**

YATIR, VIOGNIER, 2007: Made entirely from Viognier grapes, some intentionally harvested early, some quite late and wisely unoaked to maintain the fruity and aromatic nature of the variety. Rich, ripe and crispy dry, a generous mouthful of pear, green apple, melon and summer fruits, those backed up by crisp acidity and a hint of cream. Drink now–2011. Score 92. **K**

Ye'arim ✳✳✳

Located in the village of Givat Ye'arim near Jerusalem, this small winery is owned by Sasson Ben-Aharon, who is also the senior winemaker for Binyamina Wineries. With vineyards in the Judean Mountains, the winery produced 1,000 bottles from the 2000 vintage and is currently releasing about 3,000 bottles annually.

YE'ARIM, CABERNET SAUVIGNON, SASSON'S WINE, 2006: Dark ruby toward garnet, full-bodied, with firm tannins and gentle wood integrating nicely. Still in its extreme youth but already showing fine balance and structure. On the nose and palate blackberries, currants and blueberries, those on a lightly spicy background. On the long finish an appealing hint of tar. Drink now–2012. Score 90.

YE'ARIM, CABERNET SAUVIGNON, SASSON'S WINE, 2005: Garnet toward royal purple, medium- to full-bodied, with caressing tannins and gentle wood parting to reveal blackberry, blueberry and cassis notes, those on a background of Oriental spices and a note of red licorice. Drink now–2011. Score 90.

YE'ARIM, CABERNET SAUVIGNON, SASSON'S WINE, 2004: Dark garnet, medium- to full-bodied, with silky smooth tannins and a gentle hand with spicy wood, opening to show generous red currant, berry and cherry fruits, those matched nicely by spices and hints of licorice that come in on the long finish. Drink now. Score 89.

YE'ARIM, MERLOT, SASSON'S WINE, 2005: Medium- to full-bodied, with soft, caressing tannins and a moderate hand with spicy and vanilla-rich wood. Opens to show black cherry, red and black berries, and a generous minty note on the finish. Drink now–2011. Score 89.

YE'ARIM, MERLOT, SASSON'S WINE, 2003: Merlot blended with 10% Cabernet Sauvignon grapes, garnet toward purple in color, well balanced and medium-bodied. With soft tannins, and reflecting 16 months in French oak with a gentle touch of spicy wood, the wine shows aromas and flavors of cherries, wild berries and tobacco as well as an appealing hint of minty-chocolate on the finish. Drink now. Score 87

Yehuda *

Located on Moshav Shoresh in the Jerusalem Mountains, this winery was founded by Avi Yehuda in 1998. Cabernet Sauvignon, Merlot and Sauvignon Blanc grapes come from the winery's own nearby vineyards as well as from Moshav Shoresh. Current production is about 5,000 bottles annually.

YEHUDA, CABERNET SAUVIGNON, 2005: With chunky tannins, a generous dose of green vegetables and a few cherry-berry notes, a simple and distinctly country-style wine. Drink up. Score 76.

YEHUDA, CABERNET SAUVIGNON, HILAH HASHIRAZ, 2005: Blended with 12% Shiraz and oak-aged for 18 months, a dark garnet, medium- to full-bodied wine with firm tannins integrating nicely with spicy wood. Opens to show appealing black fruits on a light leathery and earthy background. Drink up. Score 85.

YEHUDA, MERLOT, 2005: Dark royal purple in color, medium- to full-bodied, with firm tannins that seem to not want to integrate and a few berry, cherry and cola notes. Drink up. Score 75.

YEHUDA, MERLOT, JACOB'S LADDER, 2005: Oak-aged for 18 months, an appealing if not overly internationalized little Merlot. Dark ruby toward garnet, medium-bodied, with soft tannins and easy-going berry, cherry fruits. An entry-level wine. Drink up. Score 82.

YEHUDA, MERLOT, 2004: Opens with juicy black cherry and cola aromas and flavors but goes bitter and herbal as it lingers on the palate. Showing age. Drink up. Score 75.

Yiftah'el ✶✶

Founded in 1999 in the community of Alon Hagalil in the Upper Galilee, owner-vintners Tzvika Ofir and Avner Sofer rely on Cabernet Sauvignon, Merlot, Petite Sirah, Shiraz, Mourvedre and Sangiovese grapes from their own vineyards. Current production is about 10,000 bottles.

YIFTAH'EL, CABERNET SAUVIGNON, 2006: Dark ruby, medium- to full-bodied, with chunky tannins and moderate spicy oak. On the nose and palate blackberries and blueberries with overlays of roasted herbs. Not complex but a pleasant little country-style wine. Drink now. Score 84.

YIFTAH'EL, CABERNET SAUVIGNON, 2005: Ruby toward garnet, medium-bodied, reflecting its 12 months in American oak with soft tannins and hints of vanilla. Opens to show blackberry and currant fruits along with notes of Mediterranean herbs and minerals. Round, soft and with good length. Drink now. Score 86.

YIFTAH'EL, MERLOT, 2006: Medium-dark garnet in color, medium-bodied, with chunky tannins and spicy oak, opens to show blackberries, blueberries and earthy-herbal notes. Drink now. Score 83.

YIFTAH'EL, MERLOT, 2005: Ruby to garnet, reflecting its time in *barriques* with spicy cedarwood. Medium-bodied with chunky tannins, a simple but appealing country-style wine with berry and cassis fruits. Drink up. Score 80.

YIFTAH'EL, SHIRAZ, 2006: Dark, almost inky-garnet, full-bodied, and with soft, mouth-coating tannins. Opens to show black fruits, and goes on to reveal black pepper, licorice and spicy wood, all coming together and lingering nicely. Drink now. Score 86.

YIFTAH'EL, SHIRAZ, 2005: Dark garnet, medium- to full-bodied, with chunky, country-style tannins and appealing plum, herbal and earthy minerals that linger nicely. Drink now. Score 85.

YIFTA'HEL, SANGIOVESE NOUVEAU, 2007: Light enough ruby red that one might take it for a rosé, with super-soft tannins and simple but pleasing red berry and cherry flavors. A pleasant summertime quaffer. Drink up. Score 83.

YIFTAH'EL, SANGIOVESE, 2006: Dark royal purple in color, with soft tannins and showing berries, prunes, freshly picked mushrooms and spices on a background of citrus-flavored chocolate. Drink now. Score 84.

YIFTAH'EL, SANGIOVESE, 2005: Light ruby in color, with soft tannins and simple but appealing berry and red cherry fruits on a light licorice background. Drink up. Score 80.

YIFTAH'EL, PETITE SIRAH, 2006: Full-bodied, with firm tannins in good balance with spicy wood. On first attack licorice, chocolate and tobacco, those followed by red berry and cherry fruits. Generous, mouth-filling and moderately long. Drink now. Score 85.

YIFTAH'EL, PETITE SIRAH, RESERVE, 2005: Firm, full-bodied and concentrated, almost inky-black in color showing intense tannins and spicy wood, both needing time to integrate, but even now opening to show blackberry, currant and licorice aromas and flavors. Drink up. Score 85.

YIFTAH'EL, PETITE SIRAH, 2005: Although aged in new oak for only four months, this full-bodied, dark garnet wine is showing remarkably firm tannins and surprisingly full-bodied. The chunky tannins give the wine a distinct country style, and the black fruits here are largely hidden by a heavy iodine/medicinal overlay. Past its peak. Drink up. Score 76.

Zauberman ★★★★

Founded in 1999 by Itzik Zauberman and located in the town of Gedera in the Southern Plains, this small winery draws on organically raised grapes from its own nearby vineyards as well as grapes from Karmei Yosef. Current production is about 3,000 bottles annually.

ZAUBERMAN, LIMITED EDITION, 2005: Cabernet Sauvignon made in the system of Italian Amarone. With a whopping 15.4% alcohol content, reflecting generous sweet and spicy cedar from its aging in *barriques* for 22 months. Almost chewy, with raspberries, dried cherries and blackberry jam on the nose and palate, those supported by hints of black tea and licorice on the finish. Missing the deep bitterness of true Amarone, but an "interesting" wine and one of the most expensive on-release prices in the country. Drink now–2015. Score 90.

ZAUBERMAN, CABERNET SAUVIGNON, LIMITED EDITION, 2004: Deep royal purple, fullbodied, intense and concentrated, with generous soft tannins, moderate spicy oak and showing raspberry, blackcurrant, chocolate and light earthy herbaceousness. Drink now–2011. Score 91.

ZAUBERMAN, CABERNET SAUVIGNON, LIMITED EDITION, 2003: Dark garnet, full-bodied, with generous tannins starting to integrate and equally generous spicy wood. Showing blackberry, plum and cassis fruits, all leading to a long, intense finish. Drink now–2012. Score 91.

ZAUBERMAN, CABERNET SAUVIGNON, LIMITED EDITION, 2002: Deep garnet-red, full-bodied, with intense tannins and generous, almost powerful wood integrated nicely with plum, raspberry and currant fruits along with spicy and earthy aromas and flavors. On the long finish generous hints of well-roasted nuts. Consider decanting before drinking. Drink now–2012. Score 90.

ZAUBERMAN, CABERNET SAUVIGNON, LIMITED EDITION, 2001: Dark royal purple toward black, full-bodied, concentrated and tannic, with aromas and flavors of dried plums, cherries, red berries, chocolate, honey and spices. This powerful, near-massive and complex wine, made by drying the grapes before pressing them much in the *ripasso* method, is approachable now if given at least 30 minutes in the glass to open. Drink now. Score 91.

ZAUBERMAN, MERLOT, SPECIAL EDITION, 2006: Full-bodied, dense and concentrated, with a more than generous 15.2% alcohol content and an almost intense presence of spicy wood. A wine so tightly wound that it opens very slowly even after decanting, and then goes on to show aromas and flavors of plums, red currants, mocha, anise and espresso coffee. Starts and finishes with muscular tannins. A well-crafted wine, but one primarily for those who prefer to chew their wines. Drink now–2015. Score 90.

ZAUBERMAN, MERLOT, 2004: Dark, almost impenetrable garnet, full-bodied, with soft tannins, spicy oak, and plum, currant and berry fruits. Long and generous. Drink now. Score 89.

ZAUBERMAN, MERLOT, 2003: Dark ruby toward garnet, medium- to full-bodied, with good balance between generous smoky oak, firm but caressing tannins, black and red berry fruits and hints of coffee and chocolate. Drink now. Score 89.

Zemora ✻✻✻

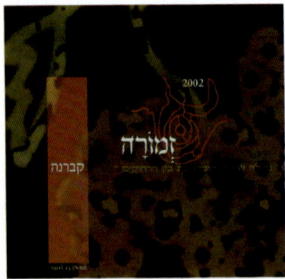

Set in a facility in Moshav Beit Zayit in the Jerusalem Mountains, winemaker Baruch Yosef released his first wines from the 2000 vintage. Grapes are drawn largely from the Jerusalem Mountain area and include Cabernet Sauvignon, Merlot, Cabernet Franc, Shiraz, Petit Verdot, Sangiovese, Viognier and Chardonnay, some of which are being raised organically. The winery releases wines in three series: Special Reserve, the Bordeaux blends in the Castra series and single-variety wines in the Zemora series. Current production is about 50,000 bottles annually. Starting with the 2004 vintage, the wines have been kosher.

Among problems to be noted are that several wines have been released with similar labels but with different blends, so that it has sometimes been difficult to determine which wine is being sampled at any given moment (see, for example, the first tasting note that follows), and, as this guide goes to press, the winery is for sale and future plans are uncertain.

Special Reserve

ZEMORA, SPECIAL RESERVE, 2004: An oft-discussed wine, in that it seems so vastly different on every tasting occasion and because the winemaker has released at least three different versions of the blend. In general, a dark garnet wine, medium- to full-bodied, with chunky, sharp-edged tannins and showing blackberry and purple plum fruits. A distinctly country-style wine. Drink up. Score 84. **K**

Castra

CASTRA, RED, 2004: Deep inky garnet, this full-bodied blend of Merlot, Cabernet Sauvignon, Cabernet Franc, Shiraz and Petit Verdot (65%, 20%, 10%, 3% and 2% respectively) spent 24 months in new French oak. Generous toasty wood balanced by firm tannins. On the nose and palate purple plums, blackberries and cherries, those leading to a long, spicy finish. Primarily for those who like their wines with an ample overlay of oak. Drink up. Score 87. **K**

CASTRA, BLACK, 2004: The mirror image of the Castra Red, in this case with the amounts of Merlot and Cabernet reversed, containing 65% Cabernet and 20% Merlot. Full-bodied, with generous wood and firm tannins complemented by blackberries, black cherries, currants and dark chocolate and, on the moderately long finish, a hint of smoked meat. Drink up. Score 88. **K**

CASTRA, 2003: Almost impenetrably dark garnet, medium- to full-bodied, with still-firm tannins integrating nicely. A well-balanced blend of 75% Cabernet Sauvignon, 20% Cabernet Franc and 5% Merlot, showing up-front cherry and blackberry fruits, those complemented by spicy, smoky cedar. Showing signs of aging. Drink up. Score 87.

Zemora

ZEMORA, CABERNET SAUVIGNON, 2005: Full-bodied, deep royal purple in color, with somewhat chunky tannins and reflecting its 14 months in medium and heavy-toasted French oak with a generous, toasted cedar overlay. On the nose and palate opens to reveal blackberries, blueberries, cassis and vanilla. Developing a marked note of bitter herbs and the fruits fading on the finish. Drink up. Score 84. **K**

ZEMORA, MERLOT, 2005: Blended with 10% Cabernet Sauvignon, and to my palate, as happens from time to time with Zemora, a vastly different wine than when earlier tasted. Dark garnet, reflecting its 21 months in oak with generous spicy wood and smoke, and somewhat chunky tannins that give the wine a distinct country style. On the nose, berry, black cherry and plum fruits. Drink up. Score 84. **K**

ZEMORA, SYRAH, 2005: Youthful royal purple, medium-bodied, with somewhat sharp tannins and perhaps too-generous spicy oak. On the nose and palate berry and black cherry aromas and flavors, but overall one-dimensional. Drink now. Score 84. **K**

ZEMORA, CABERNET FRANC, 2006: Ruby toward garnet, medium-bodied with chunky, country-style tannins. A very quiet nose and on the palate no trace of the variety, but a basic spicy, black fruit personality, that with a too-heavy green vegetable overlay. Drink up. Score 82. **K**

ZEMORA, CABERNET FRANC, 2005: Deep garnet, full-bodied, with now softening tannins and smoky oak opening to reveal plum and black cherry notes, those supported by leather and cedar all leading to vanilla and spices on a moderately long, near-sweet finish. Drink up. Score 87. **K**

ZEMORA, PETIT VERDOT, 2005: Dark purple, medium- to full-bodied, with sharp-edged tannins and quite generous spicy oak. Currant and blackberry fruits here, but those outweighed by the oak and a sharpness that cannot be avoided. Drink up. Score 83. **K**

ZEMORA, BLENDED RED, 2006: Oak-aged for 20 months, a blend of 65% Merlot, 25% Cabernet Sauvignon and 10% Cabernet Franc, that manages somehow to hide any varietal traits whatsoever. Medium- to full-bodied, with soft tannins and blueberry, blackberry and plum fruits. Smooth, soft and round, an entry-level wine. Drink now. Score 84. **K**

Zion ✳✳✳

Founded in the old city of Jerusalem in 1848 by the Shor family, until recently this winery produced primarily wines for sacramental purposes. Managed by the ninth generation of the family, starting four years ago the winery began to release dry, more upscale wines aimed at a more sophisticated market. Now located in Mishor Adumim, not far from Jerusalem, the winery produces about 2,200,000 bottles annually of which 100,000–150,000 are dry, those in three series, Armon, Tidhar and Erez. The winery's better wines rely on Cabernet Sauvignon, Merlot, Carignan, Petite Sirah and Emerald Riesling grapes from the Galilee, the Judean Hills and the Central Plain. Vineyards with Chardonnay, Sauvignon Blanc and Viognier are under development.

Armon

ARMON, CABERNET SAUVIGNON, 2006: Dark, almost inky-garnet in color, full-bodied and generously tannic, and at this early stage opening with a somewhat medicinal aroma that blows off after a few moments in the glass. On the nose and palate traditional blackcurrant, blackberry and spices followed by a hint of vanilla. Drink now. Score 85. **K**

ARMON, 2005: Aged in partly new and partly one- and two-year-old American *barriques* for 24 months, a medium- to full-bodied blend of 65% Cabernet Sauvignon, 30% Merlot and 5% Petite Sirah. On the nose and palate generous currant, blackberry and purple plums, those supported nicely by notes of spices, espresso coffee and earthy minerals. Drink now–2011. Score 90. **K**

Tidhar

TIDHAR, CABERNET SAUVIGNON, 2006: A medium- to full-bodied blend of 85% Cabernet Sauvignon, 10% Merlot and 5% Petite Sirah. Shows silky tannins and opens in the glass to reveal aromas and flavors of blackberries, black cherries and plums. Not overly complex but a good quaffer. Drink now. Score 86. **K**

TIDHAR, CABERNET SAUVIGNON, 2005: A garnet-red, lightly oaked, medium-bodied and softly tannic blend of 85% Cabernet Sauvignon, 10% Merlot and 5% Petite Sirah. Black and red berries, ripe purple plums and light spices that run throughout. Drink now. Score 85. **K**

TIDHAR, MERLOT, 2006: Medium-bodied, dark ruby toward black cherry in color, an unoaked red with soft tannins and showing notes of berry, black cherry and wild strawberry notes, those on a lightly spicy background. A blend of 90% Merlot and 5% each of Cabernet Sauvignon and Petite Sirah. Soft, round and easy to drink. Drink now. Score 85. **K**

TIDHAR, CARIGNAN-MERLOT, 2006: An unoaked blend of 70% Carignan, 25% Merlot and 5% Cabernet Sauvignon. Dark royal purple in color, with soft tannins and generous blackberry and raspberry fruits, those on a lightly spicy and earthy-mineral background. Drink now. Score 85. **K**

TIDHAR, CARIGNAN-MERLOT-CABERNET SAUVIGNON, 2005: Dark ruby red in color, this lightly oaked, light- to medium-bodied wine shows soft tannins and opens with light minty aromas and flavors going on to raspberry and plums. A refreshing quaffer. Drink up. Score 84. **K**

Erez

EREZ, CABERNET SAUVIGNON, 2006: Dark garnet toward royal purple, medium-, perhaps medium- to full-bodied, with somewhat chunky country-style tannins, but those yielding in the glass to show blackberry, black cherry and purple plum fruits, those on a background of nutmeg-flavored dark chocolate. Drink now. Score 86. **K**

EREZ, MERLOT, 2005: Blended with 15% of Cabernet Sauvignon, this medium-bodied, dark ruby wine shows soft tannins and straightforward red berry and currant fruits. Drink up. Score 84. **K**

EREZ, PETITE SIRAH, 2007: Dark royal purple, full-bodied, showing the onset of spicy wood influence and with gripping tannins just starting to settle in. Opens to show black and red berries along with black pepper, anise and hints of Mediterranean herbs. Drink now. Score 84. **K**

EREZ, CABERNET SAUVIGNON-MERLOT, 2006: Dark garnet toward royal purple, medium- to full-bodied, a blend of 50% Cabernet Sauvignon, 45% Merlot and 5% Petite Sirah. Reflecting 12 months of development in *barriques* with gently spicy wood, and opening on the nose and palate to show an array of currant, blackberry, citrus peel and red licorice. Turns a bit astringent on the finish. Drink up. Score 85. **K**

EREZ, PETITE SIRAH-MERLOT, 2006: Developed partly in new, partly in 1–2-year-old *barriques*, a blend of 60% Petite Sirah and 40% Merlot. Dark royal purple, medium- to full-bodied, with softly caressing tannins parting to show plums, wild berries and currants, all on a lightly spicy background. Turns a bit astringent on the finish. Drink up. Score 85. **K**

EREZ, PETITE SIRAH-MERLOT, 2005: Petite Sirah and Merlot in equal parts. Ruby to garnet, clean and fresh, with soft tannins, a hint of spicy wood and generous red fruits. Not complex but an acceptable entry-level wine. Drink up. Score 83. **K**

EREZ, CHARDONNAY-CHENIN BLANC, 2007: An unoaked blend of equal parts of Chardonnay and Chenin Blanc. Light gold with green and orange tints, medium-bodied, with summer fruits and melon highlighted by floral and apple notes. Just enough complexity to get our attention. Drink now. Score 86. **K**

Late Additions

Among other recent tastings were wines from three new producers, the wines available in both Israel and the United States. Although details about the wineries were not available at press time, the tasting notes follow so that they may be of use. Full details on each of the wineries will appear in the 2011 edition of this book.

FLEGMANN, CABERNET SAUVIGNON, JUDEAN HILLS, 2006: Not so much an independent winery as a set of private label wines made especially for the Flegmann family at the Psagot Winery. Dark garnet, medium- to full-bodied, with somewhat chunky country-style tannins. On the nose and palate traditional Cabernet currant and blackberry fruits and, on the moderately long finish, hints of licorice and green olives. Drink now. Score 87. **K**

FLEGMANN, MERLOT, JUDEAN HILLS, 2006: Ruby toward garnet, medium-bodied, with soft tannins and well-balanced, a pleasant albeit somewhat internationalized Merlot, opening to show blackberry and black cherry fruits, those on a lightly spicy and minty background. Drink now. Score 86. **K**

DOMAINE VENTURA, CABERNET SAUVIGNON, GRAND VIN, LIMITED EDITION, HAUT JUDÉE/JUDÉE-SAMARIE, 2006: Lively garnet toward royal purple, medium- to full-bodied, with soft tannins. Quiet on the nose but opens in the glass to reveal appealing wild berries and currants on a spicy background. On the finish a note of freshly turned earth. Drink now. Score 85. **K**

DOMAINE VENTURA, MERLOT, GRAND VIN, LIMITED EDITION, HAUT JUDÉE/JUDÉE-SAMARIE, 2006: Garnet toward royal purple in color, medium-bodied, with soft, near-sweet tannins, and developed in French *barriques* for 12 months. Opens to show aromas and flavors of raspberries and red currants, those on a light earthy-herbal background. Put aside its somewhat grandiose labeling information and you will find a pleasant enough quaffer. Drink now. Score 86. **K**

VORTMAN, NETIV OFAKIM, 2007: From a mini-winery and from grapes harvested in the Carmel Hills, not far from Haifa, a blend of 70% Carignan and 20% Merlot, the balance made up of Cabernet Sauvignon and Petit Verdot. Medium- to full-bodied, reflecting its ten months in French oak with light spicy overtones and soft tannins. Opening to reveal generous blackcurrant and blackberry fruits and, rising on the finish, a note of ripe purple plums. Drink now. Score 88.

VORTMAN, SHAMBOUR, 2007: Dark garnet in color, aged in French oak for ten months, a somewhat unusual blend of 50% Merlot and 25% each of Petite Sirah and Pinotage, but don't let that hold you back. Low on the nose, but the wine opens to reveal flavors of rich black fruits and Mediterranean herbs along with a hint of green olives. Tannins and fruits rise nicely on the finish. Drink now. Score 87.

Afterword

A Guide to Tasting Wines

Wine tasting is not a complex or difficult task. All that is required is the use of one's senses of sight, smell and taste. Before setting out to taste wines, try to eliminate as many distractions as possible. During the actual tasting, for example, extraneous aromas (e.g., food, perfume and aftershave lotion) should be avoided as they interfere with the ability to appreciate the aromas and bouquet of the wine. Also, during a tasting, try as hard as possible to ignore the comments by others in order not to be influenced by their opinions. Be sure to use high-quality glasses (ideally of thin crystal) as this enhances the flavors and aromas of wines. A separate glass should be provided for each wine, this allowing the taster to return to earlier tasted wines in order to make comparisons. The glasses should be, of course, perfectly clean, without any aroma of soap or detergent. Glasses should be filled to no more than 20% of their capacity as this will give ample room for swirling the wine, that process serving to aerate and release the more subtle aromas and flavors of the wine being tasted.

Basic Rules for Tasting Wines

Professionals can sample fifty or more wines at a single sitting, but it is widely agreed that in a private tasting, alone at home or at a friendly gathering, the number of wines for tasting should not exceed eight.

White wines should be tasted before reds, and within each group wines that are light in body should be tasted before fuller-bodied wines. When tasting wines of the same variety, such as Cabernet Sauvignon or Merlot, always start with the youngest wines and end with the most mature.

Wines should be served at their proper temperatures. Young reds should be opened about fifteen or twenty minutes before the tasting, and more mature reds about half an hour before they are poured.

You can either place the bottles on the table with the labels exposed or place each bottle in a paper bag, each bag identified only by a number, for a blind tasting. I prefer blind tastings, for the power of suggestion is strong and it is difficult to be entirely objective vis à vis a label of a prestigious Chateau.

Wines should be arranged on the table in the order they are to be tasted. I suggest using a felt-tipped pen to put a number on each bottle and then to mark the corresponding number on the base of each glass in order to avoid any confusion.

Professional wine tasters spit the wine in order to avoid intoxication, but there is no need to spit at a home tasting where much of the pleasure comes from drinking the wine. For those who choose to spit, prepare adequate receptacles (clay jugs, low vases and Champagne buckets are ideal).

Allow half a bottle per person. That is to say, for eight people you will need four bottles. When pouring during the tasting, remember that the average sampling should be small enough to allow room for swirling the wine in the glass. Whatever wines are left over after the actual tasting can be served with the meal or snacks afterward.

Use a tasting form, such as that illustrated in the following section, or record your impressions on a piece of paper. Making notes helps people make up their minds before they commit themselves.

Food should be served after a wine tasting and never before or during because food changes the taste of wine. If you must have something on the table, use unsalted and sugar-free white bread.

Wine Appreciation

1. VISUAL APPEARANCE

In order to best see the color and clarity of a wine, hold your glass against a white background (a white tablecloth or even a blank sheet of white paper will do) and tilt the glass away from yourself slightly so that the exposed surface is larger. Red wines can be anywhere from bright cherry red in color to dark and opaque, in fact almost black. Although most white wines will have a light golden straw color, they can range from almost colorless to deep golden, and rosé or blush wines are only rarely true pink and can vary from purple-pink to orange or even bright ruby red. Whatever the color, the wine should be perfectly clear. Wines that have thrown a sediment will become clear as the sediment settles.

Consider whether the color is deep or pale and whether it is vivid and youthful or browning and perhaps showing age. While the glass is tilted look as well at the rim (that point where the wine meets the glass), for it is not generally a positive sign if the color at the rim fades to an almost watery consistency. After noting the qualities of the color, swirl the wine in the glass gently and then hold it up to see the legs or tears—these are the threads of wine that appear and linger on the inside of the glass. These are an accurate indicator of the alcohol level in the wine; the broader and more viscous the legs, the greater the alcohol content and, according to many, a good indicator of the wine's ability to age. At the same time, note whether the wine is *frizzante*, that is to say, whether it has tiny little bubbles in it. Although this is acceptable in some white wines (e.g., Muscadet de Sevres et Maine *sur lie*, Vinho Verde, Moscato d'Asti), and occurs in many white wines when they have been overly chilled, such bubbles indicate a fault in nearly all red wines. When evaluating Champagnes or other sparkling wines, the bubbles should be sharp, small and long lasting, rising from a central point in the glass.

A hint: Never taste wines under fluorescent light as this makes all red wines appear brown.

2. SMELL

It surprises many to realize that people with a normal sense of smell can identify more than 1,000 different aromas. That should not be daunting, however, as the process of identifying aromas is a largely automatic one, and, although we may sometimes "struggle" to distinguish between the aroma of a blackberry or raspberry, our associations with aromas are quite strong. In order to best evaluate and appreciate the aromas of a wine, swirl the glass rapidly for a few seconds, place your nose well into the glass and inhale deeply through your nostrils.

One of the first sensations to be evaluated is the alcohol content of the wine. If the wine appears to be highly alcoholic, ask yourself whether it is a fortified wine (e.g. Sherry, Port, Madeira) or whether the strong alcoholic aromas reflect a fault. After that, consider whether the wine smells as youthful or as mature as it appears to the eye, whether the aromas are smooth and harmonious, whether they are distinctive, bland or reticent, and whether they are simple or complex. Consider as well whether there is a creamy, spicy or vanilla note to the aromas as this may give a hint about whether the wine was aged in oak. Also consider whether the wine has any "off" aromas that may indicate a fault. With a bit of practice it becomes possible for many to identify from aroma alone the variety of the grape used and even the region in which the wine was made.

A hint: A slight musky aroma can add great charm, but when exaggerated almost always reveals a fault in the wine.

3. TASTE

When actually setting out to taste the wine, take a good mouthful, close the lips firmly and swirl the wine vigorously in order to coat the entire mouth. This is important because different taste sensations are perceived by different parts of the mouth (sweetness on the tip of the tongue, sourness on the sides, bitterness on the back and the roof of the mouth, saltiness on the front and sides of the tongue). Some tasters also draw a bit of air into the mouth, believing this will accentuate the flavors.

The first thing to be noted is whether the flavors are in accord with the aromas of the wines. Then, with the wine lingering in the mouth, identify the various taste sensations imparted. Ask yourself: Are the flavors pronounced and easily identifiable or somewhat confused; is the wine clean or muddy; are the tannins, acidity, wood and fruits in balance; are the tannins and wood in good proportion to the fruits; is the level of sweetness appropriate for the wine?

Keep in mind that the major goal of tasting is not only to evaluate a wine but to determine whether it is to your taste. Wine tasting is not a guessing game but with increased practice and repeated tastings, many come to the point where they can identify and discuss the grape variety, area of origin and age and quality of the wines they are tasting.

A hint: A wine dominated by a single flavor is one-dimensional and thus lacking excitement.

Among the fruit aromas and flavors to be sought in white wines: citrus (especially lemon, grapefruit, lime and citrus peel), apple, melon, pear, peach, apricot, grapes, figs and, especially in sweet dessert wines, dried fruits. Also in white wines look for hints of grassiness, herbaceousness, honey and a creamy sensation. Fruits to be found in red wines include, among others, black and red currants (sometimes referred to as cassis), plums and a variety of berries. Other taste sensations that may be imparted by red wines are chocolate, coffee and tobacco. In both reds and whites look for aromas and flavors imparted by oak aging, those including spicy or smoky oak, sweet cedar, asphalt and vanilla. Be aware that some of the aromas and flavors traditionally found in a red may appear in a white and vice versa.

TASTING FORMS

Because few of us have perfect memories, one of the very best aids in tasting wines is to use an organized sheet for keeping notes. Such sheets, used by professional wine tasters as well as amateurs, help to organize our thoughts and to leave a permanent record for future reference with which to compare the same wine or similar wines. The act of writing our reactions down also serves to implant our thoughts in long-term memory.

The tasting form that is illustrated on the opposite page (and is in larger format on the inside of the dust jacket of this book) is meant for those purposes. Readers may feel free to reproduce this form for their own use or for the use of friends, and should the original be lost, a downloadable and printable copy can be found at:

www.tobypress.com/rogov/tasting.pdf

Several Words about Scores

A great many people walk into wine stores and order this or that wine entirely on the basis of its high score. This is a mistake. A score is nothing more than a critic's attempt to sum up in digits the overall quality of a wine. Scores can provide a valid tool, especially when awarded by experienced critics, but they should not be separated from the tasting notes that precede them; for although a score may be a convenient summary, it says nothing about the style, personality or other important traits of the wine in question and therefore cannot give the consumer a valid basis for choice.

There are, however, three major advantages to scores. First of all, scores can serve as initial guides for the overall impression of the wine in question. Second, scores also give an immediate basis for comparison of that wine to others in its category and to the same wine of the same winery from earlier years. Finally, such scores give valuable hints as to whether the wine in question is available at a reasonable value for one's money.

The scores awarded in this book should be taken as merely one part of the overall evaluation of the wine, the most important parts of which are the tasting notes that give details about the body, color, aromas, flavors, length and overall style of the wine. It is also important to keep in mind that scores are not absolute. The score earned by a light and hyper-fruity wine made from Gamay grapes, a wine meant to be consumed in its youth, cannot be compared to that given to a deep, full-bodied wine made from a blend of Cabernet Sauvignon, Merlot and Cabernet Franc, the peak of drinking for which may come only five, ten or even thirty years later on. Numerical comparisons between the wines of the great Chateaux of Bordeaux and those meant to be consumed within weeks or months of the harvest is akin to comparing, by means of a single number, the qualities of a 1998 Rolls Royce and a 1965 Volkswagen Beetle.

Even if there was a perfect system for rating wines (and I do not believe such a system exists), no two critics, no matter how professional or well intentioned they may be, can be expected to use precisely the same criteria for every facet of every wine they evaluate. Even when similar scoring systems are used by different critics, readers should expect to find a certain variation between them. The trick is not in finding the critics with whom you always agree, but those whose tasting notes and scores give you direction in finding the wines that you most enjoy.

My own scoring system is based on a maximum of 100 points, interpreted as follows:

95–100	Truly great wines
90–94	Exceptional in every way
86–89	Very good to excellent and highly recommended
81–85	Recommended but without enthusiasm
70–79	Average but at least somewhat faulted
Under 70	Not recommended

A Few Words about Wine Bottles

Wine bottles are so taken for granted that we rarely give much thought to their history or design. All of which is rather odd, because wine bottles as we know them have only been in regular use since the 17th century. Prior to that time, wines were stored in clay vats or wood barrels and then sold and served in ceramic or metal pots or jugs, many of which resembled cooking pots far more than they did the kinds of bottles we know today. In some cases, well into the 18th century, wines continued to be stored and sold in containers made from the skins of animals.

Wines stored that way even in the best of conditions did not last very long, but in the 18th century, when wineries learned how to use cork to seal wine bottles, a whole new range of possibilities opened up. Wines, finally, could be made in such a way that they could last and mature over a period of many years. By the 1850s, wine bottles had become such a world standard that wines were being sold in bottles considered traditional for different regions. As can be seen today, for example, the wines of Bordeaux come in bottles with square shoulders, those containing Burgundy wine have sloping shoulders, and those containing the wines of Alsace and parts of Germany are especially tall with gently sloping sides and no shoulders whatsoever.

In addition to their different shapes, wine bottles also come in a variety of sizes. Most people have become accustomed to wines that come in "standard bottles" that contain 750 ml. Even though such bottles have been accepted for generations as the most convenient size for two, when they were originally designed in the early 18th century, they were considered an ideal portion for one person. The truth is, however, that there are times when such standard bottles are far from ideal, even for two. Sometimes, for example, a couple wants only a glass or two of wine with their meal. There are also those occasions when a person dining alone wants wine, but hesitates to order a bottle in a restaurant because he knows that most of the wine he has paid for will go to waste. Even at home, we have learned that if we recork a half-used bottle (even using vacuum sealing tools) it will rarely be as good the next day, and there is a good chance that it will have gone bad two, three or four days later. And, as we become more sophisticated about wine, there are many times when we would like to have two or more different wines with our meals but hesitate to order or open two bottles, also knowing that we will be unable to finish an entire bottle of each of the wines we are drinking.

The French discovered the solution to these problems in 1885 and the Americans followed suit in 1901, when they started to make bottles that held 375 ml. of wine and were thus well suited to those who felt that a standard or full bottle was simply too much for them.

That half-bottles are convenient is undeniable, but they do have a limitation and this should not be ignored. Because wines age better and their life-span is increased when they are stored in larger bottles, one should not purchase half-bottles of wines that are going to be stored for a prolonged period of time. The simple truth is that with the exception of wines that are meant to be consumed fairly young, the ultimate life expectancy of any wine increases in direct proportion to the size of the bottle in which it is stored. When buying French wines that one wants to store for many years, for example, many knowledgeable drinkers prefer to buy at least some of their wines in "magnum"-sized bottles, that hold the equivalent of two regular bottles. In fact, in addition to the half-bottle, whole bottle and magnum, wines also come in bottles named "Marie-Jeanne," "Double-Magnum," "Jeroboam" and "Imperiale," that have capacities, respectively, for three, four, six and eight regular bottles. Because bottles larger than the magnum are hard to handle, it is rare to find them except in the cellars of well-known Chateaux who bottle them for their own private use. Those building wine cellars should keep in mind, especially when buying fine French wines, that it is considered good logic that for every four regular bottles one stocks, one should also purchase one magnum, the magnum invariably to be drunk last as it will last the longest and age the best.

The range of bottles that hold Champagne is even broader, with a total of ten different sizes. Even smaller than the half bottle is the "split" or quarter bottle, generally intended for a single drinker. Larger than the regular bottle and the magnum (and keep in mind that the standard Champagne bottle holds about 30 ml. more than other wine bottles) are a series of bottles, all named after Biblical Kings. The "Jeroboam" holds four bottles; the "Rehoboam" holds six; the "Methuselah," eight; the "Salmanazar," twelve; the "Balthazar," sixteen; and the "Nebuchadnezzar" holds twenty standard bottles of champagne. Anyone who has ever seen a Nebuchadnezzar knows that it takes at least three strong and completely sober people to pour from such bottles.

What About the "Hole" in the Bottom of the Bottle?

Many people have wondered about the "hole" or indentation in the bottom of some wine bottles. The use of such indentations, correctly known as "punts," has its roots in the earliest days of bottle-making, when the Romans found that this would make bottles stronger. As glass-making improved, however, the punt was no longer necessary for strength, but continued as it made the stacking and shipping of wine easier.

Today deep punts are found most often in Champagne bottles and only on occasion in other bottles. The simple truth is that it is merely a question of style—the punt serving no purpose whatever unless one is cynical enough to think it is used to make some bottles appear slightly larger. It says nothing about the quality of the bottle or the wine therein.

As some have pointed out, the punt allows for an elegant way of serving wine with just one hand by putting your thumb into it. Some, with a bit of humor, also point out that the punt makes it easier to dance with a bottle on your head.

Glossary of Wine Terminology

ACIDIC: A wine whose level of acidity is so high that it imparts a sharp feel or sour taste in the mouth.

ACIDITY: An important component of wine. A modicum of acidity adds liveliness to wine, too little makes it flat and dull, and too much imparts a sour taste. The acids most often present in wines are tartaric, malic and lactic acids.

AFTERTASTE: The flavors and aromas left in the mouth after the wine has been swallowed.

AGGRESSIVE: Refers to the strong, assertive character of a young and powerful wine. Aggressive wines are too high in acidity, have harsh tannins, or both, and often lack charm and grace.

ALCOHOL CONTENT: Percent by volume of alcohol in a wine. Table wines usually have between 11.5–13.5% in alcohol content but there is an increasing demand for wines as high as 15–16%.

ALCOHOLIC: A negative term, referring to wines that have too much alcohol and are thus hot and out of balance.

AROMA: Technically, this term applies to the smells that come directly from the grapes, whereas bouquet applies to the smells that come from the winemaking process. In practice, the two terms are used interchangeably.

ASTRINGENT: A puckering sensation imparted to the wine by its tannins. At a moderate level, astringency is a positive trait. When a wine is too astringent it is unpleasant.

ATTACK: The first sensations imparted by a wine.

ATYPICAL: A wine that does not conform to its traditional character or style.

AUSTERE: A wine that lacks fruits or is overly tannic or acidic.

BACKWARD: Describes a wine that is not yet ready to drink, or a wine that has not yet developed its maximum potential.

BALANCED: The term used to describe a wine in which the acids, alcohol, fruits, tannins and influence of the wood in which the wine was aged are in harmony.

BARNYARD: Aromas and flavors that call to mind the barnyard, and when present in excess impart dirty sensations, but when in moderation can be pleasant.

BARREL: The wood containers used to ferment and hold wine. The wood used in such barrels is most often French or American oak but other woods can be used as well.

BARREL AGING: The process in which wines mature in barrels after fermentation.

BARRIQUE: French for "barrel" but specifically referring to oak barrels of 225 liter capacity, in which many wines are fermented and/or aged.

BIG: A term used to describe a wine that is powerful in flavor, body or alcohol.

BLANC DE BLANCS: White wines made entirely from white grapes.

BLANC DE NOIRS: White wines made from grapes usually associated with red wines.

BLEND: A wine made from more than one grape variety or from grapes from different vintages. Some of the best wines in the world, including most of the Bordeaux wines, are blends of different grapes selected to complement each other.

BLUSH WINE: A wine that has a pale pink color imparted by very short contact with the skins of red grapes.

BODY: The impression of weight or fullness on the palate. Results from a combination of fruits, alcohol and glycerin. Wines range from light to full-bodied.

BOTRYTIS CINEREA: Sometimes known as "noble rot," this is one of the few fungi that is welcomed by winemakers, for as it attacks the grapes it shrivels them, drains the water and concentrates the sugar, thus allowing for the making of many of the world's greatest sweet wines.

BOTTLE AGING: The process of allowing wine to mature in its bottle.

BOUQUET: Technically, the aromas that result from the winemaking process, but the term is used interchangeably with aroma.

BRETTANOMYCES: Often referred to simply as Brett, a side effect of yeast that causes a metallic or wet-fur note to develop in a wine. In small amounts Brett can add charm, but in large amounts it is a serious fault.

BRILLIANT: A wine whose color is clear and has no cloudiness.

BROWNING: When a red wine starts to develop a brown edge or a brownish color. Such wines are generally fully mature and will almost surely not improve.

BRUT: Bone dry. A term used almost exclusively to describe sparkling wines.

BUTTERY: A positive term for rich white wines, especially those that have undergone malolactic fermentation.

CARAMELIZED: A wine that has taken on a brown color, and sweet and sour aromas and flavors, often due to exposure to oxygen as the wine ages.

CARBONIC MACERATION: Method of fermenting red wine without crushing the grapes first. Whole clusters of grapes are put in a closed vat together with carbon dioxide, and the fermentation takes place within the grape berries, which then burst.

CHARACTER: Balance, assertiveness, finesse and other positive qualities combine to create character. The term is used only in the positive sense.

CHEWY: Descriptive of the texture, body and intensity of a good red wine. A chewy wine will be mouth-filling and complex.

CLONE: A vine derived by vegetative propagation from cuttings, or buds from a single vine called the mother vine.

CLOSED: A wine that is not showing its potential and is holding back on its flavors and aromas.

CLOYING: A wine that has sticky, heavy or unclean aromas or flavors.

COARSE: A wine that is rough or overly alcoholic. Appropriate in some country-style wines but not in fine wines.

CONCENTRATED: Wines with intense flavors, depth and richness. Synonymous with deep.

CORKED: A wine that has been tainted by TCA (2, 4, 6-Tricholoranisole), increasingly caused by faulty corks. TCA imparts aromas of damp, moldy and decomposing cardboard to a wine. Sometimes only barely detectable, at other times making a wine unapproachable.

COUNTRY-STYLE: A simple wine that is somewhat coarse but not necessarily unpleasant.

CREAMY: A soft, silky texture.

CRISP: A clean wine with good acidity

CUVÉE: A wine selected by a winemaker as special, and separated out for bottling under a special label.

DELICATE: Wines that are valued for their lightness and subtlety.

DENSE: Full in flavor and body.

DEPTH: Refers to complexity and intensity of flavor.

DESSERT WINE: A sweet wine. Often served as an accompaniment to goose liver dishes at the start of a meal.

DIRTY: A wine typified by off aromas or flavors resulting from either poor vinification practices or a faulty bottling process.

DRINKING WINDOW: The predicted period during which a wine will be at its best.

DRY: The absence of sugar or sweetness.

DUMB: A wine that has gone into a dumb period is one that has closed down and is holding back on its aromas and flavors. A natural process in many red wines 12–18 months after bottling.

EARTHY: Clean sensations of freshly turned soil, minerals, damp leaves and mushrooms. Can be a very positive trait.

ELEGANT: A wine showing finesse or style.

EVERYDAY WINES: Inexpensive, readily available and easy-to-drink wines, lacking sophistication, but at their best pleasant accompaniments to food.

FAT: A full-bodied wine that is high in alcohol or glycerin but in which the flavor overshadows the acidity, giving it a heavy, sweetish sensation. A negative term.

FERMENTATION: A process by which yeast reacts with sugar in the must, resulting in the creation of alcohol.

FILTRATION: Usually done just prior to bottling, the process of filtering of the wine in order to remove large particles of sediment and other impurities. Over-filtration tends to rob wines of their aromas and flavors.

FINESSE: Showing great harmony. Among the best qualities of a good wine.

FINISH: The aromas and flavors that linger on the palate after the wine has been swallowed.

FIRMNESS: The grip of a wine, determined by its tannins and acidity.

FLABBY: The opposite of crisp, often a trait of wines that lack acidity and are thus dull and weak.

FLAT: Synonymous to flabby.

FLINTY: A slightly metallic taste, sometimes found in white wines such as Chardonnays. A positive quality.

FORTIFIED WINE: A wine whose alcoholic strength has been intensified by the addition of spirits.

FORWARD: Can be used in three ways—wines that border on being flamboyant; wines that have matured quickly; or wines that are delicious and well developed.

FRIZZANTE: Lightly sparkling.

GARRIGUE: A wine that hints of scrub brush, Provençal herbs and light earthy notes. A positive term.

GRASSY: A term often used to describe white wines made from Sauvignon Blanc and Gewurztraminer grapes.

GREEN: In the positive sense, wines that are tart and youthful but have the potential to develop. In the negative sense, a wine that is unripe and sour.

HARD: A sense of austerity usually found in young, tannic red wines before they mellow and develop with age.

HARSH: Always a negative term, even more derogatory than "coarse."

HERBACEOUS: Implies aromas and flavors of grass, hay, herbs, leather and tobacco.

HOT: The unpleasant, sometimes burning sensation left on the palate by an overly alcoholic wine.

ICE WINE: A dessert wine made by a special method in which the grapes are left on the vine until frozen and then pressed while still frozen. Only the water in the grape freezes and this can be removed, leaving the must concentrated and very sweet. In warm weather areas the freezing process may be done in the winery.

INTENSE: A strong, concentrated flavor and aroma.

INTERNATIONALIZED WINES: Reds or whites that are blended to please any palate. At their best such wines are pleasant, at their worst simply boring.

LATE HARVEST: In such a harvest, grapes are left on the vines until very late in the harvest season, the purpose being to obtain sweeter grapes that will be used to make dessert wines.

LEES: Sediments that accumulate in the bottom of the barrel or vat as a wine ferments.

LEGS: The "tears" or stream of wine that clings to a glass after the wine has been swirled.

LENGTH: The period of time in which the flavors and aromas of a wine linger after it has been swallowed.

LIGHT: Low in alcohol or body. Also used to describe a wine low in flavor.

LIVELY: Clean and refreshing.

LONG: A wine that offers aromas and flavors that linger for a long time after it has been swallowed.

LONGEVITY: The aging potential of a wine, dependent on balance and structure.

MALOLACTIC FERMENTATION: A second fermentation that can occur naturally or be induced, the purpose of which is to convert harsh malic acid to softer lactic acid.

MATURE: A wine that has reached its peak after developing in the bottle.

MELLOW: A wine that is at or very close to its peak.

MÉTHODE CHAMPENOISE: The classic method for making Champagne by inducing a second fermentation in the bottle.

MID-PALATE: Those aroma and taste sensations felt after the first attack.

MOUSSE: The foam and bubbles of sparkling wines. A good mousse will show long-lasting foam and sharp, small, concentrated bubbles.

MOUTH-FILLING: A rich, concentrated wine that fills the mouth with satisfying flavors.

MUST: The pre-fermentation mixture of grape juice, stem fragments, skins, seeds and pulp, that results from the grape-crushing process.

NOSE: Synonymous with bouquet.

NOUVEAU: Term that originated in Beaujolais to describe very young, fruity and light red wines, often made from Gamay grapes and by the method of carbonic maceration. Such wines are always meant to be consumed very young.

N.V.: A non-vintage wine; a term most often used for sparkling wines or blends of grapes of different vintage years.

OAK: The wood most often used to make the barrels in which wines are fermented or aged. The impact of such barrels is reflected in the level of tannins and in its contribution to flavors of smoke, spices and vanilla to the wines.

OAKED: A wine that has been fermented and/or aged in oak barrels.

OFF: A wine that is spoiled or flawed.

OXIDIZED: A wine that has gone off because it has been exposed to oxygen or to high temperatures.

PEAK: The optimal point of maturity of a given wine.

PERSONALITY: The overall impression made by an individual wine.

RESIDUAL SUGAR: The sugar that remains in a wine after fermentation has been completed.

RICH: A wine with full flavors and aromas.

RIPASSO: A second fermentation that is induced on the lees of a wine made earlier.

ROBUST: Assertive, full-bodied and characteristic of good red wines at a young age, or country-style wines that are pleasingly coarse.

ROTTEN EGGS: Describes the smell of hydrogen sulfide (H_2S). Always an undesirable trait.

ROUND: A wine that has become smooth as its tannins, acids and wood have integrated.

RUSTIC: Synonymous with country-style.

SHARP: Overly acidic.

SHORT: A wine whose aromas and flavors fail to linger or to make an impression after the wine has been swallowed.

SILKY: Synonymous for lush or velvety. Silky wines are never hard or angular on the palate.

SIMPLE: A wine that has no nuances or complexity.

SMOKY: A flavor imparted to a wine from oak casks, most often found in unfiltered wines.

SMOOTH: A wine that sits comfortably on the palate.

SOFT: A wine that is round and fruity, relatively low in acidity and is not aggressive.

SPICY: A wine that imparts a light peppery sensation.

STALE: A wine that has lost its freshness, liveliness or fruitiness.

STEWED: The sensation of cooked, overripe or soggy fruit.

STINGY: A wine that holds back on its aromas or flavors.

SULFITES: Usually sulfur dioxide that is added to wine to prevent oxidation.

SUR LIE: French for "on the lees." A term used to describe the process in which a wine is left in contact with its lees during fermentation and barrel aging.

TANNIC: A wine still marked by firm tannins. In their youth, many red wines tend to be tannic and need time for the tannins to integrate.

TANNINS: Phenolic substances that exist naturally in wines and extracted from the skins, pips and stalks of the grapes, as well as from development in new oak barrels. Tannins are vital for the longevity of red wines. In young wines, tannins can sometimes be harsh, but if the wine is well balanced they will blend with other substances in the wine over time, making the wine smoother and more approachable as it ages.

TASTED FROM COMPONENTS: A barrel tasting done before the final blend was made.

TCA: 2, 4, 6-Tricholoranisole. See "corked."

TERROIR: The reflection of a vineyard's soil, altitude, microclimate, prevailing winds, and other natural factors that impact on the quality of the grapes, and consequently on the wines produced from them.

THIN: Lacking in body or fruit.

TOASTING: Searing the inside of barrels with an open flame when making the barrels. Heavy toasting can impart caramel-like flavors to a wine; medium toasting and light toasting can add vanilla, spices or smokiness to the wine, all positive attributes when present in moderation.

VANILLA: Aroma and flavor imparted to wines from the oak barrels in which they age.

VARIETAL TRAITS: The specific colors, aromas and flavors traditionally imparted by a specific grape variety.

VARIETAL WINE: A wine that contains at least 85% of the grape named on the label.

VEGETAL: An often positive term used for a bouquet of rounded wines, in particular those made from Pinot Noir and Chardonnay grapes, whose aromas and flavors often call to mind vegetables rather than fruits.

VINTAGE: (a) Synonymous with harvest; (b) A wine made from grapes of a single harvest. In accordance with EU standards, a vintage wine must contain at least 85% grapes from the noted year.

VOLATILE: A volatile wine has a vinegar-like aroma. A serious fault in a wine.

WATERY: A wine so thin that it feels diluted.

WOOD: Refers either to the wood barrels in which the wine ages or to a specific aroma and flavor imparted by the barrels.

YEAST: A kind of fungus, vital to the process of fermentation.

Contacting the Wineries

Achziv Winery
Rehov Rokach 5/11A, Kiryat Motzkin 26376
Tel: 050 7713687 Fax: 04 8772112
gmark5@bezeqint.net
www.guberman.net

Agur Winery
Moshav Agur 99840
Tel/Fax: 02 9910483
 shukiya@017.net.il
www.agurwines.com

Alexander Winery
POB 8151
Moshav Beit Yitzhak 42970
Tel: 09 8822956 Fax: 09 8872076
a_wine@netvision.net.il
www.alexander-winery.co

Aligote Winery
Moshav Gan Yoshiya 38850
Tel/Fax: 04 6258492
aligote@aviv-flowers.co.il

Alon Wineries
Moshav Alonei Aba 36005
Tel: 04 9535251 Fax: 04 9800727
alonwinery@walla.co.il

Alona Winery
Moshav Givat Nili 37825
Tel: 052 2425657
ap_azoulay@hotmail.com

Amphorae Vineyard
POB 12672 Herzliya 46733
Tel: 04 9840702 Fax: 04 9704318
info@amphorae-v.com
www.amphorae-v.com

Amram's Winery
Moshav Ramot Naftaly 13830
Tel: 050 5222901 Fax: 04 6940039
amramswine@gmail.com
http://amramwinery.com

Anatot Winery
POB 3390
Givat Ze'ev 90917
Tel: 02 5860187 Fax: 02 5362565
 info@anatotwinery.co.il
www.anatotwinery.co.il

Asif Winery
POB 413 Na'ale 71932
Tel: 052 5932200 Fax: 077 3217070
oryah@zahav.net.il
www.asifwinery.co.il

Assaf Winery
Moshav Kidmat Tzvi 12421
Tel: 054 4779722 Fax: 04 6820292
kedemas@walla.com

Avidan Winery
Kibbutz Eyal 45840
Tel: 09 7719382 Fax: 09 7712679
avidanwine@walla.com

Bar Winery
22 Ha'avoda St.
Binyamina 30500
Tel: 04 6388545
alanbar@zahav.net.il

Baram Winery
Kibbutz Baram 13860
Tel: 052 8313208
baram.winery@gmail.com

Barkai Vineyards
Moshav Neve Michael 99865
Tel/Fax: 02 9993281
barkaimi@bezeqint.net

Barkan Wine Cellars
POB 146
Kibbutz Hulda 76842
Tel: 08 9355858 Fax: 08 9355859
winery@barkan-winery.co.il
www.barkan-winery.co.il

Bashan Winery
Moshav Avnei Eitan 12925
Golan Heights
Tel: 054 4603213 Fax: 04 6762618
bashanwinery@013.net

Bazelet Hagolan Winery
POB 77
Moshav Kidmat Tzvi 12421
Tel: 04 6965010 Fax: 04 6965020
bazelet@netvision.net.il
www.bazelet-hagolan.co.il

Beit-El Winery
Beit-El 90628
Tel/Fax: 02 9971158
hmanne@netvision.net.il

Benhaim Winery
34 Ben-Zvi Ave.
Ramat-Gan 52247
Tel: 03 6762656 Fax: 03 5741089
benhaim@benhaim.co.il
www.benhaim.co.il

Ben Hanna Winery
Moshav Gefen 99820
Tel: 052 5434253
shlomi@ben-hanna.com
www.ben-hanna.com

Ben-Shoshan Winery
Kibbutz Bror-Hail 79152
Tel: 08 6803321 Fax: 08 6803667
niva_yuval@walla.com

Ben-Zimra Winery
Moshav Kerem Ben Zimra 13815
Tel/Fax: 046 980056
ashk_y@netvision.net.il
www.yekev-benzimra.com

Binyamina Wine Cellars
POB 34
Binyamina 30550
Tel: 04 6388643 Fax: 04 6389021
info@binyaminawines.co.il
www.binyaminawines.com

Birya Winery
Birya 13805
Tel/Fax 04 6923815
drporat@zahav.net.il

Bnei Baruch Winery
POB 1552
Ramat Gan 52115
Tel: 054 6696704 Fax: 03 9226741
Boris_beloter@yahoo.com

Bustan Winery
POB 55
Moshav Sharei Tikva 44860
Tel: 054 4892757
bustanwinery@yahoo.com

Bustan Hameshusheem Winery
Moshav Had Ness 12950
Tel: 052 4358407

Carmel Winery
Rishon Letzion, Zichron Ya'akov
Tel: Rishon Letzion 03 9488888
Tel: Zichron Ya'akov 04 6390105
www.carmelwines.co.il

Carmey Avdat Winery
Midreshet Ben Gurion 84990
Tel: 08 6535177 Fax: 08 6535188
Carmey-avdat@bezeqint.net
www.carmey-avdat.co.il

Domaine du Castel
Moshav Ramat Raziel 90974
Tel: 02 5342249 Fax: 02 5700995
castel@castel.co.il
www.castel.co.il

The Cave
POB 34
Binyamina 30550
Tel: 04 6388643 Fax: 04 6389021
thecave@zahav.net.il

Chateau Golan Winery
Moshav Eliad 12927
Tel: 04 6600026 Fax: 04 6600274
winery@chateaugolan.com
www.chateaugolan.com

Chillag Winery
12 Shabazi St.
Yehud 56231
Tel: 03 62032290 Fax: 03 6325473
chillag@netvision.net.il
www.chillagwinery.com

Clos de Gat
Kibbutz Har'el 99740
Tel: 02 9993505 Fax: 02 9993350
harelca@netvision.net.il
www.closdegat.com/intro.html

Dalton Winery
Dalton Industrial Park, Merom Hagalil 13815
Tel: 04 6987683 Fax: 04 6987684
info@dalton-winery.com
www.dalton-winery.com

Dico's Winery
Moshav Ginaton 73110
Tel: 08 9243135

Ein Nashut Winery
Moshav Kidmat Tzvi
Tel: 052 27991457
www.bellofri.co.il

Ein Teina Winery
Moshav Givat Yoav 12946
Tel: 050 8217554 Fax: 02 6920414
Yotam76@yahoo.com

Ella Valley Vineyards
Kibbutz Netiv Halamed Hey 99855
Tel: 02 9994885 Fax: 02 9994876
www.ellavalley.com
ella@ellavalley.com

Erez Winery
Har Bracha 44830
Tel: 02 9409026 Fax: 02 9400402
Yekev-erez@barak.net.il

Essence Winery
Ma'aleh Tsvia 20129
Tel: 04 6619058 Fax: 04 6619054
essencewines@zvia.org.il

Flam Winery
9 Avshalom St.
Rishon Letzion 75285
Tel: 02 9929924 Fax: 02 9929926
golan@flamwinery.com

Gad Winery
Moshav Sdot Micha 99810
Tel: 050 5601886
ohad1478@walla.com

Galai Winery
Moshav Nir Akiva 85365
Tel: 08 9933713 Fax:08 9933622
info@galai-winery.co.il
www. galai-winery.com

Galil Mountain Winery
Kibbutz Yiron 13855
Tel: 04 6868740 Fax: 04 6868506
winery@galilmountain.co.il
www.galilmountain.co.il

Gat Shomron Winery
Karnei Shomron 44855
Tel: 052 7264855
lior@walla.co.il

Gesher Damia Winery
2 Hatavor St.
Pardes Hannah-Karkur 37011
Tel/Fax: 04 6377451
damiya@walla.co.il

Ginaton Winery
Moshav Ginaton 73110
Tel/Fax: 08 9254841
ginaton1999@walla.co.il

Givon Winery
POB 140
Givon Hachadasha 90901
Tel: 02 5362966
info@givonwine.com
www.givonwine.com

Golan Heights Winery
POB 183
Katzrin 12900
Tel: 04 6968420 Fax: 04 6962220
ghwinery@golanwines.co.il
www.golanwines.co.il

Greenberg Winery
51 Hameginim St.
Herzliya 46686
Tel: 052 3237689
elegant@netvision.net.il

Gush Etzion Winery
POB 1415
Efrat 90435
Tel: 02 9309220 Fax: 02 9309156
winery@actcom.co.il
www.gushetzion-winery.com

Gustavo & Jo Winery
19 Marvah St.
Kfar Vradim 25147
Tel: 04 9972190
boia@netvision.net.il

Gvaot Winery
POB 393
Shiloh 44830
Tel: 09 7921292 Fax: 09 7921086
info@gvaot-winery.com
www.gvaot-winery.com

Hakerem Winery

POB 645
Qiryat Arba 90100
Tel: 052 4621390

Hamasrek Winery

Moshav Beit Meir 90865
Tel: 02 5701759 Fax: 02 5336592
hamasrek@netvision.net.il
www.hamasrek.com

Hans Sternbach Winery

Moshav Givat Yeshayahu 99825
Tel: 02 9990162 Fax: 02 9911703
sk-Gadi@zahav.net.il

Hatabor Winery

POB 22
Kfar Tavor 15241
Tel: 04 6767889
ssiecodo@zahav.net.il

Hevron Heights Winery

Moshav Geulim 42820
Tel: 09 8943711 Fax: 09 8943006
mm@churchill.fr

Kadesh Barnea Winery

Moshav Kadesh Barnea 85513
Tel: 08 6555849 Fax: 08 6571323
winerykb@012.net.il
www.kbw.co.il

Kahanov Winery

Feinberg 4, Gadera
Tel: 0523936999
info@kahanov.co.il
http://kahanov.co.il

Kadita Winery
POB 1052
Safed
Tel: 050 6933219
winery@kadita.co.il
www.kadita.co.il/winery/intro.html

Karmei Yosef Winery
Karmei Yosef 99797
Tel: 08 9286098
bravdo@bravdo.co.il
www.bravdo.com

Katlav Winery
Moshav Nes Harim 99885
Tel/Fax: 02 5701404
yosss@bezeqint.net

Katz Winery
Moshav Mesilat Tzion 99770
Tel: 050 2573950   Fax: 02 5855356
jossi@katz-winery.com
www.katz-winery.com

Kfir Winery
POB 4125
Gan Yavne 70800
Tel: 08 8570354   Fax: 08 8673708
meirkfir@gmail.com
www.kfir-winery.co.il

Kitron Winery
Kibbutz Ma'abarot
Tel: 050 5250035
kitronwinery@gmail.com

Kleins Winery
19 Tchelet Mordechai St.
Jerusalem 94396
Tel: 02 5022946   Fax: 02 5022947
yomtov@kleins1.com

La Terra Promessa Winery
Moshav Shachar 79335
Tel: 08 6849093 Fax: 050 5684775
laterrapromessa@bezeqint.net

Lachish Winery
Moshav Lachish 79360
Tel: 054 7920151
galiam@bezeqint.net

Domaine de Latroun
Latroun Monastery 99762
Tel: 08 9220065

Lavie Winery
15 Shemen Zeit St.
Ephrata 90435
Tel: 02 9938520

Levron Winery
10 Orbach St.
Haifa 34985
Tel: 04 8344837 Fax: 04 8246724

Maccabim Winery
Maccabim-Re'ut 71908
Tel: 050 8503362
info@maccabimwinery.com

Maor Winery
Moshav Ramot 12948
Tel: 052 8515079
danny@maorwinery.com
www.maorwinery.com

Margalit Winery
POB 4055
Caesarea 38900
Tel: 050 5334433 Fax: 04 6262058
a_m_n_l@netvision.net.il
www.margalit-winery.com

Meishar Winery
Moshav Meishar 76850
Tel: 08 8594759
zosh_s@netvision.net.il
www.meishar.co.il

Meister Winery
33 Schunat Hashalom,
Rosh Pina 12000
Tel: 054 4976940
meister@bezeqint.net
www.ruth-meister.co.il

Miles Winery
Moshav Kerem Ben Zimra 13815
Tel: 050 6233014
miles013@013.net.il
www.miles-winery.com

Miller Winery
114 Ya'alom St.
Sha'arei Tikva 44810
Tel: 050 5211079 Fax: 09 7687761
yekev@gomiller.co.il

Mond Winery
Moshav Mishmeret 40695
Tel: 050 5243328
www.mond-winery.co.il

Mony Winery
Dir Rafat Monastery
POB 275
Beit Shemesh 99000
Tel: 02 9916629 Fax: 02 9910366
monywines@walla.co.il
www.monywinery.co.il

Na'aman Winery
Moshav Ramot Naftaly 13830
Tel: 04 6944463 Fax: 04 6950062
rami@naamanwine.co.il
www.naamanwine.co.il

Nachshon Winery
Kibbutz Nachshon 99760
Tel: 08 9278641 Fax: 08 9278607
winery@nachshon.co.il
http://winery.nachshon.org.il

Nahal Amud
Moshav Kfar Shamai 20125
Tel: 04 6989825

Nashashibi Winery
Kfar Eehbelin 30012
Tel: 054 6387191
nash_win@hotmail.com

Natuf Winery
Kfar Truman 73150
Tel: 052 2608199
natuf@012.net.il

Neot Smadar Winery
Kibbutz Neot Smadar 88860
Tel: 08 6358111

Noga Winery
POB 111
Gedera 70700
Tel: 08 8690253
nogawinery@bezeqint.net

Odem Mountain Winery
Moshav Odem 12473
Tel/Fax: 04 6871120
megolan@012.net.il

Pelter Winery
POB 136
Kibbutz Merom Golan 12436
Tel: 052 8666384 Fax: 04 6850343
tal@pelterwinery.co.il
www.pelterwinery.co.il

Poizner Winery
71 Hameyasdim St.,
Zichron Ya'akov
Tel 052 3202323
poizner.winery@gmail.com
http://poiznerwinery.wordpress.com

Psagot Winery
Psagot 90624
Tel/Fax: 02 9978222
info@psagotwines.com
www.psagotwines.com

Ra'anan Winery
Moshav Ganei Yochanan 76922
Tel: 08 9350668
orsss@zahav.net.il

Ramim Winery
Moshav Shachar 79335
Tel: 054 4608080 Fax: 08 6849122
enrade@multinet.net.il

Ramot Naftaly Winery
Moshav Ramot Naftaly 13830
Tel: 04 6940371 Fax: 04 6902661
Yitzhak3@012.net.il

Recanati Winery
POB 12050
Industrial Zone, Emek Hefer
Tel: 04 6222288 Fax: 04 6222882
info@recanati-winery.com
www.recanati-winery.com

Red Poetry Winery
Havat Tal
Karmei Yosef 99797
Tel: 08 9210352
talfarm@bezeqint.net

Rosh Pina Winery
Rosh Pina 12000
Tel: 04 6827062
bloom_r@walla.com

Rota Winery
Havat Rota 85515
Tel: 054 4968703 Fax: 03 9732278
rotawinery@walla.com

Rozenbaum Winery
Kibbutz Malkiya 13845
Tel: 050 5423046 Fax: 09 8996316
aviroz@bezeqint.net

Ruth Winery
Kfar Ruth 73196
Tel: 050 6980098
maortal@012.net.il

Salomon Winery
Moshav Amikam 37830
Tel: 04 6380475

Saslove Winery
POB 10581
Tel Aviv 69085
Tel: 09 7492697 Fax: 03 6492712
info@saslove.com
www.saslove.com

Sassy Winery
24 Ha'atzmaut Ave.
Bat Yam 59378
Tel: 052 2552012

Savion Winery
41 Bareket St.
Mevaseret Zion 90805
Tel: 02 5336162

Sde Boker Winery
Kibbutz Sde Boker 84993
Tel: 050 7579212 Fax: 08 6560118
winery@sde-boker.org.il
www.sde-boker.org.il/winery

Sea Horse Winery
Moshav Bar Giora 99880
Tel: 050 7283216 Fax: 02 5709834
info@seahorsewines.com
www.seahorsewines.com

Segal Wines
Kibbutz Hulda 76842
Tel: 08 9358860 Fax: 08 9241222
segal@segalwines.co.il
www.segalwines.co.il

Shdema Winery
Kibbutz Revivim 85515
Tel: 050 5255128 Fax: 08 6562397
motis@revivim.org.il

Shfeyah Winery
Tel: 04 6399520 Fax: 04 6299858
ormik@walla.com

Shiloh Winery
Shiloh 44830
Tel: 050 6422268

Sifsaf Winery
Moshav Safsufa 13875
Tel: 06 7498928
eazywine@bezeqint.net

Smadar Winery
31 Hameyasdim St.
Zichron Ya'akov 30900
Tel: 04 6390777

Snir Winery
Kibbutz Snir 12250
Tel: 04 6952500 Fax: 04 6951765

Somek Winery
16 Herzl St.
Zichron Ya'akov 30900
Tel: 04 6397982 Fax: 04 6391194
barakdhn@netvision.net.il

Soreq Winery
Moshav Tal Shachar 78805
Tel: 08 9450844 Fax: 08 9370385
soreq@barak.net.il

Sraya Winery
Moshav Tomer 90680
Tel: 02 9944704 Fax: 02 9944705
brosho1@netvision.net.il

Srigim Winery
POB 174
Moshav Srigim 99835
Tel: 050 6991398 Fax: 02 9991512
ursr10@netvision.net.il

Stern Winery
Kibbutz Gadot 12325
Tel: 054 6737423
stern.johnny@gmail.com
www.stern-winery.co.il

Tabor Winery
POB 422
Kfar Tavor 15241
Tel: 04 6760444 Fax: 04 6772061
twc@twc.co.il
www.taborwinery.co.il

Tanya Winery
Ofra 90627
Tel: 050 9974949
tanyawinery@gmail.com
www.tanyawinery.co.il

Teperberg
POB 609
Kibbutz Tzora 99803
Tel: 02 9908080 Fax: 02 5340760
office@efratwine.co.il
www.efrat-winery.co.il

Three Vines
Moshav Ramot Naftaly 13830
Tel: 052 2660933 Fax: 04 6940462
gbbarak@gmail.com

Tishbi Estate Winery
33 Hameyasdim St.
Zichron Ya'akov 30900
Tel: 04 6389434 Fax: 04 6280223
tishbi_w@netvision.net.il
www.tishbi.com

Trio Winery
Tel: 050 5333765 Fax: 03 5748861
triowinery@gmail.com

Tulip Winery
Kfar Tikva
Kiryat Tivon 36081
Tel/Fax: 04 9830573
tulip@tulip-winery.co.il
www.tulip-winery.co.il

Tzora Vineyards
Kibbutz Tzora 99803
Tel: 02 9908261 Fax: 02 9915479
info@tzorawines.com
www.tzorawines.com

Tzuba Winery
Kibbutz Tzuba 90870
Tel: 02 5347678 Fax: 02 5347999
winery@tzuba.org.il
www.tzubawinery.co.il

Vanhotzker Winery
Moshev Meron 13910
Tel/Fax: 04 6989063
Elivan1@bezeqint.net

Villa Wilhelma Winery
Moshav Bnei Atarot 60991
Tel: 054 4564526 Fax: 03 9721988
motti_goldman@yahoo.com
www.villawilhelma.co.il

Vitkin Winery
POB 267
Kfar Vitkin 40200
Tel: 09 8663505 Fax: 09 8664179
info@vitkin-winery.co.il
www.vitkin-winery.co.il

Yaffo Winery
15 Rozov St.
Tel Aviv 69716
Tel: 03 6474834
yaffowine@zahav.net.il
www.yaffowinery.com

Yatir Winery
POB 5210
Arad
Tel: 08 9959090 Fax: 08 9959050
y_yatir@zahav.net.il
www.yatir.net

Ye'arim Winery
Moshav Givat Ye'arim 90970
Tel: 052 5791080
sassons_wine@hotmail.co.il

Yehuda Winery
Moshav Shoresh 90860
Tel: 054 4638544 Fax: 02 5348100
yekev_yehuda@neve-ilan.co.il

Yiftah'el Winery
Alon Hagalil 17920
Tel: 04 9861466 Fax: 04 9501350
Habikta2@bezeqint.net
www.yfw.co.il

Zauberman Winery
50 Piness St.
Gedera 70700
Tel: 08 8594680
www.zaubermanwines.com

Zemora Winery
POB 451
Mevaseret Tzion 90805
Tel: 02 5701402 Fax: 02 5346166
info@zmorawinery.co.il
www.zmorawinery.co.il

Zion Winery
Rehov Charuvit 45
Mishor Adumim
Tel: 02 5352540 Fax: 02 5355535
yossi@zionfinewines.co.il
www.zionfinewines.co.il

Index of Wineries

About the Author

Daniel Rogov is Israel's most influential and preeminent wine critic. He writes weekly wine and restaurant columns in the respected newspaper Haaretz, and contributes regularly to two prestigious international wine books—Hugh Johnson's Pocket Wine Book and Tom Stevenson's Wine Report. Rogov also maintains a wine and food forum, which can be found at www.tobypress.com/rogov.

The fonts used in the book are from the Chaparral family

Other works by Daniel Rogov
available from *The* Toby Press

Rogov's Guide to Kosher Wines

Rogues, Writers & Whores:
Dining with the Rich and Infamous

The Toby Press publishes fine writing,
available at bookstores everywhere. For more information,
please contact *The* Toby Press at www.tobypress.com